JEWISH CATTLE TRADERS IN THE GERMAN COUNTRYSIDE, 1919–1939

JEWISH CATTLE TRADERS IN THE GERMAN COUNTRYSIDE, 1919–1939

ECONOMIC TRUST AND ANTISEMITIC VIOLENCE

STEFANIE FISCHER

TRANSLATED BY JEREMIAH RIEMER

INDIANA UNIVERSITY PRESS

This book is a publication of

Indiana University Press
Office of Scholarly Publishing
Herman B Wells Library 350
1320 East 10th Street
Bloomington, Indiana 47405 USA

iupress.org

Originally published in German as *Ökonomisches Vertrauen und antisemitische Gewalt*
© Wallstein Verlag, Göttingen 2014
https://www.igdj-hh.de/upload/fischer_vertrauen.pdf
English translation © 2024 by Indiana University Press

Manufactured in the United States of America

First Printing 2024

Cataloging is available from the Library of Congress.

ISBN 978-0-253-06871-2 (hardcover)
ISBN 978-0-253-06872-9 (paperback)
ISBN 978-0-253-06873-6 (ebook)

CONTENTS

ACKNOWLEDGMENTS

Writing a book takes a lot of time and patience. It also takes a community of advisers, critics, colleagues, and friends, not to mention generous financial support. This is especially true in my case. I would not have been able to undertake this research without the transatlantic network of people who stood by my side at different points during this project. It is my pleasure to take this opportunity to thank some of them.

The idea for carrying out a study of Jewish cattle traders in interwar Germany was born during a directed reading class with Déborah Dwork while I was a graduate student at the Strassler Family Center for Holocaust and Genocide Studies at Clark University in Worcester, Massachusetts, in 2005/2006. Our readings introduced me to the history of German Jews in the countryside and how it came to an end during the Nazi era. The history of rural Jewry connected me with parts of the history of the area where I grew up, namely Central Franconia in Northern Bavaria. I am grateful to Déborah Dwork and Thomas Kühne for encouraging me to delve into research about the complexities surrounding the history of Jews in the cattle business. I also owe my thanks to Wolfgang Benz, who guided my research on an earlier version of this book. Michael Wildt made many invaluable suggestions about the direction my research should take. I am indebted as well to Michael for welcoming me into his research seminar at the Hamburg Institute for Social Research on the history and theory of violence. Altogether, I am deeply beholden the numerous contributions made by this vibrant academic community, whose members encouraged me to approach my research from new directions.

The German edition of this book came out in 2014 with the Wallstein publishing house, which then gave permission to bring out the study in English. Two academic prizes for the German edition shone a much-needed light on the neglected history of German Jewish cattle traders. I therefore owe my thanks to the selection committee of the Fraenkel Prize from the Wiener Library in London and to the selection committee from the Irma Rosenberg Prize awarded by the Institute for Contemporary History at Vienna for honoring my work. In 2014, I was also invited to participate in the seminar "On the Word of a Jew," sponsored by the Advanced Jewish Studies program at the Oxford Centre for Hebrew and Jewish Studies. My discussions with the gifted scholars there about the dynamics of trust in the field of Jewish Studies encouraged me to pursue an English edition of my book. My special thanks to Mitchell B. Hart, David Rechter, and Derek J. Penslar for providing me with guidance and support in the early stages of this project.

A book of this kind, focusing as it does on the interrelationship between economic trust and antisemitic violence, could not have been written without the trust of those who shared their family histories with me. In the course of my research, I interviewed the children and grandchildren of Jewish cattle traders, now living in the United States and in Israel. I owe a great debt to all those who generously shared their recollections, including extremely painful parts of their family history. I learned more from listening to them than from any written document. My very special thanks to the Berman family in the United States and in Israel. They contributed their own family's story to this project, but they also taught me more about the culture and tradition of cattle trading and how it continued in the United States than I could ever have hoped to uncover through archival research. Daphna Berman, great-granddaughter of Bernhard Bermann from Ellingen and a professional copy editor, read the translated manuscript with a critical eye and improved it stylistically. Our conversations deepened my understanding of her family history and of the cattle business in general. The manuscript of this book benefitted tremendously from her expertise. I thank Daphna for her careful reading, editing, and comments.

I embarked on this journey after my daughter Elisabeth was born in 2016. At that time, I was fortunate enough to hold a visiting professorship at the department for German and Russian languages and literatures at the University of Notre Dame in South Bend, Indiana. There, the support of William C. Donahue, Eli Borts, and Anna Siebach-Larsen transformed the idea of bringing this study to light in English into a full-fledged publication project. During this period, I was also given the valuable opportunity of presenting my research findings to a workshop at Indiana University in Bloomington, and I thank Constanze Kolbe for inviting me to discuss my work with faculty and graduate students from the Borns Jewish Studies Program. I am grateful to Dee Mortensen from Indiana University Press for taking on this project with enthusiasm and for navigating it through its early stages and to Gary Dunham and his tremendously supportive team, who took on this project after Dee retired in 2019 and offered valuable assistance during the publication process. The Schwartz Fund for New Scholarship from the Borns Jewish Studies Program also contributed to the achievement of this edition.

The translation was made possible through the Gerald Westheimer Career Development Fellowship from the Leo Baeck Institute in New York. I offer my thanks to Frank Mecklenburg and Atina Grossmann for their support and guidance. My particular thanks go to Michael Brenner for introducing me to Jeremiah Riemer, who took on the giant work of translating this study from German into English. For four years, he accompanied me on a rewarding but sometimes also strenuous journey through English and German grammar, syntax, and style; the Franconian dialect, which was used in some of the sources, added an extra layer of complexity to this linguistic adventure. Jeremiah's rigorous and meticulous work improved the manuscript in multiple ways, and his sharp mind has given the English edition more clarity and nuance than I could have hoped to achieve without his help.

Although this book is based on the German edition, the introduction has been newly written and updated for this translation. I thank Cornelia Aust, Irit Dekel, and Frank Wolff for providing me with useful feedback on this new chapter. I am grateful to Lizzy Emerson for polishing my English. Along the way, I have been fortunate to be invited to present my work in different settings, including the College of William and Mary as its Lyon Tyler Gardiner Lecturer and the Center for Jewish Studies at the University of Florida as lecturer for the Alexander Grass Chair in Jewish Studies there.

My special thanks to Stefanie Schüler-Springorum and to my exceptional colleagues at the Center for Research on Antisemitism at the Technical University of Berlin, who welcomed me into their ranks and who provided a rich intellectual home, allowing me to expand my horizons during those years. I am so grateful to my colleagues for their strength and support.

The manuscript of this book was submitted to the press after my second daughter, Magdalena, was born in spring 2020. Rewriting parts of this book, proofreading, and editing have sometimes been exhausting, but Elisabeth's and Magdalena's joy and love have kept me going through it all. I dedicate this book to both of them. Last but very much not least, my enduring appreciation and love to my husband, Frank, who ran the household and took care of our daughters while I was working on this book in the evenings and on weekends. I could not have done it without his support.

ABBREVIATIONS

[English translations in square brackets]

Abt.	Abteilung [div. - division]
AG	Amtsgericht [local or district court]
BA	Bezirksamt [district office]
BArch	Bundesarchiv Berlin-Lichterfelde
BayHStA	Bayerisches Hauptstaatsarchiv
Bl.	Blatt [page or sheet]
BLVW	Bayerisches Landesamt für Vermögensverwaltung und Wiedergutmachung [Bavarian State Office for Asset Management and Restitution]
C.V.	Central-Verein deutscher Staatsbürger jüdischen Glaubens [Central Association of German Jews of the Jewish Faith]
DNVP	Deutschnationale Volkspartei [German National People's Party]
ELG	Einkaufs- und Liefergenossenschaft des Landesverbandes bayerischer Viehhändler e.V. m.b.H. [Purchase and Delivery Cooperative of the State Association of Bavarian Cattle Traders, registered association, limited liability]
e.V.	eingetragener Verein [registered association]
Gestapo	Geheime Staatspolizei [Secret State Police]

GLK	Gewerbelegitimationskarte [business license]
GmbH	Gesellschaft mit beschränkter Haftung [limited liability corporation]
HRA	Handelsregisterauszug [certificate of registration with register of companies]
Jg.	Jahrgang, Jahrgänge [annual volume(s)]
KZ	Konzentrationslager [concentration camp]
LBV	Landesverband bayerischer Viehhändler e.V. [State Asociation of Bavarian Cattle Traders, Ltd.].
LEA	Landesentschädigungsamt [Bavarian State Compensation Office]
LRA	Landratsamt [state district administration]
NS	Nationalsozialistisch(-e), (-er), (-es) [National Socialist]
NSDAP	Nationalsozialistische Deutsche Arbeiterpartei [National Socialist German Workers' Party]
Opf.	Oberpfalz [Upper Palatinate]
Pg.	Parteigenosse [(Nazi) party member]
RA/RAe	Rechtsanwalt/Rechtsanwälte [Attorney(s)]
Rep.	Repertorium [Archival reference work]
RGBl.	Reichsgesetzblatt [Reich Law Gazette]
SA	Sturmabteilung [Nazi party storm troopers]
Sprk.	Spruchkammer [Denazification court]
SS	Schutzstaffel [Nazi party elite elite corps: "Protective Echelon"]
StAN	Staatsarchiv Nürnberg [Nuremberg municipal archive]
USHMM	United States Holocaust Memorial Museum
WB	Wiedergutmachungsbehörde [Restitution Authority]
YIVO	Yidisher Visnshaftlekher Institut [(Yiddish) Institute for Jewish Research]

JEWISH CATTLE TRADERS IN THE GERMAN COUNTRYSIDE, 1919–1939

Introduction

"We need the Jews because, without Jews, even today I cannot get my cattle to the customer. The Christian cattle dealers just always want to sell livestock below price, which is not the case with the Jews."[1]

Gunzenhausen town council member, November 1934

From 1933 onward, it was Nazi policy that anyone caught doing business with a Jewish cattle trader faced severe punishment. By the late 1930s, this could include being taken into "protective custody" ("Schutzhaft"). Yet despite this risk, it seems that non-Jewish farmers were reluctant to stop doing business with Jewish cattle traders. Their actions contradicted the widespread belief that farmers eagerly participated in the exclusion of Jews from the cattle trade in the Nazi era. How do we explain this paradox?

This book is not about political resistance to Nazi policies. It takes one important group—Jewish cattle traders—and explains the social and economic networks in which they operated. It analyzes the informal and durable bonds between Jewish cattle traders and famers that not even incessant Nazi attacks could break. Using fresh evidence and bringing together approaches from social history, economic history, and sociology, it offers a new contribution to the history of German Jews and the Holocaust.

My work is based on a detailed study of ties between Jewish cattle traders and non-Jewish farmers and what underlay their business relationships in the interwar period (1919–1939).[2] I argue that the exclusion of Jews from the economy and society can only be fully understood if we shift our focus away from the (largely urban) Jewish economic elite and look at Jewish economic activity that took place in the German countryside. The complexity of the exclusion of German Jews comes to light when we examine the foundations of their business relationships before the Nazis took power in 1933. This study uses new evidence and approaches to explore economic relationships between Jews and non-Jews, shedding light on the role Jews played in cattle-trading—a role that challenges the long-standing cliché of the greedy, shady Jewish cattle dealer out to exploit farmers.

The place I have chosen as the focus of my study is the northern Bavarian district of Central Franconia. The selection is a careful one, made to highlight how these relationships functioned under the most intense strain. Central Franconia features several characteristics important for understanding the complex economic and social relations that underpinned the social processes of the Holocaust. Central Franconia had one of the highest proportions of Jews in its population outside Germany's urban centers such as Berlin, Frankfurt, and Breslau; at 1.37 percent of the population, or 13,719 Jews,[3] this was above the average of 0.9 percent for Germany as a whole in 1925.[4] In this region, a significant percentage of the Jewish population still lived in rural areas in 1933, and most of them made their living in the cattle-dealing business. There were numerous reasons for this. One was the aftereffect of the Bavarian Judenedikt (Edict on the Jews) of 1813, which prevented the urbanization of Jews for far longer than was the case in Prussia.[5] While many Bavarian Jews left their villages for larger German cities or immigrated to America during the nineteenth century, the rural Jews who did remain continued to follow traditional patterns of living. In Central Franconia, Jews were disproportionately prominent in the economy, including in areas like the grain and hops trade but especially in the cattle trade.

Even before 1933, however, Central Franconia was a Nazi stronghold steeped in antisemitism. Led by Gauleiter Julius Streicher, publisher of the antisemitic journal *Der Stürmer*, local Nazi leaders initiated attacks on Jews in the region well before racist laws were introduced on a national level. Streicher and his followers enjoyed great popularity from the mid-1920s onward. Some striking statistics distinguish the profile of Streicher's district. In 1925, 69.25 percent of the region's inhabitants were Protestants deeply rooted in the *völkisch* movement, whose racist and antisemitic Weltanschauung promoted the idea of a Germanic race. Central Franconia's Protestant middle class bourgeoisie followed a religiously inflected version of nationalism that was dominant in the Prussian provinces of the German Reich. This Protestant small-town milieu constituted the backbone of the early Nazi movement in Central Franconia.[6] This intersection of politics and demographics is reflected in results of the pre-1933 elections: in some areas of this district, the Nazi party had gained more than 80 percent of the vote by April 1932 (when Hitler challenged Paul von Hindenburg in the second round of that spring's presidential election).[7] Central Franconia may be considered an extreme case because of the region's early embrace of Nazism, yet its political and social developments foreshadow trends in other German regions. The argument I make about the interrelationship between economic trust and antisemitic violence therefore has important ramifications for the study of relations between Jews and non-Jews more generally, since Central Franconia's regional structure exhibits only a small number of peculiarities.

Until very recently, the history of rural Jewry has been sorely neglected in research on German Jews and the history of the Holocaust, despite the fact that rural Jews constituted one-fifth of the German Jewish population on the eve of their destruction. They were also the group most severely targeted by Nazi attacks.[8] There are three main reasons for this historiographical neglect: First, the decades-long and dominant focus of German Jewish historiography was on the urbanized and acculturated Jewry to which the majority of Jews belonged before the community was destroyed under Nazi rule.[9] Second, the small number of scholarly works that treated Jewish cattle dealers did so from the specific perspectives of either German Jewish history or Holocaust history. In these works, researchers tended to either focus on the history of cattle dealers before they acquired equal legal status or else delve solely into the history of their persecution under National Socialism. There remains a tradition in historical scholarship of setting January 1933, when the National Socialists took power, as a boundary date determining the relevant period under investigation— and thus of dividing history into two time ranges, one prior to January 1933 and one afterward.[10] Other issues have also affected the historiography in this area. The works of (exiled) Jewish historians were primarily concerned with intra-Jewish themes, and the non-Jewish scholars who came later to the study of rural Jewry tended to focus on Jewish-Christian coexistence and how this fell apart under the National Socialist dictatorship. Until the 1990s, Utz Jeggle's (1969) pioneering study of life in *Judendörfer* (as villages with Jewish populations of twenty to sometimes forty percent were called) in Württemberg remained an exception among works by (non-Jewish) historians and ethnographers in post-war Germany. The first published research to qualify as a worthy successor to Jeggle's work on Jews in the countryside came in 1997 with the comprehensive anthology edited by Monika Richarz and Reinhard Rürup.[11] In these noteworthy works on rural German Jews, Jewish cattle traders are touched on but not specifically analyzed. They get almost no treatment in studies on larger, urban Jewish communities. There has not thus far been an investigation of this group for the interwar period (1919–1939). Yet, this was a period of enormous change in the views and attitudes expressed about this group and about German Jewry more widely. At the time of the end of the First World War, Jewish cattle traders found themselves defamed as usurers, as they had been for centuries, though they had been left largely unmolested by the law. By the mid-1930s, however, Jews faced expulsion from cattle dealing under the National Socialist dictatorship. Third, agricultural history has paid scant attention to Jewish cattle dealers, despite their prominent position as the traditional middlemen between town and country.[12]

A study of Jewish cattle traders in the interwar period shows us an intersection of Jewish history with Holocaust history. An examination of the history of Jewish cattle traders reveals how business interactions and emotional ties such as trust permeated the practices of everyday life that continued even after the Nazis tried to undermine these interactions and emotions with racist hatred. A close look at these practices helps us understand the processes whereby Jews were excluded from society and the economy in Germany during the 1930s and in turn shows something that may at first surprise us: Trust often existed alongside antisemitism. They were in many cases parallel phenomena.

Thus, by looking at Jewish cattle traders, we can begin to understand the social dynamics that underpinned the violent exclusion of Jews from society and the economy in Germany during the late 1930s. Numerous studies have already emphasized the long tradition of excluding Jews from German society as well as the persistence of antisemitism in both German culture and society. This study, however, sheds new light on these established patterns of ostracism by including examples of trust instead of focusing exclusively on economic data. This approach allows us to see and understand the complexities of relations between Jews and non-Jews who were engaged in economic and social exchange, challenging our previous understandings by demonstrating that Jewish agency was an ongoing factor throughout the exclusionary process that took place under Nazi rule. The ways that cattle traders (both Jewish and non-Jewish) operated created a Vertrauensgemeinschaft (community of trust) that continued to shape their internal and external relationships as well as their day-to-day lives, even under the most extreme political conditions.

The Rural Setting

In order to appreciate the complexity and historical importance of the social and economic relationships between Jewish cattle traders and non-Jewish farmers, we need to understand the rural setting in which this study takes place. It has been widely forgotten that the heart of Jewish economic activity in German lands was in the countryside, where Jews traditionally functioned as middlemen between agricultural producers and regional markets. Cattle dealing reaches back to the beginning of Jewish life in Ashkenaz. Until settlement and occupational restrictions were lifted during the process of emancipation, the majority of Jews made a living as peddlers, traders, or merchants. In the countryside, this chiefly amounted to trade in agricultural products, such as hops and grain, but also in livestock (chicken, sheep, cattle, and horses). Cattle dealing in particular was quite widespread among Jews living in rural areas. Legend even has it, by way of stories passed down orally, that the majority of German Jews were descendants of a cattle dealer's family.[13]

Jewish cattle dealers operated on both sides of the livestock market, as buyers and sellers. They supplied their communities with kosher meat and often combined trading in cattle with kosher butchering. As cattle dealers, they also provided farmers with the domestic livestock necessary to work the fields, as the motorization of agriculture was still in its infancy. Until tractors became affordable for medium- and small-scale farmers in the 1960s, agriculture across large swaths of Europe continued to depend on livestock for farm chores like plowing and harvesting.[14] Traditionally, the cattle trade came with many economic risks for all parties involved. In the interwar period, most farmers were unable to pay in cash for their working animals; therefore, they depended on the cattle trader's willingness to grant them loans. The farmers' dependence on credit put the cattle trader in a very sensitive position; on the one hand, he was the man who provided farmers with the cattle they needed, but on the other, he was the one who could repossess the cattle if farmers proved unable to pay their debts. In other words, Jewish cattle traders depended on farmers' economic ability to pay back their debts, and farmers, in turn, depended on a dealer's willingness to grant them credit. As buyers and sellers of cattle and as creditors, these rural traders helped shape the way peasants on small and medium-sized farms lived and conducted business in the German countryside.

Until today, this important chapter of Jewish history has been marginalized by both scholarship about the places and periods discussed and historical interpretation more generally. One reason for this may be what happened during the process of emancipation, as the concomitant forces of urbanization and assimilation prompted more and more Jews to leave the cattle-trading business. Yet in the interwar period, despite this trend, there were still a significant number of Jewish businessmen engaged in the sector. Those remaining in the cattle trade were indispensable to rural Jewish communities, Christian farmers, and urban market outlets. Attempts to promote Christian traders had been part of antisemitic politics since the late nineteenth century but were widely unsuccessful. Right-wing and conservative movements had been agitating against

"Jewish usury" by promoting rural cooperatives since the end of the nineteenth century, but until the Nazi seizure of power, they had failed to gain the trust of farmers.[15] The inroads made by these forces become particularly evident in the 1930s, when Nazi influence began to favor them.

Despite the prominent position of Jewish cattle traders in Jewish history, we know very little about their everyday life and how it came to an end during the Nazi dictatorship. Disparaged as "backward Jews" in modern times, they were commonly dismissed as rural throwbacks who—unlike Jewish intellectuals, lawyers, and doctors—apparently had little to offer the "Jewish Century" (as Yuri Slezkine has labeled mostly the nineteenth century in which unprecedented Jewish upward mobility seemed a perfect match to the professional skills demanded by modernization).[16] Jews who remained in the cattle trade were often seen as being unwilling to adapt to the process of modernization and stuck in old patterns, while their apparently more advanced coreligionists took up "bourgeois" professions. Yet the history of Jewish cattle traders in the interwar period matters deeply because of the way it sheds light on an economic activity reaching back to the early settlement of Jews in German lands and extending, unbroken, to the interwar period. By studying these individuals and their networks, we gain important insights into the social and economic dynamics at work in interwar Germany and into the relationships between Jews and non-Jews in rural areas—areas where tradition and modernity collided powerfully. An examination of the evidence confirms the notion that "ethnic networks not only survive in a modern economy but may even possess certain advantages" and that a unique path of development emerged in rural areas that was closely tied to urbanization.[17] Although Jewish cattle dealers chose to remain in their pre-emancipation trade even after discriminatory restrictions on their business activity were dropped, they nevertheless underwent a dramatic process of professionalization. We learn, for example, that retaining an Orthodox Jewish lifestyle posed no contradiction to the formation of a modern entrepreneurial culture. Jewish cattle dealers, most of whom were religiously observant, operated in an important and rapidly growing field of business; they were, in a manner of speaking, both conveyors of old structures and agents of modernity in a rural society. So far, this dimension has been widely neglected by studies of German Jewish economic history that have tended to emphasize the secular character of the Jewish economic elite.[18]

The mix of the traditional and the modern becomes especially apparent when one takes the period before 1933 into consideration. Here it becomes evident that a substantial entrepreneurial middle class had emerged out of the heterogeneous group of Jewish cattle traders as the process of legal equality took its course. These middle-class cattle traders enjoyed the trust of their customers thanks to their excellent infrastructural ties and solid business equipment but also to their specific trade practices and culture. Their position in the cattle trade is even more conspicuous when one inquires not only into the role of the male protagonists, the dealers, but also into the significance of women and children. The cattle dealers' middle-class character was exhibited by the housewifely activities of their wives and by their children's schooling outside the family. By analyzing Jewish cattle dealers and their business relationships, I answer a number of questions: What were the foundations on which the position of Jewish cattle traders in agrarian societies rested? What role did trust play here—what factors were important for its creation and manifestation, and what factors stood in its way? To what extent could public institutions or parties affect this network of relationships, and what happened to the network of trust under changing political conditions? My broader aim is to determine whether economic trust was able to persist between Jews and non-Jews—and if so, in what forms—even under the impact of Nazi violence.

The Dynamics of Trust

The cattle trade was a risky business governed by rituals that followed specific, long-established rules. Deals were sealed with a handshake, not with a paper contract. The lack of written documentation created a very precarious situation that was even more insecure because of uncertainty surrounding the livestock. There was no reliable or objective information available about each individual cow; the buyer had to trust the word of the salesman. Each partner had to trust the other to keep his—and sometimes her—promise. The cattle trade business was therefore based on mutual trust.

The sociology of trust is at the heart of this study. A binding factor in any social process and a critical prerequisite of any economic exchange, trust is essential for stable relationships. As such, it was also the basis of the bond between Jewish cattle traders and non-Jewish farmers. This trust was often shaken by antisemitism that stigmatized Jews *per se* as untrustworthy, greedy business partners who aimed to destroy farmers. The dynamic between traders and farmers was further complicated by the fact that the cattle trade had been a predominantly Jewish domain in German provinces from the beginning of Jewish settlement and remained so until Jews were excluded from the livestock trade during the Nazi era.

My work draws on several important studies in economic history that have convincingly demonstrated how fundamental trust is for business relations, especially when dealing with an extremely risky commodity such as livestock.[19] This study takes up the plea for Jewish history to take an "economic turn" and also a sociological one. Gideon Reuveni has observed how the aspect of trust has so far not been given the attention it deserves in Jewish (economic) history, especially when examining trade relations between Jews and non-Jews.[20] This is especially true for research on business interactions between Jewish merchants and their non-Jewish customers. This study brings together socio-historical facts with the principles of sociological theory on trust to shed new light on this chapter of economic history.[21]

In terms of relationships between Jews and non-Jews in this period, the question is how far antisemitism stood in the way of trust. Was it wholly explosive of existing networks and relationships, or was it in some situations set aside or at least moderated? As Nina Caputo and Mitchell B. Hart have convincingly argued, in Jewish history, "the challenge is to understand the mechanics of trust, [and] how 'the Jew' and Jews move, either as subjects or objects, between trust and mistrust discursively and materially."[22] Indeed, antisemitism often had an economic basis and strained relations between Jews and non-Jews. However, as sociologist Lynne Zucker has emphasized, prejudices can be overcome by the positive experience of daily interactions, including doing business together.[23] Zucker shows how trust is a critical prerequisite of economic exchange and is essential for stable relationships. She is also clear that there must first be what she terms a trust-building process. According to Zucker, prejudice based on gender, age, and ethnicity may be an obstacle in the trust-building process but does not function as a blockage to it. These findings also can be applied to the study of Jewish cattle dealers, where trust was initially produced between farmers and traders through the process of conducting day-to-day business. Their mutual trust was built on social experiences with one another. Both cattle traders and farmers were equally responsible for the production and preservation of this trust relationship. Even so-called untrustworthy business methods—such as the *Viehhändlersprache* (the "cattle traders' language" or "cow dealer speak") that was often blamed as an argot used to fix prices clandestinely because farmers could not always understand this Western Yiddish dialect—did not function as exclusionary but rather had an inclusive dimension. Both farmers and cattle traders, Jews dealing with non-Jews as well as with other Jews, used these business practices. These long-established methods of the cattle trade incorporated all participants into a community of trust. Prejudices about the social and/or religious background of a business partner could hamper the trust-building process; however, daily interaction ultimately functioned as the strongest element in its development. Hence, farmers and cattle traders cooperated in a trust relationship as accepted—though not always as equal—business partners. Even if farmers harbored antisemitic resentments against Jews, that did not necessarily prevent them from building up economic trust with individual Jewish cattle traders.

These insights are fundamental when it comes to research on the cattle trade. Jewish cattle dealers entered into a complex and fluid network of relationships with non-Jewish peasants that could not have emerged, much less persisted, without trust. It is important to ask how self-perceptions and perceptions of outsiders influenced the relationship of trust and how prejudices about each actor's trading partner could be overcome.[24] When it comes to studying Jews doing business with non-Jewish partners, especially under the crucible of an emerging antisemitic dictatorship, these shifting perceptions take on even greater importance.

The Paradox of Violence

When we combine these understandings of trust with a more granular examination of local society, we begin to see the extent of the ambiguities and inconsistencies in the policy of Jewish exclusion and persecution in Europe. We discover in particular the role that economic motivation played in the decisions individuals made to participate in, or to resist, the genocide. Looking at the micro level allows us to see the layers of ambivalence in relations between Jews and non-Jews that emerged as Jews were excluded from the economy. This is particularly true for the countryside, where the interaction between Jews and non-Jews had been more intimate than in urban areas. Yet in the German countryside, the level of antisemitic violence was often even worse than in the towns and cities. I argue that economic trust endured even under the strain of antisemitic violence. The Nazis created social conditions that first had to be adopted by the local population. This did not happen overnight. Instead, as we see in various places around Europe as well as in this study, the forced exclusion of Jews from the economy was a complex process of adjustment accompanied by a variety of responses. These reactions ranged from cooperation with the new regime to collaboration, indifference, reluctance, and an outright unwillingness to adapt to a new political, social, and economic order.

The farmers' response to Nazi policy therefore corroborates the assertion that the Holocaust developed from a long history of relationships between Jews and non-Jews that had already come into being before racism became official policy. Through a detailed analysis of the interaction between these two groups, this study makes it clear that farmers put their economic interests first, ahead of antisemitic resentments. Process-based trust emerged out of the ways in which actors from different social, religious, or economic backgrounds dealt with each other. This kind of trust is much stronger in a high-risk field of business like livestock trading than in branches of the economy where institutions matter more, like manufacturing or the sale of brand-name products. In other words, the social relationships that traders developed with peasants mattered more than the same kinds of relationships might matter in other areas of business. An examination of the influence of antisemitic violence on this network of relationships reveals that economic trust can persist even under radically altered political conditions. It is here, in the end, that we see the great importance of Jewish cattle dealers for (early twentieth-century) agrarian society. Numerous studies on the exclusion of Jews from the German economy in the 1930s have shown that farmers' general response to interference in the cattle-dealing business was not unique; it was mirrored in other business sectors.[25] The present study, however, moves beyond these previous approaches. By including social aspects—such as trust—rather than focusing purely on economic trends, we can see the myriad inconsistencies that riddled the process of expelling the Jews from Germany. An economic analysis alone cannot answer the question as to why—even if farmers put their economic interests first—one of them would secretly sell a cow to a Jewish cattle dealer in the late 1930s when the penalty could include public shaming, the loss of benefits offered by the regime, or even being taken into "protective custody."

The Evidence

Carrying out research on Jewish cattle traders may sound like a difficult undertaking, as they left few written documents behind to help us study them. Jewish cattle traders were not illiterate, but they were not prominent writers of memoirs or diaries either. Even well-known archives of German Jewish history, such as the Leo Baeck Archives in New York, house only a handful of sources on this group in the interwar period; many more documents can be found there relating to the history of Jewish cattle traders before the First World War. Even when Jewish archives hold records on Jewish cattle traders, they are difficult to track down. One reason for this is that German Jewish cattle traders who escaped Nazism often did not identify as "cattle traders" in postwar records but as "merchants" (*Kaufleute*). Despite this lack of documentation, traces of Jewish cattle traders have been well preserved in a number of international and local government archives. But there, too, locating sources on this group can quickly turn into an adventure. Because of the small-scale nature of most cattle-trading businesses, government archives did not file their tax or trade register records. In order to obtain a precise picture of the cattle trade's structure and key actors,

I therefore analyzed files created after the passing of the 1953 Federal Compensation Law (Bundesentschädigungsgesetz) by the Bonn government.[26] This law provided financial compensation to eligible individuals whom the Nazis had persecuted for racial, religious, political, or ideological reasons. These files are highly relevant for Holocaust research, in particular when studying underrepresented groups such as Jewish cattle traders.

These records give evidence of Jewish cattle traders' personal stories and their everyday life in Germany before, during, and after the Holocaust. The files, moreover, include testimonies by neighbors, customers, and employees of Jewish cattle traders. These accounts, which help to reconstruct power relations among the witnesses, form the mainstay of the second chapter. Importantly, female voices are included along with those of the male family members, and the perspectives span the generations.

Data was collected from more than three hundred Jewish men, women, and children affiliated with the cattle trade in the interwar period. The material consulted includes vital demographic information (such as date of birth, place of birth, name at birth, married name, and number of children), as well as educational and occupational background, average business volume before 1933, business partners, and the number of employees in individual firms. These records have allowed me to draw a nuanced picture of the structure of the cattle trade and of family businesses. In addition, I have gathered primary sources from private family collections in Central Franconia, the United States, and Israel.

All these materials have offered insights into a very intimate world of encounters between Jews and non-Jews in the German countryside. This study also builds on a variety of contemporaneously published sources about the cattle trade as well as on newspapers aimed at farmers and published by cattle-trade associations. These sources shed new light on the interrelationship between institutional and social trust. Finally, I interviewed farmers, children and grandchildren of Jewish cattle traders, and non-Jewish cattle and hog traders who interacted as colleagues with one another. These interviews—despite being conducted more than seventy years after the actual events—completed the picture of the relationships of trust between Jewish cattle traders and farmers. The personal voices of historical actors offer vital insights that underscore the social dynamics of this much neglected part of European Jewish history.

Organization of the Book

The material researched here is divided into four main chapters. Chapter 1 gives a detailed description of the cattle-dealing business in the interwar period in order to explicate the dynamics of trust in the relationships between Jewish cattle traders and their business partners. This chapter sheds light on how the cattle trade functioned and sets out the structural pillars on which trust was built. In so doing, it questions the stereotypical stigmatization of the livestock trade as firmly in the hands of Jews. The inclusion of non-Jewish cattle dealers in the study reveals the commonalities shared by Jewish and non-Jewish livestock trading operations and the differences between them. The survey makes it possible to identify different types of livestock-trading businesses in order to deconstruct the monolithic image of the (stereo-)typical Jewish cattle trader. Analyzing the business profile of Jewish cattle traders draws a more nuanced picture that helps us understand their relationships with non-Jewish farmers. It shows that a variety of business operations existed at the same time, with so-called *Schmusers* (a cognate of the familiar Yiddish term *schmoozers*) working alongside middle-class entrepreneurs and wholesale suppliers. In addition to analyzing the company structure of livestock-trading firms, I also focus on the involvement of individual family members in their businesses. Looking at the roles of women and children in this area reveals that a transformation took place across three generations. It also shows how deeply rooted in the middle class these families had become. In sum, my analysis makes clear the economic and social structure of the Jewish cattle-dealing businesses that laid the foundation for trust networks and relationships.

Chapter 2 deals with the question of how trust was formed in the cattle trade. It focuses on actors who helped shape relations between cattle dealers and peasants. Sometimes the impact of these actors, customs, practices, and institutions was significant, and at other times, less so. To demonstrate the process of building trust between Jewish dealers and non-Jewish peasants, I discuss common cattle-trading practices, including the handshake and the business language spoken by dealers. I also analyze how the trust that was built up could be shaken by self-perception and the perceptions of others.

Chapter 3 deals with the question how trust was established between individual traders and institutions. The additional actors in question include all the institutions taking part in the cattle trade, such as cooperatives, trade associations, and political parties. The actions of these groups reflect the dynamics of trust within a sector where Jews and non-Jews cooperated on a daily basis. Among (government) officials, there was a high level of trust in those middle-class livestock-trading firms that met the criteria of the "trustworthy merchant" (*reeller Kaufmann*). Yet antisemitic mistrust, especially in times of economic crisis, could massively unsettle this network of relationships. One such disturbance of the trust network is illustrated by an analysis of the public debate about high meat prices at the beginning of the 1920s.

My conclusion examines the persistence of trust in the face of increasing violence as National Socialism steadily rose in popularity from the end of the 1920s. It is clear that trust was deeply rooted between Jewish cattle dealers and non-Jewish peasants. To be sure, the antisemitic hate propaganda of the National Socialists picked up on dissatisfaction in the rural population, which had suffered massively from the world economic crisis, and this propaganda characterized Jewish cattle dealers as "farm slaughterers" (*Güterschlächter*) responsible for farmers' economic distress. Yet this hate campaign did not perforce lead to a dissolution of trading ties. Despite the threats of violence, peasants stuck with their Jewish trading partners. In Chapter 4, I discuss the influence that antisemitic violence had on this web of relationships and how the network finally collapsed under the Nazi regime—even though it survived, too, in the form of ties between individual farmers and Jewish cattle traders who found refuge abroad or between individual farmers and Jewish cattle traders who resettled in their old *Medineh* (sales territory) after the war's end.

By analyzing the farmers' response to Nazi policy in the Bavarian countryside, this study brings to light the significance of Jewish cattle traders within rural society. It illuminates the limitations on Nazi policy's drive to destroy Jewish involvement in the cattle trade specifically and economic engagement more broadly and demonstrates that everyday life under Nazi tyranny was shaped not only by ideology and violence but also by long-standing relationships of trust and economic interdependence. It also shows that Jews were a crucial and accepted part of rural business culture; they were trusted business partners despite the fact that the stereotypical Jew was widely stigmatized as greedy and untrustworthy.

Together, Jews and non-Jews had created a community of trust that existed beyond racially defined boundaries and preceded the "racial state." This trust community existed in parallel with the largely imaginary but heavily propagated *Volksgemeinschaft* (the Nazi notion of a national-racial community). By showing the complexity and subtlety of the interactions between Jews and non-Jews in one region of Germany, this study exposes the falsity of the Nazis' invented community.

1

A Social History of Cattle Trading in Weimar Germany

Jewish and Non-Jewish Cattle-Trading Firms

Both in popular literature and in more scholarly publications, one encounters the generalization that "the cattle trade was firmly in the hands of Jews."[1] This is a problematic assertion because Jews, owing to their high concentration in the cattle trade, were repeatedly accused by non-Jews and antisemites of fixing prices to their advantage because of limits on competition and thereby having a negative impact on the market.[2] Because there is no reliable data to empirically confirm or refute the generalization that a big number of cattle traders were Jews, we shall start with an examination of the quantitative distribution between Jews and non-Jews in the cattle trade. We will then look at some important qualitative features of cattle-trading operations in order to arrive at a clearer picture about the structure of this business. Non-Jewish cattle traders will be adduced as a reference group in order to expose possible differences and commonalities between Jewish and non-Jewish cattle-trading businesses.

Owing to the widely fluctuating character of the trade and to sources that are often quite disparate, checking the distribution of Jewish and non-Jewish cattle traders is a tricky business. Nevertheless, in order to get a methodological handle on the group, we relied on data from the *Bayerisches Landes-Adreßbuch für Industrie, Handel und Gewerbe* (*Bavarian State Address Book for Industry, Trade, and Commerce*) for 1929–30, in which all cattle-trading firms for the region are listed. The edition for that year reflects the number of cattle traders and their settlement structure shortly before the outbreak of the world economic crisis and thereby affords a look at the composition of an occupational group at the end of a period that was relatively stable economically and politically.

Needless to say, this type of data set offers risks as well as opportunities for the historian and researcher of social history. One possible danger with using this source is that only some of the traders are captured in the records, since these kinds of directories always provide just a documentary snapshot and presumably do not include traders who operated very small businesses and sidelines. We may therefore assume that there were really more cattle traders in the selected time period than are listed in the address directory. Overall, it contains the names and contact data (address and phone number) of 430 Central Franconian cattle-trading firms.

To ensure that a meaningful statement about the distribution of Jews and non-Jews in this field of business could be made, we checked the business owners listed in the *Bayerisches Landes-Adreßbuch für Industrie, Handel und Gewerbe* to see if they had any Jewish affiliation.[3] Of the 430 Central Franconian cattle-trading firms, over half (55.58%) were owned by Christians and a good third (37.21%) by Jews; for 31 business owners (7.21%), religious affiliation could not be clearly established. Hence, most cattle dealers were Christians, not Jews. Yet Jews, based on their share of the overall Central Franconian population (1.37%), were more disproportionately represented in the field of cattle trading (at 37.21%) than in other professions stereotyped as Jewish. For example, in Bavaria in 1925, the share of Jews among lawyers was 13 percent and among physicians was 4 percent.[4] In spite of the large number of Jewish merchants in the cattle trade, therefore, one cannot—contrary to the common assertion—speak of a Jewish monopoly in the field. By definition, a supply monopoly of this sort is understood as a type of market in which "supply [is amalgamated] in a single hand"[5]—that is, in the hand of a single monopolist or group. In this case, according to antisemitic rhetoric, this single hand would be a group of Jews. In general, monopolists are suspected of forming cartels in order to give themselves an advantage in market strategy and thereby establish a favorable and anticompetitive framework. This generally involves impeding market access for other suppliers, such as, in this case, non-Jewish cattle traders. But the available data shows that this is out of the question in the case of the cattle trade. There were certainly many Jewish merchants operating in the cattle trade, yet their quantitative share was lower than that of their non-Jewish fellow professionals. Moreover, it must be added how misleading it is to impute that traders—regardless of whether they are Jewish or Christian—operate as a group solely on the basis of their religious affiliation, group-based action being an essential precondition for monopolism. Every trader—whether Jewish or not—is assumed to do business in the first place for his own profit and not for that of a group.

Table 1.1 Distribution of Jews and non-Jews in the cattle trade, 1929–30, according to data from the *Bayerisches Landes-Adreßbuch für Industrie, Handel und Gewerbe (Bavarian State Address Book for Industry, Trade, and Commerce)*.

	Number of Cattle Traders	
Non-Jews	239	55.58%
Jews	**160**	**37.21%**
Cases unaccounted for	31	7.21%
Total	**430**	**100.00%**

Since the quantitative distribution of Jews and non-Jews in the cattle trade still says nothing about their qualitative positions in this branch of the economy and thus about their importance for agrarian society, the links that Jewish cattle-trading businesses had to local business siting, transportation, and related infrastructure also need to be examined. A cattle-trading operation's infrastructural links may be regarded as the central precondition for a supraregional cattle sale. Data about these aspects of infrastructure help provide evidence about the action radius of a business transaction. To this end, we looked at the settlement structure of Jewish and non-Jewish cattle traders. The 430 cattle-trading firms registered in the *Bayerisches Landes-Adreßbuch* we used for reference are distributed across 136 sites or towns, which may be divided into five categories according to size (see fig. 1.1).

It is evident that both Jewish and non-Jewish cattle-trading firms were almost evenly distributed across all categories of town size. The biggest differences between the proportions of Jewish and non-Jewish cattle dealers can be seen in small villages (those with fewer than eight hundred residents) and in the major city of Nuremberg (more than one hundred thousand inhabitants). Non-Jewish cattle traders constituted the largest group in small villages (seventy-nine cases, or 33.05%) and in the city of Nuremberg (fifty-eight cases, or 24.27%); conversely, Jewish cattle traders were relatively underrepresented both in small farming villages and in the urban centers of Central Franconia, consisting of the cities of Nuremberg, Fürth, and Erlangen (thirty-seven cases, or 23.13%, for the villages and nineteen cases, or 11.88%, for the cities). This underrepresentation of Jews is especially noteworthy for Fürth, where only five of the twenty-nine cattle traders were of Jewish descent.[6] By contrast, Jews constituted a bare majority (50.65%) of traders in towns with eight hundred to ten thousand inhabitants (that is, in small and rural towns).

Thus these figures show that Jewish cattle traders cannot generally be categorized as rural Jews. Although about half (50.03%) of them really were

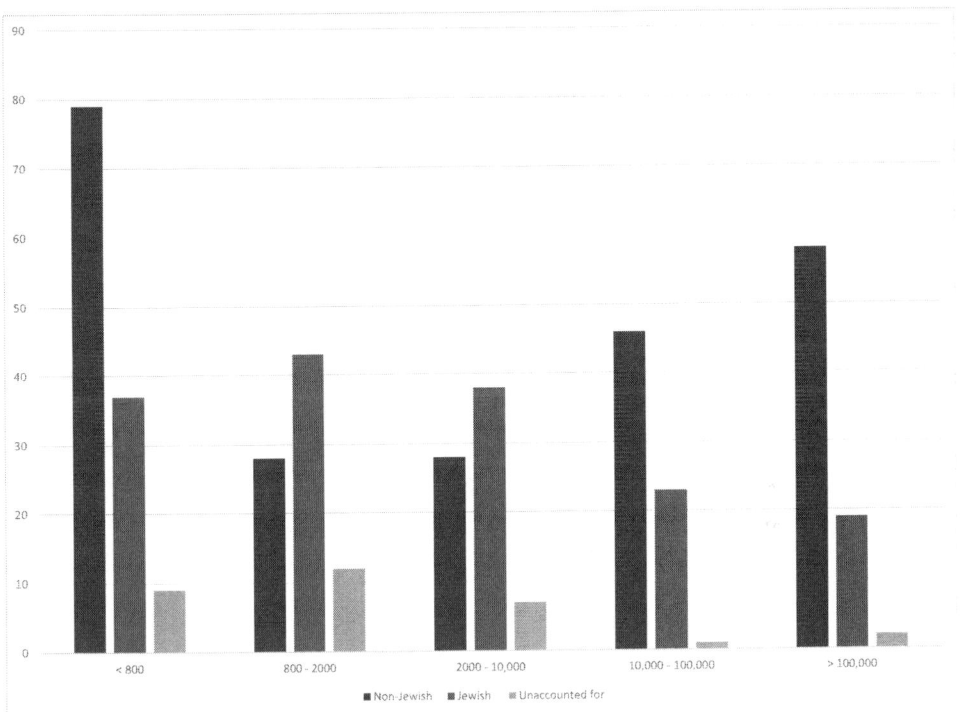

FIGURE 1.1. Distribution of the 430 cattle-trading firms sorted into five categories based on size of town (according to number of residents), 1929–30.

residing in towns with fewer than two thousand inhabitants, and thus in rural areas, almost as many (49.97%) lived in places with more than two thousand inhabitants, in medium-sized towns and big cities.[7] A large number of Jewish cattle traders, accordingly, lived in localities larger than the towns their rural and small-town clientele inhabited.

A connection to the railway network was of central importance to the livestock business. The livestock could be sent to and obtained from supraregional market outlets by rail, and the data about rail access give us information about a business's radius of action.[8] Rural regions in general and rural businesses in particular, like the cattle trade, experienced major structural change owing to the expansion of the railway network. That network now connected small rural communities to urban centers, and places not linked to the rail system were marginalized.[9] In the course of industrialization, the railway—and with it those cattle traders who availed themselves of this new transportation mode—became "for critics and admirers alike the instrument and symbol

Table 1.2 Connection of 315 cattle-trading firms from small towns and villages to the railway network, 1929–30, according to the data from the *Bayerisches Landes-Adreßbuch für Industrie, Handel und Gewerbe* (*Bavarian State Address Book for Industry, Trade, and Commerce*).

	Jewish Cattle Traders		Non-Jewish Cattle Traders		Cattle Traders, Religious Affiliation Unaccounted For	
Railway Connection: Yes	116	87.88%	87	56.13%	26	92.86%
Railway Connection: No	16	13.79%	60	38.71	2	7.17%
No Indication	–	–	8%	5.16%	–	–
Total	132	100.00%	155	100.00	28	100.00%

of the new 'system' of connections in industrial production, commerce, and perhaps even communication beyond conventional geographic barriers and political borders."[10]

Accordingly, it is important to examine the 136 communities where the 430 cattle-trading firms in Central Franconia were located for their connections to the railway network. The foundation for this examination is provided by the data in the place index of the *Bayerisches Landes-Adreßbuch*. One hundred fifteen additional cattle-trading firms from the cities of Nuremberg, Erlangen, and Fürth are not considered here, since, as larger cities, they provided structural preconditions for the cattle trade that differed from those in small towns and villages. Nuremberg was mainly a site for wholesale merchants who traded in animals for slaughter that they purchased from cattle traders in medium-sized firms. These traders had no direct contact with farmers.

More than one-third (38.71%) of non-Jewish cattle traders resided away from central trade routes, and their trade radius and market outlets were restricted to the area immediately surrounding where they lived. Documents from business, commercial, and trade registries that might provide more detailed information about the structure and size of the non-Jewish cattle-trading businesses are not available for Central Franconia. Therefore, we drew on sources from community archives where a registration sheet from the State Office for Livestock Traffic for the period before the First World War could occasionally be found. From these sources, it is possible to obtain some limited information about the business structure of the non-Jewish cattle-trading firms. For example, it can be shown for the old Imperial city of Rothenburg ob der Tauber that non-Jews in the livestock business were mostly restaurant proprietors or butchers practicing the cattle trade on the side, making them inconsequential in terms of supraregional cattle sales.[11] This was confirmed by the contemporary witness Kurt B., who gave this answer to a question about non-Jewish cattle dealers: "The [non-Jewish] butchers traded a bit, but they never really got their turn" to place bids.[12] On the one hand, he is alluding to the cattle trade as a sideline for the non-Jewish butchers. On the other hand, the accusation of cartelization finds expression in his statement when he says "they never really got their turn" (in Franconian dialect, *"net so richtig zum Zug gekommen,"* meaning that the Jewish butchers controlled the market and never let the non-Jewish butchers participate in the competitive game). This suggests he was trying to say that Jewish cattle traders had prevented non-Jewish cattle traders from expanding.[13]

What stands out among the Jewish cattle traders is their high concentration in localities with a railway connection: almost 90 percent (87.88%) of Jewish traders lived in localities that were connected to the railway network (see map. 1.1, Central Franconia, 1928). As such, they were using a modern form of locomotion, the railway, to supply farmers with a "backward" mode of transportation—cattle. Jewish cattle traders had thus adapted to the demands of the times, and their customers profited as well. Farmers participated indirectly in the transformation of rural areas, even while they continued using the premodern means of animal power to work their fields. As the railway networks grew denser, urban markets expanded, and agricultural production encountered increased demand.[14] At the same time, farmers lost direct contact with urban markets for their commodities. However, localities with a railway connection presented traders with an ideal intermediary site between remote farming villages and the major urban markets in big cities like Nuremberg, Munich, and Frankfurt am Main.

The combined attributes of a connection to the railway network and location in a small or medium-sized town was thus a basic qualitative attribute of the way Jewish cattle-trading businesses were sited, and a feature that made them very attractive for their peasant customers and distinguished them from where their non-Jewish colleagues resided. This leads to the question of whether mobility toward places with a railway connection is a dynamic that can be ascertained inside Jewish cattle-trading families and, if so, what consequences this pattern of mobility and location entailed.

In general, once restrictions were lifted on places of residence in the nineteenth century, the Jewish population urbanized to a greater extent than any other population group.[15] To what extent did this trend also encompass Jewish cattle traders as a group? May we draw conclusions about the decision to settle at a site with a railway connection? To answer these questions, we collated birthplaces with later residential sites for seventy-one cattle traders, all of whom had been born between 1860 and 1900; this analysis revealed that places of birth differed from the later home and business locations for thirty-one traders (43.06%). This stands out most notably for the group of Jewish cattle traders in Nuremberg. None of the nineteen had been born in Nuremberg, and six had been born outside Franconia. They had all moved to Nuremberg around the time of their marriages.[16] Residential and commercial territories had, accordingly, shifted since the expansion of the railway network and the end of residential restrictions for Jews. These traders had been born in smaller communities that were frequently located in their familial *mediene* (a Hebrew term meaning "state" or "land," here used to mean an inherited trading area or a kind of early modern sales route).[17]

The urbanization process of the Mann family provides an especially clear and emblematic case of this type of development. The Mann family had lived for several generations in the little village of Ermetzhofen, near the old Imperial city Rothenburg ob der Tauber. The lifting of restrictions on settlement in 1871 made regional mobility possible for them, and Rothenburg's connection to the railway network in 1873 provided the necessary precondition for economic prosperity, setting in motion their move to the next biggest city. Frequently, wealthy Jews were the first to migrate to the cities, and once they were established, less affluent Jews followed in their tracks.[18] That is also what happened with the Mann family; brothers Josef and Theodor Mann left the little village of Ermetzhofen in May 1899 for the district capital of Rothenburg ob der Tauber, and between then and 1908, three additional family members and their spouses and children joined them.[19] Individual members of the social and business network were therefore resettling to the cities at staggered intervals, but for the family as a whole, this would ultimately represent a collective move.

Migration from villages to small towns was accompanied by the purchase and renovation of houses that met the traders' altered commercial needs (see fig. 1.2).[20] Housing chronicles indicate that the transfer of ownership from one homeowner to another was not based on whether buyers and sellers were Jewish or non-Jewish; instead, the choice of a house was oriented toward its usefulness for professional practice.[21] Expansion of the business was often followed by handing it over to the next generation, which usually happened when the firstborn son was married. This allowed the simultaneous expansion of the cattle-trading business to include trading in goods. Thus, upon taking over their father's business and moving to Rothenburg in June 1899, Josef and Theodor Mann supplemented cattle trading with trading in goods at the time.[22] The synergy that resulted from this cooperation caused sales to grow, which gave

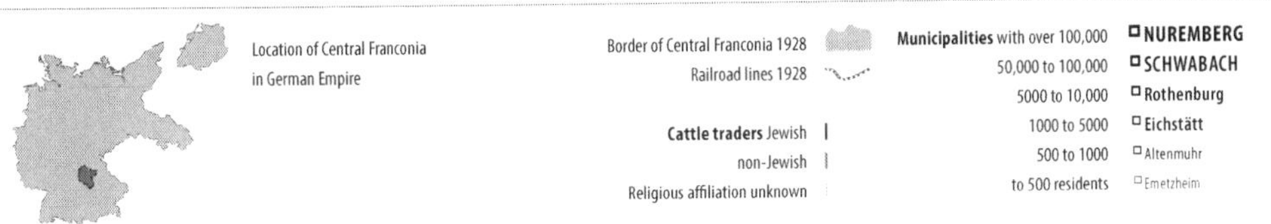

MAP 1.1. Central Franconia, 1928. Design: Tobias Stiefel; source: author.

the brothers flexibility in granting credit to farmers and allowed them to offer more favorable prices.

As the example of the Mann family shows, the process of urbanization for the professional group of cattle traders and for the Jewish population more generally often began for business reasons.[23] This pattern of mobility differed from that of the non-Jewish population; by contrast, the poor agrarian population primarily migrated to the cities to become workers.[24]

The Jewish cattle traders had thus freed themselves from pre-emancipatory structures of settlement and found themselves in an accelerating process of urbanization under National Socialism until it was abruptly and decisively ended under Nazi rule.[25] However, the process of continuing urbanization for the cattle traders often faltered after they resettled from villages to small towns. In other professions with high concentrations of Jewish traders—for example, in textiles—the move often proceeded from the countryside to the next biggest town and from there to the district or state capital.[26]

Geographic mobility cannot be reduced to something done solely for business purposes, however, as the case of the Bermann family illustrates. This cattle-trading family had resided for generations in the little market town of Markt Berolzheim, which lay along an important railroad line from Treuchtlingen via the district capital of Ansbach to Frankfurt am Main. In 1901, David Bermann moved from Markt Berolzheim to the nearly same-sized rural town of Ellingen, where there was another Jewish community dating back to 1540.[27] Following this move, he joined his brother and two other Jewish cattle traders in founding the firm Bermann & Oppenheimer at the two locations of Markt Berolzheim and Ellingen. With this move, the co-owners hooked up with an additional railway line, namely the one from Munich to Berlin. Their business was thereby able to expand further, evidenced by the construction of a new house with stables on the main street shortly after the move to Ellingen.[28] A few years later, the entrepreneurs expanded the business to include locations in nearby Eichstätt and even in the city of Breslau.[29]

Yet we still have to ask why David Bermann and his family resettled in the small rural town of Ellingen and not in the nearby district capital of Weißenburg (Bavaria), where there was even a small-town culture and a secondary school to which he could have sent his children. Presumably, religious motives prevailed here, for there had not been a Jewish community in the old free Imperial city of Weißenburg (Bavaria) since the late Middle Ages. In Ellingen, by contrast, the cattle-trading families could continue to practice their religiously orthodox way of life while simultaneously trading cattle nationally through the link to the Munich-Berlin railway line.

FIGURE 1.2. Stable of the former cattle-trading firm Simon Behr & Söhne (Simon Behr & Sons); the stable was built in 1923 next to the Behrs' residence in Mönchsroth. Courtesy of Pastor Gunter Reese.

A change in the settlement structure is also discernible if one takes a look at the residential area within a particular town. In the case of the rural Mann family's move to Rothenburg, it can be shown that in choosing a residence in their new home, quick accessibility to the train station (the loading point for the urban cattle market) was a more important factor than geographic proximity to the small-town cattle market, which had become peripheral to the supra-regional cattle trade by the 1920s.[30] The new building with stables belonging to brothers Theodor and Josef Mann was no longer downtown (that is, close to the old cattle market) but at the edge of town, near the railway station. The new residential area had the advantage of not requiring cattle to be driven through the narrow backstreets of the town; instead, they could be loaded directly at the train station. Jewish textile traders, by contrast, continued to settle downtown, close to their businesses. We can thus observe a weakening

FIGURE 1.3. Detail of the barn owned by Simon Behr & Söhne, Mönchsroth, left wall of the house. Courtesy of Pastor Gunter Reese.

of the traditional Jewish "rural ghetto."[31] Often, several cattle traders lived on the same street, with their houses side by side.[32] Communication among colleagues in the cattle trade was therefore of central importance for managing the business. Among the peasants in the farming population, this form of settlement chosen by Jewish cattle merchants could easily create the impression of a closed trading community, arousing suspicions of cartel formation. Settling in small and medium-sized towns also facilitated, in addition to better trading conditions, enhanced participation in the life of the town and access to secondary education for children. In towns of this size, the children could be sent to a trade school or gymnasium, which also opened the door to university training later on.[33] For Jewish cattle-trading families, the link to a railway and the gymnasium were "vehicles for upward social mobility."[34]

In purely quantitative terms, therefore, Jews did not have any kind of monopoly on the cattle trade. Yet a qualitative concentration of Jewish cattle-trading families may be discerned within small rural towns linked to the railway network, giving rise to infrastructural advantages that gave Jewish

FIGURE 1.4. Detail of the barn owned by Simon Behr & Söhne, Mönchsroth, entrance gate to stable. Courtesy of Pastor Gunter Reese.

traders an important starting position in this branch. This means that, following the theory of Edward Hastings Chamberlin,[35] we can say that Jews adopted a monopoly-like position within a specific group of cattle traders, namely the structurally strong, medium-sized cattle-trading firms, which we examine in the following section.

The Social Stratification of the Businesses

Two conclusions about Jewish cattle traders emerged from the preceding analysis. First, we may discern a pattern of geographic mobility and relative urbanization occurring after restrictions on places of residence were completely lifted in 1871. Second, by no means can cattle traders be understood as a homogeneous group. We will now map out the heterogeneity of the group in greater detail by taking a closer look at social stratification, which will provide a more differentiated picture of the cattle traders' living environments and their social and economic positions within agrarian society.

Information about the structure and size of cattle-trading businesses is only available through fragmentary records of contemporary sources. In Central Franconia, relevant tax and commercial registers and company documents were largely destroyed by the staff of the revenue authorities and by National Socialists at the end of the Second World War. Large portions of the revenue offices' files on Jewish citizens fell victim to these acts of destruction, so the availability of these kinds of primary sources remains limited. But on the Jewish side of things, too, only a few documents about their former businesses have been preserved. Although the state authorities started to demand in 1923 that records be kept about business transactions in the cattle trade, only one such record book could be located.[36] Jewish victims of Nazi persecution rarely took their record books with them to their places of emigration, where they could have been held for safekeeping and perusal by following generations. Interestingly, however, isolated cattle-trading books from the nineteenth century did survive in genizot.[37]

In order to close the gap left by the loss of so many sources, it is necessary to look beyond the material that has come down to us directly. An evaluation of documents from post–Second World War restitution and compensation files lends itself to this extended search. On the basis of the data on business size found in these documents, it is possible to reconstruct the economic relationships of Jewish families prior to their persecution under the Nazi regime. Overall, it was possible to consult case files on 103 people formerly operating in the cattle-trading business; these people belonged to one of the 160 former Jewish cattle-trading businesses.[38] These documents yielded detailed information about the social and economic position of the former business owners that made it possible to recognize a pattern of social stratification among the traders. The different types of enterprise ranged all the way from the small traders (*Schmusers*) through the medium-sized family business to the metropolitan wholesale establishment. Our analysis begins with the minority group of Schmusers and wholesalers and then shifts to the group of dealers from medium-sized firms to which the majority of the traders belonged.

The Small Schmuser Business

The term *Schmuser* comes from the Hebrew word שמועות (*shmuot*). The noun can mean "rumors." But the verb, which means "to hear" or "to listen" in Hebrew (from the infinitive לשמוע), was often understood (both by Jews fluent in Western Yiddish and their Gentile interlocutors who understood a smattering of Judendeutsch) as "to coax" and "to negotiate." The term thus refers to two things: a trader with very little business activity (that is, a business that has stayed small) and a classic middleman (a livestock intermediary between trader and farmer). The Schmusers, who could be either Jews or non-Jews, scouted out possible livestock transactions for cattle traders in medium-sized firms on a commission basis.[39] They did not operate cattle trades on their own accounts and were therefore exempt from the local business tax; hence they did not have to report transactions to the business registration office. As a result, they did not need a business identity card to practice their trade and were not subject to any commercial supervision.[40]

The activity of the Schmuser goes back to the prototype of the cattle trader, namely of someone trading in livestock in order to provide the rural Jewish community with meat. The prototypical Schmuser dealt only with as much livestock as was needed to supply the rural Jewish community with meat. As a result, he frequently combined livestock trading with kosher slaughter. As independent businessmen, Schmusers were also able to observe Jewish holidays. At the beginning of the twentieth century, Schmusers could still be found in small villages and old rural Jewish communities. The sale of meat was not restricted to the Jewish population but also included the non-Jewish population in that they were sold the meat not fit for kosher consumption (meat that was טרפה, *treyfa*).[41] Jewish butcher stores were therefore divided into two sections, the kosher and the treyf department; in the latter, nonkosher meat was sold to the non-Jewish population. These slaughter practices based on Jewish ritual and law were frequently the target of antisemitic attacks based on claims that the best meat from animal flesh was sold to Jews and the offal was deliberately disposed of by selling it to non-Jews.[42]

The slim volume of livestock sales, which usually amounted to little more than one or two heads of cattle per week as well as the small turnover in meat, provided only a meager livelihood for Schmusers. For example, through 1930, David Levite, a Schmuser from Mönchsroth, earned an annual income of approximately seven thousand reichsmarks from his cattle trade and butcher's shop, a sum that was barely enough to subsist on.[43]

The meager livelihood of the Schmuser may also be gathered from the evidence of their home furnishings and office equipment, which were barely distinguishable from those of peasants with small landholdings. Their home and office furniture was restricted, as in the case of Max Fleischmann from Altenmuhr, to the bare essentials.[44] Schmuser businesses were one-man firms, employing no personnel as a rule, although occasionally wives assisted with selling at the meat counter. These firms usually represented a family tradition, as in the case of Adolf Fleischmann's operation in Altenmuhr. When his father, Joseph Fleischmann, died in 1896, Adolf continued running the cattle-trade business along with the family butcher shop. After his wedding in 1903, he took over the farm, including a small amount of arable and grazing land. In 1912, he added a room for selling the slaughtered meat.[45] Schmusers like Fleischmann, because of the intra-Jewish role they exercised, were dependent on the social environment of their congregations. Even as late as the Weimar era, their homes were located in the old centers of the rural Jewish communities. As small traders, they were not supplying urban markets, so proximity to the railway station was of no importance to them.

Their meager livelihoods and small-merchant status brought these traders, in contrast to those with a larger business volume, very little in the way of prestige.[46] In the course of technicalization and rationalizatioin of the cattle-trading business, the activity of the "Schmusers" kept fading ever further into oblivion, and the number of Schmuser businesses continuously declined.

The Wholesale Establishment

In the course of industrialization, a well-financed wholesale branch had emerged that, taken together with the Schmusers, represented a minority (in purely numerical terms) among Jewish cattle-trading operations. The majority of wholesalers were Christians. The wholesale establishments were almost exclusively located in the city of Nuremberg and, owing to their focus on metropolitan markets, rarely had direct contact with farmers.[47] Wholesalers played a key role in supraregional livestock sales, and they frequently bridged the distance between town (wholesale livestock markets) and country (medium-sized cattle-trading firms where there was personal contact with customers) by way of family ties. For example, brothers Jacob and Justin Steinberger had divvied up the trade between Nuremberg and the village of Colmberg; while one sibling was running the business in Colmberg, the other operated the supraregional wholesale trade in Nuremberg. The brothers traded jointly at such a large scale in both domestic livestock and cattle for slaughter that, in addition to their general trading in cattle, they were able to send an extra wagon of livestock (equaling eight cows) every week to the markets in Frankfurt am Main and Nuremberg. The yield from this and from the brothers' other business was, according to estimates from the Bayerische Landesentschädigungsamt (Bavarian State Compensation Office), an average annual profit of at least 37,500 reichsmarks.[48] An income like this allowed wholesalers to enjoy a refined way of life that might even reach into the realm of the haute bourgeoisie, as was the case with Louis Feldmann from Nuremberg. He owned an automobile and occasionally hired, in addition to the maidservants permanently in his employ, a private chauffeur. Every year, together with his family, Feldmann took "up to three trips to all sorts of regions in Germany." In addition, his wife, Else, visited her mother in Baden several times a year.[49] The Feldmann family was thus cultivating a modern traveling lifestyle that served the purpose of recreation or pleasure and symbolized the affluence of the comfortably bourgeois middle class.[50] Another expression of this refinement was the fostering of a private salon culture in which, as one family friend recalled, the family's six-room home was used for purposes of prestige and social representation, with guests routinely welcomed at weekend receptions.[51]

Families like the Feldmanns were descended from typical country traders doing business from day to day, but by the 1920s and 1930s, they had long since outgrown this background, both economically and as a matter of custom. All in all, these wholesalers cultivated a lifestyle that now had little in common with that of the Schmusers. The link between the Schmusers and the wholesalers were the owners of medium-sized companies.

Even if the group of wholesalers represented a minority among the Jewish cattle traders, by the beginning of the twentieth century, their business transactions were no longer a rarity among horse and hops traders, who also belonged to the traditional rural trading class. The wholesale trading group was able to develop in line with the market situation faster and further than the cattle trader, who tended to operate more regionally.[52]

The Medium-Sized Family Business

Of all the Jewish cattle-trading firms examined here, this group constituted the largest and most important one. Out of 103 firms overall, the majority could be put in this category. Medium-sized cattle-trading businesses were primarily located in small and medium-sized towns, where Jews were most frequently represented in the livestock trade and constituted the majority of traders. In this, they were no different from Germany's Jewish population overall, a majority of which was involved in trade and commerce and belonged to the middle class (or owned medium-sized businesses).[53] As quasimonopolists, the Jewish cattle dealers running medium-sized businesses were therefore not only at the center of relations between Jewish cattle dealers and farmers; they were also directly in the line of fire for antisemitic attacks.

In contrast to the low sales figures for the Schmusers, a medium-sized cattle-trading business would have a turnover of between twenty and thirty heads of cattle a week. From 1930 to 1932, this yielded an annual net profit of approximately ten thousand reichsmarks. This meant that in compensation cases, they were given the same status as salaried employees at the clerical grade or sometimes even higher-level civil service rank.[54] The number of cattle sold varied according to season. In the spring, farmers needed domestic livestock to cultivate the fields, whereas beef cattle for slaughter was traded all year.[55] Depending on the focus of the business, the number of livestock was divided into cattle for slaughter and for domestic farming. The beef cattle were sold by the traders at the major urban markets in Nuremberg, Munich, or Frankfurt am Main. Domestic cattle for use on the farm were resold directly to the peasants. Their high turnover in cattle sales made it possible for the medium-sized firm owners to grant farmers urgently needed credit.

Cattle sales volume determined more than just the amount of credit made available; it also decided living standards (things like residential area or home and office furnishings) and the number of salaried employees hired. The individual trader's living standard was measured against the prevailing living standard in his line of business and his village or small-town environs and especially against that of his farm customers. An evaluation of the archival material from the Bayerisches Landesamt für Vermögensfragen und Wiedergutmachung (the Bavarian State Office for Property Issues and Reparations), the Wiedergutmachungsbehörde (Reparations Authority), and the Landesentschädigungsamt affords the historian an unusual insight into the domestic furnishings of Jewish cattle traders' homes and places of business. Of course, we cannot assume that the information contained in these files accurately reflects the actual state of the furnishings.[56] In the analysis to follow, therefore, the aim is not to verify this information by looking at matching inventories or by checking the truthfulness of statements by non-Jewish witnesses. Instead, the aim is to analyze the pictures witnesses created in these records. The sources are scrutinized by asking how non-Jewish witnesses described the home furnishings of Jewish claimants. How did the non-Jewish witnesses portray themselves in relation to Jewish claimants, and what does their testimony tell us about the social hierarchy between those providing these external statements and the Jewish claimant? Such an examination also helps reveal the status of the cattle trader in the social structure of the local community.

In these descriptions from the archival sources, the subjective boundaries separating the world of the traders from the perceptions of their neighbors become discernible. Of particular interest were items of furniture that contemporaries emphasize or frequently recall. This fact points to the exceptional value of these furnishings at the time—especially as the traders' non-Jewish neighbors construed these possessions as reflecting differences of wealth and status. This, in turn, can help us draw some conclusions about the relationship

those giving testimony had with the cattle traders' families and about the traders' status within the material culture of rural society.[57]

Home Furnishings

Since those giving outside testimony about the home furnishings of Jewish
cattle-trading families largely came from the rural, Christian lower class, it
made sense that, in reparations cases, they would emphasize the objects they
could not themselves afford. Their testimony reveals the importance attached to
these objects as expressions of social status in rural society. From the narratives
of non-Jewish neighbors and customers—and particularly from their choice of
certain terms—their views about Jewish merchant families may be discerned.
Despite the time lapse between the period when Jews and Christians were still
living next to each other and the postwar years when these former neighbors
spoke about their former neighbors, the testimony highlights the presence of a
hierarchy related above all to status. Thus, the non-Jewish witnesses frequently
characterized the households of Jewish cattle-trading families as "comfortably
middle class" (*gut bürgerlich*) and "well" (*gut*) or "modernly furnished" (*modern eingerichtet*).[58] The former household employee of the Löwensteiner family, Lina Kirsch, described the living conditions of her former employer from
Markt Berolzheim, a rural farm town, as follows: "The furnishings were, in any
event, better than those in a farmhouse."[59] Above all, the postwar witnesses
emphasized those furnishings that were not required for everyday living or
subsistence, whose primary function was not utilitarian but rather decorative
and thus also for show, such as paintings.[60] Some cattle-trader families even
owned a piano, the instrument that symbolized a bourgeois lifestyle like no
other piece of furniture. For the villagers giving testimony, an instrument that
was this expensive and took up so much space in the home signaled affluence.
In rural areas, the use of musical instruments was something people only knew
from church services or village festivals. Cattle-trader families, however, did
not just use the piano for musical entertainment; the instrument also played
a role in the musical education of their daughters—entirely in line with the
bourgeois ideal of the well-educated daughter. For example, Hilde Jochsberger,
the daughter of Nathan and Sophie Jochsberger from the rural town of Leutershausen, started receiving piano lessons at the age of eight from Miss Seibold,
who lived thirteen kilometers away in Ansbach.[61]

But other furnishings also played a leading role in the testimony procedure.
Living rooms, according to these witness reports, were not infrequently furnished with upholstered furniture and rugs,[62] and in these accounts taken from
memory, there was a special emphasis on leather seats, which (more than any

other piece of furniture) symbolized capitalism and financial power. Maria Andlinger, who for a time was employed as a maid by the Mohr family in Altenmuhr, explained: "The Mohr house was elegantly furnished, and I remember an oak smoking room (hand-carved), nice leather club chairs, and nice carpets."[63] In her communication with the Landesentschädigungsamt, Rosa Bermann, a cattle trader's wife from Markt Berolzheim, emphasized that her well-equipped home included an ample supply of wine and liquor.[64] She did not say anything about whether the wine and liquor were meant for private use or as gifts for clients. Whatever the case, the inventory indicated by this testimony brings to light the status-shaping role of such possessions.

Home furnishings like leather chairs, carpets, and pianos were, however, only innovative, urban, or exotic to the degree that they departed from norms of utility or prestigious display in the eyes of those testifying about them. Only when they seemed conspicuous as measured by these norms did they come across as extravagant in the witnesses' descriptions.

Two findings clearly emerge from this examination of the home furnishings of Jewish, middle-class cattle-trading families. Their style of home furnishing was fundamentally different from that of the smallholding peasantry and rural lower class, so it functioned in a way that signaled social exclusion. One function fulfilled by dwellings for merchant families was always that of displaying prestige, whereas in peasant circles, residential living was traditionally simple and functional, something that is summed up in the 1878 edition of the *Oeconomische Encyklopädie*: "A peasant has to furnish his house according to the comfort and utility that his status and his way of life demands; everything superfluous, which only costs him something without giving him any hope of usefulness or decent comfort, is to be advised against."[65] This restriction to the bare essentials, though, was also a reflection of the poverty among the peasant population, which was especially widespread in regions with small farms like the structurally weak economy of rural Central Franconia. Not infrequently, farmhouses there did without any kind of abundance; for example, the bedrooms of farmhands lying right next to the stable wall would be frozen over "from top to bottom with ice."[66] The rural lower class that worked as domestic servants or farm laborers for Jewish cattle-trading families took part in the more bourgeois lifeworld of their Jewish neighbors when they visited the merchants' homes and admired things that they could either not afford or would not grant themselves, as reflected in their witness statements.[67]

Jewish ritual objects were another feature that set Jewish cattle traders apart in their Christian surroundings. As the evaluation of inventory lists from Jewish cattle-trading families in the files of the Landesentschädigungsamt revealed, home furnishings always included such ritual and decorative objects as menorahs for display and for lighting on Chanukah or Torah scrolls as symbols of the family's status within the Jewish community. Thus, the Engel family from Markt Berolzheim owned its own Torah scroll, which it kept stored in the synagogue.[68] Just how closely residential living was associated with religious practice in small rural communities, where a number of Schmuser firms were still located, is something indicated by the particular features of a few synagogue buildings. At the beginning of the twentieth century, there were still some Orthodox barn synagogues in which the tradition of separating women and men at prayer was maintained. In Schnaittach, once home to one of Franconia's largest rural Jewish communities, there was a very richly appointed synagogue next to the cowshed of a cattle trader. We even know of one synagogue located above the cowshed of a cattle trader in the Swabian region.[69] One Jewish cattle trader's son, Fritz Frank, recalled how closely religious life was tied to the everyday life of cattle trading: "Their synagogue [in Horb am Neckar], that's two adjoining rooms above the stable of the cattle trader Schwarz. The mooing blends in with the prayer service, without this being regarded or even noticed as any kind of disturbance by those at prayer, who (in a manner of speaking) grew up along with the cattle."[70] In small towns, these forms of very rural Orthodox Jewish life are no longer to be found by the time of the Weimar Republic; cattle traders may still adhere to Jewish dietary and prayer rules, but the residential and liturgical spheres of life are now clearly separated from each other.

To be sure, the way these trader families lived simultaneously conveyed a message of social exclusion and inclusiveness. Their homes were public as well as private and thus were part of the trading business. All of the aforementioned furnishings had, in addition to their purely utilitarian character, another equally important function that had to do with public display. A trader's house furnished in the proper bourgeois manner conveyed a message to customers that this was a well-managed, sound business. This kind of impression led customers to have higher expectations than they would have after seeing a dilapidated trader's house. How important this kind of positioning was for a trader's family is something emphasized by the defense attorney for the Walz family from the small town of Gunzenhausen in a letter to the Landesentschädigungsamt in 1960. After Hugo and Recha Walz got married in 1922 and Hugo took over his father's business, their home furnishings were renovated and modernized. Dr. Bayer, the family's attorney, described the development this way:

A year after the modernization of the house [1928], a series of new furniture pieces in the then-current modern style was purchased. . . .

FIGURE 1.5. Front door of a former cattle-trader's house in Burghaslach. Next to the doorpost on the top right, the diagonal notch for the mezuzah may be seen. Photo by the author.

The dining room furnishings were purchased in 1922 and consisted of a table, buffet, armoire, corner bench, several armchairs, all newly acquired in 1929. In each of the two bedrooms there were two beds with mattresses and night tables, a linen cupboard, and a vanity with a seat. One set of furnishings was bought in 1922, the other in 1929. They were all modern period furniture. Even the kitchen furniture was the most modern that was manufactured at that time. It consisted of the usual buffets, kitchen cupboards etc., obtained in 1929. The furnishings for the maid's room with bed, mattress, linen cupboard, and night table had been procured in 1922.[71]

The Walz couple, according to this account, was trying to elevate their living standard to a bourgeois level by way of acquiring new period furniture that looked distinguished.

In some Central Franconian rural communities at the beginning of the twentieth century, the trading class was made up almost exclusively of Jewish families, as was the case in Ermetzhofen.[72] There, owing to social conventions that made them look different, these Jewish families stood out sharply from the neighborhood. Yet, such conventions functioned in a way that was extremely inclusive in small and medium-sized towns like Gunzenhausen. With the kind of home furnishings the Jewish families favored, they inscribed themselves into the bourgeois culture of Franconian small towns. Their residential culture represented ascendency into the bourgeoisie, even though the occupation of trader remained completely unbourgeois. To be sure, they were still recognizable as Jews; for example, they retained the custom of posting a mezuzah on their doorposts,[73] a visible mark of distinction. Nonetheless, acculturation and social mobility did not put an end to the use of mezuzot. As Jews moved from rural villages to small and medium-sized towns, the habitual marks of distinction that set them apart from the non-Jewish population were blurred. As tradesmen, they did not stick out in these towns to the same degree they did in peasant villages. Here, it was not so much cultural as economic and social marks of distinction that now played a role.

Business Equipment and Furnishings

Even at the beginning of the twentieth century, residential and business spaces in the cattle trade were united under one roof. This residential form still reflected premodern styles of family life in which everything was usually concentrated in one room.[74] In this way, commerce and residential living were linked to one another at a single site, and families often embraced several generations simultaneously. In addition, every family member assumed an economic role within the business. This was advantageous because there was no need to walk to work and family and commercial life were tied together in a daily routine. Houses of this kind offered ample space for several generations as well as room for service personnel, most of whom (from time to time) lived with the family in their house.[75]

How high the standards were for office furnishings and how many people were employed depended on sales, and both grew along with the turnover. Owning a medium-sized cattle-trading enterprise also meant being in possession of meadows and fields to cultivate animal fodder. Not infrequently, the land held by a medium-sized cattle trader, like the property of Emanuel Engel from Markt Berolzheim, was comparable to that of a medium-sized farming operation.[76] In his postwar application for compensation, this cattle trader sought to reclaim 7.6 hectares of fields and meadowlands.[77] Along with his house, his property included a washhouse, courtyard, vegetable garden, grass garden, and pasture. On economic grounds alone, these families supplied the cattle they were selling with fodder the traders cultivated on their own, but frequently they also cultivated fruits, vegetables, and potatoes in their private gardens for self-consumption. To cover their domestic requirements, they adhered to the basic forms of peasant life. Kosher beef was procured via the Jewish community, while eggs and poultry were not infrequently acquired by bartering with peasants in a sort of payment-in-kind economy used to settle interest payments for livestock debts.[78]

The stables were annexed to the residential and business houses. Often, cattle dealers would also rent stables outside town, near the railway station or close to the market square.[79] This guaranteed the quickest possible transport from one place to the next, from customer to buyer, from farm to slaughter-house. Yet even in the stable, the rule applied that status was to be on display: former cattle hands reported that the stable and farmyard were regarded as the cattle dealer's calling card and therefore always had to be kept clean. A well-kept stable communicated the message that the operation was hygienically flawless and posed no source of danger for spreading epizootic diseases. Stables thus also functioned as sales and show spaces, where customers could examine the cattle. In an interview, two contemporary witnesses recalled additional practices involving presentation: Leonore E. noted, "My father said . . . things were already very modern around 1930, when [the Jewish cattle traders] had very young calves, they presented them so properly, they didn't just keep them in the stable, they elevated them, i.e., when the peasant came in, then the cattle was standing higher, there was already a different [more modern] way of presenting [the livestock]." Walter B. added, "They [the cattle-trading business of the Behr family] had such a beautiful stable, there weren't many stables like that!"[80]

For the cattle dealers, therefore, stables were not just utilitarian in character; they had a representative function as well, displaying the wares for sale while also signaling quality and safety. Johann Horn, the former mayor and master carpenter of Altenmuhr, gave this report in 1954 to the Landesentschä-digungsamt: "The barn and the stable were in better condition than the house, it was first in 1925 or 1926 that these buildings were newly constructed by using the old stable and the old barn that was already there."[81] Although these stables served only as accommodations for the animals in transit, they needed to be well maintained while the livestock were present there. The physically demanding work done in these stables, which would contain six pieces of livestock on average,[82] was taken over by farmhands, and in smaller operations, it was also performed by the wives of cattle traders. They mucked out the manure, fed the cattle, and were responsible for maintaining hygiene. The milk from the commercial cattle was also sold and provided an additional source of income.

FIGURE 1.6. Safe of non-Jewish cattle dealer Hans Eigenthaler, acquired around 1920. Courtesy of Karin Eigenthaler.

The middle-class character of the residential business was discernible not only because of how the commercial stable was equipped but also because of what the domestic furnishings revealed. Located in the house was the office, which was managed in smaller firms by the housewife and in larger operations by a bookkeeper hired especially for this job.[83] The office work included such tasks as keeping the accounts in order, establishing contacts with customers, placing ads in the daily paper or in agricultural periodicals, and organizing the transport of cattle to the markets. The offices were frequently equipped with a telephone line, a typewriter, and a safe in which, not infrequently, all the cattle dealers' financial assets were kept. Since cattle trading was traditionally a cash business, lots of cash needed to be kept on hand at home.[84]

The connection to the telephone network is worth noting because, more than almost any other technical innovation, it provides information about links to supraregional communication structures, thus acting indirectly as

Table 1.3 Connections of 315 Jewish and non-Jewish cattle traders to the telephone network, 1929.

	Jewish Cattle Dealers		Non-Jewish Cattle Dealers		Religious Affiliation Unknown	
Telephone Line: Yes	105	79.55%	46	29.68%	20	71.43%
Telephone Line: No	25	18.94%	105	67.74%	8	28.57%
Telephone Line: Unknown	2	1.52%	4	2.58%	–	–
Total	132	100.00%	155	100.00%	28	100.00%

Note: Cattle traders from the major cities of Nuremberg, Fürth, and Erlangen were removed from the table. The figures were taken from Bayerische Industrie- und Handelskammer, *Bayerisches Landes-Adreßbuch für Industrie, Handel und Gewerbe: Bayernbuch* (Munich: Adreßbuchverlag der Industrie- und Handelskammer, 1929).

an indicator of the cattle-trading business's scope and radius of action. So that we might be able to say more about how cattle-trading businesses were equipped with a telephone connection, the *Bayerisches Adreß-Verzeichnis* was searched for patterns of telephone usage among Jewish and non-Jewish cattle traders.

From the data collected, we can see that far more Jewish (79.55%) than non-Jewish (29.68%) cattle traders had a line connecting them to the telephone network. Once again, this reinforces the finding that Jewish cattle traders were firmly anchored in the middle class (and to medium-sized business), and it indicates the supraregional radius of their business. With the phone, arrangements and agreements could be made directly with somebody on the other end of the line. Since most firms involved in agriculture and forestry at that time were not yet tied to the telephone network,[85] we can assume that the telephone lines did not chiefly serve the purpose of communicating with farmers but rather with urban markets or other business partners.

Owning a telephone line meant that Jewish cattle traders were much in demand among their contemporaries. Non-Jews who were unable to afford a telephone themselves profited from being able to use the line of their Jewish neighbors. For example, Berta Hahn, a non-Jewish neighbor of the cattle-trading couple Eugenie and Hermann Levite from Dinkelsbühl, said, "Almost every day I went into the Levite residence because we got along very well with each other. I also went into this home became there was a telephone available there and this was used by us for business."[86]

Historian Ulrich Baumann arrived at a rather different conclusion for the Southern Baden region. He found that in 1925, Jewish cattle traders were hardly hooked up to the local telephone network when compared with Jewish textile traders. He attributes this to the importance of personal commercial ties between cattle traders and peasants, which were maintained by visits.[87]

Baumann may indeed be right to point out that immediate contact with farmers was indispensable in the cattle trade. In the context of the time, however, when the cattle trade was woven into a supraregional production network, we can assume that the telephone was used primarily for communicating with business partners, buyers, cattle commissioners, urban slaughterhouses, and railway administrative offices in order to coordinate the next cattle transport to the city cattle market and less for communicating with farmers. Baumann's finding leads one to suspect that the rural Southern Baden cattle traders he studied were not yet integrated into a supraregional network of buyers and that they sold their livestock in the immediate vicinity.

This finding cannot be established for Central Franconia. Peasant customers profited indirectly from the use of the new technology, and cattle could be transported faster and at a lower cost. The telephone had a catalytic function for agrarian society. It was the symbol and expression of a cultural-technological advantage disproportionally used by Jewish cattle traders.[88] Owing to their outward orientation, traders were more attached to technological innovations than was the peasant population.[89]

But it was not just the telephone that symbolized technical advantage and modernity; new means of locomotion like the automobile or the motorcycle also were expressions of mobility and status. Cattle traders needed to be mobile all the time in order to get from one place to another as fast as possible. The development of the automobile seriously changed the trader's everyday routine, enabling him to return home every evening instead of having to be on foot from Sunday to the beginning of the Sabbath, Friday afternoon, in his mediene.[90] With the introduction of the motor vehicle, cattle traders could now return home to their families daily and share in everyday life. In addition, they no longer needed to stay overnight at unfamiliar inns, which made them less exposed to dangers there.[91]

But here, too, the kind of social stratification that existed among cattle traders made itself felt, since poorer cattle traders or Schmusers were still using a carriage in order to get from one farm to another or even a bicycle like the one operated by Hermann Bechhöfer. His nephew Jerry Bechhöfer recalled vividly, "I have a pleasant memory of my Onkel Hermann coming down on a hill into town on his bicycle, with his grey-beige 'shop coat' flying behind him."[92] Cattle traders with a larger sales volume were frequently among the first in town to own an automobile, which gave them a higher status within the local hierarchy.[93] From the proceedings of denazification courts and contemporary witness accounts, it emerges how jealous non-Jewish neighbors looked at the owners of these automobiles. They were repeatedly making malicious comments about villagers who were allowed to ride along in the Jews' "little strolling wagons" (*Spazierwägelchen*).[94]

New technological achievements like the automobile and the telephone streamlined the cattle trade and heightened the traders' mobility. Cattle could be sold directly, and new cows could be obtained immediately. Time-saving modern technology also meant that fewer traders were needed than in the days when cattle dealers were still traveling by foot from Sunday to Friday along their mediene.

Employees

It was possible to gauge the cattle traders' social status and the economic standing of their businesses not only by the material furnishings in their homes and business quarters but also by the number of employees working for them, a number that was also primarily geared to sales figures. A livestock entrepreneur with a medium-sized business usually employed at least one servant who looked after the animals in the stable and helped with work in the field as needed. Cattle drovers, by contrast, were employed as day laborers (as needed). Driving cattle, a job both women and men from the rural lower classes practiced, was quite laborious (especially in winter when there was snow and ice). These hired hands drove livestock that had been purchased to the cattle trader's stable, the markets, or the next train station. One thing former cattle drovers especially recalled was when their employer would buy them a warm meal at a restaurant, as in the case of Wilhelm Sperr, who, as late as 2008, gave a wide-eyed account of how cattle trader Hermann Behr paid for cattle driving at the Kalter Markt in Ellwangen with a hearty lentil soup at a tavern.[95]

Employees included not only ordinary journeymen like drovers and farm-hands but also trained bookkeepers and, in larger operations, chauffeurs.[96] Even if a majority of the employees in the firms I researched were Christians (with more Catholics than Protestants among them), chores were also carried out by Jewish employees, who frequently came from the immediate or extended family circle. In many households, young unmarried women assisted as maids. They often came from peasant families with whom the cattle traders had had business relations for generations. They lived in the house of the cattle-trading family, and their payment consisted of free room and board along with a modest weekly wage.[97] These young girls assisted in the household until they found a marriage partner, as Grete Weinberg (née Hamburger), daughter of a Jewish cattle trader from Nördlingen, confirmed:

> They [the maids] were usually girls, daughters from farmers. . . . My father had very nice farmers and when the girls did not want to be on the farm and they said, "Could my daughter work for you in your house for some while until she finds something else?" And my mother would train them, and from there they would go somewhere else. . . . They had their own rooms and when my parents, my mother went for lunch, they ate with us. . . . And when my father was home, they would not eat with us at the table.[98]

Maids, then, unlike farmhands, became part of the family for the duration of their employment. This frequently gave rise to close social relationships that were even maintained after the Jewish families were forced to emigrate. For example, Babette Baumann, who worked until 1938 as a maid for the Mann family, continued to stay in touch with the family even after their expulsion from Rothenburg ob der Tauber.[99]

Looking more closely at the social stratification characteristic of Jewish cattle-trading operations, one is struck by how deeply rooted these businesses were in a livestock trade made up of well-developed medium-sized firms. These firms' links to the railway and telephone networks gave them—independently of how large their place of residence was—structural and economic advantages.

In small rural towns like Altenmuhr or Markt Berolzheim, cattle traders running medium-sized businesses had habits that distinguished them substantially from their peasant surroundings. In places like Gunzenhausen or Rothenburg ob der Tauber, their very routines are what etched them into small-town bourgeois society. Their employment of salaried personnel not only pointed to the middle-class character of their medium-sized businesses and to their bourgeois habitus but also opened up another important area of life—that between the non-Jewish and Jewish environment.

Trader Families: Men and Women in the Cattle Trade
Family Traditions

The cattle trade was traditionally run as a family business, involving men and women alike. That means that we cannot focus solely on the male traders if we want to get a precise picture of the cattle-dealing business in the Weimar period; we must expand our analysis to include the role of women and children.

Is there a transformation that can be recognized within one or two generations, or are there discernable continuities? What role do family networks play?

In fact, almost all of the businesses I researched go back to an intrafamily tradition. It was, admittedly, customary for Jewish merchant families, depending on the economic situation, to move from one branch of business to a closely related one or to operate these different kinds of businesses simultaneously. Yet there was still a certain continuity about cattle trading, as can be seen in the case of Gustav Gutmann's business operations in Feuchtwangen. Gutmann was born in 1870 in the small rural town of Jochsberg, and in 1900, he moved to the nearby district capital Feuchtwangen, where he simultaneously registered a cattle-trading business with the local authorities. Conscripted during the First World War in 1915, he provisionally returned his trade license until he was able to make a successful reapplication following his return from the war. Alongside the cattle business, he also was a buyer of hay and straw and traded in hides, raw commodities, reeds, and bulrushes. Yet the cattle trade remained his main business. Following his death in 1932, his wife, Mathilde Gutmann, continued to run the cattle-trading business on her own authority.[100] Like Gustav, many cattle traders also had a side job (depending on the business climate) in some other, related branch. The additional trades they plied were mostly associated with the cattle business, like furs and hides. Trading in real estate, moreover, represented a suitable (side) business. Since they got to know the financial situation of their customers very well through their work as cattle traders, and because they were familiar with granting credit, they were also suited to act as consultants in real-estate matters. Linking the cattle trade to related commercial ventures had a positive effect on the traders' client acquisition, which might then result in more favorable prices for their customers.

Shifting from a cattle-trading business to a trade like textiles or ironmongery, by contrast, was not something that could be documented. More typically, trade would be divided between brothers or various branches of the family, with one son dealing in animals or animal products and another in textiles. For example, the family branch going back to Joseph Gabriel Hirsch operated in the cattle trade, whereas the branch of the family going back to Isaac Hirsch traded in draperies.[101] This intrafamily division into two completely different branches offered protection against branch-specific downturns in the business cycle. The continuity of trade in one specific product group was, moreover, a defining characteristic of these family businesses. For example, this was also the case with the cattle-trading business of the Behr family from Mönchsroth, which could look back on a more than century-old tradition of doing business, passed on for generations from father to son. Often, the change of generations was expressed by a change in the name of the business; thus, until 1928, the Behr family business was conducted under the name Firma Simon Behr (the Simon Behr Firm), but after Simon's retirement, the company was transferred to his sons, who ran it under the name Firma Simon Behrs Söhne (the Simon Behr's Sons Firm) as equal shareholders.[102] The name of the father thus remained an essential part of the firm's name in the next generation, communicating continuity and stability.

The structure of the fraternal business highlighted here represents a kind of continuity going back to the era before Jewish emancipation. The co-owners of the business, if they were not actually brothers, usually belonged to the extended family circle. It needs to be stressed that the business partnerships all derived from the Jewish family network. And, of course, although one of the things the partnership promised was an increase in economic profit, it is clear that intra-Jewish factors played a decisive role in the choice of a business partner. Only in two cases could an opening to the non-Jewish world in the form of a formal cooperation between a Jewish and non-Jewish cattle trader be documented. One of these cases is the cooperation between Moritz Engel from Markt Berolzheim and non-Jewish cattle trader Hans Stopfer from Ingolstadt. Engel used this business partnership to send livestock purchased in his mediene by rail to Ingolstadt, sixty kilometers away. From there, Stopfer resold it on the southern Bavarian markets.[103] Since Old Bavaria (the mostly southern part of Bavaria, not including Franconia or the Swabian part of the Free State), where the cattle markets of Ingolstadt and Munich were located, did not have any established Jewish rural communities, the concentration of Jews in the cattle trade there was much smaller than in Franconia.[104] In order to sell cattle and expand business there, Jewish traders needed to work with non-Jewish traders. But in places where enough Jewish business partners were available, they were preferred.[105] A question that remains unanswered, by contrast, is the extent to which non-Jewish cattle traders entered into business partnerships with Jewish cattle traders on their own initiative. It has been clearly proven that the cattle trade—even at the start of the twentieth century, and not only within Jewish families, but within non-Jewish families as well—was conducted as a family business across cultural settings.

Diverging Social and Spatial Mobility of
Women and Men from Cattle-Trading Families

The significance of Jewish networks is also apparent when we observe patterns of social and spatial mobility among individual members of entrepreneurial families. One thing that stands out here is how the retention of an Orthodox Jewish lifestyle did not at all get in the way of an embourgeoisement of cattle-trading families. This is best demonstrated by looking at male and female members separately.

Since scholarly descriptions of the cattle trade have traditionally confined the researcher's perspective to a focus on male business managers, we have lacked (to date) any systematic investigation into the role of women in this branch. It is true that scholars since the 1980s, influenced by women's studies, started bringing Jewish women into the historical literature as active participants.[106] Yet analyses of women in the cattle-trading branch are rare exceptions in the literature.[107] One reason for this may be that women were traditionally assigned the role of keepers of Jewish tradition, so that no economic role was ascribed to them. But an examination of the role of women in the cattle trade highlights a revealing social trend inside the Jewish family that simultaneously sheds light on an important economic process.

We evaluated the sociodemographic data of 138 women in the cattle trade, most of whom were the wives of cattle traders. These women were initially divided into two age groups. The first was made up of women who were born between 1859 and 1906 and had grown up during a time when Jews gradually experienced legal emancipation; these women had already started families before the National Socialist seizure of power set in. (This group included sixty-seven women.)[108] In the second group were the first group's daughters, born between 1906 and 1926. During the period under investigation here, these women were still being trained, and none of the women had already started a family of their own. Both groups will be examined here with regard to their social and spatial mobility so as to reveal differences and commonalities about their role within the cattle trade.

Marriage Politics for the Preservation of Jewish Tradition

It is important to note that the women of the older generation (born in the period 1859–1906) were all married to a Jewish spouse, so having a Jewish affiliation must have played an important role in the choice of a marriage partner. Overall, we find only two interfaith marriages among the cattle-trading couples researched, and in each case, a Jewish man had married a non-Jewish woman.[109] On the men's side, the preservation of Jewish tradition frequently seems to have been decisive for the choice of a spouse.[110]

If Jewish origins mattered a great deal for men choosing a spouse, we must also inquire into the economic motives involved in the selection of a mate. This question needs to be raised without feeding the old antisemitic stereotype that "Jews [were trading] their daughters like cattle."[111] Such bigoted clichés notwithstanding, fully understanding the marriage politics of Jewish cattle trader

Table 1.4 Distance between birthplace and later residence for fifty cattle traders' wives in kilometers (without Nuremberg).

Distance	Place of Birth & Residence Identical		Up to 50 km		51 to 100 km		Over 100 km	
Wives of Cattle Traders (n = 50)	8	16%	21	42%	13	26%	8	16%

Note: Here, too, as with the previous analyses, the cattle traders' wives from Nuremberg are treated separately.

families does require asking whether marrying into these families was intended to expand trade contacts into other important agricultural regions.[112] In order to examine this, we measured the distance of a woman's birthplace from the subsequent residence of her spouse. To make this measurement, we drew on the sociodemographic data of about sixty-four women, for whom both their place of birth and their subsequent residence were known (though the data is missing for three of these women).

The birthplace of more than half (58%) of the wives was in immediate proximity to the residence of the men who later became their husbands. Eight women (16%) even continued to reside in the town where they were born. The largest group of women (42%) moved to a place up to fifty kilometers away after their wedding. To the peasant population, fifty kilometers might seem high, since peasants frequently found their spouses in the same or in a neighboring community. For the rural Jewish community, however, which at the time was in a process of dissolution and was often several kilometers away from the next Jewish community, spatial proximity between birthplace and subsequent place of residence played a major role in choosing a partner. In thirteen cases, to be sure, the spatial distance between birthplace and later place of residence was as great as up to a hundred kilometers—and in eight cases, even more. Yet this does not provide any proof of marriage strategies involving supraregional cattle-trading territories outside Franconia. Rather, these cases indicate that no suitable Jewish spouse could be found in the immediate vicinity and that the marriages were arranged according to Jewish traditions.[113] In these rural "marrying-in communities," spatial mobility was something that lent women from communities further away a certain air that was regionally *different*—if not quite urban—in character. This provincially exotic character was chiefly manifested in a strange dialect and (presumably) also in a clothing style that betrayed the women's origins in a native region distinct from the Franconian surroundings to which they had moved.[114]

Nuremberg Wives of Cattle Traders

We arrive at a completely different set of results if we look at the group of cattle traders' wives from the city of Nuremberg. This group displays features that are different from those we find among the rural and small-town group of cattle traders wives, as table 5 makes clear.

In contrast to the cattle traders' wives from rural or small-town areas, the cattle traders' wives living in Nuremberg moved to that city from faraway regions along with their partners at the time of their weddings. A striking feature of this group is its geographic mobility, both for men and women. A majority of the wives of cattle traders living in Nuremberg were born and grew up outside Bavaria. It is unclear what might have motivated them and their spouses to move to Nuremberg, of all places. Presumably, the constantly expanding cattle market exerted a strong pull. And, unlike the situation they faced in cattle-market sites of comparable importance (such as Mannheim, Frankfurt am Main, and Berlin), in Nuremberg, Jews were only permitted to settle when full rights to do so were granted in 1850. For the old-established Franconian cattle-trading families, on the other hand, moving to the Nuremberg metropolis hardly brought with it any advantages. Because of these traders' close proximity to the Nuremberg metropolis, commuting directly to the cattle market in the city and calling on peasant customers in their mediene were tasks they could accomplish in a single day.

Since looking into the distance between birthplace and subsequent place of residence will not, on its own, give us any information about the structure and size of the birthplace and thus about the social environment of the cattle traders' wives, the next step in our investigation is to compare the size of the women's birthplace with that of their later residence.

From this observation, we learn that almost half of the women surveyed (47.83%) moved from a small town to a bigger one after getting married. Among the wives of Nuremberg cattle traders, the quotient was even higher; there, eleven of fourteen partners (approximately 79%) had been born in a town smaller than Nuremberg. This geographic mobility is also demonstrable for the men. Therefore, we can assume that both marriage partners jointly moved from a smaller to a bigger place. In general, nearly every third marriage was concluded among spouses from the same town or from towns of equal size. Only 15.94 percent of the women were born in a larger town than their partners'.[115] This is not an astonishing finding if one considers that in 1880, there was a significant surplus of women in the rural Jewish communities, so it was easy to find a female spouse in the immediate vicinity.[116] The choice of a marriage

Table 1.5 Distance between birthplace and later residence for fourteen Nuremberg cattle traders' wives, in kilometers.

Distance	Up to 50 km		51 to 100 km		Over 100 km		Unknown	
Wives of Cattle Traders (n = 14)	3	21.43%	4	28.57%	5	35.71%	2	14.29%

Table 1.6 Size difference between birthplace and place of residence for sixty-nine wives of cattle traders from the birth cohort 1859–1906, divided according to size category for town (based on number of residents), 1925.

	Size Category of Birthplace and Place of Residence *Identical*		Size Category of Birthplace *Smaller* than Place of Residence		Size Category of Birthplace *Larger* than Place of Residence		No Statement Possible	
Wives of Cattle Traders (born 1859–1906, n = 69)	20	28.98%	33	47.83%	11	15.94%	5	7.25%

Note: This classification into categories based on size of locality follows Statistisches Reichsamt, *Statistisches Jahrbuch für das Deutsche Reich, 1924/25* (Berlin: Verlag für Politik und Wissenschaft, 1925), 3.

partner from rural surroundings also increased the probability that she came from a cattle-trading family and had excellent qualifications for marrying into a cattle-trading household. This makes it clear that two things were secured with the choice of a marriage partner: the preservation of Jewish tradition and geographic and professional closeness of the family of origin to the marrying-in family. Expanding business ties into other cattle-trading regions or into important cattle markets, by contrast, was a consideration that apparently played a rather subordinate role in the choice of a female spouse.[117] How hard it was for men, on top of that, to find a suitable spouse in spite of the surplus of women is something Trude Maurer has drawn attention to. From her analysis of marriage advertisements, she concluded that cattle traders were not regarded as preferred marriage partners by Jewish women.[118]

From Village Cattle Trader's Wife to Bourgeois Housewife

The women in the group analyzed here adhered to a traditional Jewish way of life, even as they developed a simultaneous attachment to a middle-class way of life and small-town entrepreneurial culture. In this entrepreneurial culture, there was a discernable shift from the role of a wife engaged in the cattle trade to that of a gentrified (more bourgeois) housewife. Overall, the data on these wives underpin the finding that the cattle trade, in the course of urbanization, developed from a rural trading business into a middle-class kind of entrepreneurship for medium-sized small-town businesses.

Co-employed and Self-employed Traders' Wives

In those cattle-trading businesses that still had a rural character, women often took over work in the stables and fields, along with the bookkeeping.[119] These women assisted in running the family businesses in order to save on hiring additional personnel and improve the economic foundation of the family.

Collaborating in the cattle-trading business could extend as far as co-ownership of the business and self-employment. Although the cattle trade was a male domain, among the wives examined here we also find self-employed female traders; some worked along with their husbands, but some even worked alone. One exception, certainly, was Lina Eckmann from Burghaslach, who was employed on a regular basis in the business of her husband, Julius Eckmann. Because her husband had a hops business and was therefore often on the road, Lina managed the business on her own authority during his absence. Since she had commercial training, she also took care of the bookkeeping and the other office work, including all written and telephone correspondence.[120] She would get support in doing the housework from three domestic servants, and the couple also employed two cattle farmhands who helped out in the stable. At harvest time, the cattle-trading couple got support from additional personnel.[121] In addition to carrying out her managerial tasks, Lina, like peasant women, performed the hard physical labor in the fields required to produce cattle fodder. Her husband, however, only carried on the trade part of the business, as his 1959 testimony to the Landesentschädigungsamt underscores. Julius complained about the hard work he had to undertake on the orange plantations of a kibbutz, physical labor for which he believed he was entirely unsuited. He noted: "In Germany I only dealt with the commercial end of things—whereas the work on the fields . . . was taken care of by my wife together with the hired hands."[122]

The assistance given by women to the business not only substituted for somebody else's labor power; it also protected against a loss of livelihood in times of economic crisis. For example, in 1926, Josef Uhlfelder registered in his wife's name the cattle-trading business that had previously gone bankrupt so that he could keep running it. Since Frieda Uhlfelder had grown up in a rural cattle-trading household, she was thoroughly familiar with the business practices of the cattle trade and could take over the management of the business "without reservation."[123] But it was not only the bankruptcy of a firm that could lead to women becoming self-employed in the cattle trade; often this self-employment was triggered by the death of the husband. Not infrequently, widows show up in the sources as self-employed cattle traders. Thus, for example, we find Mathilde Gutmann from Feuchtwangen continuing to run her husband's business independently after his death.[124] This takeover, in contrast to Lina's case, was not prompted because Mathilde brought skills of her own into the joint business but rather because there was a threat to the family's economic livelihood upon her husband's death. There were also other women who worked in a field completely different from than that of their husbands, such as Fanny Rosenblatt from Burghaslach, who expanded the family income as a trader in draperies.[125]

In the cases presented here, the reasons women became active in the cattle-trading business were primarily economic in nature. Their collaboration saved the husband from having to hire additional labor and so contributed significantly to securing the family's livelihood. Lina's case stands out in this respect, since her training allowed her to practice the cattle trade as an equal partner, thereby facilitating her husband's sideline as a hops buyer and making it possible for him to travel to the most important hops and cattle markets in Germany. This simultaneously helped secure and expand the economic foundation of the family's cattle-trading business. In addition, these women maintained contacts with the non-Jewish world when they negotiated with customers and established relationships.[126] Even if many points of contact with the non-Jewish world arose from these transactions, these were restricted to the sphere of household business or to the family's place of residence, since only the men traveled to the urban markets where the livestock that had been bought was resold.[127]

Housewives

Alongside the group of self-employed and co-employed wives of cattle traders, the group of housewives is the largest in purely quantitative terms.[128] These women had brought themselves in line with a more bourgeois family model that distinguishes between a male world outside the household and a female one inside. In this model, the man is assigned the role of breadwinner and the woman that of nurturer, educator, and the person responsible for the family's welfare. An essential precondition for the life of a family model like this was an income that had grown large enough so that a woman's labor power was dispensable.

As housewives, these women now added to their intra-Jewish function a more Gentile-like role with which they anchored themselves in the bourgeois social majority as middle-class entrepreneurs.[129] On the women's side of things, then, we see a social change and symbolic rise into the bourgeoisie; by extension, this was also a departure from the cattle trade of the old rural Jewish communities, a process illustrated in the following pages.

One hallmark of Jewish cattle-trading families' embourgeoisement was their home furnishings, for whose design and maintenance women alone were responsible. Another distinguishing feature was the employment of maid-servants. These families earned such a large income that they could afford to do without the labor power of the housewife and delegate this to hired staff. The maids relieved these wives of a portion of the housework, including such tasks as laundry, shopping, and cleaning the home, and sometimes also work in the stable and fields. If a non-Jewish rather than a Jewish maid was em-ployed (which was frequently the case), not all housework could be delegated, including, for example, the preparation of kosher meals. Tasks that served to maintain Jewish traditions remained the sole job of the household's Jewish headmistress.[130] All the same, these women intensified the integrative role they played in contacts maintained with the domestic staff. Since the maids lived in the homes of the families, they participated both passively and actively in the cattle traders' family life.

This integrative role, however, was not something the housewives practiced only by cultivating social contacts with the Jewish and non-Jewish environ-ment, both of which were essential parts of their everyday life. This is confirmed by Grete Weinberg, who grew up in a Jewish cattle-trading household in the Swabian town of Nördlingen: "After she [my mother] got me to school, she probably talked on the telephone with some friends, or prepared some lunch or prepared for dinner, or my grandmother was downstairs. She took her for a walk or went to see some friends with her."[131] In addition, she emphasizes the social role played her mother: "My mother did nothing in this [cattle] busi-ness . . . my mother was a *Hausfrau*, you know, she visited people, she went to *Kränzchen* [coffee klatches], she took care of some friends who were sick, you know, I mean nothing *beruflich* [professional]."[132] She also remembers how her mother met up with Jewish and non-Jewish girlfriends for a coffee klatch and to play cards at a local café every Saturday afternoon.[133] This sociable custom allowed her to cultivate contacts, and it also shows us she did not worry about frequenting a business establishment to play games on a Saturday, though we do not know if she paid in advance, before the onset of the Sabbath, for coffee and cake. That this kind of social activity was part of the everyday routine of

FIGURE 1.7. Betty Bermann, Ellingen, around 1930.
Courtesy of William Berman.

housewives is something that Hilde Jochsberger also emphasizes in talking about her mother: "My mother was a very socially active person, kept a lovely clean house, was known as a terrific cook, family from Nuremberg used to come on Sundays, especially to eat with us. She had a bicycle, and was always visiting family members and friends. They called her: D.U.—*dauernd unterwegs* [constantly on the road]. Also, the young Jewish people loved to visit her and to talk to her."[134] These kinds of social contacts made it more feasible for women than for men to achieve a minimum of social integration into the non-Jewish world extending beyond the cattle trade. This was facilitated by women's social circles that, compared to those of males, were less formal and less hierarchically structured, such as needlework circles or the famous coffee klatch. The women were also assigned a socially integrative function that men did not and perhaps could not (at least not yet) perform.[135] To be sure, Jewish men also frequented inns to drink beer with farmers, but these meetings were often purely business; conversations were about prospective deals or finalizing the details of specific transactions. The social contacts of the women, by contrast, were primarily based on personal interests; they were not about society or even politics.[136]

It was not only through their numerous social contacts in the non-Jewish and nontrading world that the women were able to exercise this kind of integrative function but also via their style of clothing, which lent them (just superficially) a more bourgeois and urban air. Unlike their husbands, who usually wore the kind of full-length overcoats favored by traders and some of whom still covered their heads for religious reasons (usually by wearing a man's hat), they were not recognizable outwardly as Jews.[137]

This integrative role first gained importance with the arrival of legal equality and the concomitant disengagement of Jews from the rural ghetto they originally inhabited. For these women, geographic mobility away from small rural towns to small and medium-sized cities also entailed a shift in their role as wives of cattle traders. As a result, their living environment as well as their responsibilities had changed extensively within a single generation. It is through these women that we see the clearest expression of changes in the social disposition of cattle-trading families. The cattle traders' spouses led lives that were fundamentally different from those of peasant women; at the same time, their role as housewives did make a major contribution to anchoring the cattle traders' families in an environment that was bourgeois but small-town. This means that the social transformation of the cattle traders' wives can be viewed as a cultural transformation process in which Jewish women deliberately adhered to their own traditions, appropriated norms outside their own culture, and integrated these into both peasant and nonpeasant society.[138] They thus found themselves navigating a tension between traditional, intrafamily responsibilities and adaptation to a bourgeois way of life.

The Daughters: Breakaways from Family Tradition

This transformation continued into the next generation of women and even points to a break with the intrafamily tradition in the cattle trade. While the mothers either worked in their husbands' businesses or inscribed themselves in bourgeois small-town culture through their activities as housewives, the daughters (those born between 1906 and 1926) extricated themselves from the intrafamily cattle-trading tradition. This process was ushered in by the way the daughters in these families were educated. Many girls in this generation received advanced schooling and vocational training; not infrequently, they were sent to schools—including non-Jewish ones—that were far away. One example is Hilde Jochsberger from Leutershausen, whose parents made it possible for her, at the age of ten, to visit the *Realschule* (middle school) in Heilbronn am Neckar in Württemberg.[139] In addition, entirely in line with the bourgeois model of a proper upbringing, great significance was attached to the musical education of the daughters. For example, Betty Hellmann traveled fifteen kilometers every day by train or bicycle from Markt Berolzheim to Gunzenhausen in order "to be given instruction in painting and the fine arts."[140]

To what extent the boundaries between the Jewish and non-Jewish world were dissolving in this generation is also shown by the kinds of recreational activities undertaken during their leisure time. Karola Thormann from Altenmuhr, for example, was a member in the local Club of the Harmless, a group consisting of Jewish and non-Jewish youth who met every week during the 1920s, not at a reserved table in the local pub like most groups of regulars (which would have been too expensive), but at their parents' homes on a rotating basis.[141] Looking at this kind of leisure pursuit and at the acquisition of secondary school education allows us to see the strong trend toward the daughters' embourgeoisement and acculturation to the non-Jewish majority.

Secondary school education also opened up a larger marriage circle for these daughters than had been available to their mothers, a development that rang in the end of the intrafamily business tradition typical of the cattle trade. The Stern family from Leutershausen is a textbook example of this breakout from the old marriage tradition. The well-established cattle trader Falk Stern, whose business went back at least three generations, married Beppi Behr, who also came from a cattle-trading household. Their only daughter, Paula, however, was not married off to another cattle trader; instead, Falk sent her to the girls' secondary school in Fürth, fifty kilometers away.[142] There, family ties helped secure convenient lodgings for Paula with her aunt Bertha Fleischmann, who was married to a Jewish butcher.

At the girls' high school, Paula met teacher Louis Kissinger, who later became her husband. Two sons, Heinz and Walter Bernhard, were born. Heinz, who renamed himself Henry after the family fled to the United States, where he later became secretary of state, symbolizes like nobody else the upward mobility of cattle-trading families.[143] Even if the career of Falk's grandson Henry Kissinger is wholly unrepresentative, the biographical pathway taken by his mother does stand as a symbol for many women from her generation. Like Paula, the majority of daughters from cattle-trading families no longer married cattle traders themselves.[144]

A look at wedding dowries shows just how important it was for the families to marry off their daughters in a manner befitting their social station. For

FIGURE 1.8. Flora and Marta Winter, daughters of
cattle trader Solomon Winter, April 1938, Wittelshofen.
Courtesy of USHMM, no. 25832.

example, the Mann family from Rothenburg ob der Tauber had deposited se-
curities valued at least eighteen thousand reichsmarks in different banks as a
dowry for their daughter Dinah Grete.[145] This amount leads one to suspect that
Dinah was intended to be married into a middle-class family at the very least,
if not into a family with an even higher income. In this way, toward the end of
the Weimar Republic, cattle-trading families began to break out of a highly
developed Jewish marriage practice steeped in tradition. On the part of the
daughters, we may observe a certain social mobility, a turn to other occupations, and thus an uncoupling from the cattle-trading milieu, though not from
a Jewish background. Although the daughters did come into contact with the
non-Jewish world in many ways, no intermarriage across religious lines could
be documented even within this more open generation.

Upon marriage, these women did not abruptly break off contact with their ancestral families; they continued cultivating ties to the home community.[146] Until her forced emigration in 1938, for example, Paula spent summer vacation along with her two sons at Falk's home in Leutershausen. In his biography of Henry Kissinger, Walter Isaacson describes how formative this time in Leutershausen was for the future diplomat: "For the young Kissinger, one place was particularly magical: his mother's family home in Leutershausen, where the Kissingers spent the summer. The Stern home was stately and secure, built around a cozy courtyard where Heinz would chase the family's brood of chickens and, as he grew older, play *Völkerball* with his friends."[147]

The Sons: Preservers of the Cattle-Trading Tradition[148]

Whereas the daughters were breaking out of the cattle-trading milieu toward the end of the Weimar Republic, the sons seemed to remain in that setting, as a glance at their pattern of social mobility suggests. It is commonly assumed that the sons' social mobility was what initiated the dissolution of the "Jewish cattle trade."[149] This conclusion could be drawn from a survey published by the B'nai Brith Lodge about the situation of the Jewish rural population in Baden in 1900. From the survey, it emerges that 60 percent of all young Jewish men took up the career of merchant and only 17.2 percent remained in the cattle trade.[150] Based on the data I gathered, this assumption will now be examined in order to learn more about the status of the cattle-trading branch at the beginning of the twentieth century.

In my data sample, there is information about around two hundred men who were born between 1870 and 1926. The data on the men was divided into two groups. The first group is made up of older cattle traders (born 1870–1900) who had grown up immediately following the granting of legal equality to Jews and who were running well-established businesses prior to the start of National Socialist persecution. Their firms could all be traced back to an intrafamily tradition, meaning that they were carrying on the pre-emancipatory activity of their fathers.[151]

The next generation of sons (born 1900–1926) makes up the second group.[152] They were examined with respect to their social mobility—namely whether they would reorient away from the cattle-trading profession by acquiring some professional training other than the family education leading to a job as cattle trader.[153] For this generation of cattle traders, a new development in professional training was clearly taking place. There was, to be sure, a continued role for the traditional intrafamily transmission of knowledge, whereby the fathers, following their sons' bar mitzvahs, according to Jewish tradition, would pass on the requisite skills and knowledge associated with the cattle trade. These

FIGURE 1.9. Siegbert Bravman, Wittelshofen, around 1920. United States Holocaust Memorial Museum, courtesy of Steven Frank, no. 45551.

traditional skills included expert evaluation of the cattle, which entailed palpating the udders, determining the age of the livestock according to the condition of the horns and hoofs, and assessing the cattle's productivity based on their posture, gait, and weight. In addition, the fathers taught their sons to keep cash constantly on hand so that they would be prepared at any time to accept a new business trade, even when away from farms and cattle markets. Carrying a knife and rope was essential for tying and untying cows. It was also of vital importance to master the basic arithmetic needed to determine prices.[154]

Yet this generation did not confine itself to the premodern style of intrafamily knowledge transmission; instead, this type of instruction was expanded to include extrafamilial schooling and vocational training. Conspicuously, the majority of the sons learned their trade in Jewish firms; only a few learned in non-Jewish ones.[155] For example, Karl Freising (born 1900) from Roth attended Realschule in Gunzenhausen and Nuremberg, then received commercial training at a Jewish firm in Treuchtlingen before taking over the paternal cattle-trading business in 1918.[156] Also discernable is a professionalization of the cattle trade resulting from the expansion of intrafamilial training to include an extrafamilial and state-certified component.

Like Freising, most of the sons in the firms I researched returned to their fathers' cattle-trading businesses following the successful completion of their training. Although this generation also included some sons who took up a different occupation, like Semi Mohr from Altenmuhr, who rose to become director of the Wertheim department store in Berlin, these kinds of careers remained the exception.[157] Probably more typical would have been the professional development of Hermann Behr from Mönchsroth, who followed graduation from Realschule by joining his father's cattle-trading firm and then taking over the business in 1928 along with his brothers.[158]

The large number of young Jewish men who returned to their home community after successfully concluding an apprenticeship and then entered the family business calls into question the assertion that the lower absolute number of Jewish cattle dealers is a result of their move to larger cities.[159] It seems all the more astonishing to learn that this generation included a large number of "returners"—that is, sons who carried on the familial cattle-trading tradition even after concluding an extrafamilial commercial course of training.

The sources provide little information about the motives for the sons' return to their fathers' firms. But they do suggest that the findings of the B'nai Brith survey from Baden need to be evaluated critically, since the survey says nothing about whether the sons stayed away from the cattle trade or practiced it as merchants with commercial training following their graduation from trade school.

Possible reasons for the return of the cattle traders' sons to their paternal firms might have included antisemitism and bad economic conditions following the First World War, when it was difficult for the unemployed in general and the Jewish unemployed in particular to find jobs. In times like this, occupational access to a well-managed paternal firm might have been attractive for one job candidate or another. Cattle-trading fathers, in addition to being intellectually equipped with the requisite knowledge for practicing the trade, also provided their sons with the "customer capital" they needed, namely the mediene that was always passed on from one generation to the next.[160] A well located mediene could, in spite of the vagaries of the cattle trade, facilitate a middle-class living standard.

The cattle trade had thus experienced an impetus toward professionalization that was rung in by educational training for the younger generation. In addition, the progressive motorization of society had also provided an impetus toward rationalization that permanently reduced the need for cattle traders. Those who owned an automobile could visit many more peasants daily than they might have done on foot or on a bicycle. The decline in the number of cattle traders among the younger generation should therefore not be explained monocausally by reference to the supposedly low attractiveness of the profession but must be seen in the context of the times, in which every branch of the economy was experiencing modernization.

In Motion

The statement that Jewish cattle traders were a "backward" group of rural Jews who were staying put in their pre-emancipatory fields even after discriminatory occupational barriers had been eliminated rather than turning toward bourgeois professions must be contradicted.[161] This group of cattle traders underwent their own process of urbanization. Many of the families researched here moved to a bigger town with a railway connection once residential restrictions on Jews were lifted and had detached themselves from traditional rural settlement patterns.

From among the families researched, two basic motives emerged for their move away from smaller rural communities: (1) improved mobility because of the connection to the railway network; and (2) a business expansion involving the setup of a fraternal branch, with one brother moving to Nuremberg, where he would establish a wholesale cattle trade, while the other brother would take up residence in a smaller town, where he would buy cattle from the local farmers. Both motives resulted in a higher sales volume and enhanced profit maximization. This frequently provided the impetus for moving to the next biggest city, rather than the wish to start a new life.[162] To be sure, Jews in the cattle trade were still seen as clinging to their traditional commercial profession, yet within this profession, they continued to develop, keeping up with the requirements of the times. By the end of the Weimar Republic, therefore, they were in a process of urbanization that made them participants in the modernization process experienced by the overall Jewish population.[163] Preserving an Orthodox Jewish way of life did not stand in the way of this development.

As demonstrated, the traditional dichotomy of Jewish cattle traders versus farmers needs to be abolished. The living environment and therefore also the social environment of the cattle-trading families had become a small-town setting; in the interwar period, it was no longer a farming milieu. There, in the small and medium-sized towns, a process of embourgeoisement took place among the women in middle-class cattle-trading families, a gentrification that included these families in the social majority even if their customers remained completely rural peasantry.

Both for the sons and for the daughters, moreover, it was striking how social mobility was now acquired by way of secondary schooling. Here, however, the paths embarked on by the two genders parted. While the daughters broke out of family tradition by marrying non–cattle traders, the sons carried forward the tradition, even after receiving training outside the family. One reason for this may have had to do with the economic viability of the cattle trade, which resulted from the huge demand for productive cattle of both kinds, for domestic farming and for slaughter. From this we may conclude that the decline in Jewish cattle-trading businesses since Jews were granted legal equality needs to be viewed not just against the backdrop of sons moving away to the cities—as previous historical research had assumed—but also in the context of developments in the cattle trade specific to that branch of the economy.

2

Trust and Cattle Trading

The cattle trade had changed dramatically in the course of industrialization; through the expansion of the railway network, the trade had been woven into a larger customer base and thereby rendered more anonymous. Yet the social relations that the trader had with his customers remained the decisive factor for a successful cattle-trading business. The importance of social relationships may be deduced from a rejection letter sent by the Bayerisches Landesentschädigungsamt (the postwar Bavarian State Compensation Office) to a cattle-trading family's lawyer concerning compensation for the goodwill—meaning compensation for the business or company value—of a cattle-trading business. The office rejected in principle all applications of Jewish cattle traders to be compensated for the pure goodwill of their cattle-trading businesses destroyed because of Nazi persecution. They argued that the sustainability of relations between the cattle trader and his customers was the decisive determinant of a cattle-trading company's value and not, say, the intrinsic value of the firm's machines or transport fleet. In a letter of rejection to Hugo Walz from Gunzenhausen, the office argued:

> The question as to whether a cattle trade involves goodwill must be negated
> in principle. A prerequisite for the compensatory eligibility of goodwill
> is that it has existed independent of the person persecuted and could be
> transferred to a business successor. There can be no question of goodwill
> in this sense in the case of the business of the applicant and of his partner
> Salomon Walz. The business relationships (customer base), reputation
> of the company, and the importance of the livestock trading business in
> the procurement and sales market were based on the personalities of the

business owners and their personal acquaintance with the rural population and buyers. These relationships, which made up the company value of the cattle-trading business, were associated with the persons of the owners and therefore not capable of transfer to a possible acquirer of the business.[1]

Of course, one may argue that the Bayerisches Landesentschädigungsamt might have rejected this application in order to keep compensation payments to Jews persecuted by the Nazi regime as low as possible. Apart from this, we can conclude from this explanation that cattle-trading businesses really did possess an added value that extended well beyond their pure intrinsic material value. That added value, moreover, arose from the quality of the personal relationships between the business owners and their customers. In the compensation office's conclusion, a third party, a successor firm, could not have continued running the business in the same way as the original business owner.

Business success, therefore, depended essentially on the company's owner and on the relationships he established with his customers. Margot Grünberg, who wrote a dissertation on the German cattle trade in 1932, confirms that the cattle trade was a business resting on the quality of the trader's personal relationships with his customers. She argues that although it requires "a lot of capital, the cattle trading branch is nonetheless strongly based on individual capabilities. The efficiency of the individual trader is decisive. In trading circles, there is little inclination toward concentration. Centralization is unprofitable, since trading with cattle depends too much on individual places and on personal relationships and acquaintances."[2] Accordingly, it was not just material sales equipment and infrastructure links that were decisive for the operating income of a cattle-trading business and thus for their importance in the agrarian community but also the kind of business relationships that the cattle trader cultivated with his customers.

The quality of business relationships was particularly significant because cattle, as a living commodity, entailed a variety of risks and great legal insecurity. Since it was impossible at the point of sale to guarantee whether the cow would deliver the amount of milk promised, for example, and also because important information about the livestock being traded, such as weight, cannot be fixed in writing,[3] the uncertainty inherent in the transaction could only be compensated for by the level of trust that existed between buyer and seller. As Abe Gutman, son of Max Gutmann from Ellingen, explained: "The cattle business, it's all about trust." This trust served as a link substituting for the lack of reliable information about the object of trade (the cattle), which as a living commodity provided no guarantee that a promised trade could be redeemed.[4]

The importance of trust in this sector is further underscored by the custom of forgoing a traditional written contract, since the cattle trade was conducted as a handshake-only business. The cattle trade was thus, like no other business, a matter of trust.[5]

Trust as a Constitutive Element in Social Relationships

Trust is not only an essential prerequisite for economic success in the cattle trade; it is also a constitutive element of social relationships. Philosopher Annette Baier understands the concept of trust as an attitude in which the person who confides trust is consigning care to other people about a matter that is "dear to one's heart."[6] She thus draws a distinction between trust and reliability, which is morally neutral. When one trusts, one makes oneself dependent on the benevolence of one's counterpart, since one is surrendering the expectation of fulfilling a promise into the hands of a third person, the person whom one trusts. As Baier emphasizes, the granting of trust is attached to different conditions, such as bridging the gap in time between the giving of trust and its fulfillment. In concluding a contractual relationship, this is especially necessary when the contractually negotiated service is exchanged with a time lag. In this context, trust is indispensable because the two contractual parties do not know in advance if the outcome will be a fulfillment of the contract or trading agreement, such as whether an ox is going to deliver its promised tractive power. Within a contractual context, accordingly, trust functions as a kind of time bridge.[7]

Trust is thus decisive for the establishment of business relationships in general, specifically those that are high-risk. Trust in trading partners makes it possible to bypass the risks and uncertainties that some kinds of transactions entail. Trust therefore closes the gap that cannot be closed by a purely instrumental rational calculation and so facilitates high-risk trades.[8] If, however, the trust placed in the transaction does not pay off—so that a farmer gets an old instead of a young cow, for example—this can lead to the dissolution of trade relationships and ultimately also to the ruin of the business. Trust is accordingly an indispensable component in business relationships and critical for their success. For merchants, this means that trust represents a kind of social capital that they convert into economic capital and can use to influence the business value of an enterprise.[9]

As a soft category, trust at first glance seems hard for a historian to capture, since it only shows up implicitly in sources. And yet it is a decisive factor for the development of social processes. Before the concept made its way into historical scholarship, it was already being used in sociology, political science, and philosophy.[10] The concept of trust refers to action and was therefore widely applied in the action-oriented sociology of Pierre Bourdieu.[11] Similarly, German systems theorist Niklas Luhmann offered far-reaching reflections on trust as "a mechanism for the reduction of social complexity."[12] Before the discipline of history picked up on this and other conceptual approaches, it steered clear of the concept of trust as a historical category for many years.[13] Only with the advent of cultural history did trust enter the discipline as a historical category. Cultural historian Ute Frevert, however, has investigated the history of trust as a concept and the changes in its meaning over time.[14] Her working assumption is that what we characterize as trust can mean different things at different times and places. Frevert illuminates the concept of trust from a number of angles in a variety of contexts and divides it into political trust, which she characterizes as vertical, and citizen trust, which she calls horizontal.[15] In addition, she speaks of intimate trust in the private sphere, among family and friends. Ultimately, though, she is rather vague about formulating her understanding of trust as a historical category and leaves many of the questions arising from her observations open.

Hillen supplements Zucker's categories with that of character-based trust, highlighting it as a constitutive element within an entrepreneurial family. According to Hillen, trust has a strong utilitarian component in economic contexts. If trading relationships are built on trust, this saves (in his opinion) "transaction costs and serves—assuming a certain willingness to take risks—the actors as a means to maximize their own 'profit.'"[16] Nevertheless, trust in economic contexts should not be understood one-dimensionally; rather, it assumes different forms in different contexts. According to Hillen, these different forms can show up separately, alongside each other, in succession (one after another), or interwoven with one another. Hillen's thinking about this thereby touches on what Frevert and Zucker have to say about the subject.

While cultural history operates with a wide-ranging concept of trust, economic historian Christian Hillen further differentiates the concept. In the anthology he edited on the relationship between trust and economic history, he asks whether there is a unique form of trust among the parties to business transactions and how this might be distinguished from other types.[17] For their ideas about this, the economic historians around Hillen take the theoretical essays of sociologist Lynne Zucker as a foundation. She argues that trust between two subjects is not just something that exists (that is, not something that is already there) but is rather first built up through negotiations with each other. She sees trust not solely as an emotional tie but also (like Baier) as an attitude or expectation that (in our case) a customer can show a trader. But as Zucker makes clear, that expectation can similarly be denied, since respect and trust must first be earned.[18] She divides trust into three categories: trust based on *characteristics* of the exchange partners (family or ethnic background), trust based on the *process* of exchange (often indicated by reputation), and trust based on *institutional* "guarantees" (such as professional certification or escrow accounts). All three categories can exist alongside each other simultaneously and, depending on the situation, complement one another. Such features as age, sex, religion, and ethnicity can stand in the way of building up characteristic-based trust, according to Zucker, but these obstacles can also be wholly or partly overcome by process-based trust built up from the common experience of negotiating with each other.

Trust, then, is indispensable for economic relations in general and trading relationships in particular. The application of approaches from economic and cultural history to the history of the cattle trade allows us to ask how trust was built up in the relationships between cattle traders and farmers, what forms it developed, and where it ran up against its limits.

Establishing Trust in the Private Cattle Trade

Taking Zucker's approach as a starting point, it follows that trust between two partners is not a given of its own accord; rather, it must first be produced under specific conditions and in certain contexts.[19] The cattle trader's outward appearance, his lifestyle, and the reputation of his business constituted a basic requirement for building a relationship of trust with his customers.[20] Once a first contact was established, additional gestures and trading ceremonies contributed decisively to the development of trust. Establishing trust in the cattle trade was, accordingly, no one-sided matter; it was not just the customer who needed to trust the trader—the trader also needed to trust the customer. For a business to succeed, the trader had to be able to size up risk and know whom, when, and how much he could trust. For this reason, a cattle trader needed sound business practices to protect himself from possible losses arising out of high-risk cattle trades. These techniques, which included the cattle-trading language, have been treated as disruptive practices inhibiting trust between cattle traders and farmers. In the following sections, we examine how trust between the trading partners was built up and how long it continued to exist when crises and conflicts emerged.

Establishing Trust through Clothes

Zucker's reflections also play a key role in Bourdieu's descriptions of habitus (personal appearance and bearing), in that he incorporates these descriptions

FIGURE 2.1. Bernhard Bermann, Ellingen, around 1930.
Courtesy of William Berman.

into one of his social fields. According to Bourdieu, subjects (meaning traders and farmers, in our case) act within a field in which their own rules apply. These rules shape their conduct and social practice and influence everyday communication. When merchants follow these rules, their cultivated, serious demeanor serves to establish a relationship of trust with their customers. As writer Gottfried Keller stated in his novella *Kleider machen Leute* (*Clothes Make the Man*), clothing not only protects against wind and weather but also functions as a nonverbal means of communication.[21] On the one hand, the type of clothes worn distinguishes the wearer from other groups (in this case, it distinguishes the trader from the population of farmers engaged in physical labor); on the other hand, it assigns him to yet another group (in this case, that of traders and merchants). Clothing therefore has both an exclusionary and an inclusionary function.

In looking at the clothing worn by rural Jews, and especially by Jewish cattle traders, previous historical research has focused only on analyzing the way this clothing functioned to differentiate Jewish traders from their rural peasant cohort, which has frequently been equated with the non-Jewish milieu.[22] Regina Schmid maintains, for example, that the clothing of Jewish rural traders was primarily a means of expressing the difference in their status compared with their rural surroundings.[23]

As both research and oral tradition have emphasized, cattle traders wore clothing that was more commercial-looking than rustic.[24] Dark trousers, a beige coat, a white shirt sometimes worn with a tie, and a broad-brimmed man's hat were regarded as typical clothing for cattle traders.[25] At first glance, this clothing made them recognizable to the outside world as merchants, although each of these articles of clothing communicated a different—yet somehow similar—image. By wearing white shirts, cattle merchants let it be known that they were not performing any physical or even dirty work and could afford a freshly washed shirt every day, even if they came into contact with filthy livestock. This signaled to others that they were in possession of an established and secure livelihood, which inspired confidence. One willingly entrusts one's cattle to someone who communicates an impression of being clean and well-off. At the same time, this kind of appearance communicates rigorous hygiene, which leads one to expect protection against livestock diseases.

The hat, which was a telltale sign of belonging to the middle class, was also an expression of social status (see fig. 2.1). The hat clearly differentiated cattle traders from farmers but also from farm laborers (on the right side of the picture), who covered their heads with caps. Doing so allowed farm workers to perform physical labor, like driving livestock off the wagon. As we see in figure 2.1 the man wearing the hat stands in the center of the scene (unloading cattle from a wagon), while the farmhands stand at some distance from the merchant and close to the livestock. All in all, this picture depicts both the hierarchy and sense of group affiliation that existed. The hat identified its wearer as a merchant, and for religious Jews, it also served as a religious head covering and substitute for a kippa.[26]

As can be seen in the picture, the cattle trader's outfit included a cane, which could have fulfilled two functions; as a bourgeois walking cane, it was a status object, but it also served the purely practical purpose of driving cattle. In case of an attack on the street or at cattle markets, the cane could also be employed as a weapon. The daughter of a former cattle driver from Burghaslach stresses the symbolic status of a cane—and the ways it was mocked. She recalls one verse from a song that the villagers sang when cattle trader Adolf Rosenblatt

FIGURE 2.2. Cattle traders inspecting cattle at the market in Augsburg, around 1930. Source: Hans Riedl, *Die genossenschaftliche Viehverwertung in Bayern* (Munich: Bayerische Viehverwertung, 1930), 33.

was on his way to the cattle market in Würzburg: "When he swings his little cane."[27] Swinging a cane creates the impression of a bon vivant, someone who strolls across the boulevard in order to display his wealth and who cultivates a lax attitude toward money. This sort of lifestyle contrasted with that of the rural peasantry, which was characterized by Protestant austerity in which any show of affluence was scorned.[28]

This verse also underscores the perceived power relationship between the farming population and traders in rural society. In the eyes of the farmers, the cattle trader earned his money "casually swinging the little cane," while they earned their living laboriously in the field with a plow and a hoe. According to Bourdieu, the cattle traders' clothing can be ascribed habitual value, whereby the traders' outward appearance already distinguishes them from their farming clientele both symbolically and functionally.

Nevertheless, alongside the exclusionary character of cattle traders' clothing—as brought to light in the verse of that song—the inclusionary side should be highlighted as well. As contemporary author Oswald Bauer argues, the clothing of an "honorable and trustworthy merchant" needed at all times to be clean, orderly, and serious.[29] Above all, clothing should not appear showy, so as to avoid the impression that the trader is enriching himself from the way he does business.[30] The merchant's choice of clothing and his lifestyle, along with such factors as good manners, proper comportment, and a sense of tact, were critical for establishing a relationship of trust with customers.[31] Creating a trustworthy impression is what makes business transactions of both money and cattle possible in the first place, and making such an impression includes, in Bourdieu's sense, both the choice of clothing and the reputation of the business. This means that the exclusionary aspect of clothing, frequently a component of antisemitic descriptions, also served to promote business in social practice.[32] Clothing served as a means of establishing trust between cattle traders and their clients. By choosing clean and respectable clothing, they identified themselves as trustworthy and honorable.[33] And so, while nonpeasant clothes could act in an exclusionary fashion—signaling a distinct identity at the social level and within the village community—they also opened up customer contacts, resulting in further sales in the context of trade and business. For cattle traders, therefore, the exclusionary character of clothing thus had an economic function that had a positive impact on their relationship with farmers.

Trust-Producing Gestures and Symbols

Producing a trustworthy impression by wearing a certain kind of clothing is especially important for establishing initial contact. Once this has been accomplished and a trade is underway, additional trust-building gestures and behaviors are critical to the successful conclusion of a trade. These nonverbal forms of expression may be elusive, methodologically speaking, as objects of research. But, owing to the function they perform in building trust and thus promoting sales, including them in our historical analysis is critical.

The Handshake as a Gesture of Trust

As both historical research and oral tradition repeatedly emphasize, the handshake between the customer and the trader was regarded as the decisive trust-building gesture in the cattle trade when it came to sealing a deal.[34] While shaking hands is customary in the first instance as a ritual of greeting in Western culture, it is simultaneously regarded as the oldest traditional gesture of agreement between two trading partners and was still customary in the cattle trade in the twentieth century.[35]

Praising and Touching

Before the cattle trader and farmer shook hands, they first had to establish a trusting relationship. One instrument for building up this kind of atmosphere was the praising and trustful palpating of the head of livestock. Here, at the beginning of the trading negotiation, the trader stroked the animal across the instep and the back and tapped the head and legs.[36] By touching the cow, the merchant gained an impression of the animal's condition and value while simultaneously communicating to the farmer that he would treat the livestock well and that the farmer could, after all, entrust him with the commodity he had so laboriously raised.

The practice of closely inspecting the cattle could also stand in the way of building trust between the trader and the farmer, however, because some peasants viewed the act of examination through the lens of antisemitic prejudice. As antisemitic writer Franz Kayser recalled, "My mother . . . said to me: When a Jew goes into the stable and praises the cattle, one should always say: 'Dear God preserve us.' For the Jew's praise harbors something ominous, and with this little prayer one breaks the tip off this bane."[37] A certain ambivalence comes to light in this statement; the farmer's confidence or *self*-trust in the situation he experiences individually with the cattle trader becomes contaminated by antisemitic *mis*trust toward Jews in general. Apparently, the "Jew's praise" flattered the farmer, inspiring an inclination to trust; on the other hand, the farmer mistrusted the intention of the compliment and imputed something "ominous" to it. This accusation expresses the antisemitic prejudice about the "greedy Jew" enriching himself on the backs of the peasantry.[38] The turn toward God, moreover, illustrates how the trust-building measure of carefully touching and praising the head of cattle under consideration had an ambivalent effect: it made the farmers receptive to a possible sale. The very intimacy of this physical gesture could also arouse feelings of antisemitic suspicion. Yet it seems as if, on balance, the farmers' sense of mistrust was overcome by these kinds of trust-building measures, thus opening up business options.

The trustful palpating of the cattle could be followed by a thirty- to forty-minute conversation about everything under the sun.[39] This was a way for the trader to signal to the farmers that the contact he was establishing was about more than just selling cattle. It was also a way to find out about the opinions and preferences of the other party and thus gain an impression of a potential trading partner. If the conversation showed that the trader had the same views as the farmer or was simply lending him an open ear for his economic and personal situation, the trader might gain the sympathy of the customer. If they agreed on this or that bit of village gossip, it was also easier to agree on a deal.[40]

If the farmer finally acquired confidence in the trader and signaled interest in a trade, the actual price negotiation could begin. With his right hand, the buyer grasped the palm of the seller's right hand until the seller ultimately squeezed powerfully and thereby sealed the deal.[41] The haggling over the best price could last several minutes, and the hands of the trading partners would be touching the entire time. The bodily contact this produced helped to create a feeling of safety and security, which was of central importance for the production of trust. The seller sealed the trade with a handshake. Putting this trade in writing happened only by registering the name of the customer, the animal, and the price in a kind of appointment book, a simple type of commercial bookkeeping that facilitated examination by the revenue office.[42]

Although authorities were constantly urging, and sometimes also requiring, that records of trades be kept, the ritual of the oral agreement trusted by both sides remained a widespread trade practice well into the twentieth century.[43] The son of a Christian hog dealer vividly recalls the significance of the handshake for the livestock trade when he describes the conclusion of a sale in his memoirs: "It was a loose and colorful atmosphere, but one in which things proceeded very seriously and properly as far as the outcome was concerned. The word and the handshake were regarded, as elsewhere in business life, much like the signature on a purchase agreement."[44] It was in this trade promise and the gesture of the handshake—precisely because the parties dispensed with putting their agreement in writing—that trust was expressed.

Mutual trust is regarded as an informal, interactive process tied to a moral commitment, while formalizing a trade deal, as in contracts, can be experienced as something that upsets relationships of trust or even as an insult.[45] Even the authorities recognized the practice of the handshake as a legally valid form of transaction, as the following example illustrates: When cattle trader Samson Wurzinger concluded a horse trade in 1923 with a handshake in the name of his brother and horse trader Siegmund Wurzinger, he was indicted for this, since there was a legal prohibition on cattle traders simultaneously practicing horse trades.[46] Samson did not acknowledge his offense as such and defended himself by claiming that the horse trade had not been committed to writing but only came about by handshake. Yet the constable from Rothenburg ob der Tauber, Otto Deissenberger, rejected his argument on these grounds: "It is a well-known fact that the conclusion of a sale is confirmed by handshake that binds both parties to the conditions of sale."[47]

In contrast, formalizing a transaction through a written contract was deemed unenforceable and even seen as an obstacle to trade. After the First World War, the state lifted controls on the economy, and in May 1922, consequently, the State Office for Livestock Commerce (Landesamt für Viehverkehr) once again abolished the contract note obligation (*Schlussscheinpflicht*), the commitment to putting trades in writing. In a circular, the office now declared: "For future livestock trades, as was the case before the introduction of controls, the only valid regulations will be general legal provisions and special customs (bargain money and handshake)."[48] The handshake was also regarded by the legislature as the valid conclusion of a trade; it counted as a contract in the livestock trade as it did in other commercial branches. It was an oral contract based on trust. Insisting on a written contract was regarded in the cattle trade as indicative of a lack of trust and thus as damaging for business.[49]

Payment Practices: Cash Transactions

Yet even as clothing identified the trader as trustworthy and the handshake expressed faith in the trading partner, it was ultimately the payment practice of the cattle traders that cemented trust between the two parties. As both scholarly research and oral tradition confirm, the private cattle trade was conducted as a cash business from the time it came into being. Part of the cattle trader's reputation was based on giving the farmer a cash-in-hand payment of the purchase price upon acquiring a head of cattle.[50] Since large sums were spent in the cattle trade, this business practice presupposed high liquidity on the part of the buyers. Cattle trader Moritz Engel from Markt Berolzheim, for example, declared cash assets of 5,700 Reichsmarks in his financial statement to the tax office at Gunzenhausen in 1931.[51] Such substantial sums could result in envy and resentment on the part of the farmers. For those with small and medium-sized farms, handling such large amounts of money often symbolized a financial power they did not have themselves. The sense of financial inferiority they felt in such cases could be expressed in rabble-rousing antisemitic images, as in the clay figures from Zizenhausen or during the "Green Week" agricultural fair in Berlin, where a cube was exhibited where "on one side a slavishly exploited simple peasant was portrayed holding an empty wallet in his hand, and on the other side, a fat merchant smirking while holding up the full purse."[52] Even if we are dealing here with the dissemination of an antisemitic stereotype about "*the* Jewish cattle trader" as "the exploiter of the peasant," the practice of carrying around money sacks was generally regarded as typical for cattle traders.[53] The son of a non-Jewish hog trader confirms this business practice and counters the envious gaze some peasants fixed upon the cattle and hog traders' amply filled money bags by noting that these usually contained their entire fortune.[54]

In fact, another reason traders practiced this payment method was to lower the price in their favor. As the son of a non-Jewish hog trader confirmed, it was a technique that helped some livestock traders make a favorable trade.[55] Peasants from small and medium-sized farms, in particular, who depended on cash

FIGURE 2.3. Zizenhausen figurine, *The Cow Trade*, n.d., painted terracotta, 17.5 x 19.5 cm. Antisemitic portrayal of two "Jewish cattle traders" extolling the virtues of a cow to a potential buyer. The inscription reads: "Upon my life, it gives 2 pails full of milk every . . ." Source: Jüdisches Museum Hohenems, ed., *Antijüdischer Nippes und populäre 'Judenbilder': Die Sammlung Finkelstein* (Essen: Klartext, 2005), 23.

in order to keep their assets, were ready to be bargained down to a lower price upon seeing a large sum of cash.

Although paying in cash lowered prices for cattle traders, the trust-producing effect of this practice should also be underscored. While cash payments and large purses frequently roused antisemitic resentment and thus had an exclusionary effect, it was simultaneously a cornerstone for the establishment of trust; receiving the entire payment up front offered the farmer protection against losses or depreciation owing to possible payment delays that may have resulted, for example, from installments. This distinguished the cattle trader as an "honorable merchant" who was measured by whether he "promptly fulfilled all obligations and conducted his transactions with 'the most unconditional solidarity.'"[56] Accordingly, both parties profited from this trade practice. It conveyed reliability and honesty, which in turn are fundamental to the establishment of trust.

Foundations for Granting Trust: Trading Techniques

For a successful cattle trade to occur, however, it was not enough for only the farmer to trust the cattle trader; obviously, the reverse had to be true as well. Traders were not only buying animals from farmers but also reselling them to farmers. While traders paid directly in cash when making a purchase, farmers were frequently not equipped to settle an account immediately when they were on the buying end.[57] In order to do business with financially weak farmers anyway, cattle traders offered them extremely flexible payment models, such as an exchange of cattle, installment payments, or a so-called cattle loan. In the case of the latter, the borrowed cattle remained the property of the trader, but the farmer was able to use it for work or to sell its milk.[58]

These trading practices, when coupled with many farmers' economic distress, harbored numerous risks for cattle traders. Conceivably, one or another of the peasants might not repay his debts or might even go bankrupt. Since credit transactions are not possible without trust in the borrower, cattle traders had to estimate the business risk as accurately as possible. But to grant trust, a purely emotional commitment of the kind acquired in a conversation with the customer was not sufficient, as Anthony Giddens has explained in his fundamental theory of trust. An essential precondition for the granting of trust rests to a greater degree on information about the person to be trusted and about the commodity.[59] Cattle traders thus needed to possess a number of skills—including expert knowledge about the commodity trade and market conditions and basic knowledge about their clientele's financial well-being—in order to keep the business risk as low as possible.[60]

Both sides usually profited from this knowledge, as a case from the farming village of Oberhochstatt illustrates. In 1927, Jewish cattle trader Bernhard Bermann offered bachelor Andreas Auernhammer, the son of a farmer, a piece of land because it adjoined additional plots of land belonging to his family and thus promised to be advantageous in many ways to Auernhammer.[61] In order to present an offer like this, Bermann must have been very familiar with local property conditions. Auernhammer initially rejected the offer, since, as an unmarried man at the time who lacked liquidity, he did not yet control his own assets. According to oral sources, Bermann answered (as young Auernhammer recounted): "I said you're taking the field, not buying it. You're taking the field!" ("Ich habe gesagt, du nimmst den Acker, nehmen, nicht kaufen! Du nimmst den Acker!").[62] Although it remains unclear whether Bermann uttered this sentence exactly in this way, two conclusions may be drawn from the sentence: For one, the form of address he was reported as using, the familiar *du* in German, indicates a relationship of trust between the two partners to this conversation, since addressing someone as *du* is generally regarded as a way of "relativizing social hierarchies."[63] In village communities, the only ones exempted from this familiar form of address were pastors, teachers, and outsiders. When the cattle trader addressed the farmer with *du*, then, this symbolized that the trader belonged to the *Duz-Gemeinschaft*—the community of those calling each other *du*—and thus was also part of the rural community of trust. This made it possible for him to gain access to a familiar kind of information about the social and economic status of Auernhammer.

The bill of sale for the field testifies to the conclusion of this transaction: "The buyer is the fortuneless, single farmer's son."[64] No further information has come down to us, however, about how and when Auernhammer settled his debts with Bermann. What matters, though, is that Bermann's trust in the unmarried farmer (as a kind of pledge or collateral, so to speak) was sufficient enough to have finalized the business transaction. Trust is generally created when the giver of trust acts without self-interest and when the recipient of trust recognizes that the trust giver is not interested in enriching himself but rather in providing an advantage to the other.[65] Through the trust he gave in advance, Bermann communicated that he was not just concerned with his own self-interest; he also cared about the unmarried farmer's welfare.[66] This pleased the farmer and created a certain emotional commitment between the two parties, both of whom profited in the end.[67] As Frevert stated, trust is Janus-faced. Receiving trust, as the example of Auernhammer made clear, is usually perceived as positive. By contrast, having to give trust can be experienced as burdensome, since (as in the case of Bermann) it harbors a risk.[68]

These trading practices show how important it was for cattle traders to find out as much as they could about the financial and social conditions of the clientele in their *medienes* (sales territories).[69] For that reason, cattle traders, even while they were still young, became thoroughly acquainted with the farmers in their *medienes*. This was confirmed by William Berman, grandson of Bernhard Bermann. He reported that his father, Theo Bermann, from Ellingen, always knew who had a good harvest in his *mediene*, who needed money to marry off a daughter, or who wanted to buy a cow. William also recalled that his father, upon entering a pub, got to know the social and economic circumstances of the tavern's patrons within a very short time. If he did not get to hear enough news, he would leave the inn disappointed.[70] Visiting inns was important to cattle traders for two reasons: For one, they were suitable places to explore prospective business. For another, the information and observations acquired there helped them appraise their clientele and, as a result, their credit risk. Tavern gossip could be more reliable than the accounting books banks used to calculate their credit risk.

Visiting a pub was a man's business, taking place at the location where men met after finishing work in the fields or on their way home. The village community took shape over beer, sauerkraut, and bratwursts. Here, alcohol played an important role in the meetings and conversations with customers. By buying so many rounds of beer for his Gentile customers, a Jewish cattle trader could give the tavern gossip a jump start. In this way, the trader learned not only about village secrets but also about the drinking behavior of his clientele. Not a few of the farmers drank away their entire fortune in the taverns, so these were granted credit only reluctantly by traders.[71] From the oral and written records, it also emerges that the Jewish cattle trader ate and drank in these taverns[72]— despite the religious dietary constraints that many of them faced—and thus became a member of the tavern society.[73] Nevertheless, as Elfie Labsch-Benz argues, they would have imbibed little themselves and always kept a clear head, which would have allowed them to have the upper hand in a bargaining situation with drunken farmers. Labsch-Benz even maintains that Jewish traders would quickly disappear from the tavern when farmers insisted on having a drink together after concluding a trade, thereby extricating themselves from the (drinking) affair.[74] If the traders remained sober, they could keep the situation under control even if this placed them firmly outside this relaxed drinking society. Viewed negatively, this could lead to an assessment that the sober trader was keeping his distance from the drinking community in order to gain an economic advantage from the loose tongues and concomitant generosity of the tipsy peasants. Seen from yet another perspective, this was a case of peasants losing self-control in their chummy communal drinking and blaming their "aberrant behavior" on the trader who stayed sober. We leave aside the question of whether Labsch-Benz is making use of the stereotype that Jews did not drink any alcohol.[75] Based on both oral and written records, it can be demonstrated that visiting taverns was indispensable to cattle traders for scouting out and concluding trade deals. By participating in village gossip, cattle traders became part of the community and thus earned trust, though they also remained excluded to a degree, due to their different drinking behavior—if this was the case at all.

Nevertheless, as Hillen powerfully emphasized, the act of eating and drinking together is a major vehicle for creating trust between two business partners. Hillen substantiated his statement by describing the eating behavior of entrepreneur Ludwig Knoop, who literally "'inundated' himself with and 'ingested' trust" ("'er-tank' und 'er-aß' sich Vertrauen") and thereby built up a variety of friendly relationships from which, in turn, business relationships emerged.[76] Cattle traders also dined with their customers at their farms, as one contemporary witness was able to report. She recalls that her father would have breakfast in the morning with farmers before they got around to doing business.[77] For that moment of joint eating, the stranger at the table became part of the family. Jewish merchants who observed Jewish dietary laws were set apart by their different eating behavior, and they could only participate in a limited share of the eating ceremony.[78] However, even if they did not consume the same meal as the farmers, they were sitting at the same table, which testifies to the trust between host and guest.

In addition to partaking in tavern gossip, mastering basic kinds of mental arithmetic helped cattle traders estimate their business risk and thus place trust in a farmer. This put them in a position to participate in price setting and move prices in their favor. To do this, they needed the ability to work out a quick mental calculation of all fees and taxes, minus any rebates granted.[79] Fathers were already teaching their sons these skills at a very early age. In particular, one of the skills in this repertoire was calculating using Hebrew numbers, a practice originally intended to keep price agreements secret in front of the farmers.[80] This was another skill whose practice was confirmed by William Berman, whose father, Theo Bermann, managed to flee at the beginning of the 1940s (after first finding refuge in Cuba in the late 1930s) to the United States, where he again practiced the cattle trade. He reported that as a small boy, he was taken on business trips by his father and was always given complicated arithmetic problems to solve as a way of preparing him for the business of cattle trading on these journeys.[81]

The ability to make mental calculations even played a decisive role when it came to choosing a profession for their children, as another cattle trader's son confirms. Yizachar Berman recalls some family lore about a conversation his grandparents had about determining which one of their children was smart enough to become a cattle trader:

> There is a story in our family, when my father grew up, and his family [Bernhard] Bermann, where they talked a lot about him, and when they had to decide how . . . to direct their children to find their way, their jobs, their profession in life, so with [my father's brother] Theo there was no question, because he was interested in cattle dealers since he was 16 [years old] or maybe earlier, with [Theo], there was no problem [he would become a

cattle dealer, nor was there any problem] with his sister, for sure that she won't be a cattle dealer, but they had to decide if my father [Max Bermann] can be a cattle dealer, and then, so they spoke between themselves, and they decided that at the end, that maybe he is not clever enough to be a cattle dealer, so he can be a rabbi, he should be a rabbi.[82]

Mental calculation was thus a fundamental precondition for practicing the cattle trade; it helped with making quick calculations about and influencing the bargaining over the price. If a farmer was vehement about insisting on his desired price, the cattle trader could simply "calculate dumb" (*dummrechnen*) with the farmer, as one old cattle trader confirmed. If, for example, a farmer demanded 1,400 marks for four cows and the trader knew that these cows only had a market value of 1,200 marks, he would first try to bargain down the farmer. After a lengthy talk about the trade, the trader would offer the farmer 1,000 marks, and if the farmer did not accept the offer, he would shift from the total price to the price per head and say: "Well, what do you want for the head?" If, for example, the farmer said he wanted "1200—for four head," the trader could respond, "Well then, you must be crazy. You can't demand 250 marks per head." If the farmer was not able to check this mental calculation that the price per head was lower than the total price ($250 \times 4 = 1{,}000$, not 1,200) quickly enough, he might simply end up agreeing, and the cattle trader would have made a good deal. The contemporary witness justified this method by saying: "That's legal, that isn't fraud—sure, basic schooling back then was a lot worse, including arithmetic, so you could calculate dumb with a farmer."[83] The trading technique of Dummrechnen was also employed by cattle traders in order to reach an agreement on a trade with "stubborn" farmers. On the part of the farmers, this could trigger a feeling of inferiority and betrayal that, combined with antisemitic mistrust, found expression in the saying that "the clever Jew had pulled a fast one on the stupid peasant" ("der g'scheite Jud haut den dummen Bauern übers Ohr").[84]

Trust-Destroying Trade Practices

Symbols and practices had the potential to create trust, but they could just as easily upset and sometimes even destroy it, as seen with the trade practice of *Dummrechnen*. According to Zucker and Luhmann, the opposite of trust is not mistrust, and the two terms are not treated equally in philosophy.[85] Zucker explains that trust can be disturbed or irritated, but this does not mean it will be transformed into mistrust. Mistrust only develops when the expectation of redeeming a promise comes under suspicion that it cannot be fulfilled, intentionally and generally. Whereas a disturbance of trust could be a one-time occurrence, perhaps brought about by a negative experience, mistrust depends (from the outset) on prejudices and ignorance that stand in the way of trust.[86]

On closer examination of trading practices in the cattle trade, it is easy to see that there were a number of practices that could have led to a disturbance of trust. Trust-inspiring symbols and techniques coexisted alongside practices that upset trust and consequently had a detrimental impact on relationships between cattle traders and farmers. The allegedly trust-disturbing trade practices examined in this book have been divided into two categories: practices that were intentionally exclusionary and those that were manipulative.

Undermining Trust through Language?
The Cattle Traders' Language

Communication takes place nonverbally through gestures and habitual modes of expression and verbally through language. Just as nonverbal communication, like a handshake or the careful palpating of cattle, could establish a trusting atmosphere, the use of a business language often had the opposite effect. In the cattle trade, it was often said that the cattle-trading language disturbed trust and established itself as a form of communication that perpetuated misunderstandings and upset the commercial relations between the two parties.

As a matter of linguistic history, the cattle traders' language belongs to the Jüdisch-Deutsch dialect, a remnant of Western Yiddish. It consists of Hebrew, Yiddish, and German elements and is regarded as the only traders' language that was still spoken in the twentieth century.[87] Although the cattle traders' language was widely used nationally, it nonetheless had a strong regional cast and was shaped by different dialects, which underlines the local character of the cattle trade.[88]

In Franconia, moreover, there existed a special form of Jüdisch-Deutsch, namely Lachoudisch, which was composed of elements from Hebrew and Rotwelsch (a slang used by vagrants, thieves, and itinerant craftspeople).[89] The cattle traders' language consists of a limited number of words, idioms, or proverbs relevant to the practice of the trade but insufficient for everyday use.

At the beginning of the twentieth century, Jüdisch-Deutsch was still widely used, especially among cattle traders.[90] By contrast, in the uppermost Jewish stratum, that of lawyers, physicians, and manufacturers, Jüdisch-Deutsch was scorned, as it was regarded as a sign of insufficient assimilation or acculturation.[91] Jüdisch-Deutsch continued to be used as a living language only among

those strata of Jews who had remained behind in pre-emancipatory occupations.[92] In these circles, the language generally functioned as a distinguishing
mark demarcating a boundary to the non-Jewish world.

Especially at markets, the language was an important tool with which cattle
traders could set prices and protect themselves against sizable losses. It allowed
traders to exchange information with each other about the quality of a cow, for
example—details that were decisive for appraising goods and their value.[93] If,
for example, a trade was underway and the farmer was not ready to pay the requested price, one trader could use the cattle traders' language to communicate
with another about the price he had just negotiated with the farmer. That way,
he could prevent the farmer from going to another trader and telling him that
he was offering him a higher price than the previous trader.

Both Jewish and non-Jewish traders understood and used the cattle traders'
language.[94] A non-Jewish hog trader explained how he employed the language
in order to set prices with his father. If, for example, a farmer drove to market
with a wagonful of piglets, he would jump onto the wagon as it pulled in, while
his father began a conversation with the farmers. In the meantime, he could
survey the condition and value of the animals on the wagon and shout out to
his father in Jüdisch-Deutsch: "Jus kaserum, mem schuk ka rosh, tov" ("Ten
piglets, ten marks apiece"). This information gave the livestock trader an orientation as to the sum with which he should enter into negotiations.[95]

It was precisely this sort of exclusionary moment that could arouse suspicion
on the part of farmers. But farmers were not entirely powerless in confronting
this business practice, as confirmed by the existence of numerous dictionaries
that provided them with some comprehension of the cattle traders' language.
One example is the *Hebräisch-deutscher Dolmetscher* (the *Hebrew-German
Translator*), which had been published in Gunzenhausen going back at least
as far as the eighteenth century.[96] The high demand for this little booklet is
illustrated by the fact that the only copy that could be located was already in
its eleventh edition.[97] The cattle traders' language even had the status of being
the only second language farmers were prepared to learn,[98] as linguist Werner
Weinberg confirms. Based on an oral transmission, he wrote down the following conversation between a Jewish cattle trader and a farmer:

Jewish trader: "Ich gebe *bëis mëis schiwwem schuck* für die *behëime*."—"I'll
give you 270 marks for the cow."
Christian farmer: "Willst mich *besëibeln*? *Mëi ratt* oder kein *masse-
matten*!"—"Are you trying to hoodwink me? A hundred thalers [300 marks]
or no deal!"[99]

The terms cited in the *Hebräisch-deutscher Dolmetscher* make it clear which areas this language covered. In the first of two parts, the book explains the German and Hebrew (Western Yiddish) numbers that were important for agreeing on prices. The second part contains the most important vocabulary concerning persons, livestock, and other subject matter in both the cattle traders' language and German.[100] This included terms that were directly related to the livestock trade, such as *massumen* for "money" or *resach* for "profit," as well as vocabulary that might provide information about social life, such as *Er is a Schaßknisch*, "He's a drinker." This also allowed traders to use the language for telling jokes or stories about their contemporaries while on the road—stories that outsiders (especially non-Jews, like farmers and servants) were not meant to understand. In private, the language was possibly also employed to carry on conversations without disturbance in the presence of a non-Jewish maid. One testimony to this is the expression *stieke, die schickse*, which was the rough equivalent of "be quiet, the [Gentile] girl!"[101] Traders on the road also used Jüdisch-Deutsch to exchange views about women. The expressions needed for these sexualized conversations could also be found in the *Dolmetscher*. For example, one trader could secretly remark to another, "Segete hat kurante zomes" ("The woman has pretty legs").[102] A non-Jewish pig trader also testified to this use of the cattle traders' language to communicate about women. He offered this example of some vocabulary: "'Die isha is tov,' that is, the isha was the woman; or: 'Die lave isha,' she was either ugly or not as she should have been, and 'die tove,' she was intelligent and 'die hey tove' meant she was sexually very active."[103]

Nevertheless, the cattle traders' language was not exclusively for men; even if this happened only rarely, women also used it. This is backed up by the sister of a non-Jewish cattle trader who was herself occasionally active as a livestock trader. She proudly gave an account of how she—to the astonishment of some biased men—had mastered the language.[104]

At the same time, the cattle traders' language draws attention to trade practices that, owing to the poor state of written transmission for these customs, would be lost forever to posterity had they not survived in some of the language's concepts that have come down to us.

In particular, these include so-called unfair trading practices, ways of doing business that reflect the relationship of traders to the world outside of trade. One example is the term *Kaljes machen* (related to the Yiddish expression *kalye makhn*, meaning to "spoil" or "damage"). It refers to "extolling" or "bad-mouthing" a head of cattle. This was a job that could be assumed by so-called *Sasserers* (also known as Schasserers) or *Schmusers*, who worked for the cattle traders by keeping their ears open for buying opportunities on behalf of their bosses in a particular locality.[105] If a farmer expressed an interest in a livestock purchase, in the process of Kaljes machen with the farmer, the Schmuser would name a price well below the real price. Shortly thereafter, the cattle trader would drop by for a personal visit to the farmer and offer a price much higher than the one offered by the Schasserer hours or days before. This was meant to give the farmer the impression that he was striking a favorable deal. But the method of Kaljes machen was also applied by traders in order to influence a trade already in progress. In this case, the Schasser might, for example, highly praise a lower-grade cow in order to sell it at the highest possible price to the farmers.[106] The business practice of Kaljes machen made it possible for cattle traders to come to an agreement with farmers; at the same time, it could lead to a disruption of trust if the farmers recognized the manipulative nature of this tactic.

That a certain degree of chutzpah was needed to carry out a business practice like this is evidenced by the comment of a cattle trader's son, who summarized his thoughts about his father's job this way:

> But in the end, I can say [my father] was very good in business. I am not sure if he was so good in what we call cattle dealer business, because there, you know, you have to sometimes to make things not so direct. If you want to sell a good cow—let's say it is not a problem—if you want to sell a bad cow, you have to tell the one who buys it, you see what a nice cow you buy, see what a nice leg, what a nice hair, what a nice head, it wasn't for him, because he was a very honest man.[107]

The cattle traders' language separated them from the world of nontraders, since it primarily served to help them exchange information—regardless of whether they were Jewish or non-Jewish—about livestock as an object of trade in order to avert (or minimize) any loss in value for the merchandise on offer.[108] The language's use in the presence of nontraders nurtured the impression of a conspiratorial community of traders that excluded farmers from the price-formation process and thus also from a trusted inner circle. It is therefore not surprising that linguist Rudolf Post characterizes the cattle traders' language as a *langue de complicité*—a language of complicity or secret collusion—thus emphasizing the internal group effect it had and the reassurance it provided within the company of cattle traders.[109] The large share of Jewish and Hebrew elements in the language indicates how strongly anchored Jews were in the cattle-trading business.

Nevertheless, the cattle traders' language is not a specifically Jewish trading apparatus. As noted earlier, all the groups participating in the cattle trade used the language, including Jewish and non-Jewish merchants in equal measure, as

Hebräisch=deutscher Dolmetscher.

Sammlung der gebräuch-lichsten Handelsaus-drücke der israel. Han-delsleute auf Viehmärkten und im Privalver-kehr. Verdeutsch-ung der Zahlen von 1—10 000 und Um-rechnung des Karolin in Mark.

11. Auflage.

Verlag von Leo Schwarzbeck's Buchhandlung in Gunzenhausen.

Nachdruck verboten, wird gerichtlich verfolgt.

— 6 —

Deutsch.	Handelssprache.
Das Pferd ist scheu und schlägt	Die Suß is ä Stußer und makeiert
„ ist geduldig	Die Suß is fromm
„ ist ein Kopper	„ ä Kopper
„ ist trächtig	„ pattisch
„ war beim Militär	„ war bei die Balmagunes
Die Stiere sind jung räutig	Die Ekel sin jung räutig
„ lausig	„ häbe Kinnem
Dein Pferd ist auf ein Aug blind	Dei Suß reunt af än Aag niz
Ich gib dir 87½ Karolin	Ich gib dir Lamed sojen chuzen Juser
„ 27½ Karolin	Ich gib dir Kaff sojen chuzen Juser
Der Knecht	Maschores
Der Bauer	Kaftigem
reich	betug
Der Preis	Erach
rechnen	käsperna
Das Pfund	Littere
Die Mark	Schuck
es wiegt	mischkele
billig	mezzia
hergeben	nossen
fortgehen	seifrach
ruhig	stickem
horchen	roin
Der Streit	Oseras

— 7 —

Deutsch	Handelssprache
Der Nachbar	Schocher
Das Fleisch	Busser
Der Knochen	Zumes
Das Unschlitt	Kälef
Die Haut	Ores
Etwas Neues	Kittisch
Der Hopfen	Dini
Freundschaft u. Verwandtschaft	Maschbuge
Das Geld	Massumen
Die Arbeit	Maloge
Das Bier	Schäacher
Das Haus	Bajes
Das Wirtshaus	Juschpesbajes
bezahlen	maschulme
stehlen	gansen
Der Mann	Isch
Die Frau	Ischa
Der Bräutigam	Der Kusen
Die Braut	Die Kalle
Der Pfarrer	Gallach
Der Lehrer	Mallumeter
heiraten	schittige
Garantie	Oreff
trinken	schabkana
essen	achle
Der Fehler	Kasorem
verraten	matabre
Er ist ein Trinker	Er is a Schabkenisch
Der Soldat	Balmagom

— 8 —

Deutsch.	Handelssprache.
Der Profit	Resach
Teuer	Jocker
verteuern	verjockern
Schön	Toff
Nicht schön	Loloss
Schmus	Sasseres
Betrügen	Marama
Schwer Gewicht	Doff Mischkel
Leicht Gewicht	Lass Mischkel
Bankerott	Machulla
Nicht bankerott	Lass Machulla
Arm	Dalles
Vermögen	Kuzen
Ich bin Bürge	List mamen ja
Gut reden	Lass häffig
Kronentaler	Güttilrad
Preußentaler	Melachrad
Pfennig	Pschident
Karolin	Juser
Das Vieh ansehen	Soniga

Umwandlung der Karolin in Mark und Pfennig.

Karol.	M.	Pf.	Karol.	M.	Pf.	Karol.	M.	Pf.	Karol.	M.	Pf.
1	18	86	10	[illegible]	57	19	[illegible]	29	28	528	—
2	37	71	11	207	43	20	377	44	29	[illegible]	[illegible]
3	56	57	12	226	29	21	[illegible]	[illegible]	30	566	71
4	75	43	13	245	11	22	[illegible]	[illegible]	31	[illegible]	[illegible]
5	94	29	14	264	[illegible]	23	[illegible]	71	32	[illegible]	[illegible]
6	[illegible]	14	15	282	86	24	452	57	33	[illegible]	[illegible]
7	132	[illegible]	16	301	71	25	471	43	34	[illegible]	[illegible]
8	150	86	17	320	57	26	490	29	35	618	57
9	169	71	18	339	43	27	[illegible]	14	36	637	[illegible]

FIGURE 2.4A AND 2.4B. *Hebräisch-Deutscher Dolmetscher (Hebrew-German Translator).* Courtesy of Stadtarchiv Gunzenhausen.

Markt= & Handelssprache

der

Viehhändler auf deutschen Märkten, in Privatgeschäften und Stallungen.

Zahlen.

Nr.		Nr.	
1	Oleph	25	Kaff He
2	Bes	26	Kaff Fof
3	Gimmel	27	Kaff Sojen
4	Doleth	28	Kaff Ges
5	He	29	Kaff Tes
6	Fof	30	Lamed
7	Sojen	31	Lamed Oleph
8	Ges	32	Lamed Bes
9	Tes	33	Lamed Gimmel
10	Jus	34	Lamed Doleth
11	Jus Oleph	35	Lamed He
12	Jus Bes	36	Lamed Fof
13	Jus Gimmel	37	Lamed Sojen
14	Jus Doleth	38	Lamed Ges
15	Jus He	39	Lamed Tes
16	Jus Fof	40	Mem
17	Jus Sojen	41	Mem Oleph
18	Jus Ges	42	Mem Bes
19	Jus Tes	43	Mem Gimmel
20	Kaff	44	Mem Doleth
21	Kaff Oleph	45	Mem He
22	Kaff Bes	46	Mem Fof
23	Kaff Gimmel	47	Mem Sojen
24	Kaff Doleth	48	Mem Ges

Nr.		Nr.	
49	Mem Tes	80	Schmunem
50	Nun	81	Schmunem Oleph
51	Nun Oleph	82	Schmunem Bes
52	Nun Bes	83	Schmunem Gimmel
53	Nun Gimmel	84	Schmunem Doleth
54	Nun Doleth	85	Schmunem He
55	Nun He	86	Schmunem Fof
56	Nun Fof	87	Schmunem Sojen
57	Nun Sojen	88	Schmunem Ges
58	Nun Ges	89	Schmunem Tes
59	Nun Tes	90	Tischem (Tattick)
60	Sammach	91	Tischem Oleph
61	Sammach Oleph	92	Tischem Bes
62	Sammach Bes	93	Tischem Gimmel
63	Sammach Gimmel	94	Tischem Doleth
64	Sammach Doleth	95	Tischem He
65	Sammach He	93	Tischem Fof
66	Sammach Fof	97	Tischem Sojen
67	Sammach Sojen	98	Tischem Ges
68	Sammach Ges	99	Tischem Tes
69	Sammach Tes	100	Mees
70	Schiffen	101	Mees Oleph
71	Schiffen Oleph	102	Mees Bes
72	Schiffen Bes	103	Mees Gimmel
73	Schiffen Gimmel	104	Mees Doleth
74	Schiffen Doleth	105	Mees He
75	Schiffen He	106	Mees Fof
76	Schiffen Fof	107	Mees Sojen
77	Schiffen Sojen	108	Mees Ges
78	Schiffen Ges	109	Mees Tes
79	Schiffen Tes	110	Mees Jus

Nr.		Nr.	
120	Mees Kaff	500	He Mees
130	Mees Lamed	600	Fof Mees
140	Mees Mem	700	Sojen Mees
150	Mees Nun	800	Gesa Mees
160	Mees Sammach	900	Tes Mees
170	Mees Schiffen	1000	Olepha Luffin
180	Mees Schmunem	2000	Besa Luffin
190	Mees Tischem	3000	Gimmela Luffin
200	Bes Mees	4000	Doletha Luffin
300	Gimmel Mees	5000	Hea Luffin
400	Doleth Mees	10000	Jusa Luffin

Deutsch.	Handelssprache.
Die Kalbe ist gesund	Die Ekel ist koscher
„ „ krank	„ „ kuhle
„ „ geht gäll	„ „ pattischt net
„ „ ist zu teuer	„ „ ist zu jocker
„ „ ist billig	„ „ S' is ä Mäzia
Gieb ihm 12 Karolin	Jus bes juser
Biet ihm 14	Jus doleth juser
Der Mann ist hart im Handel	An dem Mann is ka proge
„ läßt mit sich reden	Der Mann is net unbekufet
Die Kuh ist alt	Des is an alte Bora
„ gibt wenig Milch	Die Bora gibt net Gutes
„ viel	„ „ viel Gutes
„ ist gewöhnt im Zug	Die Bora garantier dir ich, as gewöhnt is

Deutsch.	Handelssprache.
Die Kuh ist trächtig	Die Bora pattischt
„ ist nicht trächtig	„ pattischt net
Die Ochsen sind mager	Die Ekel sind laff schummen
Kauf die Ochsen um jeden Preis	Kaff die Ekel um jeden Erach
Der Ochse ist fett	Die Ekel ist schummen
Ich gewähr Alles	Ich bind ir oraf, für Alles
Nichts	Oraf bin ich dir für Niz
Ich werde dich verklagen	Ich bin dir oraf, daß ich dich verkofel
Er verdirbt mir den Handel	Er ist mir mäkatrig gewetzt
Ich rede dir gut im Handel	Ich schmus dir gut
Er ist ein Lump	Er is ä Gaschtbündel
Er ist ein braver Mann	Er is ä bekuferter Mann
Gib sie her	Nonsensen
Er macht mir krumm	Er is mir makattei
Die Kuh mit dem Kalb ohne Kalb	Die Bora hat an Ekele kan Ekele
Die Kuh is wert: 200 Mark	„ „ ist wert: Bes Mees Schuck
Die Pferde sind eingefahren	Die Suß sind gewöhnt
Die Pferde gehen einspännig	Die Sutz gehn einspännig garantier dir ich
Das Pferd knappt	Suß hat schlechte Jasleiemer
„ ist blind	Suß reunt net

FIGURE 2.4A AND 2.4B. (*continued*)

well as farmers. This makes the language a specific feature of the cattle trade. Therefore, it did not function so much as an exclusionary or even manipulative trading practice but more as an inclusionary one that incorporated everybody who used it into the cattle trade's "circle of trust."[110] How useful it was for the traders is demonstrated by the fact that it was still taught in the 1950s at cattle-trading schools, although by this time, there were only a few isolated Jews still active in the cattle trade.[111]

The Trade Practice of "Cow Tapering"

The widespread practice of "cow tapering" (*Kuhverjüngung,* more literally "cow rejuvenation"), also called "horn tips" (*Hörnerspitzen*), was also regarded as a manipulative tactic.[112] In this practice, the calves' rings of a cow, which made it possible to draw conclusions about the number of births associated with a cow and thus its approximate age, were sanded down. One contemporary, who worked as a blacksmith for a well-established cattle-trading business in Mönchsroth, recalled how he would remove the calves' rings on cows for his employer:

> So I . . . then trimmed and fixed the critters' hooves, and then the horns were also trimmed and shaped, and they were tapered . . . I was still an apprentice and [my boss] said, you have to rejuvenate the cow . . . and so, up front, you sawed off the piece and with a rasp and with glass shards you made it look younger again . . . and then it was rubbed down with water[,] and then you never saw this again[,] and then the cows were also made a bit more expensive than before, for when one [cow] has calved twice[,] it's worth more than when it has calved five times.[113]

In this case, not only could the deceptive practice lead to a disruption of trust; it also required an accomplice, namely the blacksmith, to carry out the deception.

The person who made this statement also reported that the cattle trader reimbursed him for the cow tapering with an extra tip. The fact that the cattle trader paid the blacksmith for this job with a supplement to his actual wage points to the unusual nature of the assignment. The tip was a kind of hush money. But farmers also availed themselves of this deceptive business practice in order to conceal the real age of a cow from the buyer.[114] Among farmers, it was also customary to saturate an animal for slaughter with water before a sale in order to put as much weight as possible on the scale. Hence, it became important for cattle traders to arrive early in the morning at a farm in order to see a head of cattle before it had been primed for sale.[115] A bit of mistrust was an intrinsic part of the cattle trade on both sides. If, however, the business partners were familiar with these practices, their use did not necessarily lead to a disruption of trust relations and could be overlooked during the social experience of mutual negotiation.

This depiction of different trading practices provides some insight into the culture of the cattle trade in which both farmers and traders were equally involved. Even if price-fixing in a special traders' language, the cow tapering methods, and "dumb calculating" were commonly seen as trade practices that disrupted trust, they still could not be reduced to their partly manipulative and partly exclusionary character.

More to the point, these practices reveal the coarseness of the business and the concomitant difficulty of concluding a good trade. There was a reason that peasants (not just traders) were compelled to resort to such practices; small farmers, who were financially very weak, struggled for every penny and tried mightily to keep prices down. Trust in the cattle trade was thus a thorny issue. On one hand, trust in one's trading partner was necessary precisely because of the numerous dubious business practices; on the other hand, these very practices posed an obstacle to building trust. When farmers realized that they had received less money per head of cattle than they had expected or that a deal had resulted in them receiving an old cow and not a young one, the relationship suffered and trust was disrupted.

Hence, one may question whether the unequal distribution of power resources, such as money or intellectual abilities, hindered the production of trust. But, as philosopher Thomas Hobbes explains, trust is expressed not only in relationships between equal partners who engage in a mutually profitable exchange; it is also expressed in those relationships where the realistic expectation of a mutually profitable exchange is absent because the partners have access to completely unequal power resources. And trust can also shape relationships where expectations of mutual profit are not necessarily the reason for partners to contact each other.[116] Accordingly, this partly unequal distribution of power resources should not have stood in the way of building trust between farmers and cattle traders. Both the trade practices producing trust and those disrupting trust must therefore be viewed as a constituent component of the cattle trade.

Cases of Conflict: Erosion of Trust

The business practices of the cattle trade produced a thick network of reciprocal social and financial dependencies that could place a heavy burden on the relationship of trust between the actors. Since the person granting trust is letting another person handle his worries about a matter that "lies close to his heart,"[117] an unfulfilled trade promise is more than the mere disappointment of expectations—it is also always a personal slight. This affront can be expressed in very different ways, but it can also be avenged. In cases of conflict, accordingly, the sustainability of trust in cattle-trading relationships is something that emerges with particular clarity.

Conflicts are thereby understood as a product of social action and thus also as a form of relations in which processes of social negotiation are manifested.[118] Here, the analysis of conflicts will proceed on the basis of substantive criteria, which (for the sake of a better presentation) will be divided into two groups. First comes the group of social conflicts—for example, those that resulted from violations of honor (insults and defamations). Then there is the group of financial conflicts, such as those resulting from economic damages (nonrepayment of debts). These examples show how trust between participating actors could be challenged and when an erosion could possibly have begun.

Methodology

The practice of settling a cattle trade by a handshake (and thus dispensing with having to put a purchasing contract in writing) draws attention to the methodological difficulty involved in investigating cases of conflict. Written traces bequeathed a record of conflicts only when the parties to the dispute brought in a third, independent authority to settle matters. Testimony regarding cases of conflict like these—evidence that would allow conclusions to be drawn about how the conflicts proceeded, what strategies of avoidance there were, and who the participating actors were—are largely absent from the files of public administration at the provincial, district, and municipal level, since these institutions rarely got involved in conflicts between farmers and cattle traders. Independent authorities brought in by disputing parties to solve their conflict were legal advisers who would bring the case to court if the occasion arose. However, since most of these cases dealt with civil trials and not with the kind of penal law trials heard at local district courts, we also have no records of them.

To some (very small) extent, it was possible to close this gap in the documentary holdings by evaluating the files of attorney Dr. Richard Herz, kept in the state archives in Nuremberg (Staatsarchiv Nürnberg). Records there show numerous instances of disputes between cattle traders and farmers, making it possible to garner important case studies for the following investigation. The imbalance between the economic conflicts, which were frequently negotiated by a higher authority, and the social conflicts, which were mostly settled privately by the disputing parties themselves, is dealt with here by using evidence from oral history. The analysis of interviews with former trading partners of

Jewish cattle traders brings to light certain "master narratives" that provide insight into power relations among the actors as they dealt with each other and thus also into the potential for conflict and into strategies for settling disputes.[119] The way evidence about these points of conflict has been transmitted to us reveals their meaning for the interlocutors in these interviews and thus facilitates conclusions about patterns that exist. This evidence derived from oral histories was not viewed in isolation but rather was matched against and underpinned by the written sources that have come down to us.

Since Herz's files deal exclusively with the years between 1927 and 1943, there is a gap for the period before 1927 that could not be closed, as there is a lack of civil case files. This warrants critical notice inasmuch as the Nazi party was already enjoying strong backing from the populace in Central Franconia at this time, and this support needs to be considered when looking at these cases of conflict. At this point in the analysis, though, the focus is on depicting conflicts typical of the cattle trade. The influence of the Nazi party on this web of relations will be investigated elsewhere in this book.

Slights to "Male Honor": Questions of Virility

In the cattle trade, a masculine domain, it often happened that conflicts were fought out as a battle over slights to "male honor."[120] Or it might also happen that conflicts started in the first place because male honor had been slighted in some way. In general, injuries to male honor are an essential component of the culture of conflict in a rural society,[121] though they certainly acquire another dimension when the actors belong to different ethnoreligious and social groups. An old anti-Jewish prejudice propagates the myth that Jewish men could commit transgressions with Christian women without violating the Talmud. This prejudice about the "lecherous Jew," which acquired a new dimension and more far-reaching consequences owing to the kind of racism and antisemitism that developed in the course of industrialization, is reflected above all in oral traditions.[122]

In the oral history interviews I conducted with farmers who were still in contact with Jewish cattle traders during their youth, many whispered off the record that in the neighboring village X, there was a certain Y who was the illegitimate son of a Jewish cattle trader. Nobody was supposed to know this; it was meant to be a big secret.[123] One interview partner even claimed that a farm widow had paid off her livestock debts through a sexual relation with a Jewish cattle trader.[124] Another contemporary, an old farmer, added that Jews were able to regulate this kind of "indiscretion" out of court owing to their better financial situation. He concluded: "But I assume that Jews mostly regulated this under the counter; for the Jews, after all, it was usually not a sin, I've been told, when the blood gets passed on" (i.e., when a Jewish man fathers a child with a non-Jewish woman; the farmer is expressing a common racist stereotype about Jewish attitudes toward sexual relations with non-Jews).[125]

For centuries, non-Jews repeatedly presented Jewish men as "lecherous men" who assaulted Christian women.[126] This meant Jewish cattle traders were often used as screens onto which the Christians projected their own sexual desires or even fears. Because of their different lifestyle, cattle traders were often perceived by farmers as having greater potency in terms of appearance and financial or even social prowess. All day long, the cattle traders were on the road from one farm to the next and thus were more mobile than the farmers themselves. They dressed like merchants, knew how to calculate prices in their heads, and always had a lot of cash on hand. Frequently, they would conduct their business with a peasant woman or farmer's wife at the farmstead while the farmer was busy in the fields, a business practice that stimulated male fantasies. The male farmer's own desire for potency, both sexual and status-related, could thus be projected onto the Jewish trader. The subjective feeling of inferiority toward the different lifestyle of the trader could be compensated for by a sense of injury and a rebuke to the trader's allegedly dishonorable behavior (extra-marital sexual intercourse with a non-Jewish farm woman). How greatly these accusations reflected the fantasies of those reporting about them in interviews is suggested by the fact that these kinds of stories were broached exclusively by male contemporaries but never by the females interviewed for this book.

Jewish men also settled conflicts about a sense of injury to the "male honor"—and sometimes the "soldier's honor"—of their opponent, as shown by one case from the town of Ellingen. There, in 1921, procurator Franz Buchner sued Jewish cattle trader Max Oppenheimer for slandering his "soldier's honor." As a cause for the suit, he mentioned his belief that Oppenheimer had publicly slandered him as a "war shirker" at a restaurant in front of several patrons.[127] Jewish traders also looked down on the lax sexual behavior of some farmers, as the dispute between farmer Josef Seehofer and Jewish cattle and real estate trader Siegfried Weinmann illustrates. In 1928, a fierce dispute erupted between these two about repaying loans. When Seehofer did not settle his debts with Weinmann in spite of numerous notices demanding payment, Weinmann accused the farmer of having frittered away his assets through excessive drinking and "the enchanting company of ladies," which explained why he was in arrears with Weinmann.[128] Seehofer then took Weinmann to court for defamation of character.[129]

The suit hardly put an end to the quarrel. Seehofer continued to inflame the dispute with more antisemitic prejudices and by insinuating that the Jewish cattle trader was being pushy. Apparently (so he claimed), the farmer was not capable of warding off Weinmann's terms for the loan he so desperately needed. Instead—so Seehofer argued—he was completely at the mercy of the Jewish merchant's loan offer. Seehofer, in effect, was making the cattle trader responsible for his own financial dependence and thus using the classic antisemitic stereotype that Jewish merchants plied a trade of "fishing for customers," which the Protestant ethic regarded as un-Christian and therefore immoral.[130]

We may certainly assume that Weinmann's loan to Seehofer came about through trust. Yet at the moment when business relations were put to a test, both parties aggravated a conflict with mistrust fueled by prejudices. To settle the matter, the parties to the dispute called in an independent authority; yet the legal remedies of a court did not suffice, as far as Seehofer was concerned, to restore his reputation. As a result, Seehofer had Weinmann beaten up on January 13, 1932, in the Lower Bavarian town of Mainburg.[131] Seehofer availed himself of the law of the jungle in order to retaliate for the injury to his honor— a time-honored practice for solving conflicts in the countryside.[132] This ended the conflict. Sources do not indicate whether Jewish cattle traders also employed methods like this to defend their honor against farmers. Yet one orally transmitted case from Mönchsroth shows that Jewish cattle traders also used physical force as a disciplinary measure. In one case it was reported that a Jewish cattle trader slapped a farmer's son after the latter had interfered in a trade that was already underway.[133]

On both sides of the trading partnership, therefore, conjecture about the sexual activity of the other and affronts to male honor provided fuel for conflict, though these suspicions also functioned as methods for restoring each party's injured sense of "male pride." Both sides would use an injury to the potency of the other party as a reason for conflict and an instrument of power. In this way, farmers and cattle traders confronted each other as accepted, if not always equal, parties to a conflict.[134] In the cases observed here, such imputations and reputational injuries did not seem to have resulted in a dissolution of business relations. This indicates how deeply such components of conflict were anchored in cattle-trading relationships.

Economic Conflicts about Financial Transactions

Conflicts could also arise among trading partners owing to unfulfilled trade promises, such as payments in arrears. This kind of dispute showed up with greater intensity in times of economic crises, as in 1923, in the wake of Germany's hyperinflation, or during the Great Depression of 1929–1930. While most farmers emerged from the hyperinflation as winners, the Great Depression was devastating for them.[135] Drastically fallen livestock prices created huge financial difficulties for many rural family farmsteads.[136] In this situation fraught with tension, the cattle traders assumed a dual role vis-à-vis the farmers: they functioned simultaneously as "kindly" lenders and as "merciless" money collectors.

As lenders, cattle traders either granted or negotiated financing options to farmers so they could obtain the cattle urgently needed to manage their operations. As security, the farmers would confer a guarantee on their farm. One piece of evidence for this practice is the tax office file preserved for cattle trader Moritz Engel from Markt Berolzheim. In that file, he recorded an item in which livestock debts were converted into long-term debts.[137] In the worst-case scenario, farmers who were unable to settle these debts would face the breakup of their farm. Since many middle-class traders running medium-sized firms combined their cattle-trading operations with trading in real estate, they would function in this situation as "merciless slaughterers of [farm] estates" (*unbarmherzige Güterschlächter*).[138] The term *Güterschlächter* (estate slaughterer) refers to a trade practice that drew a great deal of criticism. Jewish and non-Jewish cattle traders would often resell a bankrupt farm to several interested parties; they literally dismembered agricultural estates, such as the property of the Höfelsauer family from Margarethentann in Lower Bavaria, a farm in the *mediene* (sales territory) of cattle and real-estate trader Leopold Weinmann from Treuchtlingen. In October 1930, Josef and Elisabeth Höfelsauer had taken on a mortgage with Weinmann for the couple's property of 13.6 hectares.[139] A few months after the nearly bankrupt Josef did not meet his obligations, Weinmann took legal measures to repossess his cattle. The farmer thereupon had to give the cattle trader two oxen, two cows, and a bull calf. If one bears in mind that, at this time, a farming operation the size of the Höfelsauers' estate included only one milk cow on average, it becomes clear that the livestock sued for in this case amounted to the farmer's entire stock.[140] How drastic experiences like this could be for a farm family is evidenced by the way they are embedded in the town's oral history. In interviews with contemporaries, many reported about the moment when Jewish cattle traders "quickly took the last head of cattle [out of the cowshed]."[141] This moment often represented symbolically the financial end of a farm family, as in the case of the Höfelsauer family. In fact, Weinmann and the other creditors auctioned off the entire property shortly after confiscating the livestock.[142] Although Jewish cattle traders in situations like this were following the law as they collected their debts, the National Socialists in particular presented them as "usurers" or as the embodiment of "parasitic capital" (*raffendes Kapital*) and as thus responsible for the misery of the farmers.[143]

If there was a compulsory auction leading to foreclosure, the farmer's frustration about his own failure could be unloaded onto the lender. In these cases, it was easily forgotten that even the destruction of a farm estate did not protect the lender from losses incurred in the credit transaction. Demanding payment for liabilities was, in any event, an extremely unpleasant business that entailed numerous personal and financial risks. Cattle traders ran the danger of having the debtor's rancor about his desperate situation directed against them. Not infrequently, farmers experienced the circumstance of insolvency as a personal defeat that had to be kept secret.[144]

In addition, the cattle trader was frequently the only one in the know about the financial situation of the farmers in the village. As the bearer of a banking secret, the trader could get into a very delicate social situation. From a defense deposition by Siegfried Weinmann, it may be inferred that he preferred booking appointments with his debtors in restaurants in order to collect his receivables. There, he could negotiate the terms for extending debts in public, with other patrons of the tavern as witnesses. This protected the creditor from potential emotional outbursts from the debtor. If cattle traders demanded repayments of debts directly in the farmers' homes, the situation was different; they risked facing outbursts of rage and violent assaults by the indebted farmers. In a letter to his lawyer, Weinmann forcefully describes how dangerous such situations could become for him: "Besides, it was not at all suitable associating with this [Michael Inderst] in [his] home, since he was very rough."[145] Restaurants also provided a neutral space for debtors, far from the curious glances of suspicious neighbors. Inderst, the farmer in question in this case, informed Weinmann that he wanted to meet with him in a restaurant. In his letter to his own lawyer, Weinmann conveyed the farmer's rationale: "I should not meet him [at home], the neighbors are not to know that he owes me, and that the cattle were delivered to me on credit. . . . Yet this [the fact that Inderst bought on credit] was known in Mainburg, and it was also [known] personally about me that I sold cattle on credit."[146] Inderst, who was ashamed of his money problems, preferred restaurants as a meeting place, as then he could hide his money problems from his wife.[147]

In general, taverns were the sites best suited to complete cattle trades. Farmers stopped there after finishing work to drink beer and exchange news. Thus, according to witness testimony, the farmer Wegner sat at a table in the Waldsperger Tavern with several farmers in August 1931 and related how he had a fat cow at home that he wanted to exchange for a fresh milking cow, since he was in urgent need of milk. The cattle trader Thormann, who overheard the conversation in the restaurant, according to the report of the defense attorney, seized the opportunity, sat down at the table with the farmer, and extolled a fresh milking cow, which had recently delivered a calf and was milking again. The cow, he was told, was in Thormann's sales stable at the Waldsperger Tavern, and Wegner could look at it right away. According to the letter of the defense attorney, both of them then went out to the stable, examined the cow and the calf, and sealed the deal, exchanging their cattle later that day. Shortly thereafter, the farmer accused the merchant of sticking him with a fake mother cow, since the calf was not drinking the milk of the cow. On top of that, it was not Thormann's name at the head of the barter agreement, but rather that of cattle trader Louis Feldmann from Nuremberg.[148] The cattle trader, in other words, had repeatedly cheated the farmer and thus abused the trust shown in him.

Unlike personal slights, economic conflicts affected the material livelihood of the involved parties. The conversion of livestock debts into long-term debts could lead to the loss of family property. Conversely, creditors also had to swallow painful losses when their customers became insolvent. Misconduct that was either their own fault or somebody else's could damage their own livelihood or that of the other party to the conflict. As these cases indicate, the involved parties frequently brought in an independent authority to solve the dispute. This meant surrendering trust in their own potential for conflict resolution to an overarching authority. This authority was certainly capable of issuing a "judge's verdict" but not of restoring the sense of trust that had been damaged. Reclaiming that could only be done by the parties to the conflict. To what extent an overarching, "neutral" authority was even capable of influencing the relationship of trust between farmer and cattle trader is the focus of the next chapter.

3

Constituting Trust through Official Authority

The private cattle trade had its own regulations. Reciprocal trust between the trading partners compensated for the risk caused by the uncertainty surrounding cattle as a commodity. Cattle-trade regulations had emerged out of long-standing social experience in dealing with each other over many years, and the resulting process-based trust proved a guarantee for reliability and economic success. Yet even this kind of process-based trust is precarious, since it can (for example) be undone by increased cultural diversity or by alienation between the actors, as might be created by an influx of immigrants. In order to keep the economy going, process-based trust can be replaced by trust that is institution based.[1] In other words, via the constitution of official trust, economic subjects would no longer be trusting in their social experience or in something they gained from negotiating with each other; instead, they would rely on the pronouncement of an official authority that identifies the trading partner as "trustworthy." As a result, through the intervention of authorities, a formalization and standardization of the trust-building process between the economic subjects takes place.

In the cattle trade, such a shift occurred after the First World War, as a major crisis befell the agricultural and livestock economy. The crisis subjected this tried-and-tested network of relationships to a critical ordeal. The steadily growing urban population demanded ever more meat and milk products, which jacked up the demand for high-quality animals for slaughter and fatstock.[2] This need could not be satisfied, however, since a large share of the hog supply had been slaughtered during the First World War.[3] Because of the resulting shortage of pork, cattle inventories were impinged upon, which led to additional inflation in the prices for beef cattle in large urban markets.[4] These shortcomings gave consumers and producers occasion to lay blame for these miserable circumstances on the cattle trade. They accused the cattle trade of burdening prices with an excessive markup. The cattle trade became a political issue.

All of the institutions responsible for the cattle trade tried using different measures to settle the conflict in an effort to avoid social tensions.[5] The lost trust was to be restored by official regulation laid down by authorities. In observing this process, two things become clear: how much trust farmers had in the cattle traders described as "old" and "trustworthy" (*alt* and *reell*) and how the attempt of the authorities to institutionalize trust was stretched to its limits.

The Institutionalization of Trust

An essential reason for the erosion of trust in the cattle trade after the First World War was the large number of new cattle traders who were operating on the market alongside those who were established. As a result, within a few years, the total number of cattle traders skyrocketed by 62 percent. While there were around 6,000 cattle traders in Bavaria before the First World War, by 1922, the number of traders was already 9,716.[6] After the First World War, there were many veterans practicing the cattle trade who had returned from the war and were unable to gain a foothold in the occupation they had learned. Among the new cattle traders, there were also many farmers who had lost their farms.[7]

This development was met with fierce criticism. The new cattle traders were accused of not having mastered their occupation's "trustworthy trade gestures" and of using unfair business practices to enrich themselves by exploiting the special circumstances of the times.[8] In the eyes of the critics, the cattle trade had turned into a receptacle for all kinds of failed characters. The chairman of the Bavarian Meat Supply Office, Undersecretary Dr. Johann Attinger, even suspected that around 80 percent of all cattle traders had prior convictions, most of them for fraud.[9] He also found fault with these traders' poor training: "Today the farmer who's gone broke usually becomes a cattle trader, traveling from village to village, tavern to tavern. Most of these people can barely read."[10] This was also something about which Margot Grünberg complained in her dissertation, published in 1932, on the German cattle trade. She wrote that among the small traders, there were "so-called 'shady characters.' Often they are farmers or butchers who have gone broke. They represent the excrescences of merchant commercialism and greatly damage its reputation. Through their conduct, they have brought proper cattle trading into serious disrepute. They are frequently to blame for the spread of disease and constitute a danger to the population engaged in agriculture."[11] It was not only the cattle trade, however, but the entire merchant profession in general that was suffering from the reputation that its ranks now included people who were "less talented."[12] As Oswald Bauer was already complaining in his treatise on the honorable merchant in 1906, the profession of merchant offered people "a hideout" when they "did not appear suitable . . . for a 'higher profession.'" These black sheep were deemed damaging to the entire profession.[13] Since these new cattle traders had neither sufficient knowledge of their wares nor an official business license, they were also called "wild cattle traders."[14] In this way, they were competing with middle-class cattle traders operating small and medium-sized firms steeped in tradition.

An increasing number of traders also began coming onto the home market from outside because of Germany's increasing motorization (more cars on the road).[15] Because of favorable cattle prices in Bavaria, these new traders were able to buy regional cattle in order to sell it in other parts of Germany.[16] These traders from outside Bavaria were responsible not only for intensified competition among the traders but also for estrangement between buyers and producers. They no longer knew the farmers personally. Their trade relationships were not based on the social experience that came from years of dealing with each other. With the beginning of industrialization—in other words, long before the 1920s—the market on which farmers and cattle traders encountered each other had become larger and more complex. This process had put the time-tested, premodern relationships between farmers and cattle traders under high-voltage tension.

Meat consumers, representatives of agriculture, the cattle-trading associations, and the provincial and district governments all disliked this development, as the author of one sensational newspaper article conveyed:

> The consequences of flooding the land with traders is [*sic*] quite extraordinary. On the farm, one [trader] hands the door handle over to the other. Since everyone wants to earn something, railway travel, overnight lodging, and other expenses are very high—also, the necessities of life for these people are usually not cheap—he needs to see to it that he gets his hands on the cattle whatever the circumstances. The old, trustworthy trader has held back and sometimes left the farmer standing there when it seemed to him that a price was too high. The traders of today need to outbid each other on price in order to get something. The farmer has his choice. And everything is paid for by the poor consumer.[17]

Three points clearly emerge from this quote: first, how intensely traders were competing with each other for possible deals; second, what a negative impact high business expenses and fees had on prices; and, third, how the traditional trading culture had supposedly gotten lost as a result of this development.

Here, all of the participating actors agreed that lost trust in the cattle trade could only be restored by "purging untrustworthy [*unreell*] elements" in the trade.[18] This plea was taken up enthusiastically by the representatives of the cattle trade. Even the State Association of Bavarian Cattle Traders (Landesverband bayerischer Viehhändler) joined in this chorus: "Our organization has fervently endeavored since it was founded almost eight years ago to unite all professional cattle traders in its ranks and to eradicate all the untrustworthy elements."[19] Dr. Franz Xaver Zahnbrecher, a member of the state parliament for the Bavarian People's Party, also associated himself with the rhetoric of the previous contributors; he called for "excluding the bad elements [from the cattle trade] and combining the good elements."[20] Critics and representatives of the cattle trade jointly espoused the view that the disruption of trust could only be addressed through strict regulation.[21] In 1920, the Bavarian state government charged the newly formed State Office for Livestock Commerce (Landesamt für Viehverkehr) with the "convalescence" of the cattle trade.[22]

Accordingly, a third—"neutral"—authority was installed to ensure that the traders and farmers could trust each other. In the discussions about the "trustworthy cattle trader" surrounding this effort, the adjectives *trustworthy, reliable, good,* and *honorable* (the first of these terms—*reell*—can also mean "fair," "respectable," or "solid") were mostly used as synonyms, often interchangeably alongside each other. The very choice of these adjectives points to the difficulty arising from any attempt at institutionalizing trust. Although the aim was to have farmers rebuild their trust in the cattle traders, an official institution cannot restore trust between economic actors, since it lacks "reliance on another's goodwill."[23] Hence, the public authorities charged with the job of constituting trust in an official way circumvented the issue by focusing on the concept of reliability; from now on, cattle traders hoping to ply their trade would have to demonstrate reliability in order to count as trustworthy.[24] With this in mind, the authorities were supposed to make a rational calculation based on the most precise estimate possible by retrieving hard facts. The State Office for Livestock Commerce charged district authorities with this task, which meant that a personal file was created for each cattle trader.[25] The cattle traders deemed reliable were those who fulfilled the standards set by the office—standards meant to provide a foundation for developing a relationship of trust between the two trading partners.[26] With the introduction of the construct of the *trustworthy cattle trader,* the cattle trade was to be made reliable in an unreliable world.

A look at the different measures and directives by which the trustworthy cattle trader was invented reveals that the goal was to strengthen the established, medium-sized cattle-trading operations while simultaneously weakening the new traders and those for whom this business was a sideline.

Inventing the "Trustworthy Cattle Trader" (Reeller Viehhändler)

The State Office for Livestock Commerce promulgated a number of different directives to strengthen the "trustworthy cattle trade" and combat the "wild" and "untrustworthy" cattle traders. It was regarded as "untrustworthy business conduct" when, for example, a trader abandoned a head of cattle that he had purchased but not yet paid for with the farmer because he had determined belatedly that he "could no longer earn anything off of [his] wild purchase."[27] Influential polemicists like Attinger blamed the cattle traders for any shortcomings and sought to solve the conflict in a negative way by finding reasons to exclude traders. By contrast, representatives of the cattle-trading profession highlighted positive measures emphasizing inclusionary rationales. They criticized the bias of some courts toward the cattle trade.[28] In addition, the legal adviser to the State Association of Bavarian Cattle Traders, Dr. Graminger, complained about the "permissive" practice of the authorities when it came to issuing official business licenses. Decisions were mainly made according to social criteria, so that returning war veterans in particular—independently of their professional qualifications—were favored.[29] Hence, he called for the awarding of business licenses to be regulated primarily according to professional standards (such as solid specialized knowledge and professional experience) rather than social criteria. In yet another circular, the State Office for Livestock Commerce requested that determining the "unreliability" of a trader not be based on "mere assumption" but instead rest on "established facts" and asserted that "suspicions and rumors do not suffice"; accusations of criminal offenses had to be examined and proven.[30]

The State Office for Livestock Commerce joined the call for trustworthy cattle traders to have both solid experience and knowledge about the profession. The demands made of these cattle traders echo philosopher Anthony Giddens's compelling theory of trust, in which he emphasized that the absence of complete information—rather than the absence of power—was a precondition for the erosion of trust. Following Giddens, a lack of professional knowledge or insufficient information about the cattle trader would cause an erosion of trust necessitating the intervention of the authorities, who would demand that the trader demonstrate the necessary professional knowledge to ply his trade.[31] In this way, they were submitting the cattle trade to a process not only of regulation but also of professionalization, which was vehemently supported by the cattle traders' associations.[32]

In general, membership in a profession subject to government accreditation is crucial for the establishment of trust between economic actors.[33] A process of modernization, rationalization, and thus of bureaucratization—including a thrust toward professionalization in various fields such as the cattle trade— was underway by the end of the nineteenth century.[34] In the course of these associated processes, trade associations, which provided information in professional journals about current developments and represented their members in political bodies, were also founded.[35] Although we have no evidence of cattle-trading schools for the time period examined here,[36] a look at the biographies of cattle traders' sons reveals that many of them, in addition to training inside the family, completed a commercial apprenticeship.[37] This training provided them with the necessary qualifications to run a modern and successful business in accordance with managerial principles—all of which helped them be regarded as professional and trustworthy merchants. In the authorities' attempt to ensure that the cattle trade be "made reliable," one objective was combatting the trade's premodern character, which had been shaped by numerous forms of social negotiation. The aim was also to adjust the cattle trade to the demands of the times now that it was possible for many outside cattle traders and farmers to encounter each other in business dealings.

The State Office for Livestock Commerce also supported those cattle-trading operations that had already been conducting their business before 1910—that is, before the economy had suffered numerous downturns because of the war and other crises. These cattle traders were characterized as the "old trustworthy" traders who, for that reason, were entitled in principle to practice the cattle trade.[38] Tradition and experience were thus regarded as a guarantee of reliability both in the branch itself and with the public authorities. By contrast, the authorities showed no trust toward those traders who tried to enter the cattle trade after the First World War, like innkeepers or farmers who had gone broke. In this sense, tradition can be understood as process-based trust. It was a kind of trust that had emerged from mutual trading, and the new kind of institution-based trust would only be able to assert itself with difficulty against the older, process-based kind.

The official authorities' fortification and promotion of the medium-sized (middle-class) cattle-trading firms also found expression in the discussion around whether cattle traders needed an itinerant trade license or business license to operate. One condition for awarding a business license was that the applicant own a stable for his cattle trade. In other words, he should not "only" be conducting business on the road (his business should not be a hauling trade) but rather be in possession of a domiciled (retail) shop. The commercial practice of closing a deal on the street or on the fields—far away from any official control—was emphatically combatted.[39] The great lengths to which many cattle traders went to meet these requirements is demonstrated by a glance at the nomenclature used to describe their business relationships. Middle-class medium-sized firms called themselves "cattle-trading enterprises" (*Viehhandelsunternehmen*) or even firms, as in the cases of Firma Max Aal & Sohn (the Max Aal & Son Firm) or Firma Bermann & Oppenheimer Grosshandel in Vieh, Hopfen und Grundstücken (the Firm Bermann & Oppenheimer, Wholesalers in Cattle, Hops, and Real Estate). In this way, they drew a linguistic distinction between themselves and "merchant commercialism" (*Händlertum*), which was regarded as dubious and also as "Jewish." The term *Firma* (company), by contrast, stood for modern entrepreneurship and thus trust.

In addition, the State Office for Livestock Commerce prohibited practicing the cattle trade as a sideline. The government of Upper Palatinate demanded that cattle traders without a sales stable of their own be stripped of the *trader* designation, since they were just cattle *Schmusers* and not "trustworthy cattle traders."[40] This measure deprived not only the Schmusers but also farmers, butchers, and innkeepers of an important source of income, since these groups frequently plied the cattle trade as a secondary occupation, meaning that they were also practicing the much-maligned *Schmuserei*. Butchers were especially hard hit by this regulation. This refusal to grant them a business license for their sideline business drove them underground, for now they could only trade in beef cattle on the "black market."[41] Most of those affected by this regulation were non-Jewish cattle traders who were marketing beef cattle as a sideline to their occupations as butchers or farmers.[42] Jewish butchers did not suffer in the same way under this regulation, since it was often the case that two brothers or brothers-in-law within one family divided up the business of kosher slaughter and cattle trading between them.[43] With this measure, the State Office for Livestock Commerce was also strengthening the established, medium-sized cattle-trading businesses, where a large number of middle-class Jewish merchants were found.

The Bavarian State Ministry for Agriculture prohibited butchers not only from practicing the cattle trade as a sideline but also from trading cattle and horses at the same time.[44] This measure, unlike the previous one, mostly affected Jewish business owners.[45] Within a Jewish family business, it was customary for two brothers or a brother and brother-in-law to divide the horse and cattle trading between them.[46] This entailed many advantages for farmers.

If, for example, a farmer could not afford a new horse, one could be purchased from a cattle and horse trader by using one head or a pair of cattle to pay for the horse.

The new directive rendered this business practice impossible and thereby made it harder for farmers to obtain horses or cows on favorable terms. On the part of the authorities, there were reservations about this form of business because of the potential for a high concentration of traders in this field. The Bavarian State Ministry for Agriculture feared that the combination of "two such lucrative trades in one hand might mean, with a view toward the economic difficulties of the current era, an unjustified preferential treatment for the persons or firms concerned vis-à-vis other, more economically disadvantaged parts of the population."[47] Lurking behind this statement may be a thinly veiled antisemitic trope, whereby Jewish traders form a cartel and act as a group to influence pricing in their favor.[48] The cattle and horse traders affected by this measure—like the ones in Ansbach—protested against this ban. In this case, however, the State Office for Livestock Commerce dismissed their complaint.[49]

This directive cut deeply into the business practice of the brothers Samson and Siegmund Wurzinger from Rothenburg ob der Tauber. For years, they had jointly run a cattle- and horse-trading business. Once the State Office for Livestock Commerce prohibited them from combining both activities in 1921,[50] Samson worked alone as a cattle trader while his brother traded horses on his own. The separation of the two trading sectors was strictly monitored by the officials. When a conflict emerged in 1922 because Samson was accused of having concluded a horse trade in the name of his brother Siegmund, the State Office for Livestock Commerce promptly withdrew his trading license for three months.[51]

Another act regulating the cattle trade and cementing the position of it being "trustworthy" was the requirement, introduced in 1923, that cattle-trading firms keep accounts. With this measure, the State Office for Livestock Commerce was directing traders to keep registers about purchases and sales of cattle in book form, with every head of cattle sold or acquired having a consecutive number and an entry declaring the names and addresses of seller and buyer, the date of business transaction, and the weight and price of the animal. This record-keeping requirement made it easier for authorities and courts to monitor cattle trades. For the cattle-trading firms, this decision required that they use knowledgeable personnel. If the wife of the cattle trader did not have the necessary commercial education, a bookkeeper had to be hired. Employing a bookkeeper created additional costs, which could only be covered by firms with higher cattle sales. The accounting requirement brought with it greater transparency about taxes and business management but also additional operating costs, which were then reflected in a higher markup.[52]

To be sure, licensing the cattle trade was hardly enough to guarantee "purging the cattle trade of dishonest elements."[53] In 1923, Dr. Georg Heim from the State Chamber of Agriculture (Landesbauernkammer) criticized what he saw as insufficient neutrality between the applicant (the cattle trader) and the officials from the district administrations, who he deemed personally vested and prejudicial in their decision-making.[54] In order to secure the necessary objectivity between applicants and the officials in charge, Heim called for transferring the processing of applications to a higher central authority.[55] Thus, when sociologist Lynne Zucker emphasizes how a major divergence between different actors could lead to a disruption in the production of trust, a multilayered interaction can be seen at work here. While personal interaction was of the utmost importance when it came to establishing trust between cattle traders and farmers, in small town milieus, a district office administrator's decisions could influence that trust either positively or negatively. In the end, this administrative tipping of the scales could call into question the neutrality of that higher third authority.

The policy of the State Office for Livestock Commerce and of the individual trade associations ensured one outcome in particular: the strengthening of those medium-sized cattle-trading firms that were able to meet all the demands placed on a "trustworthy cattle trader." Because of their intrafamilial tradition, these firms had solid expertise about the basics of commercial management, were familiar with trade customs, and ran the kind of business that had a fixed address. Consequently, the office regarded the medium-sized cattle-trading firms, the majority of which were run by Jews, as reliable trading partners that farmers and meat consumers should trust. On the part of the authorities, therefore, there was enormous trust in the middle class running these medium-sized businesses. Tradition and the preservation of old structures were being challenged. The goals of strengthening long-established firms steeped in tradition and combatting the new cattle traders made it clear that the State Office for Livestock Commerce was doing two things simultaneously in its effort to regulate the cattle traders: institutionalizing trust while also counting on the more informal pathways of trust that had already grown between cattle traders and farmers from their joint experience trading with each other.

Antisemitic Rhetoric in the Debate about the Trustworthy Cattle Trader

Even if the authorities put considerable trust in small- and medium-sized business, this trust was suffused with antisemitic suspicion on all sides. Critics of the cattle-trading group, which above all included representatives of the farmers' associations, further inflamed the debate with anti-Jewish polemics, as they had been doing long before the 1920s.[56] Antisemitic resentments had always poisoned economic relationships. Antisemites regarded Jewish merchants as untrustworthy (*unreell*) and blamed Jewish traders alone for the erosion of trust in the cattle trade. As a report from Attinger showed in a special issue of the *Süddeutsche Landwirtschaftliche Tierzucht* (*South German Agricultural Livestock Breeding*) from 1920, there had been vehement calls at farmers' assemblies for the elimination of the "Jewish cattle trade" as early as during the First World War.[57] These farmers attributed irregularities in the cattle trade to the high concentration of Jewish traders in this branch.[58] Among the antisemitic attacks of this kind was the query of a Landtag (Bavarian State Assembly) representative addressed to the Bavarian Ministry of Justice in 1926 about whether "ways and means might be found" to dismiss the currency revaluation claims (referring to adjustments in assets accompanying the stabilization of the reichsmark ending the postwar hyperinflation) made by "cattle traders of the Jewish race."[59]

But it was not only trade associations and members of the Bavarian Landtag who resorted to such slanderous methods; National Socialist cattle traders also did this. For example, there is a case recorded in the tiny rural village of Altenmuhr about a National Socialist trader in small livestock, Johann Müller, who exploited the highly charged atmosphere at the climax of the German hyperinflation in the autumn of 1923 in order to stir up the authorities against his Jewish colleagues. Müller reported his colleagues to the State Anti-Profiteering Authority (Landeswucherabwehrstelle). He claimed that they were hoarding beef cattle in their stables instead of making the animals available to the public as meat supply. To the chagrin of the Nazi cattle trader, the resulting police investigation of the resident cattle traders determined that the inspection books of the Jewish traders were "meticulously proper" and that the traders only had domestic cattle used as farm animals, but no beef cattle. The case took an ironic twist after Müller himself was found guilty of limiting the supply of sheep available to meat consumers.[60]

While representatives of the farmers' associations and National Socialist cattle traders unloaded their frustrations on the Jewish cattle traders, public authorities deliberately placed their trust in the middle-class cattle traders running medium-sized firms, most of which were operated by Jewish merchants. Even though the debate around the "trustworthy cattle trader" in the years following the First World War was heavily loaded with antisemitic rhetoric, the bureaucratic category of the "trustworthy cattle trader" constituted a collective idea about how the cattle-trading class might adjust to the demands of the times and modernize—a process other branches of the economy were going through simultaneously.

The Constitution of Official Trust by Way of State-Subsidized Livestock Husbandry Cooperatives

The state's promotion of livestock husbandry cooperatives was an additional attempt by the authorities to rehabilitate lost trust in the cattle trade. These cooperatives were intended, in lieu of private cattle traders, to secure meat supplies for the population by buying up beef cattle.[61] This put the livestock husbandry cooperatives, along with the new and "wild" cattle traders, in competition with the private cattle traders. Examining the policy of government support for livestock husbandry cooperatives highlights the importance and strength of medium-sized cattle-trading firms while demonstrating the limits to the official effort at institutionalizing trust.

The Origin of Livestock Husbandry Cooperatives

The cooperative movement, whose origins in Germany go back to the end of the nineteenth century, aimed to combat poverty among the rural population by creating a dense network of self-help organizations. Three actors were crucial to the emergence of the cooperative system in Germany. First and foremost was Wilhelm Haas (1839–1913), who founded the Reich Association of Agricultural Cooperatives—the Reichsverband der landwirtschaftlichen Genossenschaften—in 1883.

From the outset, this association had a decentralized organization and was compartmentalized into numerous state and provincial branches. The result was a cooperative landscape that was regionally quite heterogeneous.[62] Far better known among the cofounders of the German cooperative system is Friedrich Wilhelm Raiffeisen (1818–1888), who had philanthropic motives for his goal of promoting the construction of loan societies in order to assist a rural population seriously impoverished due to crop failures.[63] From his efforts emerged the Raiffeisen movement, which set up associations of loan societies where farmers could save but also borrow money on favorable terms, for example to purchase livestock.[64] Another cofounder of the German cooperative movement was Hermann Schulze-Delitzsch (1808–1883), who advocated cooperative organization for the craft trades.[65]

All of the cooperative movement's founders pursued a common goal: to diminish poverty among the rural population by encouraging local peasants to join together in self-help organizations. This was meant to protect farmers from economic and social changes that confronted them in the course of industrialization. Farmers were granted a loan simply by virtue of their membership in the cooperative, which meant they were not reliant on a cattle trader. The cooperative system thus competed with the private cattle trade, which had previously played a central role in the rural lending business.[66] The humanistic idea of self-help, by which farmers were meant to unite in a kind of capital-accumulating community where they might function as guarantors for each other, masked an intense antisemitic agitation against independent rural traders, but especially against cattle traders.

This agitation reached an initial climax during the agricultural crises around 1880, when the trade practice of agistment (using livestock as loans) and the taking of interest were denounced as the "usurious behavior of Jewish cattle traders."[67] Above all, Germany's leading professional association of social scientists and economists, the Verein für Socialpolitik (founded in 1873 as the Association for Social Policy but today known as the German Economic Association), placed sole blame for the rural population's lack of money on Jewish cattle traders. This was expressed in the association's publications on "Profiteering in the Countryside" (*Wucher auf dem Lande*).[68] From the outset, therefore, part of the politics of the livestock husbandry cooperatives was based on mistrust motivated by antisemitism. Abuses in the cattle and meat business during the period following the First World War provided antisemitic mistrust with a new breeding ground. The pretext for this was the high meat prices. As a representative of the cooperative system, Franz Bussen stated that a main goal of the livestock husbandry cooperatives was "to remove another ill that had been burdening little people for some time, namely profiteering in the cattle trade and the lack of a suitable institution for satisfying credit needs."[69] By eliminating the rural traders, the cooperatives aimed to narrow the price margin between meat consumers and meat producers. At the same time, they willingly accepted that this effort would endanger the livelihood of countless small and medium-sized (cattle-trading) firms.[70]

The Ambitious Goal of the Livestock Husbandry Cooperatives: Lowering Prices for Beef Cattle

Criticism of the private cattle traders focused on cattle exports out of Bavaria, which had a negative impact on beef cattle prices there. The cause of this was an agreement between Bavaria and the national government in which Bavaria committed to delivering fifteen hundred heads of beef cattle to other German states for meat supply.[71] As a result of this agreement, meat prices in Bavaria skyrocketed, which turned meat into a luxury item, especially for lower-income groups. In the public debate, cattle traders alone were deemed responsible for this deplorable state of affairs. They were publicly accused of exporting beef cattle out of Bavaria without driving it into local markets, since they could earn higher prices outside Bavaria. Local butchers complained that this robbed them of the opportunity to buy beef cattle to supply the local population.[72] In addition to the livestock husbandry cooperatives, private cattle traders who were organized in the Purchasing and Delivery Cooperative (the Einkaufs- und Lieferungsgenossenschaft, abbreviated ELG), which belonged to the State Association of Bavarian Cattle Traders, also participated in cattle exports. Nevertheless, only the private cattle traders—especially those who were Jewish—were subjected to public criticism. The private cattle traders were singled out even though they operated primarily with farm animals and were therefore not involved in the beef cattle trade. In fact, all of the actors in this dispute were involved in delivering beef cattle outside Bavaria. The private cattle traders were blamed for jeopardizing meat supplies for the Nuremberg population by driving up prices.[73] The ELG countered the accusations by claiming that the livestock husbandry cooperatives were mainly delivering to the Rhineland, which paid higher prices. Furthermore, the ELG declared that they were only supplying beef cattle to the states paying lower prices, such as Saxony. As a result of this division of territory, moreover, the private cattle traders claimed they had to accept major losses.[74] According to a newspaper report, the Bavarian livestock husbandry cooperative's share of the beef cattle exports out of Bavaria amounted to only 30 percent, while that of the ELG constituted 70 percent.[75] That meant that the Bavarian state government could not have stemmed the cattle exports; it was contractually obligated by its agreement with the central government in Berlin to let Bavarian cattle be sent to other German states. The Bavarian state government was strongly dependent on cooperation with the private cattle traders represented in the ELG, consisting of well-networked medium-sized firms, since they were the only ones able to adequately supply markets with livestock demanded by the national government. The locally active livestock husbandry cooperatives, on the other hand, were not capable of meeting that demand. Yet the anger of the population about bad conditions was directed against the private cattle traders, and this fury was mixed with mistrust about the high concentration of Jewish traders in this field of business. This mistrust was reflected in increased official inspections of their firms, as attested (for example) by a 1923 report from the gendarmerie station in Gunzenhausen to the State Anti-Profiteering Authority (the Landeswucherabwehrstelle) about cattle exports by Jewish cattle traders in their district.[76]

But it was not only consumers who complained about high beef cattle prices; meat producers also protested their inability to turn a profit, despite the high prices. De facto, prices in the beef cattle markets were usually well above farm prices. One reason for this had to do with unforeseeable price fluctuations, which created a large discrepancy between "market prices" (the prices set in public markets) and "stables prices" (the more informal prices negotiated between trader and farmer for animals sold right out of the barn) and worked to the disadvantage of the cattle producer. The farmer therefore received a much lower price for a head of cattle when it was sold on the farm or in a barn compared with a trade made on a public market.[77] Since the market price was composed of the stables price plus expenses incurred and the trader's share, a component difficult for the public to understand, the latter item was singled out for a great deal of agitation and criticism. In particular, the representatives of the farmers' associations insinuated that traders were using the trader's share to enrich themselves by exploiting these miserable conditions.[78] But members of the livestock husbandry cooperatives also pinned responsibility for the high beef cattle prices on the trade margin (markup), and as Hans Riedl, an advocate for the cooperative movement, argued: "The level of the market price and expenses can be approximately ascertained. But the trade share of the transaction is an uncontrollable quantity that depends on the business acumen of the trader and the market experience of the farmer."[79] The State Association of Bavarian Cattle Traders replied to these charges by asserting that the high fees and taxes with which the cattle trade was saddled were much more responsible for burdening meat prices.[80] The association also countered the accusations with a calculation of the fees incurred, as with the following example of an expense account from a Bavarian trader in large animals (cows, oxen, bulls, etc.). On December 29, 1932, this merchant acquired thirty-four heads of livestock as well as eleven calves so they could be slaughtered and transported to Berlin. This produced the following expenses (listed in reichsmark, abbreviated RM):

Purchase of 34 heads of large livestock	4,188.70 RM
Purchase of 11 heads of calves	364.70 RM
Total costs	**4,553.50 RM**[81]

In order to send the slaughtered cattle and calves to Berlin, he incurred the following expenses:

Slaughter tax	363.00 RM
Slaughter cards	413.90 RM

Beef cattle insurance	99.60 RM
Market cards	44.20 RM
Slaughter per head 2 marks	68.00 RM
Skinning calves	6.60 RM
Loading per head 1 mark	34.00 RM
Freight to Berlin	327.75 RM
Wagon rent	27.00 RM
Sales commission in Berlin	244.85 RM
Freight charge, labor costs in Berlin	178.50 RM
Platform fee in Berlin	10.00 RM
Telephone and telegrams	18.40 RM
Labor costs and tips in Regensburg	50.00 RM
Sales tax approximately	90.00
Expenses	**1,975.80 RM**
Expenses per drover through	340.00 RM
Regensburg, per head approx. 10 marks	
Total expenses	**2,315.80 RM**[82]

The State Association of Bavarian Cattle Traders published this bill during the association's convention in a public relations effort to highlight the relatively minimal fees that the cattle dealer himself was earning from a given trade. It wanted to make taxpayers aware that the public sector was earning a substantial amount from the fees it had raised on the cattle trade.[83]

The large difference between the stables price and market price was thus above all a result of the numerous taxes and fees that the dealer incurred in sales on the market and that increased the price of meat. In order to sell a head of cattle at a profit—in spite of the high fees and price fluctuations— a cattle seller, regardless of whether he was a farmer or a cattle trader, needed a strong knowledge of market conditions.[84] Since cattle traders were routinely keeping track of market conditions and were thus able to assess them properly, they did not, in contrast to the farmers, shy away from supplying the markets. Farmers, owing to their often-insufficient familiarity with the market and the concomitant fear of possible losses, held back.[85] Cattle traders relieved the farmers of this uncertainty and bore the sole risk for supplying cattle markets. Yet they had to factor in possible price fluctuations when calculating stables prices so that they could remain liquid in light of all the uncertainties.[86] This could lead to some very unpleasant developments, as Franz Ruhwandl, a representative of the Bavarian cooperative system, complained. He maintained that "in regions in which a trader or buyer operates more or less without competition and the farmers are dependent on him . . . downright unpleasant conditions take shape in the cattle trade, especially when prices fall on the cattle markets and there is a corresponding rise in the risk for trade, also when it comes to selling animals of worse quality that the trader takes off the hands of the farmer only as a 'favor' to him."[87] The stables trade was also a thorn in the eye of the public sector, since it took place away from any kind of official control, making tax evasion easy. In the case of conflicts in the stables trade, moreover, resorting to a neutral third authority was not possible. The livestock husbandry cooperatives thought they could counter this development by buying up cattle at a fixed price and selling them on the markets.[88] They hoped a fixed price would help the farmer calculate his expenses without having to add extra costs (market fees, taxes, etc.) on top of the actual price paid for the livestock.

Despite the ambitious price policies set forth by the livestock husbandry cooperatives aiming to lower meat prices while simultaneously increasing the proceeds flowing to producers, the private cattle trade prevailed. As Dr. Sebastian Matzinger of the Bavarian People's Party complained, what happened was the exact opposite; cattle producers received prices from the livestock husbandry cooperatives that were too low. He commented on this in a 1925 article for the *Bayerische Staatszeitung*: "Happily, the adherents of an exaggerated cooperative idea are still quite far from their goal. The superiority of the private cattle trader, something sensed by the great mass of the peasantry, is the best safeguard against the cooperatives getting out of hand with their questionable price policy."[89] The Union of Cattle Traders in Germany (Bund der Viehhändler Deutschlands) was also pleased with this state of affairs and rejoiced that the cooperatives' price policy had failed to lower meat prices.[90] The chairman of the State Association of Bavarian Cattle Traders, Lorenz Eberle, criticized the relationship between the independent trade and the livestock husbandry cooperatives. Eberle reproached the cooperatives for pushing disloyal propaganda and making false assertions in a deliberate effort to damage "trustworthy trade." Furthermore, he accused the national government of subsidizing the livestock husbandry cooperatives one-sidedly at the expense of the independent trade, which occurred in 1928, after Martin Schiele, Minister of Food and Agriculture in the national government, implemented an emergency program.[91]

The lack of backing by farmers for the livestock husbandry cooperatives is also demonstrated by a glance at the turnover statistics of the Bavarian Cattle Husbandry between 1897 and 1929:

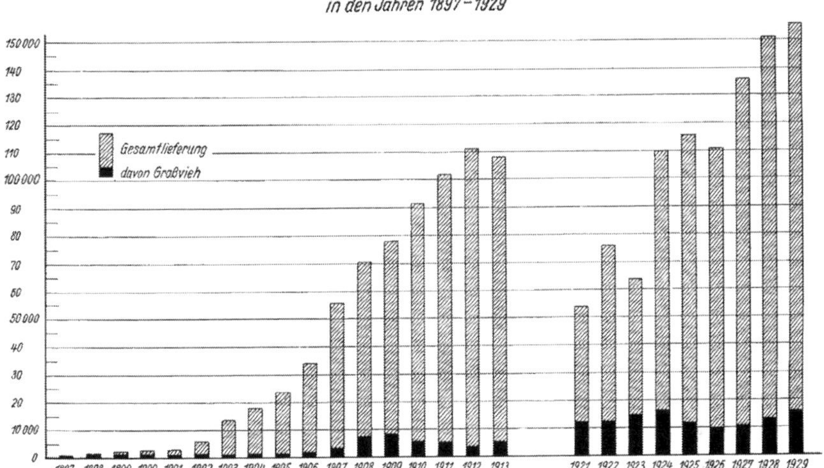

FIGURE 3.1. Turnover development of cooperative cattle husbandry, 1897–1923.
Source: Hans Riedl, *Die genossenschaftliche Viehverwertung in Bayern* (Munich:
Bayerische Viehverwertung, 1930), 55.

The diagram shows that, although the number of cattle sold in the years before
the First World War steadily increased overall through 1912, the share of large
livestock (that is, cattle) sold cooperatively remained quite low almost continuously. In the initial postwar years, moreover, the cooperative cattle husbandry
effort suffered an initial setback when it was accused of having misappropriated
beef cattle during the First World War.[92]

Only after Germany's hyperinflation ended in 1924, just as the market expanded, did cooperative cattle sales again reach prewar levels. Yet the number
of animals sold remained very small and even declined in percentage terms.
Although the share of large livestock sold in 1921 was around 25 percent, in 1929,
it had again sunk to under 10 percent.[93]

Likewise, the livestock husbandry cooperatives' share in the German
cooperative system overall was relatively low. In 1927, the Reich Association of German Agricultural Cooperatives (Reichsverband der deutschen
landwirtschaftlichen Genossenschaften e.V.) counted a total of 25,827
cooperatives—more than half of which (50.94%, or 13,040 in absolute figures)
were credit cooperatives. The share of livestock husbandry cooperatives, by
contrast, came to only 0.94 percent (or 242 in absolute numbers).[94] As these

figures imply, farmers had an unfavorable attitude toward governmental promotion aimed at expanding the livestock husbandry cooperatives. This attitude was also lamented by Attinger in an address held in 1920. In that talk, he declared that farmers mistrusted the livestock husbandry cooperatives and viewed them as part of the "war economy on the Berlin pattern," while they continued to proclaim their loyalty to the "old trustworthy trade." At the conclusion of his speech, Attinger addressed "all farmers who still have a glimmer of common sense the request that they confer trust on the new institution and avail themselves of its services."[95] In the press, Attinger was strongly attacked because of his advocacy for the livestock husbandry cooperatives. The farmers feared that expanding the cooperative system would create a state monopoly on the cattle trade, no longer offering them a diverse supply.[96] On the other side, representatives of the Bavarian livestock husbandry cooperative system criticized the farmers' unwillingness to sell their beef cattle and domestic livestock voluntarily to the cooperatives. In their opinion, this reluctance to cooperate could only be countered by an obligation to make compulsory deliveries, something already introduced in Hanover and jealously eyed by the cooperatives' representatives.[97] This view was shared by cooperatives advocate Riedl, who saw their lack of success as something caused by "the attitude of the Bavarian farmer toward cooperative collaboration, [since the farmer] is only too happy to seize the opportunity to improve his sales conditions but decisively rejects any kind of compulsion or commitment as burdensome."[98]

Bavarian farmers didn't draw any benefit from the proposed changes and therefore stubbornly opposed any deviations in the way they sold their wares. Voices were also raised in other German regions complaining about the cooperative's lack of popularity. This prompted the cattle husbandry association in Pomerania to issue a set of Ten Commandments meant to admonish the farmers. The first of these Ten Commandments said: "Deliver your cattle on a regular basis to your livestock husbandry cooperative, meaning not only the bad kind but above all the good cattle too."[99] Apparently, the farmers were inclined to give the cattle cooperatives only the lower-grade cattle that a "trustworthy cattle trader" passed on. And yet, to gain farmers' trust, the livestock husbandry cooperatives began cooperating with private cattle traders in an attempt to incorporate themselves into the ranks of practitioners of the "trustworthy trade."[100]

No Trust in the Trustees (Vertrauensmänner) *of the Livestock Husbandry Cooperatives*

To establish contact and a relationship of trust with farmers, the livestock husbandry cooperatives also employed so-called trustees (representatives called

Vertrauensmänner and sometimes also *Obmänner*, another term for spokesmen helping to avoid or settle conflicts) at every branch where cattle was purchased. These representatives—as their very name suggests (a Vertrauensmann is literally a "man of trust")—were supposed to be delegates the farmer could trust, in contrast to the independent (or, better, the "dishonest") cattle traders. The trustee was not only responsible for buying up cattle but was also meant, "within the circle of places assigned him, to . . . advertise . . . advise farmers, and . . . keep [them] up to date about the current market." The trustee, moreover, was responsible for branding "the cattle designated for delivery; in many cases he takes care of its transport to the railway and assumes the job of loading and booking. Finally, in cases where paying for the cattle is not immediately undertaken by the loan associations, he is to deliver the proceeds of the cattle [sale] to the farmers."[101] All in all, the trustee functioned as a cattle trader without personal liability, since he was a salaried employee of a state-subsidized livestock husbandry cooperative and thus neither acting as an independent businessman nor incurring any risk in supplying markets. In order for the trustee to perform his job, he needed to be acquainted above all with the trade customs of the cattle trade and have the necessary expertise about the field and its wares. On this point, U. Assel (a veterinary breeding inspector lecturing on the livestock husbandry cooperatives) commented that in "the cities and markets, well-managed branch offices [need] to be set up, presided over in all cases by a skillful managing director extremely well acquainted with the trade customs. The selection of the right expert as manager of the branch offices is decisive for their success. If he gains the trust of the participating interested parties through his substantive knowledge and professional expertise, the branch offices will also be able to prove their permanent worth for supplying the cities with beef cattle."[102] Since trust in "alien" and self-employed traders had been shaken, it would now have to be restored by recruiting people from the cooperatives' own ranks. One had to rely on one's own kind; alien traders, by contrast, were perceived as a danger. Nevertheless, farmers did not show these trustees the same degree of trust as they displayed toward the private cattle traders with whom they were already well acquainted.[103]

The process of building trust was impeded by the trustees' lack of experience in this line of business, since only a few of them had commercial experience spanning beyond a few years.[104] As the chairman, Eberle, and legal adviser, Graminger, of the State Association of Bavarian Cattle Traders jointly pointed out by way of criticism, the trustees of the livestock husbandry cooperatives were not obligated to hold a license, meaning that they were not required to have a business card or to meet the strict requirements of the authorities in order to qualify as "reliable."[105] As a result, livestock husbandry cooperatives functioned as a de facto reception center for dubious and "untrustworthy" traders. The trustees, for example, included many men to whom the district authorities had previously refused a trade license and whose reliability to practice an independent cattle dealership had been officially denied.[106] Indeed, the trustees of the livestock husbandry cooperatives were extremely unreliable and were often denied official recognition because they lacked the expertise necessary to practice their profession. As a result, they too failed to gain the trust of farmers.

The livestock husbandry cooperatives' lack of acceptance among farmers was based not only on their supposed lack of trustworthiness but also on the cooperatives' commercial practices. The anonymous livestock husbandry cooperatives functioned in a way that was more profit-oriented and capitalistic than the private cattle traders, who prioritized relationships with their customers and allowed flexible payment practices.[107] Unlike the private cattle traders, the livestock husbandry cooperatives granted loans solely based on an analysis of accounting books, so that trust and previous negotiations were rendered irrelevant. Cattle traders, by contrast, offered credit or even nonmonetary forms of payment, even when their farming customer base was short on cash.[108] For this reason alone, the cattle traders running medium-sized operations were more attractive trade partners for poorer (small) farmers than the livestock husbandry cooperatives.

An additional advantage provided by the independent (large) livestock traders was their high level of competence when it came to trading in domestic cattle for farm use. The livestock husbandry cooperatives did not successfully establish a foothold in this high-risk specialty,[109] which required a decidedly high level of knowledge about these goods, a skill set the inexperienced trustees of the cooperatives lacked compared with the highly trained cattle traders.[110]

In any event, the livestock husbandry cooperatives were competing in the first place with pork traders and not with the (large) livestock traders who focused on selling beef cattle. Traditionally, because of high pork consumption, the major component of the demand for meat animals consisted of hogs.[111] In the large cattle trade, moreover, larger sums of money changed hands, which entailed higher risks for the buyer due to price fluctuations. This gave the livestock husbandry cooperatives little incentive to operate in the cattle trade. The chief objective of the cooperatives was therefore to compete with the pork trade but not with the cattle trade.[112]

The state-subsidized livestock husbandry cooperatives failed to prevail against the private cattle trade and to gain the trust of farmers. The state's attempts to intervene powerfully in existing economic systems was ultimately unsuccessful because process-based trust triumphed over authorities' efforts to institutionalize trust. Indeed, farmers continued to prefer dealing with independent cattle dealers when buying and selling livestock.[113]

The Livestock Market Policy of Small Towns: Trust in Medium-Sized Businesses

Middle-class-owned small and medium-sized cattle-trading firms occupied a key intermediary position between the peasant villages and the urban cattle market centers and helped modernize small towns that were marginalized over the course of industrialization. On both sides, there was trust in these middle-class-owned small and medium-sized businesses. At the same time, starting at the end of the 1920s, the National Socialists used virulent antisemitic agitation to exert a powerful influence on this network of relationships that had been tried and tested for years. The Nazis aimed to drive a wedge into these established relations of trust. This placed the racist aims of the National Socialists in tension with the economic interests of the small towns and farmers.

The Declining Importance of Rural Livestock Markets

As industrialization and urbanization progressed, trade shifted away from decentralized livestock markets and toward the most important urban transportation hubs in Nuremberg, Munich, Frankfurt am Main, and Berlin. This development decreased the need for rural markets, which were thereupon gradually dismantled.[114]

The shift of trading space toward urban centers created a great deal of suspicion on the part of small towns. They were losing an important economic factor. Not only had the cattle market brought tax revenues to municipal coffers; it also increased much-needed sales for nearby innkeepers and shops.[115] As small-town cattle markets shut down, municipalities also lost a major public space. Cattle markets always exercised a social binding function; it was there that the rural population—Jewish and Christian merchants, peasant men and women, as well as onlookers and people interested in trade—met in order to exchange the latest news and current village gossip.[116]

Cattle markets also functioned as marriage markets; through the mediation of a cattle trader, a good match could be found. Cattle traders, owing to their familiarity with financial conditions among their peasant clientele, were highly qualified as marriage brokers and were reliable advisers when it came to seeking the right bride and a good dowry.[117] The abolition of the small-town livestock markets (which had happened because not enough cattle were driven there

FIGURE 3.2. Cattle market on town square (*Marktplatz*), ca. 1925.
Courtesy of Stadtarchiv Lauf/Pegnitz.

any longer) thus represented a loss for rural society. That loss was expressed in romantic-agrarian recollections of the bygone livestock market culture. In these nostalgic reminiscences, cattle traders alone were held responsible for this development.[118] For example, as early as 1914, the municipality of Ellingen blamed cattle-trading firm Bermann & Oppenheimer for its relatively idle livestock market. Officials charged the firm with selling their cattle directly out of the stable rather than at the local market.[119] The municipality also accused them of withholding cattle from local markets in order to sell it for a higher price on the national markets, thus toying with the antisemitic accusation that Jews were exploiting the economic situation for their own benefit.

Yet this process of erosion was not the result of anonymous modern forces. Nor, needless to say, did it result from Jewish businessmen withholding cattle from local markets. The causes were self-inflicted. A report from the old Imperial city of Rothenburg ob der Tauber provides some insight into the depressing condition of the small-town cattle markets. Early one morning in July 1927, according to this report, just one local farmer arrived at the town market with a pregnant cow in tow. Angered over the market's minimal activity, the district veterinarian and director of the slaughterhouse, Dr. Paul Eccard, telephoned the local cattle traders at half past eight in the morning and demanded that they promptly drive their cattle to the market, which they did. Much to Eccard's regret, however, the farmers present at the market held back from buying; they only seemed interested in coming to the market so they could inform themselves about prices.[120] As an author writing in the *Agrar-Korrespondenz*, the newspaper of the Bavarian Chamber of Agriculture (Bayerische Landesbauernkammer), stated, these small-town markets were no longer attractive for traders and farmers. He did not, however, see these towns' seclusion as the main reason for this loss of business; instead, he identified the shabby condition of the public markets as the cause.[121] While cattle markets in big cities were held in large, modern halls, the small-town cattle markets often lacked roofing to offer visitors and animals protection against sun and rain. Not infrequently, the rural cattle markets were held in an open field that turned into a swamp on rainy days.[122] This made loading at these markets a very unattractive prospect for farmers and traders alike. On rainy days, for example, they ran the risk of having the cattle slip and break a bone while being loaded. In such a case, the cow would have to be disposed of in an emergency slaughter, much to the annoyance of the seller. In the *Agrar-Korrespondenz*, Dr. Hauserhofer complained that cattle sales during bad weather lagged behind sales on sunny days by as much as 80 percent.[123]

While loading cattle at small-town markets was associated with numerous risks and had also become uneconomical, the stables trade offered both cattle traders and peasants alike numerous advantages. For one thing, it granted security against bad weather. For another, in their own stables, cattle traders could be sure that the cows they had groomed would be shown to their best advantage on the slightly raised platforms used to exhibit them. The stables trade spared the peasants an arduous journey to the cattle market and offered those traders who owned an automobile an opportunity to drive the farmers directly to the site of cattle buying and selling. Afterward, they could send the cow they had just acquired from the farming villages directly to the urban markets by rail.[124] By utilizing new technical innovations, the cattle traders weaved the local livestock trade into a national network and, as merchants, exercised a modernizing function for the entire province from which the rural population profited.

Although farmers and cattle traders preferred the stables trade, this practice encountered harsh criticism from small towns and farmers' associations, who argued that the shift left younger farmers unable to participate in the market equally because, without small-town cattle markets, they lacked the necessary experience. Moreover, they argued that peasants would get a less favorable price in a stables trade because it lacked competition. They believed that markets, on the other hand, would act to regulate prices, since there the farmer could freely choose among many different traders.[125] Finally (it was argued), the stables trade took place without official supervision—and without a neutral third office monitoring its trading activity—all of which made it possible to avoid taxes and spread livestock diseases. The lack of trust in the stables trade, its opponents concluded, had to be regained by shifting trade back to a public space.

Contending with Dwindling Importance: The Reintroduction of Decentralized Cattle Markets

The decline of the small-town markets also reflects the dwindling importance, both economic and political, of rural municipalities in the wake of industrialization, particularly as compared with the ever-growing urban centers. The social and economic revolutions that took place in the course of industrialization had a negative impact on the small town and countryside in spatial terms and on the entire middle-class business sector economically.[126] In order to counteract these impacts, at the end of the 1920s, small towns attempted to reintroduce the cattle markets that had frequently already been closed before the First World War due to lackluster demand.[127] In 1904, for example, the municipal council of Wassertrüdingen abolished the local cattle market for this very reason. Twenty-two years later, in 1926, the same municipal council applied to the district office of Dinkelsbühl to reintroduce the local cattle market in order to "improve commerce in this little town, which so urgently needs it, especially at the current time."[128]

These attempts at reviving the local cattle markets also reveal the widespread rural anxieties that had been triggered by the changes of industrialization and had become particularly acute in the crisis-ridden Central Franconian provinces. These fears found expression in anti-urban, antimodern polemics that quickly morphed into antisemitic diatribes picking on Jewish merchants.[129] Just as large department stores in major urban centers threatened small-town textile merchants, big-city cattle markets—new centers of trade built and developed with input from the middle-class cattle traders—became symbols of the threats facing small towns.[130] Jews, more than any other group, became the focus of hatred and frustration with the ailing "Weimar system," which proved incapable of protecting Germany's insecure middle class from the revolutions of modernity.[131] These resentments were seized on by an ever stronger ethnic and racial-nationalist (*völkisch*) movement, which enjoyed unparalleled popularity from the outset in the Central Franconian provinces. There, the

Protestant middle class embraced a radical form of *Nationalprotestantismus* that offered protection from liberalism and urbanization.

In everyday practice, nevertheless, these anxieties and resentments did not necessarily lead to economic trust being abruptly withdrawn, either publicly or privately, from Jewish cattle traders. Contrary to the increasing antisemitic agitation of the times, small towns in particular courted Jewish cattle traders in their effort to revive the markets that has been closed down before the First World War. The municipalities paid careful attention to making sure that the weekly schedule envisioned for the markets neither collided with a Jewish holiday nor competed with other important cattle markets.[132] Even Sunday's status as a holy day of rest could be canceled if this got in the way of efforts to have more cattle driven to the local livestock market. Thus, in 1926 and 1927, both the municipal council and the administration running slaughterhouses and stockyards in Ansbach supported the effort of Jewish businessman Ludwig Mohr and his colleagues from Altenmuhr to allow cattle to be loaded at the local train station on Sunday evening so that they could be driven to the market in Ansbach punctually the next morning.[133]

Even as stimulating the local economy in small towns became paramount—directed through an effort to promote commerce among middle-class traders—the region's steadily growing Nazi party (NSDAP, meaning National Socialist German Worker's Party) was countering this local boosterism with widespread calls to boycott Jewish businesses, both in the countryside and in the city. The NSDAP, for its part, used the social function of cattle markets to foment public disruptions by defaming Jewish traders and pitting their customers against them, blaming Jews alone for every social evil. In this way, starting around 1927, local Nazi party members routinely disrupted market operations in the region and insulted Jewish traders.[134] In June 1927, for example, Nazi party members handed out free copies of the antisemitic weekly newspaper *Der Stürmer* to farmers in Gunzenhausen.[135] These sorts of actions were a thorn in the side of the town's municipal council, since they coincided with the council's attempt to revive the cattle market with a major advertising campaign that encouraged outside traders, particularly Jews, to send their animals to the market in Gunzenhausen. The municipal council worried that the NSDAP would scare off middle-class Jewish traders and thus endanger their project.[136] In order to avoid this fate, the council promptly added a tersely worded clause to its market regulations that prohibited the "distribution of printed material at the cattle and hog market."[137]

Similar actions were taking place at the same time in the district capital Ansbach. There, too, National Socialists distributed the *Stürmer* free of cost to peasant customers of the town's cattle market. Unlike what the authorities did in Gunzenhausen, the Ansbach Municipal Council only reacted after Jewish cattle traders threatened to stop supplying cattle to the Ansbach market[138]—a disruption the council wanted to avoid at all costs. As in Gunzenhausen, the Ansbach Municipal Council had also courted nationally networked cattle traders, most of them Jews, in the past with promises of an exhibition space in the town's newly constructed, modern cattle market.[139] The Jewish middle-class traders running small and medium-sized businesses ensured an increase in market activity.[140] Unlike in Gunzenhausen, the National Socialists in Ansbach had managed to enter the municipal parliament, where they aggressively pushed their racist goals. As early as 1929, a member of the NSDAP delegation in the municipal council of Ansbach demanded that Jews be denied access to the cattle market.[141] The municipal council rejected the motion; the National Socialists did not yet have a majority in the council, and economic interests still had priority over racist goals. There was awareness in the cities of Ansbach and Gunzenhausen that only the middle-class merchants were capable of increasing the number of cattle brought to market.[142] The cattle traders' threat of a boycott had an impact, and the municipal administration banned the distribution of the *Stürmer* as a result. The municipal administrations needed the well-networked middle-class cattle traders in order to reconnect their marginalized municipalities to urban centers and therefore prioritized their economic self-interest so that cattle markets remained an important source of small-town commerce.

But there were already exceptions to this economic pragmatism even as early as the late 1920s. In Feuchtwangen, for example, the hate campaign did not stop with the submission of antisemitic proposals to the municipal council. Rather, as early as 1927, the council had already stopped making allowances for Jewish holidays when it scheduled days designated for the cattle market. Only a short time before, Jewish cattle trader Gabriel Gutmann cut his ties to the municipally owned savings bank with the explanation "that almost nobody but antisemites sat on the municipal council."[143] Here, institutional trust between the municipality and the Jewish merchants had already been ruptured, even as it remained intact in other municipalities.

Disrupting Relations of Trust with Racist Attacks

Although small towns and large sections of the peasantry generally placed great trust in middle-class cattle traders deemed "trustworthy," a campaign of antisemitic hate propaganda starting at the end of the 1920s aimed to violate relations of trust with the Jewish traders. Overall, this campaign sought to create an imagined German economy bereft of Jewish businesses. The farmers' poor economic circumstances, which had been particularly difficult since the winter of 1928–1929, gave the National Socialists an especially favorable opening for their campaign. To be sure, the Jewish population had already suffered under the atmosphere of antisemitic agitation that characterized the period between the postwar republic of revolutionary soldiers and workers' councils (1918–1919) and the Hitler putsch of 1923, when several Jewish cemeteries (as in Nuremberg in 1922) and congregational halls (as in Gunzenhausen and Scheinfeld in 1923) were desecrated.[144] There were also physical attacks on Jews during this time, such as the assault on sixty-seven-year-old cattle trader Jakob Weissmann from Sugenheim. According to a report from the Central Association of German Citizens of Jewish Faith (the Central-Verein deutscher Staatsbürger jüdischen Glaubens, or CV), Nazi farmer Johann Holzberger from Neuendorf had called out to his sons as Weissmann passed by his farm: "Take the pitchfork outside and stab the Jew pig!" The hostilities, however, did not stop at verbal attacks. As Weissmann later passed by the property on his way home, Holzberger's son (according to an account of the story) threw a wooden club as thick as an arm at the old man.[145] Yet assaults like this tended to remain the exception. In general, violence against Jews abated again after the Hitler putsch in 1923,[146] even if the CV found that hostilities persisted under National Socialist influence in the regions around Scheinfeld and in the Aischgrund area.[147]

The Starting Point for the NSDAP in Central Franconia

As the distribution of the *Stürmer* at the cattle markets underscores, the NSDAP in Central Franconia had begun an effort as early as 1926—considerably earlier than in other regions—to win over the peasant population to their racist goals.[148] Wilhelm Stegmann, founder of the local Nazi party group in Schillingsfürst, was particularly prominent, and his efforts—both in type and scope—earned him early notoriety. During an early 1926 protest against the provincial health insurance fund, which was despised by local farmers, he succeeded in mobilizing four hundred peasants, which drew attention to Stegmann well beyond the borders of Schillingsfürst.[149] Shortly after Stegmann's action against the provincial health insurance fund, Julius Streicher, editor of the *Stürmer*, made his debut appearance as a speaker on the Hesselberg, Central Franconia's highest hilltop peak, which served (through 1939) as the site of racist pseudoreligious rallies known an *Frankentage*. These gatherings, like the Reich Party Congresses held by the Nazis at Nuremberg (begun in 1927), were high points of National Socialist propaganda that attracted numerous attendees from beyond the region.[150]

In spite of all these efforts, the peasant milieu remained by and large closed off to the NSDAP, as an analysis of the Central Franconian Nazi party's membership structure makes clear. Through 1930, the farm population remained significantly underrepresented among the NSDAP membership, at 6.5 percent compared to a share of 8.7 percent among the overall population. Representation was even weaker, at 1.8 percent, for family members who helped out with farm work, although they made up 20.2 percent of the total population. Significantly overrepresented were entrepreneurs, artisans, merchants, owners of small businesses, and freelance professionals, who together made up 21.1 percent of NSDAP members and thus constituted almost double their share of the overall population, which was 10.3 percent.[151] The bulk of NSDAP membership at this time consisted of the owners of small and medium-sized commercial firms as well as of civil servants, white-collar employees, and freelance professionals. The NSDAP was thus the party of the small town and petit bourgeois middle class but not of farmers.[152]

The farming population's voting preference continued to be for the Bavarian Rural League (Bayerischer Landbund). In order to counteract that loyalty, the NSDAP fought the Rural League with various methods. For one, it infiltrated the Rural League from within by smuggling in National Socialist farmers. It also agitated openly against the Landbund by means of defamatory press campaigns.[153] As early as 1928, the Rural League, which the NSDAP had "accused of insufficient antisemitism," entered into a parliamentary alliance with the Nazi party in the Central Franconian district assembly (Kreistag), a move that signaled the end of the Rural League's predominance in the farming milieu.[154]

Because of the Great Depression, the situation for the NSDAP in the countryside changed suddenly, and starting in 1930, the Nazi party was able to exploit the insecurity of the farming population, which had been profoundly affected by the crisis. One factor triggering the change was market stagnation in grain, which occurred because of the depression and created cash-flow problems for the owners of many small and medium-sized farms. On top of that, a shortage of animal feed aggravated the situation, which gave rise to an oversupply of beef cattle, in turn causing cattle prices to nosedive. As a result, small farmers whose main source of income included the annual sale of one or two heads of cattle had to accept a painful drop in sales of beef cattle.[155] Another blow to the economic situation of the farmers was dealt by an outbreak of hoof-and-mouth disease in 1929. Although these external circumstances had a disastrous impact on peasants, the outbreak alone was not ultimately responsible for the National Socialists' gains in popularity. Peasants, after all, had been accustomed for centuries to animal diseases, while the novel and little-understood "market conditions" represented a previously unknown and unfathomable threat.[156] To farmers, it was inconceivable that an international sales crisis could render them unable to feed their families, even with a good harvest. As they discovered, hard work and good soil were suddenly no longer a guarantee of economic prosperity—and these upheavals called into question time-tested mechanisms. As these economic difficulties continued, there was a concomitant increase in "their inclination to lay blame for the 'unexpected deterioration' of economic conditions on (Jewish) traders or on other dark powers like the 'Sozis' [socialists] and the (old Bavarian) ultramontane movement."[157]

The Protestant middle class, a social stratum especially pronounced in Central Franconia and one that included parts of the farming community, saw itself as particularly endangered by these changing conditions.[158] Their anxieties found expression in an ethnic-nationalist ("völkisch") and later racist antisemitism combining antimodern and anti-Jewish ideas and promoting the restoration of the "old order" and thus the ouster from the economy of everything described as "Jewish," "capitalist," and "modern." Like no other contemporary political current, National Socialism seized on this mood and incited the resentments entrenched in this Protestant milieu.

In order to win over the unsettled peasantry as voters, Hitler even went so far as to appear in person in July 1930 at the Frankentage gathering on the Hesselberg and give a speech addressed directly to farmers. A report from the *Illustrierter Beobachter* (the Nazi party's illustrated monthly magazine) offers an impression of what kind of success the party expected from his appearance:

> What we should actually be describing on the Hesselberg was a pilgrimage.
> Whoever has experienced a National Socialist gathering on the Hesselberg...
> has had these pictures leave an indelible impression on him, and every
> participant had the sensation that, for us National Socialists, nature is the
> most noble gathering place. ... Everyone who has eyes to see or ears to hear
> knew what was spoken there; it will bear fruit a thousand-fold, for when
> the tenacious Frankish peasants climb back [down] into the valley, they will
> assist in carrying the idea of our movement from place to place, from house
> to house.[159]

The party newspaper used the meeting for its own propaganda, and in the wake of Hitler's successful appearance on the Hesselberg, peasants established numerous local associations affiliated with the party.

Even in villages where hardly a single vote had gone to the NSDAP, many peasants began to take part in Nazi party gatherings.[160] Election results from 1930 underscored the growing popularity encountered by the National

Socialists in this region. In the September election to the Reichstag, the NSDAP had already reached a new peak in the town of Gunzenhausen with 35.6 percent of the vote.[161] In addition, about one-fourth (23.8%) of all Central Franconian voters—a much higher share than the national average (18.3%)—had opted for the NSDAP.[162] In that year, the NSDAP achieved a breakthrough not only in the Reichstag elections but also in the elections to the Chamber of Agriculture (Bauernkammer), where in early 1930, it was finally able to assert itself against the Green Front (the Grüne Front, a loose alliance of agrarian associations put together in 1929) and the Bavarian Rural League.[163] In the Reichstag election in April 1932, the party's popularity continued to soar, with its highest support in Central Franconia's core Protestant regions, such as Nuremberg, Rothenburg ob der Tauber, and the vicinity of Ansbach. The region that stood out most prominently was the electoral district Rothenburg-Land (the area surrounding Rothenburg where, in 1932, 87.5% of those at the polls voted for the National Socialists).[164]

The NSDAP also owed this major electoral success to its favorable starting conditions in Central Franconia, where the party had survived the stabilization phase of the Weimar Republic (1924–1929) better than in other parts of the country. As a result, the party had an easier time extending and fortifying its activities when the moment of economic crisis arrived, particularly as compared with other regions.[165] The insufficient resistance put up by the right-wing conservative DNVP (German National People's Party) also favored the NSDAP's penetration not only into Protestant nationalist communities but also into the farming milieu of Central Franconia.[166] As the Nazis' electoral outcomes improved, party organization advanced painstakingly, resulting soon in a dense network of party structures and branches that ultimately functioned like a state within the state.[167] This gave the NSDAP success in Central Franconia's rural sector earlier than in other regions of Germany.[168] Yet this success was also regionally limited within Central Franconia. In the Catholic areas further to the south (as in Eichstätt), the NSDAP was still denied the electorate's favor. In general, the party had an easier time achieving breakthroughs in small towns rather than in peasant villages,[169] even if Nazi slogans were meeting with the approval of younger farmers.[170]

The Start of Racist Agitation against Jewish Cattle Traders

With the Nazi party's electoral victories came a rise in antisemitic attacks on Jewish institutions and people, especially in the countryside. From that point on, the experience of violence became the order of the day for Jews living in

Franconia.[171] In the NSDAP strongholds of Ansbach, Gunzenhausen, and Nuremberg, there were repeated attacks and insults hurled at individual Jews, either openly on the street or in taverns.[172] This went hand in hand with a flurry of propaganda against Jewish cattle traders, who were accused of committing atrocities and blamed as the sole cause of the farmers' misery. The large number of Jewish merchants in the cattle trade served the National Socialists well as a foil for Nazi propaganda, and the cattle dealers became the target of insinuations that they were exploiting their position to manipulate prices and thereby enrich themselves on the backs of the peasants. In this way, the National Socialists skillfully tied their agitation in the countryside to traditional anti-Jewish and ethnic-national stereotypes, propagating a causal connection between the Great Depression and the economic position of Jewish traders.[173] The National Socialists invoked the horrifying image of the "money-grubbing Jewish cattle trader," which closely resembled the image of "international financial Jewry" in the nonfarming milieu.

The first antisemitic assaults for which we have reporting in the sources were not physical, but rather verbal, attacks from National Socialists against Jewish cattle traders in public spaces, at cattle markets, and in the press. They served to disseminate antisemitic mistrust and thereby break up the relationship between farmers and Jewish cattle traders.

The Spread of Racial Antisemitism

To spread their racist ideas in the countryside, the National Socialists made use of the still-widespread and notorious accusation that Jewish men sexually assaulted non-Jewish women.[174] While this kind of slander drew on a long tradition reaching back to the 1870s, it became clear that there was a new quality to it. The National Socialists built on this tradition and violently promoted the "purity of the Aryan race."[175] The weekly newspaper *Der Stürmer*, edited by the self-styled "Antisemite No. 1," Gauleiter (Nazi district leader) Streicher, served as the Nazi party's central medium for agitating against the Jewish population, destroying relations between Jews and non-Jews, denouncing Jews in public, and spreading racist ideas.[176] A major component of the *Stürmer*'s sensational coverage was its sexualizing of Jews and in particular its use of "racial defilement" as a theme.[177] These sexualized animosities toward Jewish cattle traders were typified by a *Stürmer* article with the title "Die Kipperjuden" (the "Tricky Jews"—a *Kipper* is someone who puts debased coins in circulation), which Karl Holz, a "pupil" of Streicher and deputy Gauleiter of Nuremberg, placed on the front page of the February 1930 edition.[178] In this inflammatory article,

Holz accuses all Jewish traders from Leutershausen, among them Henry Kissinger's grandfather Falk Stern,[179] of cheating peasants and raping Christian women. In extremely vulgar language, he describes how cattle trader Sigmund Enslein from Leutershausen allegedly and repeatedly raped war widow Barbara Sander in 1925. Holz goes on to assert that Enslein impregnated Sander and then refused to contribute child support. A similar case was said to have taken place in Uffenheim, where Adolf Schneider, another Jewish cattle dealer, supposedly raped a female employee, who, according to the *Stürmer*, also gave birth to a child thereafter. The article was illustrated—as was characteristic of the *Stürmer* in this phase of its publication[180]—with a huge black-and-white cartoon showing a fat spider with supposedly typical Jewish facial features. In its tightly meshed net, the animal is holding several emaciated peasants, some of whom it has just greedily sucked dry.

Unlike the conflicts about male honor discussed earlier, stories like these aimed to exploit an event for the party's racist propaganda. Holz's article in the *Stürmer* was an attempt to stir up racial antisemitism among the peasants by accusing Jewish men of violating Aryan women.

Yet Holz's antisemitic agitation did not go unpunished; the rule of law still had traction. Fourteen Jews from Leutershausen, eight of whom were cattle traders, took Holz to court on charges of libel and malicious gossip. The district court in Ansbach sentenced Holz to a fine of either six hundred reichsmarks or fourteen days in jail, but even that punishment was unable to restore the Jewish trader's sullied reputation.[181] Indeed, the reputation of a business—alongside the honor of its proprietor—was critical for success in the countryside. But in the wake of these public defamations, reputations were often ruined. There was also a feeling of marginalization and helplessness in the face of arbitrary accusations against a merchant's personal dignity and honor. This sense of vulnerability could still cling to successful Jewish plaintiffs because of damages no court could possibly defray: the accusations themselves, however unfounded, placed the plaintiffs under suspicion of actually having done something disreputable or even prohibited. By using over-the-top depictions of alleged sex crimes by Jewish men, "*Der Stürmer* was suggesting the universality of Jewish sexual menace as not limited to specific subsectors of 'German-Jewish' coexistence—such as the economic sector—but that supposedly threatened German society from the inside."[182] In this way, the cattle traders were no longer functioning only as traders and as lenders either loved or hated by the peasantry; from that point on, they represented a menace to the entire family that the *Volksgemeinschaft* (ethnic-racial national community) pushed by Nazi propaganda had an obligation to protect.

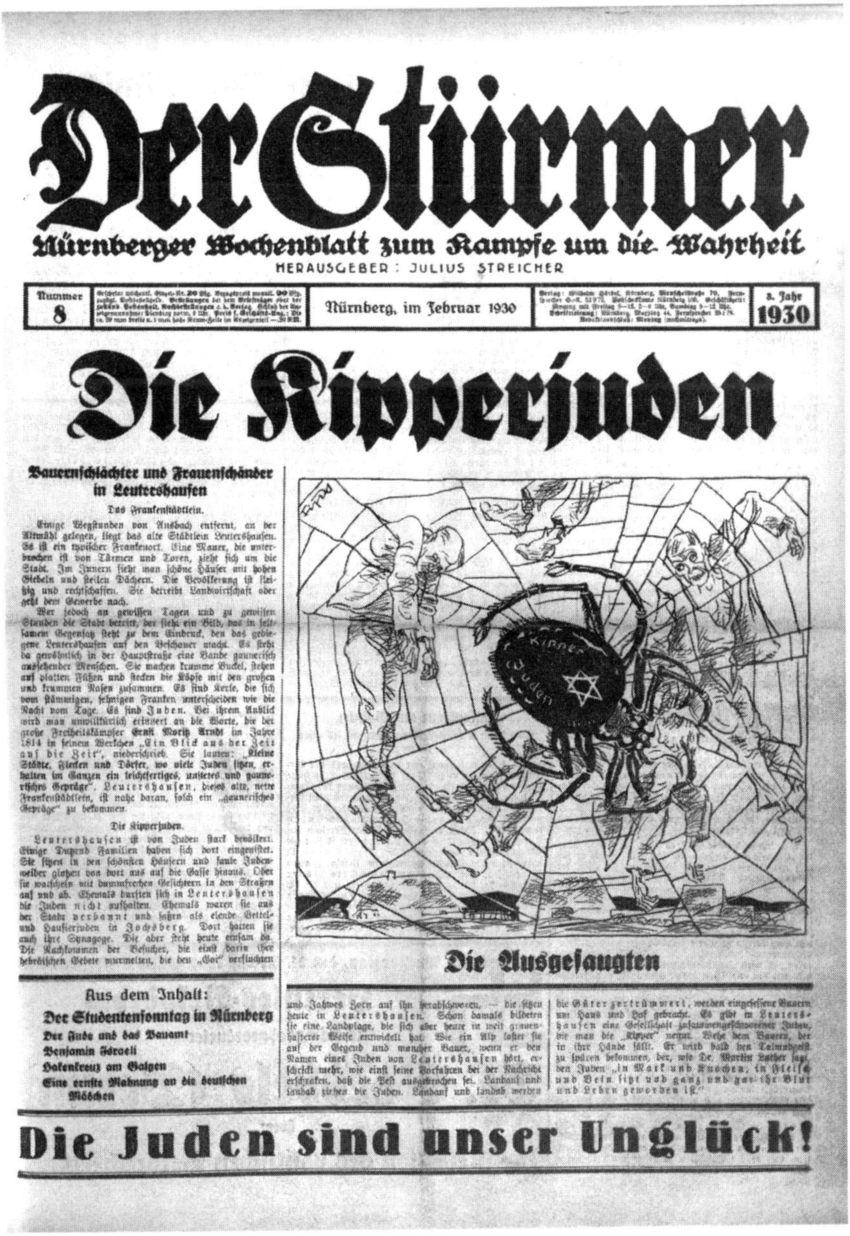

Der Stürmer

Nürnberger Wochenblatt zum Kampfe um die Wahrheit

HERAUSGEBER: JULIUS STREICHER

Nummer 8 | Nürnberg, im Februar 1930 | 8. Jahr 1930

Die Kipperjuden

Bauernschlächter und Frauenschänder in Leutershausen

Das Frankenstädtlein.

Einige Wegstunden von Ansbach entfernt, an der Altmühl gelegen, liegt das alte Städtlein Leutershausen. Es ist ein typischer Frankenort. Eine Mauer, die unterbrochen ist von Türmen und Toren, zieht sich um die Stadt. Im Innern sieht man schöne Häuser mit hohen Giebeln und steilen Dächern. Die Bevölkerung ist fleißig und rechtschaffen. Sie betreibt Landwirtschaft oder geht dem Gewerbe nach.

Wer jedoch an gewissen Tagen und zu gewissen Stunden die Stadt betritt, der sieht ein Bild, das in seltsamem Gegensatz steht zu dem Eindruck, den das gediegene Leutershausen auf den Beschauer macht. Es steht da gewöhnlich in der Hauptstraße eine Bande gaunerisch aussehender Menschen. Sie machen krumme Buckel, stehen auf platten Füßen und stecken die Köpfe mit den großen und krummen Nasen zusammen. Es sind Kerle, die sich vom stämmigen, sehnigen Franken unterscheiden wie die Nacht vom Tage. Es sind Juden. Bei ihrem Anblick wird man unwillkürlich erinnert an die Worte, die der große Freiheitskämpfer **Ernst Moritz Arndt** im Jahre 1814 in seinem Werkchen „Ein Blick aus der Zeit auf die Zeit", niederschrieb. Sie lauten: „**Kleine Städte, Flecken und Dörfer, wo viele Juden sitzen, erhalten im Ganzen ein leichtfertiges, unsteten und gaunerisches Gepräge**". Leutershausen, dieses alte, nette Frankenstädtlein, ist nahe daran, solch ein „gaunerisches Gepräge" zu bekommen.

Die Kipperjuden.

Leutershausen ist von Juden stark bevölkert. Einige Dutzend Familien haben sich dort eingenistet. Sie sitzen in den schönsten Häusern und faule Judenweiber glotzen von dort aus auf die Gasse hinaus. Oder sie watscheln mit dummfrechen Gesichtern in den Straßen auf und ab. Ehemals durften sich in Leutershausen die Juden nicht aufhalten. Ehemals waren sie aus der Stadt verbannt und saßen als elende Bettel- und Hausierjuden in Jochsberg. Dort hatten sie auch ihre Synagoge. Die aber steht heute einsam da. Die Nachkommen der Besucher, die einst darin ihre hebräischen Gebete murmelten, die den „Goi" verfluchten

Die Ausgesaugten

und Jahwes Zorn auf ihn herabschworen, — die sitzen heute in Leutershausen. Schon damals bildeten sie eine Landplage, die sich aber heute in weit grauenhafterer Weise entwickelt hat. Wie ein Alp lastet sie auf der Gegend und mancher Bauer, wenn er den Namen eines Juden von Leutershausen hört, erschrickt mehr, wie einst seine Vorfahren bei der Nachricht erschraken, daß die Pest ausgebrochen sei. Landauf und landab ziehen die Juden. Landauf und landab werden die Güter zertrümmert, werden eingesessene Bauern um Haus und Hof gebracht. Es gibt in Leutershausen eine Gesellschaft zusammengeschworener Juden, die man die „Kipper" nennt. Wehe dem Bauern, der in ihre Hände fällt. Er wird bald den Talmudgeist zu spüren bekommen, der, wie Dr. Martin Luther sagt, den Juden „in Mark und Knochen, in Fleisch und Bein sitzt und ganz und gar ihr Blut und Leben geworden ist."

Aus dem Inhalt:

Der Studentensonntag in Nürnberg

Der Jude und das Bauamt

Benjamin Israeli

Hakenkreuz am Galgen

Eine ernste Mahnung an die deutschen Mädchen

Die Juden sind unser Unglück!

FIGURE 3.3. *Der Stürmer* 8, no. 8 (1930).
From the holdings of the Staatsbibliothek zu Berlin, Stiftung Preußischer Kulturbesitz.

Boycott Threats and the First Livelihoods Destroyed
by the Bavarian Ban on Kosher Slaughter

At almost the same time that these public defamations were being made, boycott threats commenced against all Jewish traders.[183] In some NSDAP strongholds, especially Nuremberg, the Jewish population was particularly affected by the inflamed antisemitic mood. The Jewish community had already reacted to this hate campaign in 1925 by establishing the Association for Defense against Antisemitism, which had taken on the task of quashing the numerous antisemitic assaults.[184] One expression of the Nazis' far-reaching boycott policy was the *Verzeichnis deutscher Geschäfte* (*Register of German Businesses*); published since 1926 in Nuremberg, it was a list that excluded Jewish-owned businesses and thus indirectly called upon the non-Jewish population to avoid them.[185]

In other cities, such as Neustadt/Aisch in 1930 and 1931, the municipal council excluded Jewish tradespeople from being awarded public contracts.[186] Racist motives began to determine public policy in towns like Neustadt/Aisch—a development that stood in sharp contrast to previous efforts made by other municipalities to court Jewish cattle dealers as a way of enhancing the value of local markets. Jewish traders suffered financial losses as a result of the boycott calls. Even before Hitler took power in 1933, for example, the Levite family from Dinkelsbühl registered a dramatic decline in sales.[187] In many respects, then, Central Franconia served as a testing ground for National Socialists policies— a dress rehearsal of sorts for when they assumed power in 1933.

Though boycott calls were directed against all Jewish businesses, Jewish cattle dealers continued doing business, though on a restricted basis. For kosher butchers and Schmusers, however, the situation grew more challenging, and in 1930, a broad coalition across party lines in the Bavarian Landtag passed a ban on kosher slaughter that marked the transition from agitation to the destruction of economic livelihoods.[188] According to Jewish law, slaughter for meat has to be performed by a shochet, who ensures the painless and swift dispatch of the animal. Until the 1930s, a shochet often combined small-scale cattle trading with supplying kosher meat to his community.

The enactment of the Bavarian ban on kosher slaughter had antecedents in a long debate that had again flared up in the nineteenth century parallel to the process of Jewish emancipation. This on-and-off debate was conducted at regular intervals in public disputes—sometimes national, sometimes regional—by an assortment of political and social groups beginning in the 1930s. Opponents of kosher slaughter defamed the practice as an especially gruesome form of cruelty to animals.[189] Non-Jews also criticized the practice of dividing butchered meat into kosher and *treyf* (טרפה) cuts, with the treyf meat not re-garded as appropriate for consumption according to Jewish dietary laws.[190]

Some critics even maintained that Jews did this internationally in order to withhold the higher-quality kosher meat from the non-Jewish population and unload slaughterhouse waste onto the Gentiles. The antisemite Theodor Fritsch went so far as to polemicize that Jewish butchers preferred disposing of good meat rather than selling it to "the goys." Fritsch ranted vociferously: "In this way, during the daily kosher slaughter, a large amount of healthy meat is accumulated that is not savored by the Jews."[191] This kind of rhetoric aimed to provoke those segments of the population that could barely afford meat as a result of the Great Depression.

The debate was also inflamed by the charge that Jews were manipulating the meat market because they were so deeply entrenched in the cattle trade.[192] Antisemitic rhetoric borrowed the arguments set forth by animal protection advocates in order to equate the "gruesome trade practices" of the cattle traders with a slaughter practice they deemed grisly.[193] According to this allegation, farmers—like the cattle subjected to kosher slaughter—were being bled to death by Jewish cattle traders in a bestial manner.[194] These analogies were also employed by *Der Stürmer*, which compared the November Revolution that overthrew the Kaiserreich and paved the way for the Weimar Republic to the "kosher butchering of the German people." The Nazi paper even insinuated that, in Jewish eyes, the non-Jew was "a goy who is to be treated the same as cattle according to the Talmud."[195] On top of that, antisemites asserted that one could recognize good-hearted people by the way they treated animals—ergo, Jews were not good-hearted because they let cattle perish slowly while slaughtering them.[196]

While anti-Jewish and antisemitic undertones were present in earlier debates about kosher slaughter, they were by no means dominant, and in some cases they were even absent.[197] Only in the 1920s did debates on kosher slaughter serve as a laboratory to test whether antisemitic rhetoric might have an impact on political debate and ultimately on political practice as well.[198] After 1925, the NSDAP, like no other party, used the emotionally charged debate over kosher slaughter in order to capture votes with a call—which crossed lines of party and class—to ban the practice.[199] Yet the Nazi party hardly stood alone with this demand. The Economic Party of the German Middle Class, the Peasants Party, the German National People's Party, animal protection advocates, veterinary doctors, and slaughterhouse directors also fought, sometimes more vehemently and sometimes more moderately, to introduce the ban on kosher slaughter in Bavaria, which was finally incorporated into Bavarian law in 1930.[200] Bavaria thus assumed a tragic pioneering role. The kosher slaughter question also triggered fierce debates in other German regions. But only in Bavaria were the opponents of kosher slaughter able to prevail, after years of argument, as they did in 1930. The National Socialist government finally imposed a nationwide ban on kosher slaughter at the end of April 1933.[201]

For the Jewish community, the ban on ritual slaughter amounted to a restriction on its religious practice and eating habits.[202] If Jews did not want to dispense with kosher meat completely, they had to acquire it at a high cost from outside Bavaria. The rural Jewish community suffered especially from the ban on kosher slaughter, since proportionally there were more observant Jews in the countryside than in the cities who adhered to religious dietary laws.[203] Moreover, it was harder for them than for urban Jews to obtain imported kosher meat.[204] Hilde Jochsberger from Leutershausen, the daughter of a Jewish cattle dealer, recalls that her parents were forced by the Bavarian ban on kosher slaughter to abandon keeping a kosher kitchen.[205]

For small kosher slaughter and Schmuser operations, which in rural Jewish communities frequently combined cattle trading with kosher slaughter, the ban also entailed far-reaching financial losses. These kosher butcher shops sold barely more than one or two heads of cattle per week, little more than they needed to supply their rural communities with meat.[206] David Levite from Mönchsroth, for example, took in an average annual income of seven thousand reichsmarks from his cattle trade and butcher's shop. As a consequence of the Bavarian ban on kosher slaughter, his income sank to less than one-third, namely to two thousand reichsmarks.[207] This was an amount that barely sufficed to eke out a living.

On February 12, 1930, in reaction to the Bavarian ban on kosher slaughter, the Bavarian Rabbinical Conference called on its coreligionists to continue buying meat from Jewish butchers, who were offering kosher meat from elsewhere in Germany, in order to keep them in business.[208] While this solidarity among the Jews saved a few urban butcher shops in Fürth or Nuremberg from bankruptcy, it was of no help to the smaller, rural Schmuser businesses.

Municipal officials did not protest against the destruction of livelihoods for Jewish kosher butchers and Schmusers in the way they had previously intervened when antisemitic agitation undermined middle-class Jewish cattle traders at the markets. Small Schmusers' shops, like that of Max Fleischmann in Altenmuhr, thus became the first victims of the anti-Jewish laws. Only rarely did these shops grant loans, quite in contrast to the claims made by the burgeoning rhetoric of the times, which meant that their economic activity—unlike that of the middle-class traders running small and medium-sized businesses—was insignificant for the regional economy. The year 1930 marked a turning point not only for the Jewish population but, in many respects, also for the history of the Weimar Republic. Late historian Detlev Peukert (whose analysis of the Weimar era as a "crisis of classical modernity" has become a classic in its own right) called the last three years of the Weimar Republic its crisis years. A crisis can provide an opportunity for a fresh start. But for the Jewish population—and not only for them—this crisis marked the beginning of the end.

Relations of Trust Fall Apart

While the Bavarian state government had already withdrawn institutional trust from Jewish butchers in 1930, Jewish cattle traders continued to enjoy this trust. In view of how the National Socialists were also gaining popularity among the farming population after 1930,[209] questions emerge about how their rise affected relations of trust between farmers and cattle traders and how long these relations of trust, tried and tested over many years, were able to withstand the Nazis' efforts at driving a wedge into them.

In general, archival sources testify to numerous antisemitic assaults against individual Jews in the period between 1930 and the end of 1932. We have an account, for example, of one case from the administrative district of Gunzenhausen in which SA (Sturmabteilung) stormtroopers repeatedly harassed a Jewish merchant, whom they threatened by shouting "Beat him to death, the Jew!" before finally beating and bloodying him with a grater.[210] That same year, in Rothenburg ob der Tauber, SA leader Stegmann threw an elderly Jewish cattle trader into a cesspool and dealt him a blow to the head with a leather whip.'[211] Responding to a complaint from the Jewish community, SA Standartenführer (standard bearer with the rank of colonel in the Nazi paramilitary) Michl Fleischmann published an open letter in the local Ansbach newspaper in which he addressed the Bavarian state government and claimed that "nothing has yet happened to any Jew up to now (!)" and, furthermore, they were "still (!) all well-nourished" and "enjoying life."[212] Another scene of continuous antisemitic violence was Leutershausen, where the Jewish community suffered from an antisemitic onslaught. These included, at the end of 1931, nightly processions by the local SA in which SA men howled out "Die, miserable Jew!" ("Juda *verrecke*") or "Wake up Germany!" and smashed windows.[213] The Bavarian affiliate of the CV issued a statement saying that the "Jewish population of Leutershausen . . . has long been in a state of intimidation . . . because of the extreme agitation of the NSDAP . . . and acts of violence against Jewish inhabitants have also occurred repeatedly, without reports to the police authorities leading to any effective remedy or vigorous punishment of the perpetrators."[214] It is therefore not surprising that the share of Jews in the republican paramilitary, the Reichsbanner Schwarz-Rot-Gold, came to 20 percent in Leutershausen. This was one way that Jews sought allies in the fight against the National Socialists. Yet individual Jews rarely retaliated against the antisemitic violence hurled against them. One exception was when a Jew from Leutershausen responded to an insult by assaulting Streicher with a whip.[215]

Though these antisemitic acts of violence usually emanated from radical party supporters, farmers also began resorting to violence by 1932 (at the latest). By then, a growing number of farms had been sold off at recent compulsory auctions, resulting in a highly charged atmosphere across the countryside. The agricultural crisis had driven many farmers—mostly owners of medium-sized farms, but also smallholders—into financial ruin. Overall, the total number of compulsory auctions grew continuously between 1928 and 1932. By 1928, thirty forced auctions had taken place—a 100 percent increase over the year before. Two years later (1930), 58 farms were sold in auction, followed by 104 auctions in 1931. By the first half of 1932, the figure had climbed to 732 auctioned agricultural properties.[216]

Bavaria led Germany in the number of farms that were sold off in compulsory auctions between 1931 and 1932, with a growth rate of 62.68 percent; nationwide, the average was 22.46 percent.[217] Jewish cattle dealers who traded in these auctioned farm estates (obviously a sensitive issue) became a target of National Socialist agitation. The Nazis denounced Jewish merchants as gruesome butchers of farms who, as "rootless Jews" (with no connection to the soil—*bodenlose* Juden), were tearing the "German peasant" away from his clod of earth and thereby turning the settled peasant into a vagabond who would ultimately have no alternative but to move away from the "free land" and into the "bondage of the factories" in the cities. This sort of agitation primarily took place in public squares and tavern halls. For example, in 1932, SA leader Stegmann mocked a Jewish cattle trader from Ansbach at a public event in the city hall of Herrieden as a racketeer (*Halszuzieher*, literally "throat tightener").[218] Similar attitudes were reflected around the same time in Windsheim, where several National Socialists at a compulsory auction harassed "the Israelite merchants present with shouts and acts of violence."[219]

National Socialists were not the only ones to take advantage of the changed political climate to abuse the trust of Jewish cattle traders. From 1932 to 1933, for example, there was a conflict between farmer Georg Ströbel from Colmberg, on one side, and the Steinberger brothers, cattle traders from Rothenburg ob der Tauber, and estate trader Jakob Steinberger from Colmberg, on the other. The difficult economic climate left Ströbel unable to repay the loans he had taken on for his horse trading and livery vehicle business. As a result, his seventy-yoke property was auctioned off in January 1932. His creditors included the aforementioned Jewish cattle traders, as well as the Colmberg Loan Society and non-Jewish estate and cattle trader Johann Krämer. After the different creditors had broken up the property pro rata, Ströbel's daughter made an unsuccessful attempt in late 1932 to buy back a share of the original property from Krämer.[220] Shortly thereafter, the change of government in January 1933 provided Ströbel's daughter with an opportune moment to prevail with her putative property claim against the Jewish creditors, this time by force. Together with her brother, an SA man and Nazi party member, she asked State Secretary Hofmann to take care of Steinberger in a way that made him experience "some intimidation, so that I or my sister can have a better chance to dispense with these thieves, and so that their plan to destroy us fails."[221] Yet this threat of violence was only the beginning; Ströbel's daughter also submitted a debt relief application to the Bayerische Landessiedlung, a Bavarian state rural development authority, though the application was unsuccessful.[222] The attempt by Ströbel's daughter to capitalize on the growing antisemitic climate as a way of recovering family property failed, however, because the Nazis did not come to power and change the law until later in 1933. Relations of trust between individual farmers and Jewish cattle traders had nevertheless already deteriorated. Numerous cases of a similar nature described in the papers of Jewish lawyer Dr. Herz show that the Ströbel case was hardly an isolated incident.[223]

Between 1926 and 1933, Jewish cattle traders largely enjoyed institutional trust, even if some of the trust had been wrested from them by local municipal councils with a large proportion of National Socialists, as in Neustadt an der Aisch. The growing popularity of the National Socialists and their antisemitic ideology had an increasingly negative impact on relations of trust among Jewish cattle traders, state institutions, and farmers. Any kind of institutional trust, and thus any foundation for making a living, had already been withdrawn from Jewish Schmusers and kosher butchers in 1930. At the same time, numerous assaults on Jewish institutions, synagogues, and cemeteries testify to the inflamed antisemitic mood in the region.[224] The high level of migration—15.3 percent of the Jewish population left Germany between 1925 and 1933—suggests that life had already become unbearable for the Jewish population, even prior to 1933.[225] To be sure, we lack reliable evidence that would provide information about the motives behind this exodus. Yet a March 1932 letter from a Bavarian affiliate of the CV does suggest that the constant antisemitic assaults left Jews feeling intensely vulnerable. The chair of the Bavarian CV branch complained to the Bavarian State Ministry of the Interior: "Jewish inhabitants are so threatened by these incidents that they can hardly show up on the street any longer; they are boycotted economically and completely isolated socially."[226] In this way, the relationship of trust between individual Jewish cattle traders and farmers began to dissolve well before 1933. The establishment of trust, however, is an individual process between at least two actors. Hence, even under these altered political conditions, trust persisted between other actors who continued to benefit from trading with each other.

4

Destroying Trust by Force under Nazism

Violence and Terror as Instruments to Establish
Social Distance (1933–1935)

With Hitler's takeover of power on January 30, 1933, antisemitism became part of the governing policy in a modern state. This moment marked a major turning point in the history of violence against Jews.[1] What had previously been tried out on various occasions at the local level now spread to the entire country. To be sure, Jews had already been subjected to acts of antisemitic violence before 1933. Yet until 1933, the police had still tried to maintain law and order. The new situation was aggravated because the SA (*Sturmabteilung*) assumed the function of an auxiliary police force and acted violently against Jewish citizens. According to National Socialist racial ideology, Jews were regarded as wholly untrustworthy. The new rulers were thus withdrawing any kind of trust from Jews and proclaiming their status as the greatest "national pest" (*Volksschädling*), vermin harmful to the race who had to be ousted from German society by being ostracized socially and boycotted economically. Yet since the rule of law, which had previously helped to embed trade relations between cattle traders and farmers in a setting of institutional trust, was not dissolved overnight, the process of withdrawing trust by the state happened in a way that was asynchronous and lacked uniformity.[2] Initially, the relationship of trust between Jewish cattle traders and farmers continued to exist, but it was ultimately destroyed under the impact of antisemitic violence. What came to light in this process was a relationship of tension in which the economic interests of farmers and the goals of National Socialist racial ideology collided.

With the National Socialists' seizure of power, violence against the Jewish population in Franconian small towns and villages seemed as if it was positively exploding. The National Socialists established their power with open violence on the street, and with their ascent, force acquired a new dimension. It manifested itself in public spaces (as on the street) as well as in sites closed to the public (as in homes and prisons). From this point on, the Jewish population was no longer safe from attacks; to the National Socialists, they were regarded as fair game for persecution beyond the pale of law.[3]

Following the second Reichstag election in March 1933, the National Socialists blanketed the entire country with a wave of terror that served to consolidate the new rulers' power at all levels of society and to target their self-appointed enemies, such as Communists, Social Democrats, and Jews.[4] At the same time, the first concentration camps were set up, including one in Dachau, near Munich, on March 22, 1933. Jews active in professions regarded as *verjudet* (*Judaized*, a term intended as derogatory), such as law or retail and certain trade branches, were especially hard hit by these acts of violence. While Jewish lawyers were at the center of these violent acts in Germany's urban milieu, in the countryside, Jewish cattle traders were primarily targeted.[5] With these attacks, the National Socialists purported to stave off threats allegedly posed by these groups—threats the Nazis claimed they could only ward off by force. Individual SA or Nazi local group leaders organized "spontaneous" acts of terror against Jewish cattle traders and their families.[6] These acts of violence were directed against Jews as human beings, but their other aim was to permanently destroy the relationships of trust between Jewish merchants and their customers by establishing social distance between the two. An essential precondition for this effort was the change of government at the local level, which was implemented immediately after the National Socialists seized power on January 30, 1933, when they dismissed mayors and appointed Nazi cadres as the new municipal leaders.[7]

This change of government and shift in power provided individual local Nazi leaders in Central Franconia an opportunity to curry favor with Gauleiter Julius Streicher by engaging in some unusually brutal antisemitic acts. These violent attacks had such a devastating impact on their victims that many were forced to abandon their businesses immediately after the Nazis seized power, as happened with members of the Mann family from Rothenburg, who had long operated a cattle and real-estate trade business. One particular act of terror targeting the family stood out for its cruelty. Only a few days after the promulgation of the Enabling Law on March 23, 1933, local SA men arrested the two proprietors of the business, brothers Josef and Theodor Mann, along with their sons. While the men of the family were held for almost four weeks in the municipal court building jail, SA men held a several-week-long siege of the building containing the family home and office—in which Theodor's wife, Klara Mann, and her daughter, Dinah Grete Mann, were still located. After three weeks, on April 17, 1933, Klara took her own life. Only a few days later, her husband, Theodor, was released from jail. Shortly thereafter, Theodor suffered a mental breakdown and had to be taken to the psychiatric clinic in Ansbach.[8] He never recovered from the psychological damage caused by his incarceration.[9] As a result of this act of violence, the business experienced a major crisis; as early as April 22, 1933—just a few days after the suicide—the Mann firm could no longer make payments to its debtors. On June 10, 1933, the municipal court of Rothenburg ob der Tauber issued an order for an insolvency hearing to avert bankruptcy. The creditors were presented a proposal guaranteeing them 100 percent satisfaction. But the firm could no longer recover from this blow, since from then on, it was subjected to massive defamation and boycotted as a Jewish business.[10]

These early anti-Jewish acts of violence in Rothenburg following the Nazi seizure of power merit especially close scrutiny by comparison with other cases. Violence against local Jewish residents did not drop off, as happened elsewhere. According to a report of gendarmerie patrolman Heckel from Rothenburg, SS Captain (Sturmhauptführer) Karl Kitzinger had a special way of expressing his zeal for persecuting the local Jewish population: he would use criminal complaints against Jewish cattle traders in an attempt to incite the population against them, then use the pretext of "protecting [them from] public anger" in order to place the Jews under "protective custody" in the ensuing weeks and months.[11] In other places, too, local Nazi functionaries terrorized Jewish cattle traders by using the instrument of "preventive detention." For example, in April 1933, Jewish cattle trader Bär was arrested and detained for an indefinite period of time in the jail of the Ansbach provincial district court because he had allegedly spread rumors about Jews being mistreated.[12] Another major site where antisemitic acts of violence continued to happen was Nuremberg—the "city of the Reich party rallies"—where, in 1933, the SA beat cattle trader Justin Landecker so brutally that he subsequently spent several weeks in the hospital under medical care.[13]

The violence was aimed not only against the Jewish population but against their property as well. There are records of assaults on Jewish homes and of Jewish citizens being publicly abused in other Franconian localities at the same time. On the evening of March 29, 1933, for example, there was rioting in front of a Jewish cattle-trader's property.[14] In Altenmuhr in 1933, posters with

antisemitic sayings were affixed to the entrances of Jewish houses, and the occupants were simultaneously prohibited from removing them.[15] Starting in the
spring of 1933, in Gunzenhausen, as in other towns, the windowpanes of Jewish
homes were smashed and the walls smeared with paint.[16] Babette Gutmann,
the Christian wife of a Jewish cattle trader from Treuchtlingen, recalls how,
immediately after the Nazi seizure of power in 1933, SA men took up position
in front of their residential and commercial property, which prevented them
from doing business. Their home's windowpanes were also often destroyed
overnight. From this point on, attacks against the couple increased every year,
and they were publicly insulted as "Jud" (a derogatory abbreviation for "Jew")
or "Judensau" ("Jew pig").[17]

Though violence against Jews dropped off in other parts of Germany after
the Nazis consolidated power over the summer of 1933, the Jewish population
of Central Franconia continued to be at the mercy of violent attacks. Violence
emanated not only from SA men and Nazi party members but also from townspeople, as demonstrated in the case of the Palm Sunday pogrom in Gunzenhausen. On March 25, 1934, in this Central Franconian town, violence against the
Jewish population escalated after SA Lieutenant (Obersturmführer) Kurt Bär
delivered an inflammatory antisemitic speech that stirred up 1,500 Nazi party
members, SA men, and a crowd of curious onlookers. The mob marched to the
houses of the town's approximately 180 Jews, broke into and plundered their
homes, and battered the men. The mob that congregated there lent support
to the SA thrashings with shouts like "Beat them, beat them."[18] Two Jewish
men were killed in the pogrom;[19] all the others, including cattle traders Hugo
and Salomon Walz, were locked up in the local jail overnight on March 25
through the early morning of March 26, 1934.[20] To be sure, the Gunzenhausen
pogrom represents an exception even for Central Franconia and is hardly representative, as the district president for Upper and Central Franconia, Hans
Georg Hofmann, noted critically in a letter to the Bavarian State Ministry of
the Interior: "In none of the other 53 counties belonging to my prefecture has
there been such an accumulation of attacks as in Gunzenhausen."[21] The drastic character of the Palm Sunday pogrom is also underscored by historian Ian
Kershaw. He characterizes this outbreak of violence as the worse excrescence
of antisemitism in Bavaria prior to the November pogrom of 1938. In Kershaw's
words, the Gunzenhausen pogrom "showed that in extreme circumstances a
wider public could be whipped up into a hysterical mood against local resident
Jews."[22] In the case of the previously mentioned riots, the initiative came from
the SA, SS, or Hitler Youth; the pogrom of Gunzenhausen shows, however,
that parts of the civilian population also participated in the attacks against

Jews. These incidents make it apparent that violence was practiced not only in spaces closed off to the public, such as concentration camps or prisons, but also in plain view for all to see, in the vicinity of SA men and with the complicity of "normal" neighbors.[23]

Though segments of the population participated in these riots or tacitly accepted them, many non-Jews also objected to the numerous assaults on Jews committed in broad daylight. Sometime around 1934, for example, a man named Friedrich Franz, who lived in Wettelsheim, reported to the local authorities an anti-Jewish act of violence in which unemployed herdsman Johannes Knoll was returning home and pummeled cattle trader Julius Kahn with the thick end of a whipping stick.[24] Similarly, in nearby Treuchtlingen on April 27, 1934, a citizen complained to the Weißenburg/Bayern District Office about the mistreatment of Jews on the open road.[25] Since 1933, public defamations and assaults on Jews had become routine in this rural town.[26] As the examples from Treuchtlingen and Wettelsheim show, it was nonparty members who condemned the violence taking place against Jews in broad daylight. On a critical note, however, it should be pointed out that the complaint of the Treuchtlingen citizen was directed against a disturbance of the public peace rather than the use of violence against Jews per se.[27]

This negative attitude toward public violence points to the impact of that violence on the non-Jewish population. Violence in public is generally regarded as disturbing, especially when it is manifested in one's own surroundings and has a negative impact on public peace or order, as the complaint by the citizen from Treuchtlingen underscores. But participation in public violence can also create a moment of inclusiveness, in which those using force take shape as a group and clearly differentiate themselves from the "lepers" against whom their violence is aimed.[28] Violence against Jews, therefore, served the new power holders as an important instrument for the creation of a racist *Volksgemeinschaft* (national community). As emphasized in the research, constructing the Nazi Volksgemeinschaft required a range of willingness on the part of the non-Jewish population, extending from "a readiness to tolerate and approval through active participation."[29] These different facets of participation in the ostracism of Jews come to light particularly in the public denunciations involving charges of "racial defilement"—which could be arbitrarily leveled at any time starting in 1933—as well as in the public processions of shame (*Prangerumzüge*) orchestrated to pillory Jews.[30] These processions usually involved a series of humiliating rituals, like shaving the head of the victim, hanging a sign around their necks with defamatory inscriptions, and getting a rabble of local residents to drive them along in a procession through the middle of the town, as happened around 1935 to cattle trader Abraham Löwenstein[er[31]] in Markt Berolzheim.[32] According to several statements from witnesses, the cattle trader, under the pretext of having slaughtered a head of cattle illegally, was driven barefoot through the town with a sign hung around his neck. Running ahead of him with a drum was nine-year-old Adolf Schmidt, who was followed, according to witness testimony, by ten to twenty inhabitants of the town.[33] For town residents, participating in processions of shame created an inclusionary effect, which was expressed in the crowd's shared agitation against the "defiled" person. These processions of shame thus functioned as an important instrument for creating distance between the non-Jewish and Jewish population.[34]

In the case of Löwenstein[er], no pictures have survived, nor do we know what the shaming inscription on the sign said. Yet there is hardly any doubt that this act of degradation was visually exploited for propaganda purposes. Historian Alexandra Przyrembel emphasized how these processions of shame depended on photos documenting the "joy of violence" experienced by the participants.[35] In the countryside, the extent and scope of these abusive processions were often worse than in the cities.[36] Cases of "racial defilement" frequently provided the pretext for these processions of shame. Arbitrary accusations of this kind could lead to imprisonment in the Dachau concentration camp, something that happened, for example, to Heinrich Sommer from the town of Thalmässing.[37] Charges of "racial defilement" also landed people in "protective custody," as in the case of Theodor Rindsberg, a Jewish cattle trader in the city of Nuremberg who had an extramarital relationship with a non-Jewish woman, Babette Knoblach, with whom he had a child.[38]

Nationwide, violent actions rose between the spring and summer of 1935. With the passage of the Nuremberg Laws in September 1935, violence initially declined again, but in Central Franconia, it continued to shape everyday life for the Jewish population, as evidenced by the litany of criminal complaints that Jewish cattle traders lodged with local gendarmerie stations. That Jews turned to the rule of law for help is an indication they were attempting to use the issuance of a criminal charge as a way of documenting the pain inflicted on them. One example of this is the criminal complaint filed by sixty-five-year-old cattle trader Ernst Aal, who reported that a Hitler Youth group ambushed him on his way home to Ansbach. According to the police report, the group had blockaded the street so that the cattle trader was unable to ride past them in his horse-drawn carriage. Aal reportedly asked the leader of the group to let him pass, to which the Hitler Youth leader replied with his fist raised: "What did you yell, you ape? I'll just bash you in one, so you die a miserable death!" Aal apparently rode slowly behind the group until, after a while, he passed by a piece of woodland. There, according to the complaint filed by Aal, six to seven uniformed Hitler Youth jumped onto the street, and one of them shouted "One! Two! Three!" before they overturned the carriage with the elderly cattle trader. This act must have given the teenagers a feeling of dominance over the old man and power over what was happening on this deserted country road—a common experience that shaped them as a group. The cattle trader was powerless in the face of the group's action, yet he maintained his dignity by reporting the act of violence to the local police. In so doing, he documented the crime, though it remains an open question as to whether he still hoped that the police would punish this injustice. While gendarmerie Commissar Moll did take note of the Jewish cattle trader's complaint, he noted underneath it: "Out of consideration for various official obstacles, the matter cannot be pursued."[39] As Moll's statement clearly shows, the police as a state institution had stopped offering protection against arbitrary treatment and violence targeting Jews.

Violence against Jews was primarily aimed at establishing a social distance between Jews and non-Jews based on racist criteria,[40] and by extension, it also served to dissolve relationships of trust between Jews and the non-Jewish population. And yet even if violence persisted, with Jews placed firmly outside the ideological national community of the Volksgemeinschaft, trade relations, to a degree, nevertheless persisted.

Racist Cattle-Trading Policy versus Economic Trust

Immediately after taking power in 1933, the National Socialists designated the exclusion of Jews from German economic life as an essential component of their anti-Jewish policy. In line with National Socialist racial ideology, a "recovery" of the German economy could only be attained by excluding the Jewish population. In order to implement this agenda, Jewish civil servants were forced into retirement as early as April 7, 1933, with the exception of those who were categorized as frontline combatants, had lost a father or son in the First World War, or had only entered the civil service after 1914. The Aryan clause (Arierparagraph), applied here for the first time, laid the foundation for all subsequent professional debarments and for a wide variety of other persecution measures at different levels of German society.[41] Although the Aryan clause had not been introduced into the cattle trade, a look at the boycott policy and at municipal practices when it came to issuing trade licenses clearly reveals the impact of these actions on Jewish cattle dealers. Indeed, many of them abandoned their trade, even before they were mandated to by law. Even though Undersecretary Karl Kürschner from the Reich Agricultural Ministry had called for introducing an Aryan clause in the cattle trade as early as July 1933, implementing the provision nationwide dragged on until 1938.

Here, the dualism between party and state emerges with special clarity, as does their fusion into a polycratic amalgam—mixing apparent legality with antisemitic violence—something that proved to be a dangerous concoction to the victims of Nazi persecution.[42] Neither the legal situation, not clarified until 1938, nor ongoing business relations with farms provided any protection against bureaucratic condescension and physical violence. Hence, Jewish cattle traders were hardly spared the effects of the Nazis' anti-Jewish economic policy prior to the legal clarification of this policy in 1938, even if the Reich government held back for a long time from issuing a professional ban on Jewish cattle traders.

Exclusion from the Public Space

The expulsion of Jews from the cattle trade is not something that can be viewed in isolation. Rather, it needs to be understood in the context of the National Socialist "blood and soil policy," which aimed to feed the German population through agricultural programs designed to be racist and operate independently of the world economy. Because cattle traders were regarded as an important link in the food supply chain, they became targets of the National Socialists, especially when implementation of the blood and soil policy intensified.

To implement Nazi economic policy, the Reich government centralized the agricultural economy—in addition to all other branches of the economy— immediately after taking power. In September 1933, all agricultural organizations were hierarchically consolidated in the newly created Reichsnährstand (Reich Food Corporation) under Reichsbauernführer (Reich Farm Leader) Richard Walther Darré, the Nazi government's agriculture minister. In organizational terms, as a self-governing corporation under public law, the Reichsnährstand was an autonomous juridical entity and thus not a branch of the NSDAP (Nazi party). All persons involved in agriculture, all agricultural cooperatives, and all "workers and processors of agricultural products" were subordinated to the Reichsnährstand.[43] Cattle-trading associations were also included and assumed new names that expressed the transformation from an independent to a centrally organized cattle business. Thus, the Bund deutscher Viehhändler (Federation of German Cattle Traders) was now called the Reichsverband des nationalen Viehhandels (Reich Association of the National Cattle Trade). At the same time, the National Socialists officially banned the term *cattle trader* (*Viehhändler*) from linguistic usage and replaced it with the neologism *cattle distributor* (*Viehverteiler*). In this way, the National Socialists were trying to distance themselves from the *merchant class* (*Händlertum*), a term they scorned, regarding it as intrinsically *Jewish* and thus synonymous with greed, profit-seeking, and deceit. With the introduction of the term *cattle distributer* into the vocabulary of the agricultural economy, the National Socialists linguistically annulled the supposedly negative connotation associated with the term *Jewish cattle trader* in the chain of food producers.[44]

Exclusion from Professional Associations

At the beginning of the Nazi era, it was still possible for Jews—as people working in agriculture—to be members of this newly created compulsory organization, the Reich Association of the National Cattle Trade, and thus to continue practicing their occupation, which was dependent on membership in the Reich Association. In March 1933, immediately after the Nazi takeover, the Landesverband bayerischer Viehhändler (State Association of Bavarian Cattle Traders) addressed its members with an appeal in which it explicitly declared that it was a professional organization whose posture was one of "complete neutrality with respect to party politics" and in which there were no *Volksgenossen* (the Nazi term for fellow Germans—*national comrades*—in a racially defined community) but only *Berufsgenossen* (professional colleagues), "regardless of which religion or political conviction the individual member would have."[45]

This attitude of professional neutrality was countered by the blood and soil ideology of the National Socialists, who deemed it important to reorganize the honorable cattle trade according to racist criteria. This was also an ideology that declared everything "Jewish" in general to be dishonorable. Accordingly, the primary method for remedying abuses in the livestock and meat business was to exclude Jewish traders. The ministerial bureaucracy, therefore, had to clarify whether Jews, in the future, would be allowed to retain membership in the newly created Reich Association of the National Cattle Trade or could seek membership to the organization. Undersecretary Dr. Hofmann from the Bavarian Economic Ministry held the view that Jewish cattle traders should be permitted to remain members—or continue to be eligible to apply for membership—if they could be regarded as "reliable" according to existing rules.[46] This would also provide an opportunity for better control over them as members of a professional organization.[47] It was not until March 1934 that the Reich Association of the National Cattle Trade added paragraph 3 to its constitution, granting new membership only to Aryans but leaving old memberships unaffected by discrimination.[48]

The question of membership in the Reich Association of the National Cattle Trade was only a prelude to the racist restructuring of the cattle trade. A dense and expanding network, woven by both local and national actors, began to take shape in a way that soon caught Jewish cattle traders in its web.

The April Boycott of 1933: Singling Out
Adversaries and Unsettling Customers

National Socialists used a virulent boycott policy as the major instrument to implement their program of ousting Jewish merchants from the economy. To be sure, Jewish cattle traders had already been subjected to acts of intense hostility and boycott measures even before 1933. Yet with the change of government in 1933, antisemitic assaults acquired a new character. Economic sanctions now spanned the Reich, systematically attacking the livelihood of the entire Jewish population.[49] The nationwide call to boycott Jewish businesses on April 1, 1933, marked the starting point for the Jews' economic expulsion from Germany and has been characterized as the Nazi era's first antisemitic wave.[50] The official pretext used by the Nazi rulers for the boycott was the "hate propaganda" (*Greuelhetze*) allegedly conducted abroad against National Socialist Germany. The real reason, however, had to do with the numerous individual antisemitic actions undertaken by the party base. The party leadership reacted to these actions with the April boycott, which pooled the pressure "from below" into a single Reich-wide action.[51]

Under the leadership of Streicher and following an instruction from the NSDAP party leadership, the boycott was to "be driven into the smallest farming village so that it would hit Jewish merchants out on the rural plains in particular."[52] In special appeals, rural NSDAP groups addressed the peasant population directly by calling on farmers to cut off their business relationships with Jewish cattle traders.[53] According to a report written by the attorney for Salomon Walz, on April 1—the day the Nazi leadership issued its appeal for the boycott—SA guards patrolled the offices of the Walz brothers' cattle and real-estate business in Gunzenhausen. The attorney describes how customers reacted to this action: "Many a one of the most devoted and old customers put up resistance, went inside anyway, got photographed, and had his picture publicly displayed as a 'Jew lackey' [Judenknecht]."[54] The report sheds light on the ways that non-Jews participated only hesitatingly in the April boycott. Indeed, the boycott was deemed a failure, primarily because of restraint from a largely skeptical population.[55]

Nevertheless, these antisemitic actions conducted right in front of their businesses did succeed like nothing before in singling out these merchants, marking and stigmatizing them as Jewish. At the same time, customers got the signal that they were doing something forbidden, even "harmful to the national race" (*volksschädlich*), if they continued buying from a Jewish store.[56] From now on—and from all sides—the relationship of trust was subjected to massive stress.

Farmers' Reactions to the Racist Boycott Policy

Although there was an official declaration ending the boycott on April 4, 1933, that hardly meant there was an end to the calls for ostracizing Jewish businesses. In some regions, Jewish cattle traders reacted—much to the chagrin of farmers—to the aggressive anti-Jewish agitation and outbreaks of violence by ceasing to purchase cattle in the farming villages. The first indications of a disruption in the economic cycle came at the beginning of August 1933, when the Bavarian farming community organization (Bayerische Bauernschaft) complained to Georg Luber, State Secretary in the Bavarian Agricultural Ministry and Nazi party member. In the complaint, farmers noted the economic distress they experienced after Jewish cattle traders stayed away from public markets—since, as a result, they could only sell their cattle to butchers, who offered them lower prices. Luber complained, moreover: "So it gets to the point where many farmers, even National Socialists, are frankly longing for the Jewish cattle traders, looking at them as their salvation." As a result, the Bavarian farmers' organization called for "drawing the attention of the cooperative livestock husbandry [association], on the part of the government, to the unsustainable cattle market conditions prevailing in the former domains of the Jews in Franconia, so that, in places where Jewish trade has finally been eliminated, these organizations may intervene, both in their own commercial interest as well as in that of the farming community, in order that the idea one is already hearing not infrequently today does not start gaining more ground among the peasants: [the notion that] 'we peasants are lost without the Jews.'"[57] Additional urgent reports from the Bavarian State Chamber of Agriculture (Bayerische Landesbauernkammer) provide testimony substantiating the gravity of the situation, which elicited anger even among National Socialist farmers. In a letter to the Bavarian State Ministry of Economic Affairs (Bayerisches Staatsministerium für Wirtschaft), a disgruntled representative of the Bavarian State Chamber of Agriculture wrote:

> Complaints from National Socialist peasants are getting loud about how their cattle can no longer be brought to the customer because, at the moment, there is no demand coming from the Jewish cattle traders. In this connection remarks are being made like: "If we don't have the Jews, then there isn't anybody to buy up our cattle!" It almost looks as if the Jewish

cattle traders were staging a boycott with the intention of making agriculture ripe for advocacy in their favor. These Jewish cattle traders are frequently in possession of huge assets, and therefore it's easy for them to refrain from buying any cattle from farmers who've been accustomed to dealing with them for decades until such time as the latter, strapped for cash, run back into the house and beg them to purchase their cattle.[58]

According to additional accounts, the situation escalated to the point that there was a "noticeable stoppage in cattle sales" in the district of Weißenburg/Bayern and the adjoining region of Upper Franconia.[59] The economic position of middle-class cattle traders owning medium-sized businesses allowed them, at least initially, to hold their ground against the National Socialist boycott policy. Trust in this middle class and in well-known merchants was stronger than the newly implemented racist cattle-trade policy.

A "Franconian Specialty": Excluding Jews from the Towns

The boycott policy was designated by the Reich government "from above" as the centerpiece of its anti-Jewish policy. Boycotts were especially radical and hard-hitting when top-down policy interacted with grassroots initiatives, as they often did in Franconia.[60] One manifestation of the "Jewish policy" so harshly promoted by Streicher was the series of signs put up in front of almost every Central Franconian village starting in the spring of 1933 with inscriptions like "No admittance to Jews" or "Jews enter the town at their own risk."

Cattle trader Karl Freising from Roth reported that as early as 1933, it was nearly impossible for Jewish cattle traders to do business in towns with anti-semitic signs like these at the entrance.[61] Cattle trader Salomon Walz from Gunzenhausen, his attorney Dr. Bayer reported, also remembered the kinds of reactions he encountered: "If one entered [the locality] anyway, one would be chased out by fanatics."[62] Signs of this type soon dotted the landscape of other German regions, too. Yet the antisemitic inscriptions on these local signs were so widespread and infamous that they amounted to a "Franconian specialty."[63] Even in the Catholic-dominated southern part of Central Franconia, the practice was widespread, and NSDAP district leadership in Eichstätt boasted that there was "no locality in the district of Eichstätt that did not have its Jew sign." They went on to brag that "two new display cases for the *Stürmer*" had been put up by the city hall and that in Eichstätt, "almost every child has been enlightened about the Jewish danger, [whereas] in Ingolstadt, Neuburg, and Beilngries we find little more than imitation without a deeper understanding."[64] Franconia was considered extreme even by National Socialist standards: Swabia's

FIGURE 4.1. Town sign, Oberasbach, ca. 1935. The inscription says: "Look, people, at the peasant on his farm / What suffering from the Jew who's done him harm!"
Courtesy of Stadtarchiv Nürnberg, E 39, no. 2257/1 a a.

Gauleiter Karl Wahl, for example, dismissed the "rabble-rousing antisemitism" (*Radauantisemitismus*) of Streicher and his entourage and the "mimicking of Franconian methods" on the Jewish question as "laughable."[65] In October 1935, Reich Farm Leader (Reichsbauernführer) Darré also criticized how actions like this merely served as an "abreaction of economic envy complexes" and missed the point of what was at "the core of the Jewish question."[66]

Reactions of Jewish Cattle Traders to their Exclusion from the Towns

Jewish cattle traders were not entirely defenseless in the face of these radical antisemitic acts. They could respond to the systematic exclusion by working together with non-Jewish cattle dealers, as Jakob Aal did with his Protestant business partner Georg Stürzenhofecker. In order to buy an ox from the farmer Heinrich Geißler in the village of Aichau, which had antisemitic signs at the edge of town, the two rented a car, drove together from Ansbach to Aichau, and parked there in front of the entrance to the village. Jewish cattle trader Aal, who was prohibited from entering the town, remained seated in the car while his Protestant colleague negotiated with Geißler about the purchase of an ox. The successful cooperation between the two cattle traders came to an end, however, and ultimately both lost their authorization to take part in the cattle trade.[67] Non-Jewish cattle dealers, however, did not always mitigate the persecution faced by their Jewish colleagues and, in some cases, even served to exacerbate it. In the village of Ettenstatt, for example, two Aryan cattle traders insulted and beat Jewish cattle trader Max Gutmann from Ellingen after Gutmann attempted to buy an ox from the stable of farmer Christian Link during the summer of 1936.[68]

Other Jewish cattle traders circumvented the rigorous boycott policy in Central Franconia by shifting their trading activity into other—more Catholic—regions of Bavaria. Simon Hutzler, for example, only did business in Auerbach in the Oberpfalz (the Upper Palatinate) after countless acts of harassment made it nearly impossible for him to trade in Central Franconia.[69]

The Expulsion of Jewish Cattle Traders from the Cattle Markets

In other areas, too, Central Franconia assumed a sad pioneering role in the expulsion of Jews from the cattle trade, as demonstrated by the attempt of individual municipalities to exclude Jews from the cattle markets. These cases elucidate with special clarity an emerging conflict pitting the racist policies local decision-makers were determined to implement against the trade interests of farmers.

Since the mid-1920s, small towns had been attempting to reactivate their decentralized rural cattle markets by trying an approach to trading that was conservative and countercyclical. (A revival and refurbishing of old-fashioned local market sites, it was hoped, would counteract the boom in metropolitan concentration.) Immediately after the Nazis seized power, several of these towns renewed that effort. Unlike the 1920s, however, this time the local decision-makers behind this project of renewal were now less concerned with connecting their municipalities to urban centers they had lost in the course of industrialization and more preoccupied with pushing racist goals.[70] By reviving small-town cattle markets, the National Socialists intended to shift trade from farmers' stables back into the public. According to this line of argument, the stables trade was opening the floodgates to the deceptive trading practices of the Jewish cattle traders, who left defenseless peasants at their mercy. By switching trade out of the stables and back onto the public market square, the National Socialists were able to use the cattle markets as a machinery of control to monitor trade between farmers and cattle traders and thus to implement their racist policy.[71] For some municipalities, however, this was not enough;

immediately after the Nazi seizure of power, they were already one step ahead in their rush to implement the new policy. Their aim was not only to revive the cattle markets but to simultaneously reorganize them under racist auspices by excluding Jewish merchants completely from market activities. The first cities in the Reich to ban Jews from the municipal cattle markets were Ansbach, the district capital of Central Franconia, in April 1933, and Nuremberg (the "city of the Reich party Rallies") in September 1933.[72] Over the course of 1933, all Central Franconian municipalities followed this trend.[73] The municipalities' racist approach also met with approval from many non-Jewish cattle dealers, who saw the altered political circumstances as a favorable opportunity to shut out their Jewish rivals. On April 3, 1933, for example, immediately after the April boycott, non-Jewish livestock commissioner Fritz Wissmüller turned to the Bavarian State Ministry of Economic Affairs with a request to deny Jewish trading companies altogether any admittance to the Nuremberg stockyard.[74]

In order to ensure the successful revival of these small-town—and now also "Jew-free"—cattle markets, the municipalities started an extensive advertising campaign in the local press three to four weeks before the first market day. On large, colorful posters, farmers were told why they should attend these markets—first, in order to exclude Jews from the cattle trade, and next, to help young farmers learn about trading. The poster for the municipality of Scheinfeld propagandized further: "The Scheinfeld cattle market offers the young peasant an opportunity to examine what all the commotion is about and make use of the experiences gathered here for his own practice. The peasant will be trained again toward honest trade and become more nimble about commercial livestock, i.e., he gets more power over the Jews."[75] As an additional incentive, the municipalities even waived the pavement tax and fees for driving the first batch of cattle to the markets.[76] In addition, NSDAP representatives were supposed to help arrange the sale of cattle to the peasants at these markets.[77] In this way, they intervened directly in the independent trading activities between merchants and farmers.

While the municipalities were preoccupied with preventing Jewish traders from having access to the markets, the Bavarian state government was trying to strengthen the livestock husbandry cooperatives.[78] In contrast to the 1920s, this was no longer about stimulating competition between the middle-class, independent cattle traders and the government-subsidized livestock husbandry cooperatives to promote an ambitious price policy. Rather, it was more about implementing a racist blood and soil ideology that derived from nineteenth-century agrarian romanticism. This ideology was a mixture of *völkisch* (ethno-nationalist), anti-urban, and racist notions that idealized the settled "Aryan" peasant who would be elevated to the status of a new "nobility." Rendering homage to the Aryan peasant was simultaneously meant to exclude all non-Aryans from the agricultural process of production.[79] With this in mind, as early as August 1933, the municipal council of Ellingen was already pressing the Bavarian livestock husbandry cooperative to open a sales office in this small rural town. Local farmers were also urged to deliver their beef cattle directly to the local sales cooperative instead of continuing to sell their livestock to the Jewish cattle-trading company Bermann & Oppenheimer, a firm that operated nationally.[80]

In spite of all these efforts, the local government initiatives aimed at excluding Jews from the cattle markets were bound to fail, for two predominant reasons. *First*, the Reich government still had no legal foundation for excluding Jewish traders. Paragraph 64 from the Imperial Commercial Code (the Reichsgewerbeordnung dating back to the Kaiserreich or Bismarck era) still posed an obstacle, for its provisions guaranteed free market access and thus prohibited the exclusion of market participants on the basis of their "Rassenzugehörigkeit" ("racial belongingness"). Accordingly, the Nuremberg City Council, like other Central Franconian municipalities, had to rescind the racist cattle-market policy these local governments were trying to implement. There were similar developments in other areas of public life at the same time. Municipal decision-makers undertook a number of racist actions to prevent Jews from having access to public facilities like bathhouses, pawnshops, or trade exhibitions and fairs.[81] On instructions from the Nazi government's chief of staff, Martin Bormann, all these local racist initiatives had to be revoked again in the autumn of 1933.[82] A uniform Reich-wide solution for these actions had not yet been found.

Conversely, however, Bormann's directive did not lead to any improvement of conditions in Central Franconia. Local authorities continued to push uncoordinated antisemitic actions—even if slightly modified. At almost the same time as Bormann's directive, for example, a Nazi party member of the municipal council in the district capital of Ansbach tried to again block Jews from having access to the town's cattle market. This plan was introduced on September 1, 1933, with an article in the local newspaper headlined "Cattle Trade—without Jews." Approximately two months later, the proposal was converted into a renewed ban by the municipal council. According to Bormann's directive, the municipal council could no longer exclude Jewish traders from market activity on the basis of their racial affiliation. Hence, the council now kept Jewish cattle traders away on the grounds of preserving public peace and security. Signs in front of the cattle market announced the new ban, and Gestapo officials made sure it was implemented. Jewish traders who could produce a license from the NSDAP were apparently not affected by this measure.[83] To the Jews who were the objects of this persecution, this kind of uncoordinated harassment, varying widely by locality, left them uncertain about how much room they had to maneuver—and whether these actions had any legal standing.

Second, the goal of introducing Jew-free cattle markets ran afoul of established trading practices between farmers and cattle traders. After the Nazi seizure of power in 1933, for example, the Gunzenhausen Municipal Council attempted to implement a Jew-free cattle market. Despite a massive advertising campaign aimed at the rural population, however, the movement barely resonated with its target audience. Its previous failure notwithstanding, the Gunzenhausen Municipal Council pushed ahead with an additional racist campaign in October 1933, rounding up farmers, "Aryan" cattle traders from across the region, and master butchers in an effort to drum up support for the Jew-free cattle markets.[84] None of this proved successful. In November 1934, when there was still no detectable increase in sales at the local cattle market, a town council member summed it up this way: "We need the Jews, since I cannot get my cattle to the customer today without Jews. Because the Christian traders always want to buy the cattle below price, which is not the case with the Jews."[85] Even though this statement toys with the antisemitic stereotype about Jews luring Christians into deceptively ineluctable deals, it also brings to light the way that antisemitic laws disrupted established economic frameworks. In nearby Treuchtlingen, we observe a similar dynamic at work. There, a citizen had complained to the district authority of Weißenburg/Bayern (the administrative office in charge of Treuchtlingen) about sluggish sales of cattle owing to the exclusion of the Jews from the local cattle market.[86] The complaint was answered by the Nazi mayor and district party leader, Michael Gerstner, in the form of this political tirade:

> All decent social circles have regarded it as compatible with the dignity of a cultured nation [Kulturstaat] that, year after year, German peasants lost their hearth and home. Nobody ever stood up and grumbled: these poor German people. But when a Jew pig has so much as one little hair on his head harmed, there resounds from every corner the call "Our poor Jews!" The district leadership is certainly aware that a certain sluggishness has materialized, and it is to be expected that intensified efforts to create change here will yield results. That it is Germans who are encouraging peasants to take the view that one cannot make do without Jews is, once again, so typically German. If the struggle is proceeding apace along more respectable

tracks outside Franconia, that cannot be the occasion for having pity on "our dear Jews." The Jew knows perfectly well what is at stake in the Gau of Franconia. Victory is his who does not lose nerve.[87]

As Gerstner's harsh reaction to the letter from the citizen of Treuchtlingen indicates, the new racist policy was beginning to cause the previous structure for regulating the cattle trade to totter.

At the end of the 1920s, it had already become clear that small towns were eagerly embracing small and medium-sized cattle-trading firms in an effort to upgrade their faltering markets. Yet an even earlier attempt to introduce Jew-free cattle markets, undertaken by Hessian antisemite Otto Böckel in the 1890s, had failed because the non-Jewish competition proved economically impotent.[88] That the "exclusion of the cattle Jews" would have major consequences nevertheless gave the Nuremberg Chamber of Industry and Commerce cause for concern.[89] Even individual county farmers' associations (as organized in local chambers of agriculture) regarded the reintroduction of decentralized "minimally sized livestock markets" as economically meaningless.[90] In their attempt to introduce Jew-free and decentralized cattle markets, then, local decision-makers had intervened too deeply in existing economic structures.

Although the Nuremberg City Council temporarily rescinded its antisemitic cattle-market policy in the autumn of 1933 because it was deemed illegal, the council nevertheless continued to search (much like the Ansbach Municipal Council) for new ways to achieve its goal of a cattle market that was "judenfrei" (cleansed of Jews). It was a thorn in the side of the council to realize that "in years gone by . . . nearly two-thirds of the cattle traders" on the Nuremberg cattle market had been "Jews, and 70 per cent of the cattle sold there on average . . . [came] from Jewish traders."[91] In March 1934, therefore, the Nuremberg City Council started yet another attempt to keep Jewish cattle traders away from the local market. This time, the council assigned them segregated sales platforms at the Nuremberg cattle market, so that they stood apart from the non-Jewish traders.[92] Jewish cattle traders were therefore made recognizable and excluded from the market's other commercial activity, while their non-Jewish customers were branded "Jew lackeys."[93] As the office manager for the *Gau* (Nazi district) to which Nuremberg belonged later reported, the result was that "the number of Jewish cattle traders continuously declined. By the beginning of December 1934, when admittance was also refused for three Jewish cattle agents, the Nuremberg cattle market was completely free of Jewish traders and agents."[94] This led to a drastic decline in sales at the Nuremberg cattle market, as a report from the Nuremberg slaughterhouse management implied. The author of this report expressed his concern about how "the outstanding role that Nuremberg has played as intermediary between the surplus region of Franconia and the northern German regions where there is demand [for cattle] has definitely come to an end if another regulation is not made soon that ends up in a general ban of Jewish trading at German beef cattle markets. It is ineffective to call off an action already started. Losses in cash revenues for the city from market fees, feed business etc. are currently running at an estimated RM 1,500 weekly."[95] Earlier in April 1934, there had been an incident in which Jewish traders from Frankfurt am Main who wanted to buy livestock at the Nuremberg cattle market were physically assaulted at the railway station.[96] So long as these violent actions varied from one region to another, the municipalities in charge had reason to fear that this could prove detrimental to them. Yet this regional inconsistency did not last long; in other areas, similar measures were adopted slightly later, starting in 1935.[97] It took until 1938 for the Reich government to transform this locally tested antisemitic regulation—a racist policy the Nazis pursued in spite of its economic drawbacks—into a formal law excluding Jewish traders from trade fairs and markets.[98]

The Ban on "Jewish Business Practices"

Although there were still legal barriers against excluding Jews entirely from the cattle markets in 1934, the Bavarian Economic Ministry did succeed in August of that year at officially prohibiting something regarded as one of the most conspicuously "Jewish practices in the cattle trade"; there was a ban on using the cattle traders' language at markets.[99] For the National Socialists, this prohibition was a pretext for making the cattle trade "more honest" and thus also "more reliable." The impact of this racist measure was limited, however, as indicated by a complaint from the Landesbauernschaft Bayern (Bavarian State Farmers' Association) to the Bavarian State Ministry of Economic Affairs in June 1936 about the wide dissemination of "Jewish" trade practices in the cattle trade. At the time, access to most Bavarian cattle markets was no longer possible for Jews because of local bans. Nevertheless, according to the complaint, "at different markets for domestic and breeding cattle, the bad practice [had] become established of . . . sawing off horn tips and filing off calving rings. Here and there it has been determined that the execution of this 'rejuvenation' is taking place out in the open, so that the impression could be created that this is a permissible procedure."[100] Cutting horn tips and using the cattle traders' language were both regarded as "Jewish" and thus as dishonorable trade practices on which the National Socialists had declared war. In social practice, however, both of these things—the cattle traders' language and cutting horn tips—were regarded as key components in the commercial apparatus of the cattle trade.

They were used equally, even under the circumstances of the new political framework since 1933, by all parties participating in the market, regardless of whether they were Jews or not.[101] We have testimony from one non-Jewish hog trader about how the cattle traders' language continued to be used at livestock markets, in spite of the ban and even after Jewish cattle traders were shut out, so long as no representative of the Nazi party was in sight.[102] Indeed, non-Jewish cattle traders and farmers continued to use the Jewish trading language, even as the National Socialists squeezed Jewish traders themselves out of the public market space.

Reactions of Jewish Cattle Traders to their Exclusion from the Markets

With no national ban in place, Jewish cattle traders were able to take legal action—at least as a purely formal matter—against their exclusion or complain to the state government.[103] Moreover, Jewish cattle traders from Central Franconia were still able to sell their cattle at livestock markets in other regions for as long as that was still allowed in those places. For example, wholesaler Jakob Rindsberg from Nuremberg bought his cattle in the Lower Bavarian, heavily Catholic town of Vilshofen, where it was still possible for Jews to visit the markets, and then resold them to farmers in Central Franconia.[104] In this way, Jewish traders adapted themselves a bit to the political and social changes of Nazi rule.[105]

Jewish traders were able to sell their livestock in the Central Franconian cattle markets by cooperating with non-Jews. Often, however, they had to accept risking significant losses, as Salomon Walz emphasized: "Usually these [non-Jewish agents] were not experienced, successful traders, so that the sale was unprofessional and a bad trade, its degree of success consequently small, if it was even possible to talk about success at all. Profits were always small and getting smaller all the time."[106] Cooperative ventures like these resulted in financial losses for the Jewish traders and entailed risks for their non-Jewish helpers. The latter had to reckon with being defamed as Jew lackeys, (Judenknechte) something that happened to Georg Fischer, according to his own testimony, after his collaboration with Jewish cattle traders Nathan and Ignatz Jochsberger collapsed. Fischer had been buying cattle for the Jochsbergers at markets to which Jews no longer had access.[107] The Gau leadership of Franconia was scornful of partnerships forged between Jewish and non-Jewish traders. In a report issued in July 1935, the Gau administration boasted of having ensured that the Nuremberg cattle market was "completely free of Jewish traders and agents. To date nothing has changed about this state of affairs; we even succeeded, through careful monitoring of what was being loaded onto the markets, in eradicating some sellers who were stooping so low as to act as straw men for Jewish traders."[108] Non-Jewish traders who sold cattle at the markets for their Jewish colleagues accordingly ran the danger (as did their customers) of being denounced and ostracized themselves.

National Socialist Farmers Hold On to Existing Trade Relationships

Though it became increasingly difficult for Jewish cattle traders and their non-Jewish helpers to trade on Central Franconian cattle markets, the stables trade continued unabated. In spite of massive antisemitic propaganda, it proved exceedingly difficult for Nazi power holders to penetrate these nonpublic trading sites. Though National Socialist party members were forbidden from trading with Jewish cattle dealers under penalty of expulsion from the party,[109] the protected space of the stables facilitated continued trading—and these illicit trading sites also provided an opportunity for zealous party members to maintain their relationships with familiar Jewish business partners. In August 1934, Johann Eiffert, a farmer and local Nazi group leader for the town of Buch am Wald, joined his party comrade Georg Ebert on a bicycle ride to meet Jewish cattle trader Jakob Steinberger in the village of Colmberg, ten kilometers away. They leaned their bicycles against the wall of Steinberger's house and entered his home in order to finalize their deal with him. While negotiations were conducted inside, unidentified culprits threw their bicycles into the village pond. As it later emerged, the local Nazi group leader in Colmberg, Leonhard Leidenberger, had incited local Hitler Youth to commit this act as a warning to the two farmers, his party comrades, about doing business with Jewish cattle traders. Eiffert and Ebert, however, showed little remorse and demanded that Leidenberger defray the costs of the damage to their bicycles. Leidenberger refused to assume liability, so Steinberger, as was befitting for an honorable merchant, promptly paid for the damages that arose for his customers, the National Socialist farmers.[110] It is also likely that Steinberger paid for the damages because he feared that the National Socialist farmers might hold the incident against him even though he had nothing to do with it.

As Nazi party members, Eiffert and Ebert were strictly forbidden from trading with Jews. And yet they traveled to Colmberg specifically to meet Steinberger, presumably because they knew him well and believed they could reach a good deal together. Their business interests outweighed whatever influence Nazi ideology, which stigmatized Jews as swindlers by definition, had on them. In trading with Steinberger, therefore, they asserted the importance of the kind of process-based trust acquired through mutual negotiation, which stands in stark contrast to the antisemitism propagated by their own party. However, it is also important to note that Eiffert and Ebert's interest in dealing with Steinberger may say little about their trust in Steinberger while saying much more about the party members' overriding interest in making a beneficial trade. They knew very well that Steinberger had to sell his livestock below price because of the political situation. Moreover, party members like Eiffert and Ebert believed themselves to be at a disadvantage compared to other farmers, since their party membership meant that they were forbidden from trading with Jews and thus benefitting from their desperate situation. They were explicitly urged to sell their cattle exclusively to "Aryan" cattle traders, who, owing to their often much smaller volume of business, did not offer credit and were seldom able to offer the kind of cash that the farmers urgently needed at the conclusion of a sale. The two National Socialist farmers expressed their chagrin at the situation by suing the local party group leader for his "punitive action."[111]

It was not only National Socialist farmers who felt they were being wronged, but district farm leaders (*Bezirksbauernführer*) as well. District farm leader Götz from Forchheim, for example, was dismissed in 1935 from office by the Reichsnährstand under the charge that he was still dealing in livestock with Jewish traders.[112] In order to avoid the party's disciplinary measures, some mayors certified that certain Jewish traders could be regarded as "reliable."[113] This kind of declaration served many farmers as legitimization for continuing to do business with Jewish cattle traders. Shortly thereafter, this practice was prohibited by the Bavarian Interior Ministry.[114]

Although historian Menahem Kaufman claims in his study on rural Jews in Hesse that the National Socialists had already succeeded in severing relations between Jews and non-Jews in rural areas well before the Nuremberg Laws were promulgated,[115] there is evidence that such economic relationships continued in many areas after 1935. As the case of Eiffert and Ebert makes clear, the established trading practice of farmers and cattle traders stood in the way of implementing the Nazis' racist cattle-trading policy.

To be sure, the reactions of farmers to the racist boycott policy show the limits of Nazi ideology; a global antisemitic mistrust of Jews as a "race" can coexist alongside a strong economic interest in continuing to conduct business with well-known trading partners. The question, though, remains as to whether we may still speak about trust at this point if the kind of trust that once prevailed had already ceased to exist and been replaced by opportunistic rationalistic behavior. The process of excluding Jews from the racially defined ethnonationalist community, the Volksgemeinschaft propagated by the Nazis, was thus asynchronous with the process of excluding Jews from the community of trust that had grown around shared economic interests. Indeed, economic trust linked to the experience of trading together could continue unabated, in spite of altered political conditions and the threat of sanctions.[116]

Official Withdrawal of Trust: Denial of Commercial Permits

Though the Reich government did not formally exclude Jews from the cattle trade until 1938, the removal of Jews from this sector continued at the local level. Some individual local government decision-makers stripped Jewish cattle traders of the last remnant of institutional trust abruptly after 1933—a precipitous withdrawal that was reflected with particular clarity in the practice of awarding business licenses. Although the requirements relating to a cattle trader's reliability remained formally untouched after 1933, the interpretation of *reliability* as a concept changed quite suddenly. Nazi mayors and the civil servants under their authority, for example, denied all Jewish applicants any certification of reliability, which meant that Jews were unable to obtain the necessary commercial permits.[117] This bureaucratic harassment seriously restricted Jewish cattle traders from conducting their business. And yet because these local racist initiatives had not yet been legally validated by higher authorities, they collided with both national regulations and the economic interests of farmers and cattle traders.

The Ansbach District Office provides a good example of the kind of radical action and bureaucratic harassment undertaken by local decision-makers. In 1933, the office set up a register listing people active in the cattle trade, which it used to provide an overview of cattle traders residing in the district. It listed a total of eighty-six traders in cattle, hogs, and horses from twenty-seven localities; the tiny rural village of Leutershausen, with a total of twenty-five cattle traders, had the greatest density of livestock traders.[118] Since the names of the other livestock traders—apart from the two hog traders—do not appear in the administrative files prior to 1933, we may surmise that the district office had intentionally put the names of non-Jewish butchers and pub owners on the list in order to suggest (at least on paper) that enough Aryan cattle distributors were available. In order to check this assumption, the twenty-five cattle traders from Leutershausen were checked for their religious affiliations on the basis of the personal data gathered in the course of this book's research. The examination revealed that of the twenty-five cattle traders, fourteen could be unambiguously identified as Jewish.[119] By 1934, the total number of cattle, hog, and horse traders on the list of the Ansbach District Office had fallen by 13 percent; in Leutershausen alone, the number of Jewish cattle traders fell by 36 percent. Within a year, these Jewish merchants had been deprived of their trading permits or had decided to give up their businesses owing to the changed political circumstances.[120]

Yet the Ansbach District Office was not the only authority with antisemitic ambitions. The urgent demands made by local decision-makers to "purge the cattle trade of unreliable persons" show how much they considered the legal status quo as a hindrance to pursuing their racist goals.[121] This Nazi-era effort stands in stark contrast to the discussion after the First World War about "purging the cattle trade" because strengthening traditional small and medium-sized cattle-trading businesses in order to restore trust between cattle producers and traders was no longer at issue. Rather, these new policies aimed to reorganize the cattle trade according to racist criteria.

To this end, an amendment to the Imperial Commercial Code (Reichsgewerbeordnung) from July 1934 offered district administrations an expanded framework for action. The newly introduced clause, paragraph 57, allowed district administrations to deny licenses to traders suspected of "abusing [their] business for purposes hostile to the state."[122] The term *purposes hostile to the state* (*staatsfeindliche Zwecke*) provided a latitude that could be stretched and construed very widely when it came to interpreting the concept of unreliability. From that point on, it was possible to insinuate very generally that Jews were using their businesses for purposes hostile to the state and thereby endangering how the Volksgemeinschaft was supplied with cattle (both for farm work and for slaughter). In this way, district administrators were now able to withdraw commercial permits from a Jewish cattle trader solely on the grounds of an unconfirmed suspicion that—as they asserted in the case of Moritz Lehmann from Rothenburg ob der Tauber—"he is opposed to the National Socialist state and thus also politically unreliable; [this] justifies the assumption that he would misuse his business, which he used to travel about in the country quite a bit, for purposes hostile to the state."[123] The office that rejected the Rothenburg cattle trader's permit justified its decision by citing the following joke Lehmann was said to have made at an SA sport festival in Rothenburg on December 31, 1935: "If you take the 'i' out of arisch [Aryan], then the only thing left is 'Arsch' [ass]." Lehmann filed a complaint with the district government about the district office's denial of his commercial permit. Yet the government rejected that request as well on the grounds

> that Lehmann does not have the degree of honesty and conscientiousness that one demands of a traveler, and that he is not capable of exercising the restraint that is imperative for the members of a foreign race. The essence of the honorable German merchant remains completely alien to him. This fact justifies the assumption that he does not have the required personal reliability. His remark of 31 December 1935 also reveals that he is against

the National Socialist state and thus also politically unreliable; it justifies
the assumption that he would misuse his business, something he would be
using quite a bit to travel about in the country, for purposes hostile to the
state.[124]

Two key points emerge from this statement: For one, the district government
denied Lehmann the status of reliability in a *personal* sense because he was
not capable of "exercising restraint"; secondly, he was also deemed *politically*
unreliable because he was "against the National Socialist state." Both charges
were enough for the district government to prohibit Lehmann from continuing his business.

Amending the Imperial Commercial Code by adding paragraph 57 was a
recognizable first push toward persecuting Jewish cattle traders. On August 2,
1934, the Bavarian state government issued a ministerial resolution instructing
district offices to renew inspections of all cattle traders in possession of a business license with a view to their reliability. At the same time, the government
carried out a census of "Aryan" and "non-Aryan" cattle traders, which found
that out of a total of 6,278 cattle traders in Bavaria, 1,438 (just under one-fourth)
were in the non-Aryan category.[125]

From that point on, the municipal authorities were vehement about exploiting the leeway that this amendment to the law afforded them—a zeal manifested by the way that district offices started compiling files under the heading
"Jewish cattle traders."[126] These files included lists with the names of all the
cattle traders permitted to do business in the district, with those of the Jewish
traders marked or crossed out. Indeed, the authorities kept close tabs on Jewish
cattle traders in particular, as a way of withdrawing institutionally based trust
from them as a group based on their "Rassenzugehörigkeit." Hence, Jewish
cattle traders proved to be a target of the Nazi's rural anti-Jewish economic
policy, as did Jewish lawyers or bankers in the cities.

Nevertheless, because this racism had yet to be codified into law, municipal
leaders needed to continue demonstrating that individual Jewish cattle traders
were unreliable. In most cases, their frequently fabricated grounds for rejecting
Jewish businesses had no staying power. Despite its rigorous examination of
Jewish cattle traders, even the Ansbach District Office was unsuccessful, for example, in demonstrating the unreliability of every single one. As a result, many
of the office's rejections went unrecognized by the district or state government.
In December 1934, the Reich Association of the National Cattle Trade for the
Gau of Bavaria asked the Ansbach District Office to contact the district or
county farmers' associations about renewing business licenses for Jews, thereby

undercutting the office's authority.[127] In this way, the Reich Association of the National Cattle Trade was intervening in what had once been the district offices' exclusive authority to decide about awarding business licenses.

In order to inspect Jewish cattle traders with respect to their so-called reliability, the municipal authorities were also dependent on the cooperation of the town councils, the gendarmerie stations, and the county farmers' associations. The offices involved in this process thus found themselves in a conflict of interest between the existing legal situation, their own racist goals, and the demand for cattle among the rural population. In January 1935, for example, under pressure from the Ansbach District Office, all Jewish cattle traders in the district were supposed to have their business licenses revoked. Contrary to all expectation, however, the Leutershausen Town Council told the district office that "the Jewish cattle traders residing in Leutershausen [were] not to [be] denied the required [certification of] reliability, but that they [were to be regarded] as reliable."[128] The Leutershausen Municipal Council appealed to the Ansbach District Office to award the town's Jews the required certification of reliability, since no grounds for refusal could be found.[129]

In 1935, the Nazi mayor of Rothenburg ob der Tauber, Friedrich Schmidt, first denied Jewish traders in his district admission to the cattle trade in what became a protracted battle with regional and national authorities. Not even the Nuremberg Laws passed in September 1935, which deprived Jews completely of citizenship rights, provided any legal framework for this step. As a result, the government of Upper and Central Franconia had to agree with the complaint lodged by the affected cattle traders, forcing the mayor to backpedal.[130] As a resolution from the Bavarian Economics Ministry in December 1935 clarified, the "hereditary dispositions associated with race did not [justify] the commercial inspectorate's assumption of unreliability."[131] Nevertheless, the mayor of Rothenburg did not acknowledge defeat. In May 1936, he ordered Jewish cattle traders to give back the business licenses they had been issued for that year. Individual cattle traders, among them Emil Steinberger, thereupon filed complaints with the district government again. This time, too, the government agreed with the cattle traders, since the flimsy and racist grounds for denial presented by Schmidt still had no legal basis. Acting in a spirit of what Nazi officials called "obstinacy," the district government adhered to the legal regulations and, in this one case, stood as a bulwark against the local party bosses' racist actions.[132] Consequently, Steinberger got his business permit back after submitting his complaint.[133] Yet the restoration of his permit did not protect him against the major sales losses he incurred as a result of the mayor's radical action. Indeed, seven months passed between the denial of the business permit in May 1936 and the successful revocation of that order in January 1937, a delay resulting in significant economic damages.

The mayor of Rothenburg did not admit defeat, and shortly after Steinberger's successful complaint, in October 1937, Schmidt again attempted to prevent the cattle trader from practicing his trade. He requested Steinberger's files from the revenue office under a new pretext that Steinberger had committed an offense ten years earlier related to stamp duties and business taxes.[134] The fight over issuing a commercial permit had developed into an existential struggle between the Nazi mayor and the Jewish cattle trader, a battle that ended only (and abruptly) with Steinberger's death in November 1937; that year, in the Jewish hospital in Fürth, he succumbed to complications from an old war wound.[135]

Intensified Pressure from Above

Radical NSDAP mayors were not alone in exerting mounting pressure on Jewish cattle traders. In the autumn of 1935, the Reich leader of the SS, Heinrich Himmler, exploited a cattle-sales crisis in order to enact racist measures aimed at weakening the Jewish cattle trade. In this particular case, producers in different parts of the Reich had been paid excessively high prices for their cattle, leading butchers and cattle yards to complain about rising beef cattle prices. Although the reasons for the high prices had to do with bad harvests and a small volume of cattle imports due to a shortage of foreign exchange, Himmler and his police commanders talked about this as a "public assault by Jewry."[136] At that point, the Bavarian Political Police called on all district offices to provide it with information about the number of "Aryan" and Jewish cattle traders in each administrative district.[137] According to the plan, the political police would monitor and inspect Jewish cattle traders for price gouging (*Preiswucher*, literally "price usury"). This instruction was promptly countered by two gendarmerie stations, where the policemen pointed out that the number of "Aryan" cattle traders in their district was too small to meet the demand covered by the more numerous Jewish traders and that "it had not been observed that Jewish cattle traders were buying up cattle at inflated prices in order to bring about a shortage of cattle on the market."[138] What emerged here, then, was a conflict between radicalizing measures dictated from above and an insufficient body of evidence at the grass roots.

Officials had begun to intensify their actions against Jewish cattle traders and butchers. In October 1935, for example, the Bavarian Political Police commanded their subordinate authorities to monitor Jewish butcher shops and subject them to "severe and extensive controls." In this crackdown, the "most severe measures" were to be applied. Since many Jewish butcher shops had already shut down due to the ban on kosher slaughter from 1930, it is unclear how this order could have been carried out practically. Perhaps, therefore, this measure was aimed at Jewish cattle traders rather than butchers, since the decree demanded: "Jewish cattle traders are constantly to be monitored with respect to their behavior toward animals. In case of complaints, the severest measures are to be undertaken."[139] Shortly thereafter, the gendarmerie station in Ellingen inspected local Jewish butcher shops and cattle-trading firms. Contrary to all expectations, the gendarmerie station was unable to identify any complaints.[140] One year later, the same decree was used in other towns to place Jewish cattle handlers in "protective custody" under the pretext of cruelty to animals.[141]

County Farmers' Associations Push Ahead with the Exclusion of Jewish Cattle Traders

So long as Jews could not be denied a commercial permit solely because of what the Nazis called their "racial belongingness," they had to be charged with some kind of personal "unreliability" that could be demonstrated, such as proof of criminal activity. If that failed, the responsible authorities could either invoke criminal proceedings that had fallen under a statute of limitations or simply blow up flimsy accusations. For example, the Ansbach County Farmers' Association found a bankruptcy proceeding against Jewish cattle trader Benno Gutmann from several years back that served as a pretext for denying him a commercial permit in 1935. Nevertheless, the gendarmerie station in Dombühl had to concede to the Ansbach District Office: "But it could not be determined that [after the bankruptcy proceeding] people were once again damaged by Gutmann's cattle trade. Most of the farmers who lost money at that time because of Gutmann even continued trading with him. Some explained this by pointing out that there was just no other trader who came by. But all the farmers stated that they were promptly paid by Gutmann and no longer suffered any damages. It could also not be determined that there was any uproar among the farmers, because Gutmann was still allowed to trade."[142] Apparently, the trust that the farmers had built up over the years through their business relations with the cattle trader had not been destroyed by this bankruptcy case. To the annoyance of the local farming community organization, the district office ultimately issued a business license for 1935 to Gutmann from Leutershausen. The county farmers' association thereupon began to harass Gutmann and undertake its own effort to prevail against the district office.[143]

In other places, too, the initiative to expel Jews from the cattle trade was initiated by the county farmers' associations (the *Kreisbauernschaften*), which were affiliated members of the Reichsnährstand. In November 1935, the

Gunzenhausen County Farmers' Association pushed to make sure that the district office in charge of issuing commercial permits would deny them to Jewish applicants for the following calendar year. But chances of prevailing in a fight against the district office, as ultimately happened in Ansbach, were not always guaranteed. So the Gunzenhausen County Farmers' Association turned directly to the Bavarian State Ministry of Economic Affairs for support, "owing to the urgency of the matter." In so doing, they bypassed the district government, presumably because they had little faith in the normal process of going through official channels and expected the district office to reject the Gunzenhausen initiative.[144] The Bavarian State Ministry of Economic Affairs acceded to the request put forth by the county farmers' association and shortly thereafter instructed all Bavarian district offices to carry out "purging the cattle trade of unreliable persons" with "care and severity" across the state.[145] Although the racist ambitions of the Gunzenhausen County Farmers' Association were not articulated in the wording of the Bavarian Economic Ministry's decree, their aims were pursued in practice nevertheless. In the decree itself, the wording had to do with "unreliable persons" and not Jews.

Growing Mistrust: "And One Farmer Doesn't Trust the Other"

Though some Jewish cattle traders and farmers continued to interact despite the growing threat from National Socialist violence, there is clear evidence that intensified political pressure had successfully eroded trade relationships. One of these sources is the account book kept by Andreas Auernhammer, a farmer from Oberhochstatt. Between 1924—the year we first have records of his bookkeeping in the family archives—and 1933, Auernhammer sold his large farm animals almost exclusively to the Ellingen-based cattle-trading firm Bermann & Oppenheimer. In March 1933, Auernhammer noted, as usual: "March 16, 1933: Sold to Beermann [sic] Ellingen. 2 Kalm[s] around 250 M[arks] received amt 21 head."[146] In June 1934, his entries changed and took on a cryptic form: "June 13, 1934: Sold to B   E   2 bulls 3 annually circa 15 hundredweight around 310 M[arks] amt 23 head."[147] For the first time, Auernhammer does not write out the name of the firm in his account book; as his son explained, he feared reprisals from the NSDAP if they got wind of the fact that he was doing business with the Jewish cattle-trading firm. In fact, in other localities, the municipal council had already begun recording on a special list the names of farmers still conducting deals with Jews.[148] Auernhammer, presumably so that he could protect himself against sanctions, left just enough space between the initial letters B and E so that he could have easily inserted the remaining letters afterward. The last note of this kind he wrote on February 19, 1935; thereafter, only the names of non-Jewish business partners are recorded in Auernhammer's records.[149] An August 1935 report from Ellingen, where the cattle-trading firm of Bermann & Oppenheimer was registered, confirms that the measures Auernhammer took were hardly unique: "Cattle sales to Jews are concealed for the most part[,] and one farmer doesn't trust the other."[150] Indeed, the growing level of mistrust among the rural population often led—as in the case of Auernhammer—to the dissolution of business relations between farmers and the Jewish cattle-trading firms they had long relied on.

The National Socialists' rigorous boycott policy was thus directed against not only Jewish traders but also those in their milieu. The policy defamed non-Jews who were still in touch with Jews or even showed solidarity with them as "national pests" (*Volksschädlinge*) or "Jew lackeys." Farmers who continued to trade with Jewish cattle traders faced public acts of animosity and being branded heretics. Like no other medium, the *Stürmer*, with its pornographic language, offered those interested in acting as informers the opportunity to participate actively in Reich-wide boycotts and thus in the expulsion of Jews from the cattle trade.[151] *Stürmer* boxes, which were set up in nearly every village to ensure free distribution of the antisemitic weekly to everyone, guaranteed that the paper's public defamations would enjoy a wide distribution. Although previous research has disputed the impact of such propaganda, Auernhammer's records unmistakably underscore his very real fear of reprisals if someone were to discover his ongoing trade relations with a Jewish cattle-trading firm.[152]

His fears were indeed justified. Every week, under the rubric "Small News Items" ("Kleine Nachrichten"), the names of farmers still trading with Jews were printed, along with their home addresses.[153] District offices used the publication of these lists to exert additional pressure on farmers and warn them that transactions with Jewish traders who had their commercial licenses withdrawn would be declared invalid.[154]

The overlap of complicity, denunciation, and economic trust was underscored by a report drafted by Commissioner Sägebarth, the head of the gendarmerie in the village of Geslau,.[155] In that report, he explains that farmers were avoiding business with Jewish cattle trader Gutmann in order to protect themselves against public denunciations in the *Stürmer*, not because they mistrusted him as a person.[156] Nevertheless, as Sägebarth notes in the report, farmers often harassed Jews, while Gutmann was forced to endure a great deal of mockery, "all of which he acquiesced to without contradiction" during his visits to the villages. Gutmann would then "go silent" when farmers explained to him that they were no longer allowed to trade with Jews; he would "skip these farmers for a prolonged period, but then come back to them again."[157] Since there were no non-Jewish cattle traders in the secluded farming villages, however, farmers renewed their selling to Gutmann as soon as the danger of denunciation faded—and so he continued to trade until April 1938.[158]

While these farmers refrained from trading with Jews due to the restrictions and fears of being branded as Jew lackeys in the *Stürmer*, they sought to maintain contact with Gutmann in order to sell their cattle. They were acting out of self-protection and economic self-interest. In this way, they were willing participants in the system of denunciations, and even if they did not benefit financially, there were emotional rewards from the schadenfreude of seeing a non-Jewish neighbor denounced in the *Stürmer*. These denunciations created an atmosphere of mistrust and suspicion among the rural population that the farmers themselves helped manufacture, since the public denunciation of farmers as Judenknechte can often be traced back to other farmers informing on them.[159] Ultimately, the boycott policy pushed by party activists was effective because the non-Jewish population cooperated.[160]

These denunciations also underscore the immense pressure that the National Socialists, with their threats of reprisals, exerted on existing trade relationships. One especially impressive source documenting both the extent of these denunciations among the rural population and the pressure public authorities brought to bear on the web of relationships between farmers and cattle traders is a card index from Rothenburg ob der Tauber listing the names of non-Jews and Jews who had behaved in a way that was deviant by the standards of the National Socialists' racist boycott policy.[161] Though we don't know who compiled this index card or whether the file originally included additional lists, we do know that twenty-five out of a total of fifty-six cases deal with farmers who traded horses or cattle with Jewish traders in spite of the vigorous boycott policy, a testament to the explosive nature of this issue for Nazi leadership. The lists included names of the farmers and their places of residence, as well as names of the Jewish traders they worked with—most of whom came from Rothenburg ob der Tauber and its environs. Even if the initiator of the card file is not named, in about half the cases, the names of the denunciators are documented. They included local farm leaders (the *Ortsbauernführer*, who represented the Reichsnährstand at the town and village level), the county leadership, and the gendarmerie. This is what would be expected for a public authority, like the district office, as administrator and initiator of the card file. Among the denunciators, there are two private persons in addition to the public authorities. One of these is "Aryan" cattle distributor Leonhard Assel from Rothenburg, who accused Wilhelm Gerlinger from Rothenburg of having sold a horse in September 1937 to his Jewish competitor Siegmund Wurzinger. So not only was public pressure exerted on the relationship between cattle traders and farmers by the threat of reprisals, but all persons and institutions involved in the cattle trade were urged to actively shun the Jewish cattle traders. The list of "deviants" and denunciators illustrates how the boycott was both publicly authorized (from above) and participatory (from below).

"Protective Custody" as an Instrument of Terror to Establish Personal Power of Disposition

Individual NSDAP mayors and Nazi party district leaders were also instrumental in driving Jews out of the cattle trade, and the murky legal situation provided them with a suitable platform to extend their authority.[162]

Gerstner, the Nazi mayor and party leader for the county of Weißenburg/ Bayern, was a key actor in this regard. The Ellingen-based cattle-trading firm Bermann & Oppenheimer served as the primary target for his violent attacks. Starting with the Nazi seizure of power, Gerstner used whatever means he had at his disposal to undermine this firm. Nevertheless, he faced several setbacks, much like his fellow Nazi mayor from Rothenburg.

Gerstner's campaign began in 1935, when he first tried (unsuccessfully) to deny the firm's co-owners a renewal of their commercial permit, but the attempt failed at a higher administrative level.[163] Furthermore, farmers who had long-standing business relations with the Jewish firm rallied in its support and, in personally signed statements, told the mayor that "they still want to continue concluding deals with the Bermann firm, as before."[164] Later, in July 1936, a statement from the chief constable of the gendarmerie at the nearby village of Ettenstatt highlights the strength of the farmers' trust in Jewish cattle-trading firms. In that communication, the constable reports: "In Ettenstatt there are still farmers who just have higher regard for the Jewish cattle traders than for an Aryan one, which is something illustrated again by this case, for otherwise Link [the farmer Christian Link] would not have commissioned this Jew [Max Gutmann, co-owner of the firm Bermann & Oppenheimer] for the purchase of an ox."[165] Since Gerstner failed to expel the cattle-trading firm using either legal means or antisemitic propaganda, he resorted to physical violence in order to prevent farmers from trading with Bermann & Oppenheimer. In July 1936, he had Gutmann taken into "protective custody" in the local district court jail, on the grounds that Gutmann had allegedly spread the false claim that Gerstner had permitted him to sell cattle in the village of Kaltenbuch.[166] Ten days later, Gutmann was released from custody on condition that he no longer set foot in the village of Ettenstatt.[167] In addition, Gerstner filed a criminal complaint against Gutmann in the Weißenburg district court, claiming defamation. The district court dropped the criminal complaint against Gutmann after he declared himself willing to publish a statement in different newspapers retracting his assertion that the district leader had allowed him to trade in the village of Kaltenbuch.[168] According to Gerstner's own witness testimony, a "cat and mouse game" had developed between him and the Jewish cattle-trading firm.[169] The more the co-owners of the cattle-trading firm, which had national operations outside of Bavaria, defended themselves against Gerstner's actions—and the more that farmers also expressed their support—the more Gerstner resorted to increasingly radical measures.

Gerstner and other municipal authorities continued to apply force against not only Jewish cattle traders but also those farmers who maintained contact with Bermann & Oppenheimer. In September 1936, the county office from the neighboring town of Hilpoltstein reported that farmers who continued selling their cattle to Jewish traders in spite of the massive propaganda campaign were taken into protective custody.[170] The report continued: "In the last several months, the political management for the county of Hilpoltstein has had to make a regrettable observation. The trading relationships of farmers with Jews [meaning the firm Bermann & Oppenheimer] have assumed such a scope that the political leadership has come to see this as an occasion for energetic intervention."[171] In order to take control of the situation and consider additional measures, the county office of Hilpoltstein summoned a special assembly consisting of the mayor, county and municipal farm leaders, ("Aryan") cattle traders, relevant civil servants from the district office, the rural Raiffeisen cooperative, and a representative of the Nazi party's agricultural policy office for the Gau of Franconia—all of whom gathered to discuss possible next steps.[172] In addition, the group compiled a list consisting of every farmer who wanted to sell cattle, so that a "capable cattle trader [could be] sent into the relevant community to buy cattle from the farmers at respectable prices."[173]

Gerstner's attempts to shutter the Jewish cattle-trading firm were repeatedly thwarted, so in 1937, he escalated his campaign and placed the firm's co-owner Bernhard Bermann in "protective custody" for 108 days. Gerstner used the pretext that in March 1937, Bermann had promised ten thousand reichsmarks to farmer Leonhard Hübner from Hundsdorf if the latter would murder Gerstner, the county party leader, and the county party chair, one Herr Maderholz.[174] Though the public prosecutor called off the proceedings owing to a lack of evidence and contradictory witness testimony, the *Stürmer* exploited the murder accusation against Bermann for propaganda on its front page.[175] Immediately after his release from prison, the sixty-five-year-old cattle trader fled his home in Ellingen and sought refuge with his daughter and son-in-law in Karlsruhe.

From there, he prepared his flight from Germany, and shortly thereafter, he escaped to London.[176]

In other places, the terror instrument of protective custody also served as grounds for denying a commercial permit. For example, in 1936, the city of Nuremberg refused to let Jewish cattle trader Rindsberg renew his business license because protective custody had been imposed on him in 1935.[177] Radical NSDAP county leaders and mayors alike used the terror instrument of protective custody methodically in order to force Jewish cattle traders to give up their businesses and abandon their places of residence.[178] This allowed local decision-makers to make considerable progress in their campaign to expel Jewish cattle traders. If the beginning of the Nazi reign was marked by violent attacks on Jewish cattle traders from Nazi party members or SA men, this new stage—starting at the latest in 1935—was defined by a municipal reign of terror. From this point on, local authorities took over from these party activists and harassed Jewish cattle traders by bureaucratic means.[179]

The Impact on Jewish Traders

The unresolved legal situation placed Jewish cattle traders in a contradictory situation. On the one hand, they had become pawns in the conflict of interests between district offices, county farmers' associations, and the district government, which had a devastating impact on them.[180] This resulted, as in the case of Ludwig Kohn from the town of Wassertrüdingen, in some Jewish cattle traders losing their means of subsistence as early as 1934.[181] Even if the traders most affected were those with a small volume of business, we cannot confirm Kershaw's assertion that, in Central Franconia, all manner of harassment (but especially the denial of business licenses) succeeded as early as the end of 1934 in driving out Jewish traders.[182] On the other hand, it was precisely because of the unresolved legal situation and persistent demand from farmers that Jewish cattle traders were able to practice their business up until the definitive occupational ban was issued for Jews in 1938. But the only ones capable of maintaining their businesses were the medium-sized firms and wholesalers who flourished before the onset of National Socialism and who, in addition, had sufficient capital and customer contacts, which allowed them to set prices without competition and prevail economically, despite the bureaucratic harassment and the boycott policy.[183] Admittedly, persecution forced even this group of relatively better-situated cattle traders to accept cutbacks, and sometimes they let staff go.[184] Nevertheless, the balance sheets testify conclusively to sales being made as late as 1937 and even to some modest increases in sales, as illustrated by the balance sheet of cattle trader Hugo Walz from Gunzenhausen. This is what his earnings were like between 1933 and 1937:[185]

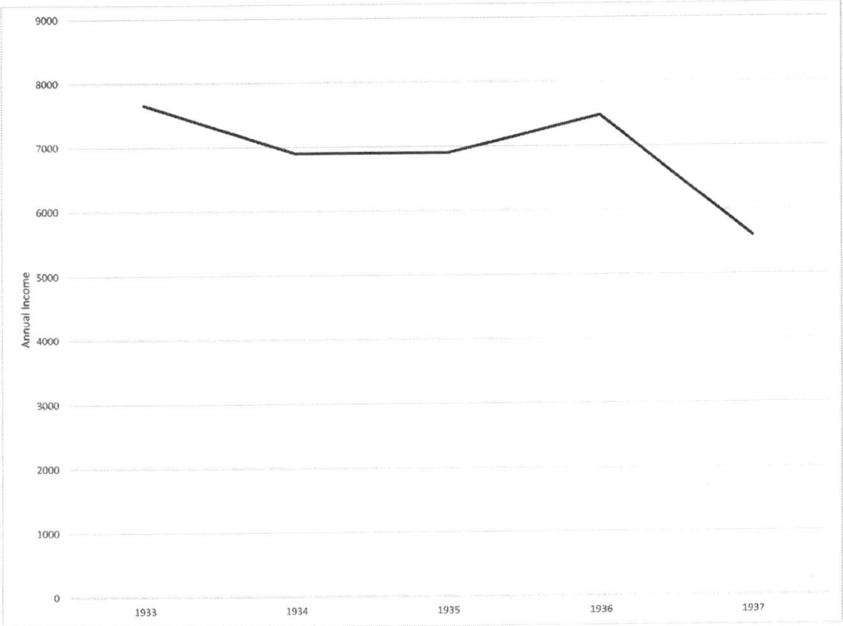

FIGURE 4.2. Earnings growth for Hugo Walz, cattle trader in Gunzenhausen, 1933–1937.

Walz continued to earn a steady stream of revenue between 1933 and 1935. In 1936, when there was an abatement of anti-Jewish policy during the Olympic games, his earnings even rose slightly compared to the previous year. It was not until 1937 that his earnings fell rapidly, yet he was able to recover them one more time until, in 1938, persecution become so severe that Walz was finally forced to give up his business.[186]

Nevertheless, this diagram of sales revenue should not obscure the abuses endured by the persecuted. Frequently, they continued to earn a living, if only "through increased commitment, flexibility, and creativity."[187] A glance at the income that Walz had earned from cattle trading and his real-estate business prior to the onset of the Great Depression in 1930 provides more detailed information about the impact of the Nazis' reign of violence on the Walz family's finances. Earlier records, for example, indicate that Walz generated an annual income of around fifteen thousand reichsmarks from his cattle trade and real-estate business in 1930. Though it is impossible to determine the breakdown between the two branches of his business,[188] by 1934, his annual earnings dropped from fifteen thousand to under seven thousand reichsmarks, underscoring the magnitude of the losses Jewish cattle traders were forced to incur because of the Nazi dictatorship.

Jewish cattle traders had little recourse in the face of violence perpetrated by fanatical NSDAP county leaders like Gerstner. Indeed, financial reserves and long-standing business relations with farmers offered even well-off traders little protection against these bureaucratic hate campaigns, which continued to have a powerful impact on rural markets for as long as the legal exclusion of Jews from the economy dragged on. In Central Franconia, too, the years from 1934 to 1937 were very much open season for the hunt on Jews, as historian Avraham Barkai noted.[189]

Preparing and Implementing the Occupational Ban

By the end of 1936, the Reich had secured full employment and the Olympic Games in Berlin had ended, prompting the Nazi government to begin planning the "de-Judaization of the German economy." Implementation of the plan was in full swing by the end of the following year.[190] In this way, the Nazi regime resumed its goal of expelling Jews from the economy—a pursuit it had postponed, albeit briefly, in the autumn of 1935. By late 1937, the regime prepared restrictions on Jewish occupational and business activity along with other economic measures.[191] At the same time, the agricultural economy was incorporated into the regime's Four-Year Plan; the aim was to enhance productivity so as to fit the farm sector into the impending war economy.[192] At this point, the Reich government began intensifying its nationwide "Jewish policy."

The Search for Opportunities to Exclude

The exclusion of Jews from the cattle trade, once and for all, was preceded by a series of directives that provided policymakers with a growing and wide-ranging set of opportunities to harass and restrict Jews. An ordinance for regulating commerce with beef cattle that passed in April 8, 1936, for example, declared that a simple warning from the livestock farming association, such as an accusation of price gouging, would be sufficient for a cattle trader to lose his commercial permit.[193] Jews were also forbidden from breeding livestock and trading in breeding cattle. Jewish traders were summarily given a message ordering them to delete records of their valuable breeding stock from their accounting books and instructing them that from then on, only beef cattle could be sold.[194]

The Reichsverband der deutschen landwirtschaftlichen Genossenschaften (Reich Association of German Agricultural Cooperatives) was concerned with the vacancy that would result from Jewish traders being excluded from livestock financing in the cattle trade. Hence, in November 1936, the association pointed out that in "excluding the Jewish cattle trade . . . the credit cooperatives would have to turn their attention in particular to the financing of breeding and domestic farm cattle purchases."[195] The relevant authorities in charge recognized that expelling Jews from the cattle trade would cause widespread problems, so they prepared the regional cooperative associations for this eventuality.

At the same time, the Viehwirtschaftsverband Bayern (Livestock Farming Association of Bavaria) placed the district offices on alert about implementing the exclusion of Jews from the cattle trade. In a circular, the association told all of the Bavarian district offices that "a regulation of farm animals" (the German term *Nutzvieh*—also sometimes translated as "productive livestock" or "domestic cattle"—refers to cows used for farm work rather than designated for slaughter) would take place in order to increase sales of beef cattle.[196] Since the livestock husbandry cooperatives assumed a key role in beef cattle sales, this regulation affected Jewish cattle traders only marginally. But, insofar as the effort to increase beef cattle sales was linked with a regulation reorganizing commerce in farm animals, the Livestock Farming Association was creating an ideal precondition for "excluding, on this occasion . . . all persons who, whether for reasons of unreliability or on grounds of national economy, have no business being in the cattle trade. . . . For the sake of verification I ask you immediately to send me a list of all persons who own a business license or itinerant trade license. In so doing, I simultaneously leave it up to you to name, with some brief information about the reasons, those persons who, based on your acquaintance with the circumstances, are to be identified as unreliable."[197] With this request, another step was taken on the path to a definitive occupational ban on Jewish cattle traders.

The reactions from county farmers' associations to complaints from "Aryan" cattle distributors make clear that in driving out Jewish traders, the authorities maneuvered themselves into an intractable situation. In order to compensate for the exclusion of Jews, the authorities desperately began soliciting Aryan cattle distributors, including even Aryans deemed unreliable. In other words, Aryans who had prior convictions were issued business licenses to trade in cattle.[198] By making an exception for Aryan traders with criminal records, the Nazi rulers revealed the utter absurdity of their previously established criteria for certifying reliability.

District Offices Push for an Instruction from the Reich Government

As these examples confirm, by the end of 1936, numerous public offices were part of a concerted campaign preparing for the expulsion of Jewish traders. Locally, municipal governments pressed for a legal directive that reorganized the cattle trade along racist lines. This push for legal clarification is reflected in the files containing complaints kept by local municipalities. In these files, for example, the category "*Jewish* cattle traders" is used for the first time on January 9, 1937, as the sole reason for rejecting a business license. On the same date, the district office in Uffenheim reported to the district government that the county farmers' association for Rothenburg ob der Tauber had refused to issue business licenses for the year 1937 to Jewish traders—without providing an explanation—and that there was also a lack of clarity about whether issuing a commercial permit could be denied solely on the grounds of "racial affiliation."[199] Shortly thereafter, the district office for the town of Scheinfeld asked the district government for a directive on the same matter, since it had learned that other Franconian district offices had already issued Jewish cattle traders business licenses for 1937.[200] The county farmers' association for Neustadt/ Aisch—in agreement with the Bavarian State Farmers' Association—favored the elimination of Jewish cattle traders in principle, but it nonetheless complained that this effort was difficult to implement: neither the county farmers' association nor the Neustadt/Aisch District Office had found Jewish cattle traders who could be labeled unreliable and who thus could legally be denied a business license.[201] The office expressed regret that the applicable regulations were still not providing any legal handle on this matter. Also, the district farmers' leader Spath's oral declaration was inadequate; he had affirmed that he wanted to assume complete responsibility for denying business licenses. Hence, the Scheinfeld District Office asked the district government for an urgent clarification.[202] Just a few days later, on January 23, 1937, the Scheinfeld District Office retracted its request for a directive from the government, because the county farmers' association for Neustadt/Aisch had been in favor of renewing business licenses for Jewish cattle traders, providing there were no grounds for refusal owing to a lack of "reliability."[203]

The situation, therefore, had become exacerbated at the lower levels of government. Local decision-makers urgently expected guidance from the Reich government about how to proceed. Guidelines were finally issued on January 25, 1937, requiring livestock business associations to issue a trade permit. This directive granted the district offices a wider range of reasons for refusal, since it required that all people working in the cattle trade be reexamined while simultaneously stipulating that trade permits were to be issued exclusively to people who had practiced as "reliable traders" for the last three years. In addition, the directive specified that "stateless proprietors" had to be of German origin.[204]

While this measure did not yet prohibit Jews from practicing the cattle trade because of their "Rassenzugehörigkeit" ("racial belongingness"), the renewed examination of all people doing business in the trade did bring an occupational purge. In addition, Jewish traders who had already been subjected to insinuations of unreliability because of the way that individual county leaders and mayors stifled them bureaucratically in the years before 1937 could now be deprived of a commercial permit solely because of a single clause (para. 3) in the new directive.

Nevertheless, the directive still failed to provide clarity at the local government level, since the decisive question as to whether Jews were forbidden to trade in principle remained open. This uncertainty was also reflected in the licensing practice of the district offices. While the county farmers' association for Rothenburg as well as the Nazi mayor of Georgensgmünd, Karl Minnameyer, used the directive as the basis to deny issuing business licenses to all Jewish cattle traders in the areas under their purview, the district offices of Scheinfeld, Uffenheim, and Neustadt/Aisch asked for clarification. It was unclear to them if this directive sufficed to prohibit Jews from practicing the cattle trade.[205] The NSDAP mayor of Georgensgmünd acted on his own authority. Only after the Schwabach District Office had directed his attention to the mayor's liability under civil law did he, at the last minute, issue business licenses to Jewish traders for the year 1937.[206]

Similarly, the Ansbach District Office denied Jewish cattle traders a renewal of their business licenses because of their "Rassenzugehörigkeit" —only to retract the decision after a series of suits filed with the court of arbitration, which instructed the office to hand out the business licenses requested by the Jewish traders "until there is a legally binding decision about the arbitration suit. . . . Apart from affiliation with the Jewish race, there are no grounds for refusal in the cases pending here."[207] Clearly, the directive of January 25, 1937, about trade with livestock failed to result in a definitive exclusion of Jews from the cattle trade.

The Erosion of Trust between Jewish Cattle Traders and Farmers

Although trade relationships between Jewish cattle traders and farmers came under intense pressure from all sides, they nevertheless continued until the occupational ban in 1938. Historian Steven Lowenstein described the process this way: "Neither antisemitism nor economic resentments were enough to stop the Jewish cattle trade, only action from above in 1936–1937 revoking the trader's licenses . . . put the Jews out of business."[208] This supposition is supported by numerous cases of denunciations, presented in the *Stürmer*, of non-Jews still trading with Jews. In 1937 alone, a total of twenty-nine people— including farmers, a non-Jewish cattle trader, an innkeeper, an attorney, and several cooperative representatives, as well as two farmers' daughters from the region—were denounced because of their dealings with Jewish cattle traders.[209]

These cases speak to the enormous pressure that the National Socialists, using threats of reprisal, exerted on the trading relationships that persisted despite Nazi policy. They also show how widely mistrust had already spread among the rural population. Jewish cattle traders and farmers adjusted to the altered circumstances they faced by shifting their business dealings from day to night and from out in the open into stables or the woods.

Several sources attest to these kinds of secret cattle deals.[210] Moreover, farmers later used their involvement in such livestock transactions during denazification proceedings after 1945 in order to present themselves as "friends of the Jews" before the courts. In 1947, for example, Ludwig Hüttinger boasted to the denazification court in Gunzenhausen that, despite his party membership, in 1937, he had still driven a cow during the night from Markt Berolzheim to cattle trader Bermann in Ellingen, thirteen kilometers away.[211]

As a Gestapo report from August 1, 1937, underscores, business relations between Jews and non-Jews were ongoing and widespread. Indeed, the National Socialists—in pushing their racist blood and soil ideology—encountered strong resistance from the rural population, as the records indicate. A Gestapo official complains, for example:

> These surveys led to startling realizations. They showed that there is still a large percentage of farmers doing business with Jews. Thus, among other things, it could be determined that, in the government district of Schwaben-Neuburg alone, there are still over 1,500 farmers with business ties to Jewish cattle traders in the years 1936–37. A cause given for this deplorable state of affairs is a lack of reliable, well-funded, Aryan cattle traders, so that the farmers are forced to conclude their deals with Jews. Thus, for example, the cattle trade at the market in Nördlingen is up to 80–90 percent in Jewish hands. But this is correct only in part.... The deeper cause, however, lies in the attitude of the farmers, which is lacking in any kind of racial consciousness. The surveys, which have not yet been concluded, are already showing that farmers, particularly in those regions where political Catholicism continues to hold sway, are so infected by the teachings of a pugnacious, political Catholicism, that they are deaf to any mention of the race problem. In addition, this circumstance shows that the bulk of the peasantry [is] completely unreceptive toward the teachings of the National Socialist worldview, and that they can only be compelled by material disadvantages

to enter into business ties with Aryan traders. For this reason, the Reich Food Corporation, Bavarian State Farmers' Association, has been getting reports about all farmers who are known to have bought from Jews, so that all the privileges of the Reich Food Corporation can be withdrawn from them.[212]

One of these farmers was presumably Hübner from Hundsdorf, who was in great financial trouble and was generally regarded as an alcoholic. Until 1936, he maintained close business ties with the Jewish cattle-trading firm Bermann & Oppenheimer in Ellingen, for which he occasionally performed small services like scouting out potential purchases or driving cattle in return for a tip. For example, Bermann would pay Hübner with a liter of beer for inquiring into a possible cattle deal.[213] Bermann also helped the financially strapped farmer as late as 1936, providing him with store cattle (young "feeder cattle" not old enough for slaughter) that he urgently needed to run his farm. These kinds of business relations were a thorn in the side of the National Socialist rulers, as a Gestapo report indicates. In March 1937, Hübner was offered the position of dairy supervisor, which seemed to solve his financial problems. Hübner immediately informed Bermann that "he [Hübner] will become dairy supervisor, and that it could harm him if he were to have one head of cattle from the Jew."[214] Even if the sources do not supply any direct evidence for this, the context points to the conclusion that Hübner was offered the position of dairy supervisor as a way of urging him to abandon his business relations with Bermann, which would, in turn, damage the Jewish cattle-trading firm. Hübner could only accept the privileges his new job offer promised by rejecting the Jewish trader, and in that moment, he opted for his own economic advantage and against the trade relationship with Bermann.[215] Personal loyalty toward Bermann or what the Nazis called "racial ideology consciousness" played a subordinate part—if it had any role at all—in his decision. That Hübner was always someone who opted for his own economic advantage may also be concluded from an earlier dispute between Bermann and Hübner, which had taken place immediately after the Nazi seizure of power in 1933. In this case, Hübner had issued a complaint against Bermann with the NSDAP county leader because of an allegedly high commission from a real-estate deal going back several years. Bermann had broken off trade contact with Hübner for about a year and a half after the complaint was lodged against him.[216] But since Hübner was in financial trouble and Bermann—presumably because of the way Jewish merchants were being persecuted—was dependent on trade partners of any kind, they entered again into a trade relationship. Bermann paid Hübner a small tip for different services until Hübner was offered the dairy supervisor job. At that point, both broke off business relations for good.

As the Gestapo report made clear, the blood and soil ideology did not end up carrying much clout among the rural population. In previous historical research, the phenomenon of farmers sticking with their trusted and familiar trade partners in spite of massive pressure from the Nazi party was mainly explained by farmers placing their economic self-interests ahead of the party's racial ideology aspirations.[217] At the same time, both Adelheid von Saldern and Robert Gellately underscore that this kind of "economic protest" can in no way be understood as a political protest. It was certainly possible to do business with Jewish traders and simultaneously be close to the regime on matters of substance.[218] Daniela Münkel emphasizes that the motivation behind the behavior of the farmers was not just purely economic; "the ties developed over the course of many years [were] also of a personal nature and . . . [were] not simply abandoned after the 30th of January 1933."[219] Since there are only a few sources that provide any reliable testimony about the "personal nature" of the relationships, the assertion is not easily verifiable. Rather, such ties rested on a relationship of trust that had arisen out of a mutual economic interest and was constantly reaffirmed through the practice of trading with each other. Economic trust can have a personal dimension, but it can also exist without one. Indeed, whether the trust that has been built has been abused is much more decisive for the relationship.[220] Farmers who continued to trade with Jewish cattle traders, even under the threat of National Socialist violence, trusted their trading partners—at least insomuch as these farmers knew that they could close a good deal with them. They opted to do business with the Jewish traders despite the regime's propaganda that depicted Jews, by virtue of their racial descent, as dishonest and untrustworthy. Certainly, many of the farmers mistrusted Jews more generally, yet in these cases, general suspicion was outweighed by a more specific trust in an individual cattle trader—trust that was, after all, required to engage in a risky business deal involving a living commodity. To be sure, farmers ran the danger of being taken into "protective custody," so their trust in cattle traders could come to cost them dearly. It is important to remember that farmers could also rely on Jewish traders' desperation to sell off their cattle, often at rock-bottom prices. To that extent, these risky deals—despite the danger farmers faced of being denounced—usually paid off economically.

Nazi files, including the previously cited Gestapo report, are limited in their ability to shed light on the kind of ambivalence—and nuance—that defined commercial relationships between farmers and Jewish traders. Indeed, a broader range of sources, including statements from Jews themselves, show that farmers continued trading with Jewish cattle traders but that many also single-handedly used force against traders. During cattle purchases in farming villages, Jewish traders ran the danger of being humiliated, cursed, or even physically attacked by local residents. This kind of violence is confirmed by a report from Alfred Eckmann, who was still buying cattle in peasant villages in 1935. As he testified in 1956, "Moreover, when I went buying in the vicinity of Burghaslach, I was seriously threatened by an inflamed populace. I recall an incident in Reichmannsdorf near Burghaslach, where I was ambushed by a crowd of Nazis, and my bicycle, which I used while shopping, [was] taken away from me."[221] Reports like this reflected the inflamed antisemitic mood in the region. Even if Jewish cattle traders were able to conduct an occasional deal, they were constantly subjected to hostile actions, including from farmers. Indeed, these attacks took place not only on their business routes but also in their private homes, as cattle trader Jonas Kahn attested in a March 1937 criminal complaint reported to the gendarmerie station in Markt Berolzheim. According to the complaint, boys from the Hitler Youth threw excrement on the windowpane of cattle trader Siegfried Schönwalter, tore down a wire screen from another windowpane belonging to cattle trader Jonas Kahn, and smashed more windows in other Jewish houses.[222] Attacks like this were directed against not only the residential property of Jewish merchants but every aspect of their daily life.

An examination of farmers' behavior in debt-relief proceedings, as well as their reactions to requests for payment made by Jewish cattle traders, provides an additional indication of their participation in the ostracizing of Jewish cattle traders. Several farmers exploited the predicament of the persecuted by refusing to settle their debts, which they knew state authorities would allow to go unpunished. In the previously cited Gestapo report from 1937, the NSDAP official writes "that farmers, particularly in those regions where political Catholicism continues to hold sway, are so infected by the teachings of a pugnacious, political Catholicism, that they are deaf to any mention of the race problem."[223] It might be concluded from this statement that Catholic farmers participated less in the exploitation of Jewish cattle traders than their Protestant counterparts. In fact, the persecution of the Jewish population in mostly Catholic as opposed to mostly Protestant areas did take place with varying degrees of severity.[224] In Catholic regions in particular, as in Swabia or Upper Bavaria, radical Nazi antisemitism was barely able to latch on to traditional antisemitic currents in the population. There, initially, a harsh antisemitic agitation—of the kind that was on the agenda in Central Franconia starting in 1933, at the latest—was even rejected by some segments of the population.[225] In Catholic regions, where the party's roots were not so deep, the Jewish population enjoyed protection from individual acts of terror somewhat longer.[226]

Nevertheless, both Catholic and Protestant debtors enriched themselves by refusing to repay their debts to Jewish creditors, as indicated by numerous debtors' lists kept by Jewish cattle traders whose *medienes* (sales territories) included majority-Catholic areas. Siegfried Weinmann from Treuchtlingen, for example, named twenty-six farmers from southwestern Central Franconia and Upper and Lower Bavaria in complaints about nonrepayment—sometimes of very high sums—proceeding from cattle deals.[227] Eleven of the twenty-six farmers came from Catholic areas, compared to six from Protestant areas; for the remaining nine debtors, there was either no indication of their home or, given the denominational mix of the population, no determination could be made.[228] A similar picture emerges from an analysis of the mediene covered by cattle trader Louis Feldmann from Nuremberg, whose trading region lay in a mixed-denomination area. A majority of Feldmann's debtors (numbering thirteen, or 62%) came from Catholic localities, and only three (or 14%) from Protestant communities. In the case of five debtors, no determination could be made about their denominational affiliation owing to the mixed-denomination character of the town.[229] Another picture emerged from an examination of the forty-two debtors listed by brothers Salomon and Hugo Walz from Gunzenhausen in their reparations files.[230] The two brothers traded in a largely Protestant area; overall, 55 percent of their debtors could be clearly assigned to Protestant districts and just 7 percent to Catholic districts, while the remaining 38 percent could not be determined.

Indeed, both Catholic and Protestant farmers owed considerable sums to Jewish cattle traders, aggravating their plight. The three cattle traders had similarly sized businesses prior to 1933, so the debt figures allow us to extrapolate about the payment habits of the population more generally. The number of debtors owing money to the Walz brothers is particularly significant. Forty-two farmers from a predominantly Protestant region owed a total of 75,084.95 reichsmarks in debts to Hugo and Salmon Walz, who were cheated out of their claims on this sum. Although a large number of Catholic farmers were in debt to Weinmann and Feldmann, the total number of their debtors (twenty-six for Weinmann, twenty-one for Feldmann) was still half the number of those owing money to the Walz brothers. It is therefore reasonable to suspect that the population in majority-Catholic regions was less inclined to enrich itself at the expense of Jewish victims of the cattle trade.[231]

Debt collection, moreover, was associated with a variety of risks, and some farmers used violence to prevent cattle traders from calling in their debts.[232]

Cattle traders, as a result, ran the danger of being chased off the farm by a peasant threatening to beat them.[233] Non-Jewish employees, attorneys, and even a farmer in one case helped Jewish cattle traders call in their claims. This was an extremely risky undertaking, as demonstrated by a case from the town of Markt Berolzheim, where a non-Jewish farmer recovered debts in the name of a Jewish cattle trader who had already emigrated—and was soon after taken into police custody for several days on a charge of "brazenness."[234] In 1937, non-Jewish attorney Dr. Bayer from Ansbach, who was also collecting on behalf of his Jewish client Theodor Mann, was even accused in the *Stürmer* of being a Jew lackey because of his efforts.[235]

Furthermore, farmers who failed to settle their debts did not fear criminal proceedings, as Bayer confirmed: "In general, propaganda was made saying that farmers no longer had to [re]pay any debts to Jews, since these debts were canceled."[236] Even if it went against the prevailing mood in the countryside to do so, Jewish cattle traders were not deterred from calling on farmers to settle their debts, as the county farmers' association for Weißenburg/Bayern was still reporting in May 1939: "Jews who still have claims on different farmers are now becoming pushy and, to some extent, they are moving ahead with coercive measures."[237]

This makes it clear that simply looking at Nazi party accounts, like the Gestapo report, does not provide a complete picture about farmers' behavior toward Jewish cattle traders. The large number of farmers who were no longer repaying their debts emphasizes their participation in the economic plundering of the cattle-trading families.

The Final Occupational Ban and Aryanization of Jewish Firms

On July 6, 1938, a new national law prohibited Jews throughout the Reich from peddling and practicing their trade outside the locality where they resided. Though this officially put an end to the cattle trade for Jews,[238] individual district offices were still issuing trade permits to Jewish traders at the start of 1938, including even the Ansbach District Office, where the crackdown had been especially radical.[239] At this point, the Livestock Farming Association of Bavaria pushed to have the authorities, including the district and trade offices as well as the Bavarian State Farmers' Association, exclude the approximately three hundred "non-Aryan cattle distributors" from the cattle trade for good.[240] In addition, the mayor of Nuremberg supported the initiative of the Livestock Farming Association. In a letter to the Ansbach District Office from March 1938, he demanded: "In agreement with the Gau leadership of the NSDAP, the Secret State Police [Gestapo]—Nuremberg/Fürth police station—regarded the Jews, owing to their membership in the Jewish race, as politically unreliable. In general, due to this opinion, no business licenses will be issued to Jews by the Nuremberg city administration at this time."[241] With this initiative, the NSDAP Gau leadership in Franconia assumed overall control of the expulsion of Jews from the cattle trade, as a summons from the Nazi Gau leadership to the Lauf/Pegnitz District Office further substantiates. Under pressure from the NSDAP Gau leadership, Jewish cattle trader Sommerich was deprived of the business license he had just received under the pretext that he had indecently assaulted an underage girl. Although the charge had to be withdrawn for lack of evidence, Sommerich was nonetheless forced to give up his business as a cattle trader because of the Reich law passed soon after in July 1938.[242]

As early as January 1938, there were no remaining Jewish cattle traders in other parts of Central Franconia. The county farmers' association for Weißenburg/Bayern boasted:

> Up to the present day there is not a single Jew in residence in the area of the district farmers' association for whom the issuance of a business license for trading with cattle has been approved. The Weißenburg County Farmers' Association did everything it could to enlighten farmers about the Jewish question. There certainly is not a single local farmers' association anywhere today where you cannot find many copies of the *Stürmer* being read, and so I also believe this enlightenment will result in the rural population coming to its senses and no longer, of its own accord, doing any more business with the Jew. I would only hope that the fight against the Jews gets underway in the other county farmers' associations the way it has been going in the case in the Franconian county farmers' associations.[243]

It is impossible to ascertain just how many cattle traders were forced to give up their firms even before the July 1938 occupational ban, since many postwar reparations files did not include precise information. Indeed, sometimes these files included only the date of emigration or departure from the hometown residence, which did not necessarily coincide with the date when the business was abandoned, since victims of persecution who forcibly abandoned their businesses often continued to live in their homes, albeit in poverty, until the opportunity to flee the country arose. At any rate, in forty cases, it was possible to make inquiries into the exact date when the business was abandoned, and the data can be broken down as follows:

From the data in this chronology of closures, it emerges that over 60 percent of cattle-trading firms gave up their business operations in 1937 and 1938. This confirms the conclusion that nearly two-thirds of Jewish cattle traders,

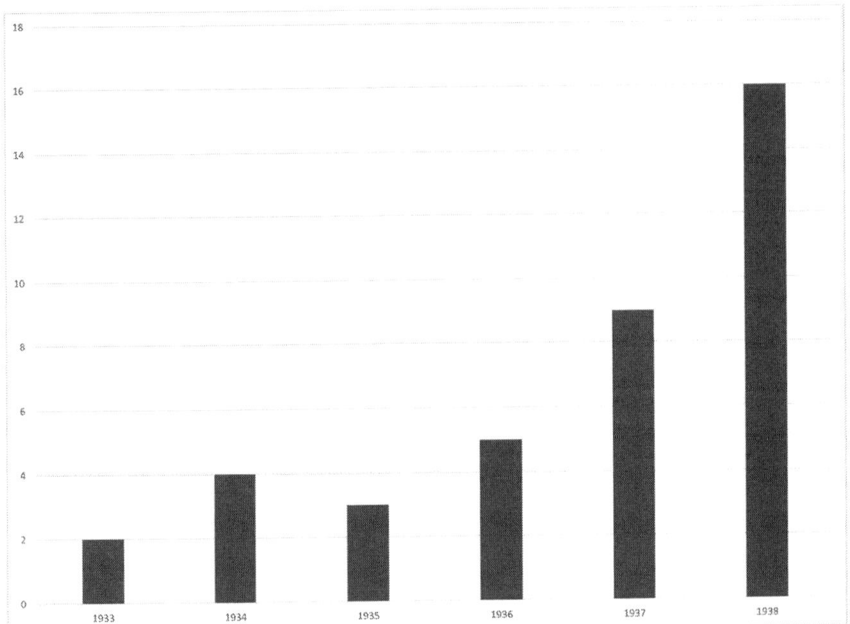

FIGURE 4.3. Chronology of thirty-nine business deregistrations in Central Franconia, 1933–1938.

because of the unresolved legal situation and the traders' ongoing economic relations with farmers, continued doing business until the occupational ban was enacted.[244] This finding is also reinforced by Maren Janetzko's detailed study about the "Aryanization" of small and medium-sized business firms in Bavaria. For the town of Gunzenhausen, Janetzko demonstrates that 59 percent of all Jewish businesses during the same time period were either liquidated or Aryanized.[245]

Nevertheless, though Aryanization in textile stores and restaurants was common, this was not the case in the cattle business; through 1938, there was not a single case of Aryanization, meaning that a Jewish trader might have been forced to transfer his business to an Aryan counterpart.[246] One explanation is that the cattle-trading businesses had no purely material value that could have been sold, since goodwill was not transferable. The value of a cattle-trading business depended much more on the cattle trader himself and the relationships he established with his customers.[247] A relationship of trust could not be sold or Aryanized. The dissolution of these businesses first started with the definitive occupational ban. In the cattle trade, there was no search for Aryan buyers; instead, as early as the beginning of 1933, Aryan cattle distributors were installed in opposition to Jewish cattle traders. As the example of the register compiled for the Ansbach District Office shows, the names of butchers and pub owners were deliberately placed on this register in order to raise (at least in purely quantitative terms) the number of Aryan cattle distributors available. There is testimony about this process from two contemporary witnesses, who said the following:

> Oliver G.: "And then these Christian-Jews, as we called them, came along."
> Kurt B.: "Then the uncircumcised came along."
> Oliver G.: "That was the butchers, the pub owners, they were the cattle traders then, they had a pub and a cattle trade, but no wholesale business— like the Behrs."
> Kurt B.: "And then there were the livestock husbandry cooperatives, like Fritz [last name unclear]; he was the one who made purchases for the livestock husbandry cooperative, and then it came to Nuremberg."
> Oliver G.: "They then bought the critters together, or brought them to the slaughterhouse in Nuremberg on commission, that was what happened after [the Jews were expelled from the livestock business]."[248]

In fact, the livestock husbandry cooperative pushed by the Reichsnährstand was able to more than triple the number of its deliveries between 1933 and 1939.[249] Only by the autumn of 1938 do we first have demonstrable evidence of forced sell-offs in which a non-Jewish buyer took over the business and property of a Jewish cattle trader. These buyers might be independent cattle traders, like Assel, who acquired the firm of the Mann brothers in Rothenburg for a price well under its actual value. Other frequent buyers included herdsmen who took over the firm of their former boss, such as Anton Schwarz, who followed in the footsteps of the cattle-trading firm Bermann & Oppenheimer in Ellingen.[250]

It is impossible to generalize about the ways in which the (compulsory) sales took place. According to verifiable records, some residential and business offices took place at a "fair" market price, while others were sold for well below the property's actual value. To be sure, the record shows that the degree of persecution in any given town or region was not of necessity reflected in the degree of Aryanization.[251]

The aim of National Socialist policy was to purge the cattle trade of "untrustworthy" elements in order to make it "honorable" and "reliable" under racist auspices. That this racist policy hardly succeeded in making relations between farmers and "Aryan" cattle traders run more smoothly, however, is indicated by the numerous complaints farmers made about the dishonorable business practices of Aryan cattle distributors. One of these complaints came from farmer and pub owner Hans Hofmann from Forth, who lodged a complaint in January 1938 against Aryan cattle distributor Heinrich Gollwitzer before the county farmers' association of Nuremberg. Hofmann maintained that in August 1937, Gollwitzer had sold him a cow that he had promised was a young cow that had calved only twice and was purportedly providing eighteen liters of milk daily. But after buying the cow, and much to the farmer's disappointment, he soon realized that she had calved not twice but eight times and provided only five liters of milk instead of the promised eighteen. On top of that, the cow suffered from rheumatism and could not even be used as a draft animal.[252] Hofmann's complaint was not isolated. The relationship between farmers and the Aryan cattle distributors remained strained, and the cattle trade had by no means become more honorable.[253] One contemporary witness described the Aryan cattle distributors in his own words (apparently unable to avoid alloying his ironic comment with an antisemitic stereotype): "O, the uncircumcised Jews [were] worse than the circumcised ones."[254]

Broken Trust: Robbing and Plundering Trusted Trade Partners

Once the occupational ban was enacted, the last Jewish cattle-trading families still living in Franconia tried to find refuge either in the next largest city or abroad. Nationwide, we have records of early "Aryanizations"—forced sales in which individual Jewish owners were compelled to dispose of their remaining property by handing them over to non-Jewish buyers—starting in the spring of 1938. These early Aryanizations culminated in the Aryanizations following the November pogrom of 1938, when all remaining Jewish businesses were transferred to Aryan owners. Numerous non-Jewish neighbors enriched themselves at the expense of the persecuted, who were in dire straits, by acquiring Jewish property at prices well below their actual value. These forced sales were the ultimate confirmation of the ways in which economic trust in a trading partner was ultimately broken. Once it became clear that Jewish cattle traders had lost their economic function as middle-class businessmen during the course of their persecution, they had nothing to offer farmers from an economic perspective other than their worldly possessions. The bonds of trust had been irrevocably shattered.

Antisemitic Violence in the Spring and Late Summer of 1938

The events related to the Anschluss (annexation) of Austria and the Sudeten crisis ushered in the end of Jewish life in the region. By the spring of 1938, the remnants of the Jewish population had been pressured into selling their remaining property, both private and congregational, to non-Jews or to the rural communities themselves. There are several recorded cases of compulsory sales from this period. In one instance, cattle trader Falk Stern from Leutershausen was forced as early as April 1938 to sell his property—consisting of a home, barn, stable, pigpens, horse shed, and courtyard, including all the local grazing and pasture rights associated with the property—well below its actual value.[255] A similar case from the town of Altenmuhr shows the extent of the plundering. In July 1938, the mayor of Altenmuhr, together with local party officials, pushed Karola Thormann, the single daughter of a cattle trader, to sell off her family property at a rock-bottom price to a non-Jewish village resident.[256] The sale price forced on her was 80 percent below the original purchase price of three thousand reichsmarks, which she had paid her brother just a few months earlier in January 1938 and which was already well below the property's earlier market value. By the summer of 1938, the persecution of Jews made it extremely difficult for them to keep up their standard of living and shield their assets from ruin. As non-Jewish master carpenter Johann Horn confirmed, after 1933, it had become nearly impossible for Jewish residents of Altenmuhr to hire craftsmen for maintenance work.[257]

The early Aryanizations of Jewish property continued through the summer of 1938 and reached a final climax late that summer. The radical actions of local decision-makers made this economic plundering especially hard on the Jewish population by driving Aryanization to an extreme.[258]

A prelude to this escalation of violence came in August 1938 from the "Franconian Führer" Streicher, who ordered that the main synagogue in Nuremberg be demolished.[259] This action quickly found zealous imitators in several rural communities. In Ellingen and Leutershausen, Jewish residents were forced during the High Holy Days in the autumn of 1938 to sell their houses along with the synagogue for a few marks.[260] Such persecution did not abate even after the forced sale of Leutershausen's synagogue. Additional acts of violence against the Jewish population included riots during October 1938, with local residents joining in. Along with the Nazis, they broke into Jewish houses, smashed household goods, and maltreated Jewish occupants.[261] In other towns, the Jewish community had already been driven out in September 1938. For example, the Jews of Bad Windsheim had to leave town on September 21, 1938.[262] In Rothenburg ob der Tauber, too, between September and October 1938, the city's remaining Jewish families were robbed of what was left of their property and banished from the town.[263]

Witness testimony from two non-Jewish housemaids who worked at the time for the Mann family in Rothenburg provides critical details that help reconstruct how this kind of expropriation played out. According to one housemaid's testimony, another antisemitic act of violence took place overnight between October 29 and 30 in front of the Mann family house. As Lisette Decker explained, a crowd assembled that night in front of the house and screamed: "Jewish pig, go away! Open up, you Bolshevists, you deserve to have your stomach slit open!" According to the housemaid's account, one of the Mann brothers called the police for assistance. Yet the state had long since ceased to protect Jews from assaults like this; instead, state power was itself a participant, in that the authorities were taking Jewish men into protective custody when they arrived at the police station. Around 1:30 a.m., the two brothers returned to their home, completely distraught but silent about what had transpired, which the housemaid concluded meant they had been mistreated at the police station.[264] The other housemaid, Babette Baumann, testified that the front steps and windows had been vandalized that night. A little later on that same night, local Nazi party functionaries Steinacker, Haberkern, Denzer, and Hitte arrived and forced Josef Mann—under the threat that he would otherwise be sent to the Dachau concentration camp—to sell his house to Aryan cattle distributor Assel. By morning, the "sale" was legally certified by a notary.[265] Subsequently, brothers Josef and Theodor Mann fled Rothenburg to Munich. Since they were already too old to emigrate, they were not able to escape the horrors of the Holocaust. On June 24, 1942, they were deported to Theresienstadt, and on September 19, 1942, they were transported from there to the Treblinka extermination camp, where all trace of them was lost.[266]

In the district capital Ansbach, too, the mood had already intensified, and in the weeks before the pogrom of November 1938, vandals hung posters on the exteriors of Jewish homes that declared, "Jew, get lost by Jan. 1, 1938!" ("Jud hau ab bis 1.1.1939!").[267] As in Rothenburg ob der Tauber, Jewish residents of Ansbach were robbed of their property before being driven out of town. On the Sabbath before November 10, several Jews in Ansbach were locked up in a bus until they agreed, in writing, to sell their houses for half their actual value.[268]

The threat to the Jewish population increased during those weeks in other places, too. As the case of the Mann brothers had already shown, the threat of imprisonment in the Dachau concentration camp provided local decision-makers with an instrument of terror to carry out their anti-Jewish policies. Consider the case of Philipp Wassermann, a cattle dealer from Forth. In September 1938, he was sent to the Dachau concentration camp under the pretext that he had spat in front of a Hitler Youth group. One month later, he was sent to the concentration camp at Buchenwald, and after he was freed in April 1939, he and his wife fled Germany for the United States of America. He was unable, however, to recover from the trauma of his imprisonment, and as his wife, Martha Wassermann, later testified in 1956, the experience of arbitrary violence and terror shattered him mentally.[269] Over the course of 1938, the attacks against Jews escalated, perpetrated not only by teams of SA men but also by local men, women, and children.[270]

Riots during the November Pogrom

The riots in the spring and late summer of 1938 had fatal consequences for the region. By late that autumn, ten of Central Franconia's twenty-two village synagogues, along with six of the region's fifteen small-town synagogues, had already been sold, damaged, or desacralized.[271]

The last remnants of the tradition-steeped Franconian Jewish communities were finally destroyed during the riots that took place throughout the Reich on November 9 and 10, 1938. The pretext used by the National Socialists for the state-initiated pogrom was the murder of Ernst vom Rath, diplomatic secretary at the German legation in Paris, committed by Herschel Grynszpan, a seventeen-year-old Polish Jew. Shortly before the assassination, Grynszpan's family, along with about seventeen thousand Jews of Polish origin, had been deported to the Polish border by the Gestapo. Grynszpan's act provided the National Socialists with a suitable opportunity to provoke a Reich-wide pogrom. Rioters in Nuremberg were well equipped for the pogrom; weeks before, crowbars and rods had been ordered from a firm in Augsburg, and these were distributed on the early morning of November 10 to the Nuremberg SA.[272] Under the leadership of Joseph Goebbels, the National Socialists initiated a Reich-wide "unleashing of popular rage" that (in the words of one historian) marked Germany's "turn to barbarism."[273] It became clear that Jews in Germany no longer had rights or the rule of law on their side.

Across the Reich, the acts of severe violence that took place overnight between November 9 and 10, 1938, followed a similar pattern. In the early morning hours of November 10, rioters torched synagogues, vandalized Jewish homes, and humiliated and assaulted Jewish residents. Teams of SA men and NSDAP members organized these acts of terror, and in many places, local residents participated.[274] In the "city of the Reich party congresses" (the Nuremberg rallies), the November pogrom took place under the direction of the city's Nazi mayor, Willy Liebel, in what was undoubtedly the most extreme manner. Liebel bragged that twenty-six Jews had been killed in Nuremberg overnight between November 9 and 10. His boasts weren't entirely accurate; according to Jewish community estimates, at least thirty Jews were murdered during the Nuremberg riots.[275]

Extreme acts of violence took place throughout Germany at this time, and for all their uniformity, they could assume very different forms locally, especially outside the major cities. The devastation and abuse suffered by Germany's Jewish citizens over the course of these two days is far-reaching, particularly in the countryside, and much of how the November pogrom unfolded in Central Franconian rural towns is detailed by the Ansbach public prosecutor's office. In Markt Berolzheim, in the Heidenheim district, for example, the November pogrom is documented through the extensive witness testimony presented to the Ansbach public prosecutor's office in 1946 during the postwar denazification process. In 1933, this town was home to 1,025 residents, of whom 91.2 percent were Protestant, 6.3 percent Jewish, and 2.5 percent Catholic. At the time of the pogrom, just twenty-four of the town's original sixty-five Jewish residents were still living there. Indeed, two-thirds of the town's Jewish residents had already fled in the period between 1933 and 1938.[276]

The pogrom was set into motion on the evening of November 9, after Goebbels conveyed Hitler's approval of a "spontaneous outbreak of popular rage" to the party and SA leaders attending a meeting of "old party stalwarts" gathered at the Old Town Hall in Munich to celebrate the anniversary of the Beer Hall Putsch. At 10:30 p.m., Nazi functionaries began to phone local offices and issue instructions to destroy synagogues, homes, and businesses.[277] When the news reached Markt Berolzheim, local SA men and village residents, including master blacksmith Georg Bickel, set the synagogue on fire. Before that, the arsonists had dismantled the synagogue's chandelier and broken into an inn, Gasthaus Stoer. Carpets and prayer books that were still in the synagogue burned along with the building. At the time, a Jewish woman named Sofie Schönwalter was staying with her mother in the home adjoining the synagogue. As the two women tried to flee the onslaught of flames, an SA man named Georg Wurmthaler prevented both of them from leaving their home.[278]

Among the SA men who mistreated Jewish men, Johannes Knoll stands out for his extreme brutality. In his denazification trial after 1945, Knoll called himself a "Jew hater" and justified his attitude and behavior by saying that he had been fired in 1931 by Julius Kahn, a Jewish cattle trader he had worked for as a cattle hand.[279] In his appearance before the denazification court, Knoll insisted that his hatred was directed only "against the Berolzheim Jews." As he said in his defense, "I had nothing to do with the Heidenheim Jews."[280] Knoll vented his hatred toward the Berolzheim Jews, particularly elderly Jewish cattle trader Adolf Bermann, for whom he had previously worked as a cattle driver. When the SA troop forced its way into Bermann's house, Knoll slit open Bermann's money sack, which (more than any other distinguishing feature of the cattle trade) represented his purported economic power. Knoll proceeded to scatter money throughout the room,[281] and in so doing, he symbolically carried out the disempowerment of the Jewish cattle trader while also demonstrating that power relations had been turned upside down. As a former cattle hand who had previously been dependent on a Jewish cattle trader, Knoll could now exploit the Jews' disadvantaged legal position in order to avenge the personal sense of injury he suffered due to his firing in 1931. Bermann, who was sixty years old at the time, feared that Knoll would escalate his attacks and wanted to take his own life.[282]

By dawn, a growing number of people assembled in front of the burned-down synagogue. At the same time, SA men, accompanied by up to thirty non-Jewish residents, including children, marched from one Jewish house to the next.[283] In desperation, the Jewish population turned to the local police station, but the senior policeman on duty, Johann Bär, turned a deaf ear to any cries for help.[284] Indeed, state authorities had long since ceased their protection of Jews against violent attacks. The riots lasted all day, whipping all the town's residents into a frenzy. An SA man, Fritz Liebhardt, depicted the mood that day in a 1946 testimony to the postwar public prosecutor: "Oh my, that was a rebellious day, we just took our time."[285] The plundering mob "took time" to seize everything that was not nailed down, including the entire stock of cattle and fodder belonging to cattle-trading couple Abraham and Martha Löwensteiner, who, as they did every year during that time, had been busy storing animal feed for the entire winter.[286]

Many of the details from those fateful days are drawn from testimony provided by the non-Jewish population to the Ansbach prosecuting attorney in the immediate postwar years between 1946 and 1948. Testimony from Jewish eyewitnesses is more fragmentary, so we are forced to rely on the postwar statements from those accused of attacking the Jews for a rough reconstruction of events. A clearer picture of the events is thus obscured by the fact that during the denazification proceedings, townspeople under indictment often attempted to exculpate themselves by shifting responsibility for the crimes onto other people from Markt Berolzheim who had died in the war.[287] As a result, many of the details from the November pogrom remain lost to history: Did the cattle-trading couple Emanuel and Berta Engel barricade themselves in the dovecote of their house for fear of being beaten by Karl Loy, an SA man, or had Loy himself locked them up there?[288] Though the answers remain unclear, one thing is certain: the incident was unsettling and continued to affect the town deeply even years after it occurred.

The fear of death that gripped Jewish residents that night is best illustrated by what septuagenarian Mr. [Siegfried] Stern and his wife [Therese] did when confronted by an agitated crowd at their doorstep; terrified, they jumped out the upper-story window of their home. The old man broke both of his legs, while his wife broke one leg.[289] In this case, too, it could not be determined whether the Sterns were forced to jump out the window or had jumped as a way to escape further harassment and abuse. Several witnesses, however, confirmed that the couple lay bleeding outside their home through the following afternoon, lodged in the narrow gap between their home and the house next door. According to eyewitnesses, several people passed by the old man and his wife without offering them medical assistance or any other form of help. Only later that afternoon was a physician finally called to attend to the old man. The couple was then brought to the Jewish hospital in Fürth, where Mrs. Stern's leg was amputated. Mr. Stern, meanwhile, succumbed to his injuries within two weeks.[290]

As the riots drew to a close by the late afternoon of November 10, many of Markt Berolzheim's non-Jewish residents lined the streets, shouting and berating the Jews who were marched through the town to the nearby train station.[291] From there, the Jewish residents of Markt Berolzheim were brought to the court prison in Gunzenhausen, and the men were transported to the Dachau concentration camp. The next day, the women were allowed to return to Markt Berolzheim, but the local SA forced them to clear away the burned-out debris of their synagogue and clean the town's vandalized Jewish homes.

After the pogrom, the villagers, under the leadership of SA man Karl Loy, auctioned off Jewish communal property as well as some individual Jewish-owned private property.[292] The proceeds went directly to the municipal coffers. Friedrich Kirsch, newly married in 1938, told the Ansbach prosecuting attorney in 1949 how he profited from the auction of property pilfered from Jewish townspeople. The sale had taken place at a very favorable time for him, he said: "At the auction of fabrics that came from Jewish holdings, I bought a pair of pants as well as the inner lining for two horse collars for a total of 10.50 RM. I acquired furniture; it was only eight days ago that I had my wedding."[293] Furnishings and valuables belonging to Jewish townspeople were left utterly in tatters. Fields and meadows belonging to cattle-trading couple Emanuel and Berta Engel were sold off to a total of eleven families from the town.[294] The local choral society auctioned off, at the ridiculously low price of fifty reichsmarks, the piano belonging to Sigmund Schönwalter's family. It remained in use for many years after the Second World War in Meyer, the local restaurant, where it was used by the choral society.[295]

A similar picture emerged from reports coming out of the postwar prosecuting attorney's office about what happened during the November pogrom in other Central Franconian localities. Indeed, across the region, residents participated eagerly in these events. In the town of Burghaslach, there is even a verse of a rhyme composed by locals about the auctioning of Jewish property that has been passed down: "There was a huge sellout here in the last fourteen days, for the Jews had to wander, put their treasure up for sale."[296] Though the verse is short, it is clear that the auction lasted fourteen days and that—as indicated by the word *sellout*—the village population paid rock-bottom prices for the "Jews' treasure." The second part of the verse—"for the Jews had to wander"—expresses a passive perspective on what happened, as if the villagers themselves had no part in the expulsion. Indeed, the ditty creates a distance from the violence, as if the event was triggered and carried out by a higher authority alone. An additional verse from the rhyme describes the greed with which the village population participated in the plundering: "Early in the morning, late in the evening, the whole public crept around in the Jews' houses, there were chairs without legs, each piece of furniture had a hole."[297] This verse leads one to suspect that the other villagers were busily seizing every last worldly possession once belonging to a Jewish family, not stopping even at furniture that had been destroyed during the pogrom.

In many local communities, as in Burghaslach, what remained of property belonging to the Jewish communities was desacralized during the weeks following the pogrom. For example, the citizens of Gunzenhausen used the synagogue from that point on as a market hall; in other places, a public park with a playing field was laid out on the grounds of the burned-down synagogue.[298] In Hüttenbach, the pogrom was followed by a celebration that the village was "Jew-free."[299]

The November pogrom riots had a devastating impact on the Jewish population across the Reich. By November 1938, it was unambiguously clear that Jewish lives were at risk. The situation was summed up by historian Kurt Pätzold when he wrote that the pogrom marked "the transition from the National Socialist persecution of the Jews by way of administrative and legislative means to open violence."[300] In the days following, up to thirty thousand Jewish men were arrested and detained in the concentration camps at Dachau, Buchenwald, and Sachsenhausen. According to conservative estimates, at least ninety-one people were killed during the riots.[301] Jewish men who were carried off to concentration camps during the pogrom could only be released if they could produce emigration papers. Goebbels took stock and measured the economic damage that resulted from the plundering. The Nazi party leadership agreed that the Jews needed to be held liable for the damages inflicted. Indeed, they imposed an additional "penalty fee" (the German term *Buße* can mean both "penance" and "fine") totaling 1.26 billion reichsmarks.[302]

Flight and Dissolution of the Jewish Communities

Some Central Franconian local authorities, like the municipality of Pappenheim, had already declared that their towns were "free of Jews" (Judenfrei) as early as September 1936.[303] In fact, Central Franconia's rural Jewish population had already shrunk by 95.2 percent between 1933 and 1939 due to the intensity of persecution, which made this region a tragic front-runner among Bavarian municipalities (since the Bavarian average for out-migration was 41%).[304] The region's violence put enormous pressure on younger Jews, in particular, to emigrate. The younger generation had already fled from the countryside to the anonymity of the closest big city or abroad as early as the first years of the Nazi regime. For example, Theodor Mann's children left Rothenburg shortly after the attack on their family in March and April of 1933 and sought refuge from SA terror in Berlin and Munich, where they arranged their emigration to England and France.[305] So far, there are few precise details known about the course of the Jewish emigration and the distribution of Jewish refugees by type of population and occupational group. Nevertheless, it was possible to determine the year of immigration for a total of seventy members of cattle-trading families (men, women, and their children). Needless to say, these figures are not representative of the entire group, yet they do give an impression about the time pattern of emigration for cattle-trading families from Central Franconia.

A high proportion of these family members succeeded in fleeing Nazi Germany in 1939 (twenty-one people). Almost as many people (twenty-four) had already left their homes in the years prior to 1938. It was possible to determine the residence of 123 people in exile. Eighty-nine people (71.2%) found refuge from Nazi terror in the United States and an additional seventeen people (13.6%) in Israel (Mandate Palestine before 1948), while the remaining 15.2 percent were distributed almost evenly across the countries of Argentina (four people), South Africa (four people), and the Netherlands (two people), with one person each in Canada, England, France, India, Italy, Liechtenstein, and Uruguay.

Behind every one of these figures lies a harrowing individual fate, each shaped by an experience of humiliation, disappointment, and violence. What tipped the scales in favor of a decision to emigrate was usually the personal experience of physical violence, as Senta Bechhöfer, the daughter of a Jewish cattle trader, confirmed. She recalls how her father came home one day in 1934 distraught. A farmer had chased him with a cane after he visited the peasant's

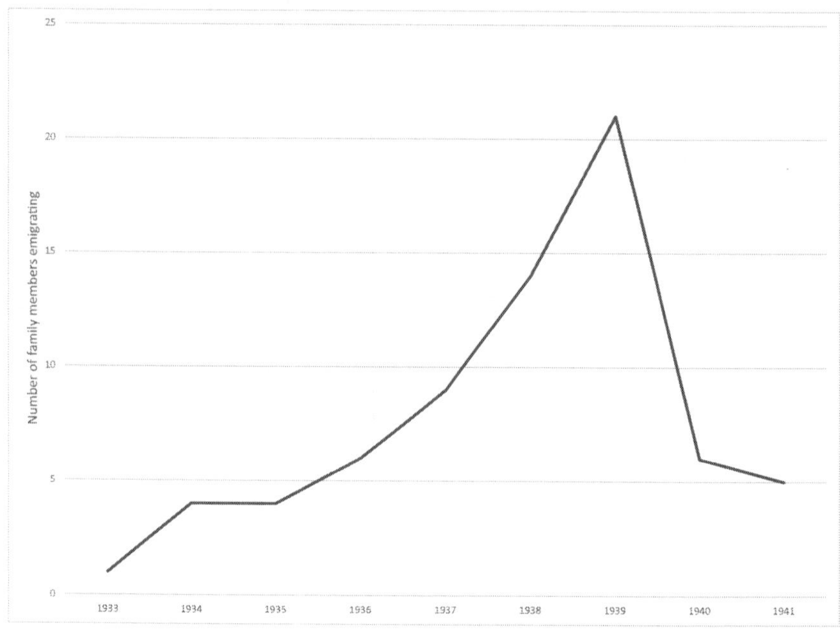

FIGURE 4.4. Development of emigration for seventy members of cattle-trading families, 1933–1941.

farm to purchase cattle. From that day on, her mother started preparing for the family's emigration to America. That same year, the family left Bechhofen for New York.[306] Like the Bechhöfer family, many Jewish cattle traders were forced by the severity of persecution to abandon their business and move to a larger city soon after 1933. A letter written by Rosalie Gutmann from Ellingen attests to the central role that religion played in choosing a place of refuge. In this letter, she asks the Free Association for the Interests of Orthodox Jewry whether her family would have access to an Orthodox religious community in Hildesheim if they took refuge there.[307]

Nevertheless, forty-three people did not manage to escape the Nazi terror in time. They were either too old to start building a new life abroad or could no longer obtain visas. Although they had all left their home villages in order to seek security in the anonymity of the big city—some as late as the days after the November pogrom—they were no longer able to flee the Reich. Ultimately, they were shipped either to Theresienstadt or to the extermination camps in Poland, where all trace of them was lost.

Continuity and Rupture in the Lives of German Jewish Cattle Traders after Fleeing Nazism

Jewish cattle traders often escaped Germany with little more than their lives and those of their families. Many of them struggled with the psychological, social, and economic repercussions of Nazi persecution. To this day, we know little about how the families of Jewish cattle traders carried on living after fleeing Germany and finding refuge abroad. So far, historical scholarship, which has elaborately worked out details of how German Jewish refugees influenced the receiving countries, has only given marginal attention to how Jewish cattle traders went on living in the various countries where they found refuge. We are offered special insight into this multifaceted history of Jewish cattle traders by documents from restitution proceedings in which many of the refugees, starting in the 1950s, discussed the background to their flight, how it proceeded, and what life was like for them in the receiving country far away from Central Franconia.

In their applications to the Bavarian State Compensation Office, the women, above all, depict the physical suffering inflicted on them by Nazi persecution. Frida Eckmann, who until 1935 had run a well-established cattle-trading business in Burghaslach along with her husband, Adolf Eckmann, managed to flee to Palestine. Upon arrival in Petah Tikva, the couple found it impossible to pick up where they had been forced to leave off and resume working at the kinds of jobs employing their previous skills. In this suburb of Tel Aviv, they were unable to establish their own cattle-trading business.[308] Frida and Adolf were only able to live quite frugally on their income as domestic help. In addition, Frida suffered greatly from the hot and humid climate in Petah Tikva. Soon after her arrival there, she was afflicted with a serious reactive depression. From a medical certificate sent by the physician treating her, Dr. A. Grotto, to the Bavarian State Compensation Office, we learn that Frida did not establish any "social relationships with residents because she did not know the language" and that she suffered greatly under her impoverished circumstances.[309] Adolf also suffered and was just as unable as his wife to establish a foothold in Petah Tikva. In 1958, twenty-three years after they fled Germany, the couple briefly returned and attempted to resume their old jobs in the cattle trade in Würzburg. They did not stay long; as early as April 1959, the two returned to Petah Tikva. The files do not tell us if political, economic, or social reasons were what motivated Frida and Adolf to leave Würzburg again. Nevertheless, we do learn from the compensation proceedings that Frida had to seek out treatment again in Israel for her psychological ailments. Yet even antidepressants were unable to alleviate her pains. On April 11, 1961, she took an overdose of sleeping pills, from which she died two days later in a nearby hospital.[310]

After she died, her husband carried on with his late wife's compensation claim; as a widower, he was eligible for payments from his wife's claim. Yet her husband was also rebuffed by the German authorities, since the Bavarian State Compensation Office refused to recognize Frida's suicide as a consequence of the suffering she endured under National Socialism. The physicians hired by the Bavarian State Compensation Office to render an expert opinion—senior medical civil servant (*Oberregierungsmedizinalrat*) and executive physician Dr. Maier and senior medical officer (*Regierungsmedizinalrat*) Dr. E. Hoffmann— argued: "Even if one assumes that there was a psycho-reactive disturbance or nervous condition of exhaustion caused by emigration . . . this was in all likelihood a temporary condition to be assessed as having subsided again after 2 years at the most (for the period 1939 to the end of 1941, one could assume a reduction in earning capacity of 30%);—then this could never be identified as the cause of a suicide chosen 25 years later. The question of causal connection between death and persecution must therefore be denied."[311] With this assessment, the two medical doctors rejected Frida's application for compensation for damages to her professional advancement. This meant that the Bavarian State Compensation Office was not only denying any right to financial compensation but also destroying any hope the couple might have had for some German authority to recognize the suffering they had endured because of their persecution and expulsion. Decisions like this opened old wounds among the persecuted and frequently exacerbated the very traumas that had been inflicted on them by the National Socialists.

In the files on compensation cases for the Jewish men who fled Germany, these kinds of psychoses as reactions to the experience of persecution and flight are rarely documented. This may be because there is, to this day, a stronger social taboo against men discussing psychological ailments. Whatever is not recognized socially was apparently also not raised in compensation proceedings.

Even if the sources frequently provided information about psychological wounds only indirectly, most of them do clearly speak for themselves about the economic damages left by the experience of flight and expulsion. Many former cattle traders in exile were not well placed to secure an independent economic livelihood, so they often lived in poverty. For example, the cattle-trading Walz family from Gunzenhausen started out in New York sharing a single room with kitchen privileges. Their meager income—derived from Salomon Walz's job as a delivery man and his wife's as a cleaning lady—enabled no other lifestyle.[312] Adolf Fleischmann, who fled Altenmuhr in 1938 for Chicago at the age of sixty-four, was no longer able to earn an independent income with his wife. In the United States, the couple was reliant on financial support from their son.[313]

The experience of economic downward mobility and dependence on family members or their own children was also shared by those who had found refuge in Palestine. Julius Eckmann from Burghaslach tried his best to keep his head above water with hard physical labor but ultimately failed to find employment in Petah Tikva. He testified about how he struggled to keep up his professional life in Palestine:

> When we arrived in Palestine, in September 1938, the country was in a serious economic crisis. There were lots of unemployed. I, at age 55, unfamiliar with the local language, was also no longer able to find a job in my profession or another trade. I had to look around for casual employment, which I found at harvest time picking oranges or in earth-moving operations when orange trees were planted. These jobs were only assigned to me as piecework, and this way, even when I worked more than others, I earned less than young people who were in better shape physically and had more experience.... Only after about 3 years, after my wife had recovered from a serious illness ... were we able to rent a one-bedroom apartment. Until then we lived in a shack without any sanitary facilities outside Petah Tikva and from which we had to walk to work or take care of our shopping on unpaved roads.... I was also no longer able to recover, have been completely unfit to work since that time, and I have to live off my wife, who works as a housemaid, and from the upkeep contributed by my sons.[314]

For Eckmann—who had always employed two workers at his cattle-trading business in Burghaslach, along with six to eight agricultural workers for his hop-trading business at harvest time and a domestic servant all year—the experience of underemployment and financial dependence on his children must have been humiliating.

We usually learn about the psychological damages inflicted on men by Nazi persecution only indirectly. Often it is the wives who speak for their husbands. From Rosa Schmalgrund, a resident of Uffenheim, we learn that her husband, Jakob, was not able to recover from the repercussions of their flight from Germany. Immediately after the antisemitic riots of November 1938, Jakob was placed in "protective custody," and then he was held for forty days in the Dachau concentration camp. After his release, he and his wife initially found refuge in Shanghai in April 1939. There, the two of them suffered from the subtropical monsoon climate and onerous living conditions. Rosa reports that her husband was kept under medical treatment in Shanghai for a long time; he weighed "only 70 English pounds, his weight was usually 1?o [sic] pounds."[315] Although they were soon able to resettle in Story, Wyoming, Jakob was never able to build a new life in the United States. He remained unemployed. His wife was only able to find work two days a week with a tiny income, so both of them were dependent for financial support on Rosa's siblings. Under these circumstances, Jakob died when he was only sixty years old. His wife held their flight responsible for his early death. Yet, in this case, too, the German authorities refused to recognize the link between such an early death and the experience of National Socialist violence.[316] Things went much the same for the couple Jenny and Hermann Bechhöfer, who had operated a securely established cattle-trading firm in Bechhofen. They could not manage to find a new livelihood after fleeing Nazi Germany for New York in March 1938. While Hermann did work for a few months in a factory producing venetian blinds, where he earned twelve dollars a week, this did not provide any long-term stability.[317] Just two years after his arrival in New York, Hermann died at the mere age of fifty-eight on December 4, 1940.[318] Bernhard Bermann from Ellingen, who managed to flee to London by way of Karlsruhe along with his daughter Bertha and son-in-law, also died at his new destination shortly after arriving at age seventy. To be sure, we will never be able to answer the question of whether men like Jakob and Bernhard might have lived longer if they had not been forced to flee. Yet their deaths shortly after escaping Nazi Germany speak their own language. Others did cling to life longer, yet for all their suffering, they never found the words to talk to their children and grandchildren about their life in Germany and about the pain inflicted on them there. Senta Bechhöfer's father snapped under the pressure he experienced from ostracism, humiliation, and persecution. At his place of refuge in New York, the established cattle trader from Bechhofen never again uttered a word about his former life in Central Franconia.[319]

In many families, the wives and mothers assumed the job of integrating into the new society and adapted more quickly to the new lifestyle and business culture of the host country. This was the case with the family of Henry Kissinger, who escaped Nazi Germany in 1938 and found refuge in New York. After the Kissinger family settled into their new home, an apartment in the Fort Washington section of New York, Paula Kissinger took up a job "as a cook at private parties, then established her own catering business." As Henry's biographer, Bruce Mazlish, concludes: "[Paula] was clearly the more energetic one by character. Her quickness and cleverness also stood her in good stead in learning the English language. . . . Clearly, it was she who became 'Americanized' first and most."[320]

The case files on indemnification that provide us with some background to these stories reveal not only how German Jewish cattle traders struggled to rebuild their lives after escaping Nazism; they also tell us something about how German Jewish cattle dealers continued doing business at their places of refuge in the United States and elsewhere, either as cattle traders or in related fields like the dairy industry. It is widely forgotten that many German Jewish cattle dealers retooled their skills by moving from cattle trading into chicken breeding, a business that allowed them to keep adhering to kashrut by trading in kosher animal products.[321] One of these traders was Ernst Gutman, who had helped his father, Max Gutmann from Ellingen, escape Nazism. Ernst first worked on commission for the Fuller Brush Company before moving on to the egg and later chicken business. Subsequently, however, he decided to return to cattle, the family business back in Germany for generations. Max, who left Germany in July 1937 and found refuge in New York, probably shaped Ernst's decision to make a living from buying and selling cows. In 1942, Max and Ernst founded a cattle-trading business in York County, Pennsylvania. These German Jewish cattle traders were probably motivated by caution in picking this site, since the farmers there spoke Pennsylvania Dutch, a German dialect that Max, who never mastered English, could easily follow in conversation.[322] Already in his sixties at the time, Max was probably too old to pick up English as a business language; he retained not only economic but also linguistic ties to his German background. Like many men of his generation, he never quite arrived either culturally or socially in the United States. His ties and sense of belonging there remained fragile for the rest of his life. Even Ernst had a lifelong habit of speaking about his time in the United States as merely a passing phenomenon, something he expected would end after setting up a new life in Israel (a move he contemplated but never actually made). When Ernst wanted to incorporate his cattle-trading business, he changed the name from E. Gutman and Co. to Logoor, Inc. The name of the business referred to the Hebrew expression *rak lagur* (found in commentaries on passages in Genesis where Abraham and later Israelites state their intention "only to sojourn" in Egypt while there is famine in Canaan), by which he wanted to express the wish to live just temporarily in the United States until he could settle more permanently in Eretz Israel. And yet Ernst celebrated his arrival in the United States annually with a barbecue on the farm, where he assured his family: "I'm only a guest here [in the United States], I'm only passing through." His feeling of only being a guest was also expressed by his voting behavior; although he became an American citizen, he never availed himself of his right to vote.[323]

But it was not only the cattle trade that Ernst "transplanted" from Ellingen to Pennsylvania; he also brought along the trust-building trade practices when it came to granting credit. Like their counterparts in Central Franconia, farmers in Pennsylvania were accustomed to flexible payment methods enabling them to finance a head of cattle. Ernst offered the Pennsylvania farmers a head of cattle on credit. A third institution—such as a bank—was not involved. Here, too, the sale of cattle was based on trust. Ernst's son, Abe Gutman, recalls how relations between farmers and cattle traders were negotiated without introducing a third party: "My father sold cows to farmers and financed them, charging them interest. . . . Back then, you never heard the word 'bankruptcy' in the countryside. If you signed a note saying that you owed somebody money and then you couldn't pay, you called and said, 'I'm short this month and I can't pay. Can we work it out somehow?'"[324]

Not only did the Gutmans relocate their business culture based on trust from Ellingen to York County; they also preserved their Orthodox Jewish lifestyle. York County, which offered ideal conditions for the cattle business, lacked a Jewish community and never really became home for the family. They built their house an hour south, in Baltimore, where they could live close to a Jewish community (the kind of place Gutman called a *"makom Torah,"* a vibrant Jewish center).

This division between work on the farm in Pennsylvania and Jewish family life in Baltimore has not changed to this day. Like "Opa Max," the Gutmans still commute from Baltimore to York County for work between Sunday and Friday each week. Max and Ernst's dictum remains as true as it was earlier: "As much as we feel at home on the farm, we would never be here for Shabbos."[325] Separation between the Jewish home and the cattle business continues to shape their lives. Preserving their Jewish tradition also meant observing daily prayers, something Max did to set an example for his children and pass on to the next generation. As Abe recalled, his grandfather prayed every morning in a minyan before starting work, and he ended each day with a prayer, even if he came home very late. Abe explained: "[Max] wouldn't eat until he davened Maariv [an evening prayer]. I took that upon myself, too."[326]

In his choice of clothing, Max picked up on the tradition of men wearing hats, something that made him recognizable as a merchant and simultaneously served as a religious head covering. His grandson confirmed how important it was for Max to be identifiable as a Jew while plying his trade: "Even on the farm, Max wore a gray hat or a smaller cloth hat, and dressed like a Jewish man; everybody in the countryside knew that he was Jewish. He said that a Yid has got to look like a Yid."[327] In his report, Abe does not discuss whether Max also experienced antisemitism while working as a cattle trader in the environs of York County. Even four generations after Max started trading cattle in York County, the business continues to thrive. Today, the Gutmans own four farms in York County, and on an additional farm in Lancaster County, they produce dairy products for the region.[328]

Between 1949 and 1952, Max, in his capacity as former co-owner of the Ellingen cattle-trading firm Bermann & Oppenheimer, wound up the firm's restitution suit with the German authorities. The other co-owner, Bermann, had already died in 1943 in London and could no longer be active in the proceedings of the firm. There are indications that, following flight to the United States, there were also ties to a third co-owner, Max Oppenheimer, and his family, but we know very little about this. Much more is known about the ties to Bermann's son Theo, who managed to enter Florida by way of Cuba. While Max and Ernst were building up their cattle trade in Pennsylvania together, Theo settled six hundred miles to the south in Florida. Within a short time, Theo established good relations with farmers there, as his granddaughter, Daphna Berman, recalled: "Though Bavaria is a long way away from Florida, Holsteins are Holsteins and farmers everywhere speak the same language. When he arrived in Miami, the area surrounding the city was still farm country. With an old pick-up truck, he slowly built a business buying and selling cows throughout the state."[329] Yet soon, Theo turned his back on the cattle trade and shifted to the dairy industry. According to his son, Theo never wanted to be a trader; instead, he always wanted to be a producer.[330] The fact that Jews were constantly portrayed in antisemitic agitation as useless traders who allegedly never pursued "honest" work but "only" traded may suggest that a kind of reaction or sensitivity to this stereotype influenced Theo's wish to be a producer rather than a trader. Essential knowledge about the dairy industry and milk production was something he could transfer from cattle trading. In building up his dairy farm, Theo got support from the Gutmans, who supplied him with high-grade cattle that he shipped to Florida by way of South Carolina. Since the Interstate Highway System had not yet been expanded for nonstop travel, it took twelve to fifteen hours for this kind of transport. The animals had to be unloaded and fed in South Carolina before they could be sent on to Okeechobee.[331]

Like the Gutmans, the Bermans down in Florida did not live on the farm. Most of the time, Theo commuted from his residence in North Miami Beach, Florida, a two-hour ride north to the farm in Okeechobee. Likewise, his son William spends much of the week on the farm, but weekends and Jewish holidays are spent in Hollywood, where the family has ties to a Jewish congregation, a shul where William meets with others for prayer to this day. Even in 2023, this is how William is running their farm, Davie Dairy.

While the Gutmans and Theo carried on in the cattle business on their own terms in the United States, others followed an appeal issued by the American Jewish Agricultural Society. In the 1940s and 1950s, this organization deliberately recruited German Jewish immigrants to settle among the small farms of upstate New York so they could contribute to dairy farming there. German Jewish cattle traders from Baden, Franconia, and Hesse who fled to the United States heeded the call and soon assumed an important role as lenders for the agricultural economy there. By the 1960s, nearly 90 percent of all cattle traders in New York State had a German Jewish background.[332] This is an episode in the history of German Jewish migration that still awaits a full-scale scholarly treatment.

In Mandatory Palestine, too, some of the German Jewish émigrés were able to resume cattle trading—or enter the related field of dairy farming—shortly upon arrival. For example, after David Levite was forced to give up his business in Dinkelsbühl in 1937, he used the proceeds to buy twenty Frisian cows that he brought to Mandate Palestine. The cows were his initial capital to start dairy farming in the agricultural settlement of Kfar-Bialik near Haifa.[333] To be sure, Levite soon had to supply himself with new, heat-resistant cattle, since the Mediterranean climate did not agree with the Frisian cows. Yet he did succeed in gaining a foothold in his old line of work. Another well-known example is that of Jewish cattle traders from Horb/Rexingen in Baden. In 1938, the local Jewish community there organized a group emigration to Mandatory Palestine. The majority of the refugees traded in cattle. In what is today northern Israel, they founded the moshav shitufi (collective moshav with some kibbutz-like features) Shavei Zion, using cattle from Baden that they imported especially for this purpose. Like Levite's cows, the cattle in Shavei Zion were unable to withstand climatic conditions in the new environment. Nevertheless, the cattle traders on the moshav were able, within a short period of time, to turn their collective into one of the most important milk suppliers for Palestine.[334]

The history of Jewish cattle traders following their flight from Germany was shaped by pain and mourning for the life that the National Socialists and their helpers had destroyed. Those who were able to resume their business as cattle traders in their receiving countries carried on the tradition of embracing the trust-building trade practices distinctive to the trade. Even in Florida or Pennsylvania, it was conducive to trust and therefore to sales when a trader held a pleasant conversation with his customers before getting down to business. In this way, Jewish cattle traders had a "significant impact on the societies and cultures of the receiving countries" as well as on their economies.[335]

As Jews were forced out of the cattle trade in Germany, non-Jews initially carried on the business with livestock. Yet the days of the independent cattle trade were numbered. In a process accelerated by National Socialist policy, the cattle trade shifted from being an independent profession to one in which livestock husbandry was organized by cooperatives—a trend that continued after the end of the Second World War. By the mid-1960s, there were hardly any independent cattle traders left in Germany. What has remained is the term *Viehjude*—"cattle Jew"—still used to this day among older farmers when referring to cattle traders, even to those who are not Jewish. This linguistic legacy testifies like nothing else to the deep roots of Jews in this field of business.

Conclusion

Though this study provides an in-depth look at the roles of Jewish cattle traders in rural Germany and how farmers responded to National Socialists' policies of exclusion in the years after 1933, it is also—in a broader sense—about larger trends of Jewish exclusion from the *Volksgemeinschaft* (ethnic-racial national community) propagated by the Nazi regime. Indeed, it is this dynamic of exclusion that became increasingly radicalized and ultimately culminated in the genocide against Europe's Jews. Inclusion and exclusion, however, are not topics that can be reduced to the National Socialist era alone; rather, they are themes running through Jewish history that assume different forms at different times and are always closely interwoven. As my studies have shown, both for urban and rural areas, the ways Jews and Christians lived alongside each other in the years after Jews were granted legal equality resembled a multilayered structure that oscillated between peaceful coexistence and social exclusion, producing the oft-cited German-Jewish symbiosis.[1]

Earlier works dealing with this subject emphasized the distinctive features of the Jewish population, such as a professional and residential pattern that distinguished them sharply from the general population. This pattern was said to demonstrate their exclusion from what has been called the "village community" ("Dorfgemeinschaft"),[2] or from what we might simply think of as the countryside.[3] An approach like this can be illuminating, yet it can also obscure our view of the opportunities for and limits to coexistence that ensued from this distinctive pattern. This approach thus blocks the way to a deeper understanding of the two religious communities' reciprocal relations. As Till van Rahden demonstrated with his concept of "situational ethnicity"—which he applied to the case of Breslau and coexistence among Jews, Protestants, and

Catholics there—individuals were constantly required to balance a variety of particular and situational identities.[4] One could simultaneously be a member of a Zionist organization (as an expression of belonging to the larger Jewish population) and the local rifle club (as an expression of belonging to the "extra-Jewish"—i.e., Gentile—population group) without having to give up one kind of membership for the other.

Until now, these insights have been largely overlooked in scholarly analyses of Jewish-Christian coexistence in the countryside.[5] Yet because relations between these two groups in small towns during the Weimar era were so particular to the rural condition, an independent investigation—one distinct from previous analyses focusing on large, urban settings—is essential.[6] Indeed, many rural Jews were still working in pre-emancipatory and stigmatized occupations. Yet the distinctive features that made Jews stand out from the general rural population, such as practicing a nonfarm occupation, did not always exclude them from the surrounding society. To be sure, Jewish cattle traders were blocked from joining many aspects of communal life in their villages because of their Jewishness and because, unlike many of their neighbors, they did not work in farming. Yet this did not stand in the way of them building trust in the economic sphere. Jewish cattle traders, by virtue of their conduct, demonstrated that they were "honorable merchants" and thus trustworthy businessmen. In doing so, they became part of a community of trust resulting from their trading relationships with farmers. Still, owing to their membership in another religious group, they remained excluded from parts of village community life. It was not only the case that an individual could develop a "situational ethnicity"; he could also experience either situational inclusion or exclusion. The development of a trade relationship or of situational inclusion depended on trust between the trader and the farmer. Both sides were equally responsible for building this trust. This process could be highlighted by a shift in perspective from the exclusionary to the inclusionary moments of the relationship. To be sure, the nature of the trade relationship was decisive for the successful conclusion of a cattle trade. Yet certain structural features, such as the middle-class character of the Jewish cattle traders' small and medium-sized firms and their businesses' links to the national railway network, also helped secure their business operations. In addition, the bourgeois furnishings used in their residential and commercial buildings fortified their position in the cattle trade.

Demographic and technological changes helped many middle-class Jewish cattle dealers develop small and medium-sized enterprises that thrived in the years before 1933. After the historic restrictions on Jewish residential mobility were lifted, for example, many Jews found themselves in a rapid process of urbanization that was in sync with such modern developments in the cattle trade as the expansion of the railway network. This means that the conceptual pairing of *Jewish cattle trader* with *rural Jew*—a coupling that, until now, has been permanently inscribed in historical scholarship—needs to be severed, as it ignores the broad modernizing trends in which the Jewish cattle trade was embedded. Indeed, Jewish cattle traders should be integrated into German Jewish historiography generally, as well as into both German agrarian and economic history overall.[7]

It is already evident from a simple analysis of Jewish cattle traders' residential patterns that many were no longer purely "rural" by the beginning of the twentieth century; while about half of the Jewish traders did indeed still live in small rural communities, the remaining 50 percent had already settled in small or medium-sized towns and large cities. And yet their place of residence is not the only criterion that should be used to measure their degree of modernization and disentanglement from old structures. Their businesses were also relatively mechanized, and many cattle-trading firms underwent a process of professionalization similar to that of other occupations at the time. It remains unclear to what extent an overwhelmingly Orthodox lifestyle and the low degree of secularization were responsible for Jews remaining in the cattle trade—or whether more economic factors might have played a role here—and answering these questions would require additional research. Yet it is clear that, unlike those pursuing "bourgeois" or academic professions, cattle traders were able to cultivate an Orthodox lifestyle that did not stand in the way of their trade or pose an obstacle to the formation of a modern entrepreneurial culture. To be sure, the term *Orthodox lifestyle* as applied to the 1920s hardly connotes strict observance of all Jewish religious laws; rather, it refers to an orientation around rabbinic tradition. By no means should it be understood as anything like Hasidic religiosity of the kind that was widespread in East Central and Eastern Europe.[8]

For many Jews, the ongoing demand for high-quality cattle for domestic farm use, slaughter, and breeding provided an external economic incentive to continue their traditional trading in livestock even after restrictions on occupational choice had been removed in modern Germany. So long as the motorization of agriculture was still in its infancy, the cattle trade remained a lucrative and attractive line of business. Those cattle traders who availed themselves of such modern means of locomotion as the automobile and the railway operated as middlemen who were providing farmers with a wholly unmodern means of locomotion—that is, cattle. In so doing, they exercised an enormous modernizing function for rural areas.

We need further research setting out to what extent developments and processes that were intra-Jewish or specific to the cattle trade were responsible for the modest presence of Jewish merchants among wholesale trade firms (see chap. 1 for more on what we do know about Jews' underrepresentation in the wholesale establishment). These additional investigations might also bring in the hops and horse trade for purposes of comparison or examine broader regional connections in a Central European context.[9] The modest presence of Jewish cattle traders among the wholesalers clearly differentiates them from the "Jewish economic elite,"[10] instead placing them squarely in the middle class along with the vast majority of German Jews.[11]

As our investigation into the changing role of women in the cattle trade has shown, adhering to an Orthodox lifestyle and remaining in a pre-emancipatory occupation hardly stood in the way of the Jewish cattle traders' partial embourgeoisement and, by extension, their partial assimilation into the larger society. Nevertheless, there were significant differences between the individual social strata of the cattle-trading families—differences that reflect specific features attributed only to "the Jewish cattle traders." The contribution made by women to the cattle-trading business was indispensable in the small operations run by *Schmusers*, but it was very much expendable in medium-sized and wholesale trade firms. This reflects not only a development within the cattle trade but also the interplay between inclusionary and exclusionary factors; while the middle-class cattle traders' wives were "allowed" to concentrate on household work in a way that set them apart from the wives of rural farmers who also had farm chores to perform, housekeeping simultaneously enabled these same women to become part of the small-town, bourgeois middle class. A sphere of domesticity was created whose boundaries were exclusionary vis-à-vis the peasantry but inclusionary with respect to the provincial bourgeoisie.

All these factors—being involved in technological developments, participating in urbanization, and conducting a (partly) bourgeois lifestyle—shaped a middle-class entrepreneurial culture that was typically German. Belonging to the middle class contributed decisively to the ability to develop a relationship of trust built not only on the traders' interplay with farmers but also on their interaction with the institutions and associations participating in the cattle trade. It's important to note, however, that owing to the small volume of their trade, it was almost impossible for Jewish Schmusers to become part of a community of trust. At the social level, admittedly, they might have been able to construct a relationship of trust with one farmer or another by the way they conducted business. Yet state authorities would not ascribe any institutional trust to them. As the analysis of the discussion surrounding the trustworthy cattle trader revealed, however, institution-based trust also had its limits. Institution-based trust could lay the groundwork for a trade relationship to start, but it could not reinforce or even sustain lasting ties. To be sure, authorities could identify a cattle trader as trustworthy, yet this did not create any trust between business partners. Transforming official trust into economic trust was the sole responsibility of the trading partners. This authority of this third, "neutral" party, however, did not have only a positive impact on the network of relations between cattle trader and farmer; the impact could also be negative. Farmers' associations and antisemites, for example, exploited economic crises in order to agitate against Jewish cattle traders. Nevertheless, the propagation of racist mistrust did not stand in the way of building trust between cattle traders and farmers, as demonstrated by the low level of popularity the livestock husbandry cooperatives enjoyed. The trust built up in the course of trading proved to have the most powerful ramifications.

Even if the findings of this study pertain only to a single region's social and cultural history, they are nonetheless representative. And while empirical findings from an examination of other German regions with similar smallholder agrarian structures may vary somewhat, the deviation from Central Franconia would be only slight. Indeed, the changes undergone by agrarian society in general and the Jewish minority in particular during the course of industrialization, as well as after Jews were granted legal equality, were apparent in other regions as well.[12] Moreover, earlier studies on Jewish cattle traders in East Frisia, Switzerland, Alsace, and Baden suggest that the evidence from Franconia about how relationships of trust are formed can be generalized, since the commercial culture of the cattle trade exhibits only a few regional peculiarities.[13]

Clear differences with other regions of Germany first became apparent during the Great Depression of the 1930s and the concomitant rise in support for the National Socialists that accompanied the global economic crisis. Here, the first ruptures in the relationship of trust between the rural population and Jewish cattle traders began to emerge earlier than they did in other regions. This process of erosion, however, happened in a way that was neither free of contradictions nor uniform. While, as late as 1933, decision-makers in local government had been wringing their hands in an effort to woo medium-sized cattle-trading firms, in 1930, Bavaria's state government had already destroyed the economic foundation of Jewish butchers by banning kosher slaughter. In social relations between farmers and cattle traders, too, signs of rupture were beginning to show up prior to 1933. Thereafter, these rifts became larger, although without abruptly destroying trade relations altogether. While economic cooperation between farmers and cattle traders endured after 1933, much to the chagrin of the Nazis, who by then had come to power, there emerged a fateful interplay between an antisemitic policy of violence that was Reich-wide and individual antisemitic actions at the local level. These hostile acts, sometimes vehement and sometimes more moderate in character, accelerated the exclusion of the Jewish population. The dynamic that became apparent here was a profound escalation of the tension between the "normative state" and the "prerogative state," to use Ernst Fraenkel's terminology.[14] The withdrawal of business licenses illustrates just how contradictory this process could be—and the kind of devastating impact this often chaotically organized apparatus of persecution could have on its intended victims. Until the Reich government completed the legal process of excluding Jewish merchants from the cattle trade, it was the antisemitic measures undertaken by local decision-makers that had the most powerful ramifications.

Initially, the commercial interests of the farming population seemed to be moving in a contrary direction. As noted earlier, this was not a regional phenomenon. Across the country, farmers held onto their trusted trading partners in spite of antisemitic propaganda. In the cattle trade, (farmers') economic interests sharply contradicted the Nazi rulers' racist aims. Historian Adelheid von Saldern concludes from this that antisemitism was less widespread among the peasant population than it was among small traders, who competed directly with Jewish merchants.[15]

But if one casts a glance beyond the trade situation alone to the way Jews and non-Jews lived alongside each other on a daily basis, it becomes apparent that the farming population participated in ostracizing and plundering Jews to the same extent as other segments of the population. The numerous antisemitic attacks that took place in the first years after the National Socialist seizure of power show that social trust between the Jewish cattle-trading families and the peasant population dissolved early, while economic trust (that is, trust in being able to conclude an advantageous trade) persisted on the part of the farmers. One could continue to do business with a Jewish cattle trader while simultaneously taking part—as a perpetrator, accomplice, or onlooker—in a parade pillorying Jews. Even a Nazi party member could do business with a Jewish cattle trader of long-standing acquaintance, no matter how zealously he pushed to implement his party's racist goals in other matters. Social and economic trust can exist alongside each other, but there is often a time lag between these two kinds of trust. To this it needs to be added that Jewish cattle traders' trust in their trading partners began to erode by January 1933. Beginning then, Jewish merchants could no longer trust that their debtors would reliably settle claims. But as the Bermann–Hübner case from Ellingen demonstrates, Jewish cattle traders also made a certain calculation by choosing trading partners who were dependent on cooperation with them.[16] (Bernhard Bermann stopped doing business with Hübner in 1933 after the farmer had reported the cattle dealer to the authorities over an allegedly high commission from a previous real estate deal. For several years, there was no contact between the two. But Hübner had always been struggling economically and was also coping with a drinking problem. So he eventually reached out to Bermann about the possibility of renewing their business relationship. Both men needed to make a living, albeit for entirely different reasons, and continued cooperating until Hübner took up a job as dairy supervisor.)

Whether Protestant or Catholic farmers took part to different degrees in the exclusion of Jews from the cattle trade remains an open question. As numerous studies on National Socialism have shown, the persecution and exclusion of Jews in the countryside was more severe in Protestant than in Catholic regions. Yet religious affiliation cannot be adduced as the sole factor explaining the degree of approval for National Socialism and the way the persecution of Jews took place in a particular region; religion was one factor among many.[17] Thus, the behavior of many farmers shows that, in the case of a conflict between their economic interests and their racist ideas, they chose in favor of their financial concerns.[18] Nevertheless, the question arises as to what motivated farmers to drive a cow for a Jewish cattle trader from one farm to the next when they ran the danger of being denounced or even taken into protective custody. In cases like these, it seemed as if social motives, not just economic ones, shaped the conduct of these actors. The trust that developed out of an economic interest had apparently broadened to include a social component that facilitated the ability of both trading partners to transcend the boundaries drawn by racism. Here, the unachievable character of the *Volksgemeinschaft*—the racial national community propagated by the National Socialists as an absolute ideal—comes to light most starkly.

This study's findings thus emphasize the impact of the process-based trust that had developed between cattle traders and farmers. In a high-risk business like the cattle trade, this type of trust is stronger than that which is institution-based and only established contingently. This can also be seen in the attempt of the National Socialists to withdraw institution-based trust from Jewish cattle traders by implementing a racist economic policy. Although the Nazi rulers attempted with all the means at their disposal to push Jews out of the cattle trade, commercial relations with farmers persisted. Economic trust can prove to be lasting even when underlying conditions have radically changed. That the relations of trust between Jewish cattle traders and non-Jewish farmers persisted even under the influence of antisemitic violence shows the great importance of Jewish cattle traders for agrarian society in the early twentieth century. As American cattle trader Abe Gutman, grandson of the Jewish cattle trader Max Gutmann from Ellingen, put it when asked about the secret to his own successful livestock trading company in Baltimore, Maryland: "You know, the cattle business: it's all about trust."[19]

NOTES

Introduction

1. "Bericht der Polizeistation Heidenheim" ["Report from Heidenheim Police Station"], 15 November 15, 1934, in Staatsarchiv Nürnberg (StAN), BA Gunzenhausen 4241, cited by Ian Kershaw, "Antisemitismus und Volksmeinung: Reaktionen auf die Judenverfolgung," in Martin Broszat and Elke Fröhlich (eds.), Bayern in der NS-Zeit: Herrschaft und Gesellschaft im Konflikt, vol. 2, ed. Martin Broszat and Elke Fröhlich (Munich and Vienna: Oldenbourg, 1979), 300.

2. In this study, the term *Jewish cattle traders* refers to persons who operated a cattle-trading business and were regarded as Jews according to the National Socialist racial laws.

3. This number comes from Christoph Daxelmüller, *Jüdische Kultur in Franken* (Würzburg: Echter, 1988), 41.

4. Statistisches Reichsamt, *Die Bevölkerung des Deutschen Reichs nach den Ergebnissen der Volkszählung 1925* (1929; repr., Berlin: Reimar Hobbing, 1978), 327–382.

5. Stefan Schwarz, *Die Juden in Bayern im Wandel der Zeiten* (Munich: Olzog, 1980), 181–296; Richard Mehler, "Auf dem Weg in die Moderne: Die fränkischen Landjuden vom frühen 19. Jahrhundert bis zum Ende der 'Weimarer Republik,'" in *Juden in Franken 1806 bis heute*, ed. Julia Hecht (Ansbach: Bezirk Mittelfranken 2007), 78; Hartmut Heller, "Juden in Franken im 19. Jahrhundert," in Hecht, *Juden in Franken*, 40; Gerhard Rechter, "Die Judenmatrikel 1813 bis 1861 in Mittelfranken," in Hecht, *Juden in Franken*, 53–66.

6. Denominationally, the overwhelmingly Protestant administrative districts of Central and Upper Franconia (where Protestants made up 69.25%

and 60% of the population, respectively) were quite distinct from Catholic
Lower Franconia (where Protestants were only 18.31% of the population);
see Rainer Hambrecht, *Der Aufstieg der NSDAP in Mittel- und Oberfranken, 1925–1933* (Nuremberg: Stadtarchiv Nürnberg, Korn u. Berg: 1976), 1.

7. Manfred Kittel, *Provinz zwischen Reich und Republik: Politische Mentalitäten in Deutschland und Frankreich 1918–1933/36* (Munich: Oldenbourg,
2000), 620.

8. Monika Richarz, "Ländliches Judentum als Problem der Forschung," in
Jüdisches Leben auf dem Lande: Studien zur deutsch-jüdischen Geschichte, ed.
Monika Richarz and Reinhard Rürup, (Tübingen: Mohr Siebeck, 1997),
1. In her pioneering study "Viehhandel und Landjuden," Richarz touches
on this twentieth-century development only marginally. Several works by
Robert Uri Kaufmann provide a good historical overview of rural cattle
traders; the most relevant of these is Kaufmann, *Jüdische und christliche
Viehhändler in der Schweiz, 1780–1930* (Zurich: Chronos, 1988).

9. Richarz, "Ländliches Judentum als Problem der Forschung," 1–2; Ulrich
Baumann, *Zerstörte Nachbarschaften: Christen und Juden in badischen
Landgemeinden 1862–1940* (Hamburg: Dölling und Galitz, 2000), 22. In the
1950s, before historical scholarship in Germany began to deal with rural
Jews, Jewish (exile) historians like Hermann Schwab were already turning
to the history of rural German Jewry; see his *Jewish Rural Communities in
Germany* (London: Cooper, 1956). These early works were often shaped
by the pain of having lost what once was home to the authors or their
subjects. The first to take an approach that was methodologically more
far-reaching was Werner Jacob Cahnman in his sociological study of rural
Jewry, which investigated this marginal group from different perspectives.
See Cahnman, "Village and Small Town Jews in Germany: A Typological
Study," in *Leo Baeck Institute Year Book* 19 (1974): 107–130.

10. Examples of this periodization that also take Jewish cattle traders into
account are, for the period before 1933: Arno Herzig, "Die westfälischen
Juden im Modernisierungsprozeß," in *Deutsche Juden und die Moderne*, ed.
Shulamit Volkov (Munich: Oldenbourg, 1994), 95–118; and Kaufmann, *Die
Beerfeldener Juden 1691–1942* (Beerfelden: Stadt Beerfelden, 2003). For the
period following 1933, see Falk Wiesemann, "Juden auf dem Lande: Die
wirtschaftliche Ausgrenzung der jüdischen Viehhändler in Bayern," in *Die
Reihen fast geschlossen: Beiträge zur Geschichte des Alltags unterm Nationalsozialismus*, ed. Jürgen Reulecke and Detlev Peukert (Wuppertal: Hammer,
1981), 381–396. In his study, Michael Wildt shows how profitable it can be
to expand the historian's perspective to include the period before 1933;
see Wildt, *Volksgemeinschaft als Selbstermächtigung: Gewalt gegen Juden in
der deutschen Provinz 1919 bis 1939* (Hamburg: Hamburger Edition, 2007).

Wildt's book is available in English as *Hitler's Volksgemeinschaft and the Dynamics of Racial Exclusion: Violence against Jews in Provincial Germany, 1919–1939*, trans. Bernard Heise (New York: Berghahn, 2012).

11. Richarz and Rürup , eds., *Jüdisches Leben auf dem Lande* (Tübingen: Mohr Siebeck, 1997). For an expanded edition of Utz Jeggle's dissertation published three decades earlier, see Jeggle, *Judendörfer in Württemberg* (Tübingen: Tübinger Vereinigung für Volkskunde, 1999).

12. Unlike in France, where the Annales school strongly influenced historical scholarship, in Germany, agrarian history took up very little room until the 1990s. See Ulrich Kluge, *Agrarwirtschaft und ländliche Gesellschaft im 20. Jahrhundert* (Munich: Oldenbourg, 2005), 67–77; and Jacques Revel, "Die Annales," in *Kompass der Geschichtswissenschaft: Ein Handbuch*, ed. Joachim Eibach (Göttingen: Vandenhoeck und Ruprecht, 2006), 23–37.

13. Richarz, "Viehhandel und Landjuden im 19. Jahrhundert: Eine symbiotische Wirtschaftsbeziehung in Südwestdeutschland," in *Menora: Jahrbuch für deutsch-jüdische Geschichte*, ed. Julius H. Schoeps (Munich: Piper, 1990), 66–88.

14. As late as 1925, throughout Germany, a total of 4,500 tractors and 1,700 trucks were used in agricultural holdings—that is, in no more than 0.08 percent of all farms. Most were used on large-scale farms where more than a hundred hectares of land were available for cultivation, most of these in East Prussia. See Statistisches Reichsamt, *Statistik des Deutschen Reichs: Landwirtschaftliche Betriebszählung. Personal, Viehstand, Maschinenverwendung* (1929; repr., Berlin: Reimar Hobbing, 1978), 17.

15. David Peal, "Antisemitism by Other Means? The Rural Cooperative Movement in Late Nineteenth-Century Germany," *Leo Baeck Institute Year Book* 32 (1987): 146.

16. Yuri Slezkine, *The Jewish Century* (Princeton: Princeton University Press, 2019).

17. Jonathan Karp, "An 'Economic Turn' in Jewish Studies?," *AJS Perspectives* (Fall 2009): 10. On this, see Shmuel N. Eisenstadt, "Multiple Modernities," *Daedalus* 129, no. 1 (2000): 1–29; Eisenstadt, *Multiple Modernities* (New Brunswick, NJ: Transaction, 2002). Thomas Mergel has drawn attention to the different shadings and asynchronies of modernity and to the application of the concept of modernity in historical scholarship; see Mergel, "Geht es weiterhin voran? Die Modernisierungstheorie auf dem Weg zu einer Theorie der Moderne," in *Geschichte zwischen Kultur und Gesellschaft: Beiträge zur Theoriedebatte*, ed. Mergel and Thomas Welskopp (Munich: Beck, 1997), 203–232. According to Shulamit Volkov, the concept of modernity should be regarded "as the result of all the processes of change in our time." Since these processes, according to Volkov, are not

only applicable to the social majority, we should not let them obscure our outlook on intra-Jewish processes of change. See Volkov, "Zur Einführung," in *Deutsche Juden und die Moderne*, ed. Volkov, x; Herzig, "Die westfälischen Juden im Modernisierungsprozeß," in Volkov, *Deutsche Juden*, 103.

18. In contrast to the literature on German Jews, the historiography of Polish Jews has convincingly shown that a religious lifestyle does not stand in the way of economic growth; see Glenn Dynners, *Men of Silk: The Hasidic Conquest of Polish Society* (Oxford: Oxford University Press, 2006), 14.

19. The state of research is explored more fully in chapter 2. For now, just three fundamental works are singled out for mention: Martin Fiedler, "Vertrauen ist gut, Kontrolle ist teuer: Vertrauen als Schlüsselkategorie wirtschaftlichen Handelns," *Geschichte und Gesellschaft* 27 (2001): 576–592; Richard Tilly, *Vertrauen = Trust* (Berlin: Akademie, 2005); Christian Hillen, ed., *"Mit Gott": Zum Verhältnis von Vertrauen und Wirtschaftsgeschichte* (Cologne: Stiftung Rheinisch-Westfälisches Wirtschaftsarchiv, 2007).

20. Gideon Reuveni, "Prolegomena to an 'Economic Turn' in Jewish History," in *The Economy in Jewish History: New Perspectives on the Interrelationship between Ethnicity and Economic Life*, ed. Reuveni and Sarah Wobick-Segev (New York: Berghahn, 2011), 9; see also Todd M. Endelman, "New Turns in Jewish Historiography?," *Jewish Quarterly Review* 103, no. 4 (2013): 589–598.

21. See also Karp, "An 'Economic Turn' in Jewish Studies?," 10.

22. Nina Caputo and Mitchell B. Hart, "Introduction: On the Word of a Jew, or Trusting Jewish History," in *On the Word of a Jew: Religion, Reliability, and the Dynamics of Trust*, ed. Caputo and Hart (Bloomington: Indiana University Press, 2019), 1.

23. Lynne Zucker, "Production of Trust: Institutional Sources of Economic Structure, 1840–1920," *Research in Organizational Behavior* 8 (1986): 53–111. There is a more extensive review of her theoretical observations in chapter 2.

24. While some historians do indeed indicate that trust plays a decisive role in business relations between Jewish cattle traders and non-Jewish farmers, they do not expand on this point. See, for example: Kaufmann, "Die Behejmeshändler: Oder der Alltag der jüdischen Viehhändler in Zentraleuropa vor und nach der rechtlichen Gleichstellung und dem Ausbau des Eisenbahnnetzes," *Geschichtswerkstatt* 15 (1988): 11; and Beatrix Herlemann, *"Der Bauer klebt am Hergebrachten": Bäuerliche Verhaltensweisen unterm Nationalsozialismus auf dem Gebiet des heutigen Landes Niedersachsen* (Hanover: Hahn, 1993), 187.

25. This was also the case in other trust-based business sectors, such as the coffee trade. See Dorothee Wierling, "Mit Rohkaffee handeln: Hamburger Importeure im 20. Jahrhundert," in *Kaffeewelten: Historische Perspektiven auf eine globale Ware im 20. Jahrhundert*, ed. Christiane Berth et al. (Göttingen: V&R unipress), 118ff.

26. Critical comments on the types of sources represented by the files on compensation are provided by Frank M. Bischoff and Hans-Jürgen Höötmann, "Wiedergutmachung: Erschließung von Entschädigungsakten im Staatsarchiv Münster," *Der Archivar* 51, no. 3 (1998): 425–438; Stefan Brüdermann and Anikó Szabó, "Tiefenerschließung von Entschädigungsakten," *Archiv-Nachrichten Niedersachsen* 2 (1998): 35–38; Bernhard Grau, "Entschädigungs- und Rückerstattungsakten als neue Quelle der Zeitgeschichtsforschung am Beispiel Bayerns," *zeitenblicke* 3, no. 2 (2004), accessed January 10, 2014, http://www.zeitenblicke.de/2004/02/grau /index.html.

1. A Social History of Cattle Trading in Weimar Germany

1. Despite a lack of absolute figures, this assumption runs through the research literature of the last several decades. See Rainer Hambrecht, *Der Aufstieg der NSDAP in Mittel- und Oberfranken, 1925–1933* (Nuremberg: Stadtarchiv Nürnberg, Korn u. Berg, 1976), 6; Falk Wiesemann, "Einleitung: Zur Geschichte der jüdischen Gemeinden seit 1813," in *Die jüdischen Gemeinden in Bayern, 1918–1945*, ed. Baruch Z. Ophir and Wiesemann (Munich: Oldenbourg, 1979), 22; Monika Richarz, ed., *Jüdisches Leben in Deutschland: Selbstzeugnisse zur Sozialgeschichte 1918–1933* (Stuttgart: Deutsche Verlags-Anstalt, 1982), 21; Avraham Barkai, "Die Juden als sozio-ökonomische Minderheitsgruppe in der Weimarer Republik," in *Juden in der Weimarer Republik: Skizzen und Porträts*, ed. Walter Grab and Julius H. Schoeps (Stuttgart: Burg, 1986), 340; Richarz, "Die soziale Stellung der jüdischen Händler auf dem Lande am Beispiel Südwestdeutschlands," in *Jüdische Unternehmer in Deutschland im 19. und 20. Jahrhundert*, ed. Werner Eugen Mosse (Stuttgart: Steiner, 1992), 276; Beatrix Herlemann, *"Der Bauer klebt am Hergebrachten": Bäuerliche Verhaltensweisen unterm Nationalsozialismus auf dem Gebiet des heutigen Landes Niedersachsen* (Hanover: Hahn, 1993), 173.

2. See Willi Wygodzinski, *Agrarwesen und Agrarpolitik: Kapital und Arbeit in der Landwirtschaft. Verwertung der landwirtschaftlichen Produkte. Organisation des landwirtschaftlichen Berufsstandes*, 3rd ed., rev. August Skalweit (Berlin: Göschen, 1928), 85–86; see also Barkai, "Die Juden als sozio-ökonomische Minderheitsgruppe," 341.

3. We checked the names of the business owners against those of Jewish business owners mentioned in the community archive. The Nazi persecution of the Jews made available extensive archival material about the Jewish population in different localities. By contrast, there was only sparse information to be found about non-Jewish business owners, so there is a very high probability that the thirty-one cases in which religious affiliation could not be identified involved non-Jews.

4. See Wiesemann, "Einleitung," 18; see also Reinhard Weber, *Das Schicksal der jüdischen Rechtsanwälte in Bayern nach 1933* (Munich: Oldenbourg, 2006). Unfortunately, there are no comparable figures for Bavaria about the share of Jews in the hops and grain trade.

5. Definition according to the article "Monopol," *Brockhaus Enzyklopädie in 30 Bänden* (Leipzig: Brockhaus, 2006), 18: 744–745.

6. Information from Roland Langer, Stadtarchiv Fürth, August 18, 2010; on the Jewish community in Fürth, see also Gerhard Renda, "Fürth, das 'bayerische Jerusalem,'" in *Geschichte und Kultur der Juden in Bayern: Aufsätze*, ed. Manfred Treml and Josef Kirmeier (Munich: Haus der Bayerischen Geschichte, 1988), 225–236; Barbara Eberhardt and Frank Purrmann, "Fürth," in *Mehr als Steine . . . Synagogen-Gedenkband Bayern*, ed. Wolfgang Kraus et al., 266–333 (Lindenberg im Allgäu: Kunstverlag Josef Fink, 2010).

7. In the research literature to date, however, Jewish cattle traders have always been assigned as a group to the category of rural Jews, as indicated just by the titles of the two standard works on them. See Wiesemann, "Juden auf dem Lande: Die wirtschaftliche Ausgrenzung der jüdischen Viehhändler in Bayern," in *Die Reihen fast geschlossen*, ed. Jürgen Reulecke and Detlev Peukert, 381–396 (Wuppertal: Hammer, 1981); and Richarz, "Viehhandel und Landjuden im 19. Jahrhundert: Eine symbiotische Wirtschaftsbeziehung in Südwestdeutschland," in *Menora: Jahrbuch für deutsch-jüdische Geschichte*, ed. Julius H. Schoeps, 66–88 (Munich: Piper, 1990). Here, to begin with, we need to clarify what is actually meant by the term *rural* ("land," as a prefix in German). In the research literature in general and according to the statistics of the German Reich, the line for rural is drawn at two thousand inhabitants. See Wolfram Pyta, *Dorfgemeinschaft und Parteipolitik 1918–1933: Die Verschränkung von Milieu und Parteien in den protestantischen Landgebieten Deutschlands in der Weimarer Republik* (Düsseldorf: Droste, 1996), 36. Richarz, however, defines *rural* differently for the Jewish population, noting it involves localities with fewer than five thousand inhabitants. See Richarz, "Die soziale Stellung," 273. In this study, we will follow Pyta and draw the line for rural at two thousand inhabitants, for if one were to follow Richarz, some old Franconian Imperial

cities like Dinkelsbühl or Windsheim would fall under the category of rural. Although these towns did have fewer than five thousand inhabitants during the Weimar Republic, their history and social and economic structure distinguished them significantly from rural towns and villages. In small and medium-sized towns, there was, both among non-Jews and Jews, a pronounced petty bourgeois culture. See also Richard Mehler, "Die Entstehung eines Bürgertums unter den Landjuden in der bayerischen Rhön vor dem Ersten Weltkrieg," in *Juden, Bürger, Deutsche: Zur Geschichte von Vielfalt und Differenz 1800–1933*, ed. Andreas Gotzmann et al., 193–216 (Tübingen: Mohr, 2001), 198–199. It therefore seems to make sense to add the concept of small-town Jews, the category to which the majority of Jewish cattle dealers belonged, to those of rural and urban Jews; see Stefanie Fischer, "Ein Beispiel für Landjuden? Jüdische Viehhändler in Mittelfranken (1919–1939)," *Aschkenas: Zeitschrift für Geschichte und Kultur der Juden* 21, no. 1–2 (2013): 105–142.

8. See also Robert Uri Kaufmann, *Jüdische und christliche Viehhändler in der Schweiz 1780–1930* (Zurich: Chronos, 1988), 83.

9. See Günter Dippold, *Eisenbahn und Kleinstadt: Auswirkungen des Knotenpunktes auf Lichtenfels im frühen 19. und 20. Jahrhundert* (Bayreuth: Regierung von Oberfranken, 2001); Ralf Roth, "Die Eisenbahn und ihre Folgen für die Mobilität im 19. Jahrhundert," in *"Auf eisernen Schienen, so schnell wie der Blitz": Regionale und überregionale Aspekte der Eisenbahngeschichte*, ed. Andreas Hedwig, 1–16 (Marburg: Hessisches Staatsarchiv Marburg, 2008).

10. Alf Lüdtke, "Eisenbahnfahren und Eisenbahnbau," in *Bürgerliche Gesellschaft in Deutschland: Historische Einblicke, Fragen, Perspektiven*, ed. Lutz Niethammer (Frankfurt am Main: Fischer, 1990), 111; see also Roth, "Die Eisenbahn und ihre Folgen."

11. Files of the Landesamt für Viehverkehr, Stadtarchiv Rothenburg o/T, Box 976.

12. Fischer, conversation with Kurt B. and Oliver G., Mönchsroth, 2008.

13. See chapter II 4.

14. Karl H. Metz, *Ursprünge der Zukunft: Die Geschichte der Technik in der westlichen Zivilisation* (Paderborn: Schöningh, 2006), 152.

15. Avraham Barkai, "The German Jews at the Start of Industrialisation: Structural Change and Mobility 1835–1869," in *Revolution and Evolution: 1848 in German-Jewish History: Robert Weltsch on his 90th Birthday in Grateful Appreciation*, ed. Werner Eugen, Emil Mosse et al. (Tübingen: Mohr, 1981), 135; Richarz, "Emancipation and Continuity: German Jews in the Rural Economy," in *Revolution and Evolution*, ed. Mosse et al., 95–96; Marion A. Kaplan, "Konsolidierung eines bürgerlichen Lebens im

kaiserlichen Deutschland, 1871–1918," in *Geschichte des jüdischen Alltags in Deutschland: Vom 17. Jahrhundert bis 1945*, ed. Kaplan (Munich: Beck, 2003), 227.

16. This emerged from an evaluation of the registration cards for Jewish residents of Nuremberg through 1945 in the Stadtarchiv Nürnberg, C 21/X.

17. See Richarz, "Landjuden und Wirtschaft: Jüdische Schlachter und Viehhändler im deutschen und internationalen Viehhandel des 19. Jahrhunderts (Kurzfassung)," *Studia Rosenthaliana* XIX, no. 2 (1985): 357; Kaufmann, *Jüdische und christliche Viehhändler*, 72–78.

18. Steven M. Lowenstein, "The Rural Community and the Urbanization of German Jewry," in *The Mechanics of Change: Essays in the Social History of German Jewry*, ed. Lowenstein (Atlanta, GA: Scholars Press, 1992), 146–148.

19. Information from the list, compiled by Oliver Gußmann, of Jewish families who lived between 1933 and 1938 in Rothenburg o/T, unpublished, around 2009, in private archive of Oliver Gußmann, Rothenburg o/T.

20. Information from Stadtbauamt Rothenburg o/T, March 28, 2011; additional evidence about new buildings may be found in affidavit by Eugenie Levite to the LEA, April 30, 1957, in BayHStA, BEG 49839, A-185; "Wiedergutmachungsbehörde III, Ober- und Mittelfranken, Fürth/Bay., 22.09.1950, wegen Rückerstattung in Sachen Aal, Arthur und Bloomfield, Ingeborg," in BayHStA, EG 78417, A-0007; Information from Stadtarchiv Ellingen, September 17, 2009.

21. Siglinde Buchner, *Ellinger Hausbesitzer zwischen 1536 und 1820* (Ellingen: Stadtarchiv, 1998), 9; Karl Kroder and Birgit Kroder-Gumann, *Schnaittacher Häuserchronik: "seit unfürdenklichen Zeiten..."* (Nuremberg: Ges. für Familienforschung in Franken, 2002).

22. "Registerakten zu Handelsregister A, Registerblatt 1459 über die Firma Gebrüder Mann, Eintrag vom 1.06.1899," StAN, HRA 1459.

23. As Lowenstein emphasized, urbanization was frequently preceded by cultural and economic change. See Lowenstein, "The Pace of Modernization of German Jewry in the Nineteenth Century," in *The Mechanics of Change*, ed. Lowenstein, 22.

24. Lowenstein, "The Rural Community," 140–141.

25. For a long time, the prevailing view in the historiography was that Jews who had remained in traditional commercial professions like the livestock and grain trade after occupational restrictions had been lifted were not participating in the Jewish minority's modernization process. In the course of emancipation, they had not adapted sufficiently (so the view goes), and they had lagged behind their urban coreligionists in keeping up with the kind of cultural and economic change (see Richarz,

"Emancipation and Continuity," 101) that preceded urbanization and thus disengagement from the old structures of German Jewish life (see Lowenstein, "The Pace of Modernization," 22). This finding is supported by Martin Ulmer, "Bedeutung und Ende des jüdischen Viehhandels," in *Zerstörte Hoffnungen: Wege der Tübinger Juden*, ed. Geschichtswerkstatt Tübingen (Stuttgart: Theiss, 1995), 215; and, for Westphalia, by Arno Herzig, "Die westfälischen Juden im Modernisierungsprozeß," in *Deutsche Juden und die Moderne*, ed. Shulamit Volkov (Munich: Oldenbourg, 1994), 103.

26. Richarz, ed., *Jüdisches Leben in Deutschland: Selbstzeugnisse zur Sozialgeschichte 1780–1871* (Stuttgart: Deutsche Verlags-Anstalt, 1976), 30.

27. On the history of the Jewish community in Ellingen, see Simone Ott et al., *Juden in Ellingen 1540–1938* (Ellingen: Hermann Seis 2008).

28. Information from Stadtarchiv Ellingen, September 17, 2009; Information from Stadtbauamt Rothenburg o/T, March 28, 2011.

29. Data obtained from the companies register of the firm Bermann & Oppenheimer, copy from November 22, 1950, in StAN, WB IIIa 4130.

30. See chapter II 4.

31. See also Jacob Toury, "Der Eintritt der Juden ins deutsche Bürgertum," in *Das Judentum in der Deutschen Umwelt 1800–1850: Studien zur Frühgeschichte der Emanzipation*, ed. Hans Liebeschütz and Arnold Paucker, 227–241 (Tübingen: J. C. B. Mohr, 1977).

32. This may be confirmed by examining the addresses of Jewish cattle-trading firms in Ellingen, Markt Berolzheim, Burghaslach, Altenmuhr, and Nuremberg.

33. Richarz, ed., *Jüdisches Leben in Deutschland: Selbstzeugnisse zur Sozialgeschichte im Kaiserreich* (Stuttgart: Deutsche Verlags-Anstalt, 1979).

34. Richarz, ed., *Jüdisches Leben in Deutschland: Selbstzeugnisse zur Sozialgeschichte 1780–1871*, 30.

35. Edward Hastings Chamberlin, *The Theory of Monopolistic Competition: A Re-orientation of the Theory of Value* (Cambridge, MA: Harvard University Press, 1965).

36. The account ledger (around 1930) for Hugo Lang may be found in StAN, "Nachlass RA Herz, no. 1381."

37. The word *genizah* (Hebrew, גניזה)—plural *genizot*—refers to a depository for prayer books that have become unusable and that, according to Jewish practice, cannot be thrown away. The books were stored in the attic of a synagogue in order to preserve their sanctity. Wiesemann looks into the trove of genizot in Wiesemann, "'Verborgene Zeugnisse' der deutschen Landjuden: Eine Einführung in die Ausstellung," in *Genizah, Hidden Legacies of the German Village*, ed. Wiesemann, 15–32 (Gütersloh: Bertelsmann, 1992); see also

Forwald Gil Hüttenmeister, "Die Genisot als Geschichtsquelle," in *Jüdisches Leben auf dem Lande,* ed. Monika Richarz and Rürup, 207–218 (Tübingen: Mohr Siebeck, 1997). The Stadtarchiv Roth still has a cattle-trading ledger of this kind from the nineteenth century.

38. For a more detailed methodological discussion about the use of restitution documents as a source, see the introduction.

39. So far, there are only a few studies on the Schmusers. One exception is the study by Susanne Bennewitz, "All Talk or Business as Usual? Brokerage and Schmoozing in a Swiss Urban Society in the Early Nineteenth Century," in *The Economy in Jewish History: New Perspectives on the Interrelationship between Ethnicity and Economic Life,* ed. Gideon Reuveni and Sarah Wobick-Segev, 79–93 (New York: Berghahn, 2011).

40. Mayor of Herrieden to LEA, March 31, 1964, in BayHStA, BEG 1146, K-752, 8.

41. See Alexandra Binnenkade, *Kontaktzonen: Jüdisch-christlicher Alltag in Lengnau* (Cologne: Böhlau, 2009), 148.

42. See Robin Judd, *Contested Rituals: Circumcision, Kosher Butchering, and Jewish Political Life in Germany, 1843–1933* (Ithaca, NY: Cornell University Press, 2007), 154–189.

43. Affidavit by David Levite to LEA, June 27, 1955, in BayHStA, BEG 26698–26699, A-183. An additional example of this kind of business is the firm of Adolf Fleischmann in Altenmuhr; see letter from Adolf Fleischmann to LEA, Chicago, March 29, 1949, in BayHStA, BEG 24946, K-861. Yet another example is the firm of Sigmund Enslein; see Mayor of Herrieden to LEA, March 31, 1964, in BayHStA, BEG 1146, K-752.

44. Letter from Mayor of Altenmuhr, Dr. Wolff, to LEA, Altenmuhr, January 8, 1958, in BayHStA, BEG 62223, K-886.

45. Copy of letter from Dr. H. Wolf to Dr. Walter Peters, n.d., n.p. [around 1952] in BayHStA, BEG 24946, K-861.

46. Utz Jeggle, *Judendörfer in Württemberg* (Tübingen: Tübinger Vereinigung für Volkskunde, 1999), 163.

47. Of the 157 Jewish firms examined, it was possible to locate at least 19 wholesale trade firms, whereas among non-Jews the figure was at least 58.

48. Karl Steinberger and Ada Maier to the LEA, New York, February 9, 1961; affidavit by Nathan Gutmann to the LEA, New York, February 18, 1961; both in BayHStA, BEG 021315, K-0421.

49. Affidavit by Else Feldmann, wife of Louis Feldmann, Buenos Aires, October 29, 1958; affidavit by Heriberto Weissenburger, Buenos Aires, June 10, 1955; both in BayHStA, BEG 11308, K-320.

50. See also Kaplan, *The Making of the Jewish Middle Class: Women, Family, and Identity in Imperial Germany* (New York: Oxford University Press, 1991), 117–136, esp. 118.

51. Affidavit by David Weinberg, Seattle, to the LEA, January 19, 1959, in
BayHStA, BEG 11308, K-320.

52. See also Herzig, "Die westfälischen Juden im Modernisierungsprozeß,"112.

53. In Bavaria in 1925, 66.8% of the Jewish population worked in the trade
sector (contrasted with 12.6% of the overall population). See Wiesemann,
"Einleitung," 18. On the occupational structure of the Jewish population
in general, see Barkai, "Die Juden als sozio-ökonomische Minderheitsgruppe," 334; Barkai, "Population Decline and Economic Stagnation," in
*German-Jewish History in Modern Times: Renewal and Destruction 1918–
1945*, ed. Michael A. Meyer and Michael Brenner (New York: Columbia
University Press, 1998), 41.

54. The total of restitution payments was based on income earned between 1930 and 1933. Since the world economic crisis had a discernable
negative impact on the income of cattle-trading firms after 1931, these
figures need to be viewed critically. See Barkai, "Die Juden als sozio-
ökonomische Minderheitsgruppe," 339; Richarz, ed., *Jüdisches Leben in
Deutschland*, 24; Axel Drecoll, *Der Fiskus als Verfolger: Die steuerliche
Diskriminierung der Juden in Bayern, 1933–1941/42* (Munich: Oldenbourg, 2009), 19–20.

55. Kaufmann, "Die Behejmeshändler: Oder der Alltag der jüdischen
Viehhändler in Zentraleuropa vor und nach der rechtlichen Gleichstellung und dem Ausbau des Eisenbahnnetzes," *Geschichtswerkstatt* 15
(1988): 9.

56. See introduction.

57. On this, see also the studies by Christoph Daxelmüller, "Kulturvermit-
tlung und Gütermobilität: Anmerkung zur Bedeutung des jüdischen
Handels für die ländliche und kleinstädtische Kultur," in *Wandel der
Volkskultur in Europa: Festschrift für Günter Wiegelmann zum 60. Geburt-
stag*, vol. 1, ed. Nils-Arvid Bringéus and Günter Wiegelmann (Münster:
Coppenrath, 1988), 233–253; and Jeggle, *Judendörfer in Württemberg*.

58. For example, witness examination of Berta Hahn before the Amtsgericht Dinkelsbühl, March 10, 1964: "The parental bedroom [of the Levite
family] and an additional double bedroom were well designed, as was the
so-called good room. There was a large carpet there, it had everything required for a comfortably middle class family; sewing machine, radio, and
the like." In BayHStA, BEG 49839, A-185, see also testimony from Christian Weissel, *Güterschaffner* (goods inspector), Markt Berolzheim, before
Amtsgericht Gunzenhausen on the home furnishings of the Bermann
family, n.d.: "Before 1938 I was often in the house [Markt Berolzheim, no.
98] because I had business there as a goods inspector. The house was very
nicely furnished, you can say that." In BayHStA, EG 92225, K-2242, and

letter from RA Dr. Adolf Bayer to the LEA, Ansbach, March 15, 1960: "The living room area in the house on Burgstallstraße 5 in Gunzenhausen is about 150 square meters. The home consists of nine [*sic*] rooms, namely living room, dining room, two bedrooms, maid's room, dressing room, storeroom for wardrobes, kitchen, larder, and bathroom. The bathroom was modern with complete bathroom furnishings, stove, bathtub etc., and sink." In BayHStA, BEG 77459, A-16.

59. Witness examination of Lina Kirsch, farmer and former domestic servant for the cattle-trading family Löwensteiner, in AG Gunzenhausen, regarding Helene Löwensteiner, Heidenheim, June 2, 1958, in BayHStA, EG 26539, K-1955.

60. For example, the testimony of Kirsch in AG Gunzenhausen, June 2, 1958: "All the commodes were filled with linen, there was lots of linen available. The closet in the bedroom was full of linen. The clothing for Herr and Frau Löwensteiner was stored in the closet of the guestroom. There was also a basket chair in the living room. In the good room there were several paintings. . . . Apart from that, there were also framed photographs." In BayHStA, EG 26539, K-1955. Leo Gutmann from Treuchtlingen also mentions the ownership of oil paintings in his application for restitution, Appendix to D, September 8, 1950, in BayHStA, EG 36221, K-36221.

61. Email correspondence between Hilde (Tzipora) Jochsberger (born 1920) and Fischer, January 13–14, 2008. In Israel, Hilde Jochsberger changed her name to Tzipora.

62. On the importance of the sofa in the countryside, see also Jeggle, *Judendörfer in Württemberg*, 200. For a description of the home furnishings of Jewish cattle-trading families, see the recollections of Julius Frank in Richarz, ed., *Jüdisches Leben in Deutschland*, 191; see also Manfred Kittel, *Provinz zwischen Reich und Republik: Politische Mentalitäten in Deutschland und Frankreich, 1918–1933/36* (Munich: Oldenbourg, 2000), 83.

63. Testimony of Maria Andlinger to the LEA, presumably in Altenmuhr, December 19, 1966, in BayHStA, EG 97419, K-50/71.

64. Rosa Bermann to the LEA, Buenos Aires, October 3, 1955, in BayHStA, EG 92225, K-2242.

65. Johann Georg Krünitz, *Oeconomische Encyklopädie*, 1878, quoted in Bernhard Deneke, "Fragen zur Rezeption bürgerlicher Sachkultur bei der ländlichen Bevölkerung," in *Kultureller Wandel im 19. Jahrhundert*, ed. Günter Wiegelmann and Dietmar Sauermann (Göttingen: Vandenhoeck und Ruprecht, 1973), 51.

66. Kittel, *Provinz zwischen Reich und Republik*, 331.

67. See also Daxelmüller, "Kulturvermittlung und Gütermobilität," 253.

68. Affidavit by Max Emanuel Herz to the LEA, New York, November 12, 1968, in BayHStA, EG093012, A-82, in which Max Emanuel Herz also states that the Torah scroll of the Engel family was burned during the night of November 9 to the early morning of November 10, 1938, in the synagogue of Markt Berolzheim.

69. See Eberhardt and Hans-Christof Haas, "Schnaittach," in *Mehr als Steine*, ed. Kraus et al., 575–596; on the link between living and commercial quarters, see also Kaplan, ed., *Geschichte des jüdischen Alltags*, 230–232.

70. Fritz Frank, "Selbstzeugnis," in *Jüdisches Leben in Deutschland*, ed. Richarz, 173.

71. Letter from RA Dr. Bayer to the LEA, Ansbach, March 15, 1960, in BayHStA, BEG 77459, A-16.

72. Richarz, "Emancipation and Continuity," 98; Jeggle, *Judendörfer in Württemberg*, 198–201. See also Regina Schmid, *Verlorene Heimat: Gailingen – ein Dorf und seine jüdische Gemeinde in der Weimarer Zeit* (Konstanz: Arbeitskreis für Regionalgeschichte, 1988).

73. The Hebrew word מזוזה (mezuzah) means "doorpost." According to Jewish tradition, a metal capsule is affixed to a doorpost containing a parchment strip inscribed with passages from Deuteronomy 6:9 and 11:20, and on the outside, the name of the Almighty is visible. See Jeggle, *Judendörfer in Württemberg*, 199. Hermann Schwab reports that Christians left the mezuzah on the houses when they were taken over; see Schwab, *Jewish Rural Communities in Germany* (London: Cooper, 1956), 50. To this day, in fact, indentations may still be seen on entrances to houses formerly occupied by Jews indicating where a mezuzah used to be. See figure 1.5.

74. Ute Frevert, "Bürgerliche Familie und Geschlechterrolle: Modelle und Wirklichkeit," in *Bürgerliche Gesellschaft in Deutschland*, ed. Niethammer, 91–92.

75. Frevert, "Bürgerliche Familie und Geschlechterrolle," in *Bürgerliche Gesellschaft in Deutschland*, ed. Niethammer, 92.

76. In Central Franconia, 26.9 percent of farmers cultivated an area between two and five hectares and 20.9 percent an area between five to ten hectares. See Statistisches Reichsamt, *Statistik des Deutschen Reichs: Landwirtschaftliche Betriebszählung. Personal, Viehstand, Maschinenverwendung* (1929; repr., Berlin: Reimar Hobbing, 1978), 20.

77. StAN, BLVW, no. 258, 259, 260, 266, 271, 272, 273, 274, 276, 277. This figure needs to be viewed critically, since the number refers to land holdings immediately prior to the process of Aryanization that commenced in 1938. It may be assumed that, at this time, land holdings had already decreased owing to anti-Jewish persecution and that the size of the holdings was larger than 7.6 hectares in 1933.

78. This business practice was corroborated in several interviews with contemporary witnesses: Fischer, conversation with Grete Weinberg (née
Hamburger), New York, NY, 2007; and Fischer, conversation with Robert
Auernhammer, Oberhochstatt, 2008. One case of settling a cattle debt
with hay deliveries is found in the communication of RA Landenberger
to the BA Weißenburg/Bay., Nürnberg, April 27, 1937, in StAN, Rep. 270,
Regierung, K.d.I, Abg. 1978, no. 3420. This payment practice is also documented by the letter from Albert Niesel & Söhne to the Reichsnährstand,
Hauptabteilung IV, Wansen in Schl., December 16, 1933, in BArch, R
3601/1803. See also Kaufmann, "Die Behejmeshändler," 10.

79. For example, Louis Mohr rented a stable for his livestock; see "Außenstelle
Fürth der Finanzmittelstelle Ansbach des Landes Bayern an das Bayer.
Landesentschädigungsamt," October 27, 1961, in BayHStA, EG 97419,
K-50/71. See also Helmut Gabeli, "'Die Männer der Gemeinde—fast alle
Viehhändler': Jüdische Viehhändler im Raum Haigerloch," in *Jüdische
Viehhändler zwischen Schwarzwald und Schwäbischer Alb: Vorträge der Ta-
gung der Arbeitsgemeinschaft Jüdische Gedenkstätten am Oberen Neckar am
3. Oktober 2006 in Horb-Rexingen*, ed. Kaufmann and Carsten Kohlmann
(Horb-Rexingen: Barbara Staudacher, 2008), 76–77.

80. Fischer, conversation with Leonore E. and Walter B., Burghaslach, 2008.

81. Testimony from Johann Horn before the Wiedergutmachungskammer,
Landgericht Nürnberg-Fürth, January 27, 1954, in StAN, WB III 3874,
vol. I.

82. Affidavit by Eugenie Levite to LEA, presumably Dinkelsbühl, April 30,
1957, in BayHStA, BEG 49839, A-185.

83. Gabeli, "'Die Männer der Gemeinde,'" 79.

84. Bruno Buff, "Warum gehen wir 'auf die Bank'? Manfred Specht, Bäckermeister in Ellingen, berichtet über die Erzählungen seiner Großmutter,"
unpublished manuscript, Ellingen, 2011, Fischer private archive, 1–2; see
also Werner Teuber, *Jüdische Viehhändler in Ostfriesland und im nördlichen
Emsland 1871–1942: Eine vergleichende Studie zu einer jüdischen Berufsgruppe in zwei wirtschaftlich und konfessionell unterschiedlichen Regionen*
(Cloppenburg: Runge, 1995), 75; Ulmer, "Bedeutung und Ende des
jüdischen Viehhandels," 224.

85. In 1922, 6.9 percent of agricultural and forestry firms had a telephone line.
See Horst A. Wessel, "Die Verbreitung des Telephons bis zur Gegenwart,"
in *Vom Flügeltelegraphen zum Internet: Geschichte der modernen Telekommunikation*, ed. Hans-Jürgen Teuteberg and Cornelius Neutsch (Stuttgart:
Steiner, 1998), 87. A more uniform distribution of the telephone network
was hindered by, among other things, high connection charges; thus,
for example, the cost of connecting to the telephone network amounted

to around half the annual income of an unskilled worker. See Clemens Zimmermann and Werner Troßbach, *Die Geschichte des Dorfes* (Stuttgart: Ulmer, 2006), 226–227. How long it took for the telephone to become more widely available is shown by the fact that it was not until the 1960s that the device became an article of everyday use in Western Europe. See Metz, *Ursprünge der Zukunft*, 340.

86. Transcript for hearing of Berta Hahn, née Rosenbauer, Dinkelsbühl, March 3, 1964, in BayHStA, BEG 49839, A-185.

87. Ulrich Baumann, *Zerstörte Nachbarschaften: Christen und Juden in badischen Landgemeinden 1862–1940* (Hamburg: Dölling und Galitz, 2000), 44.

88. See also Schmid, *Verlorene Heimat*, 106–110.

89. Schmid, *Verlorene Heimat*, 110.

90. Grete Weinberg recalls that her father came home every evening. See Fischer, conversation with Weinberg (née Hamburger), New York, NY, 2007. The son of a Jewish cattle trader, Julius Frank, describes how laborious cattle trading was before motorization in Richarz, ed., *Jüdisches Leben in Deutschland*, 191.

91. See Kaufmann, "Die Behejmeshändler," 8; Kaplan, ed., *Geschichte des jüdischen Alltags*, 242, 307–308; Barbara Staudacher, "Rexingen," in *Ort der Zuflucht und Verheißung: Shavei Zion 1938–2008*, ed. Heinz Högerle (Stuttgart: Theiss, 2008), 14.

92. Email correspondence between Jerry Bechhöfer and Fischer, February 3, 2008; see also Martina Switalski, *Shalom Forth: Jüdisches Dorfleben in Franken* (Münster: Theiss, 2012), 225.

93. Fischer, conversation with Felicita R., Burghaslach, 2008; see also Kaufmann, "Jüdische Viehhändler in Württembergisch Franken," 82.

94. Testimony by Friedrich Bickel, master blacksmith, Markt Berolzheim, before the Sprk. Gunzenhausen-Land, 13.–16.09.1948, in StAN, Sprk. Gun-Land, R-37; see also Jeggle, *Judendörfer in Württemberg*, 205.

95. Fischer, conversation with Helmut S., Mönchsroth, 2008; also Gabeli, "'Die Männer der Gemeinde,'" 77. On the significance of eating in contemporary witness reports, see also Fischer, "'Der hat irgendwie an Christen net den Hals abdreht': Erinnerungen an jüdische Viehhändler," *Alt-Gunzenhausen* 63 (2008): 226–246.

96. By way of example, see the figures in BayHStA, EG 121828, K-2720; BayHStA, BEG 11308, K-320; see also Trude Maurer, "Vom Alltag zum Ausnahmezustand: Juden in der Weimarer Republik und im Nationalsozialismus, 1918–1945," in *Geschichte des jüdischen Alltags in Deutschland*, ed. Kaplan, 389.

97. See also Jacob Picard, "Childhood in the Village: Fragment of an Autobiography," in *Leo Baeck Institute Year Book* 4 (1959): 286.

98. Fischer, conversation with Weinberg (née Hamburger), New York, NY, 2007.

99. See affidavit by Babette Baumann, London, September 18, 1956, in BayHStA, EG 46576, K-237 and BayHStA, EG 121828, K-2720.

100. Email correspondence between Ilse Vogel and Fischer, July 2009; email correspondence between Dietrich Weiss and Fischer, March 2011. On the history of the Jews from Feuchtwagen, see Dietrich Weiß, "Aus der Geschichte der jüdischen Gemeinde von Feuchtwangen, 1274–1938," in *Feuchtwanger Heimatgeschichte*, ed. Arbeitsgemeinschaft für Heimatgeschichte (Feuchtwangen: Arbeitsgemeinschaft für Heimatgeschichte, 1991).

101. Horst Steinmetz and Helmut Hofmann, *Die Juden in Windsheim nach 1871* (Bad Windsheim: Die Autoren, 1994), 114; see also Richarz, "Emancipation and Continuity," 98.

102. Letter from RA Max Stern and RA Fritz Engel to the LEA, Fürth, April 9, 1958, in BayHStA, BEG 57576, K-1138.

103. Tax records, Moritz Engel, 1934, in StAN, Finanzamt Gunzenhausen, no. 234.

104. On the history of Bavarian Jews, see Stefan Schwarz, *Die Juden in Bayern im Wandel der Zeiten* (Munich: Olzog, 1980); Wiesemann, "Einleitung," 13–29.

105. See also Daxelmüller, "Kulturvermittlung und Gütermobilität," 234; Teuber, *Jüdische Viehhändler in Ostfriesland*, 71.

106. For an overview of research on German Jewish gender history, see Kirsten Heinsohn and Stefanie Schüler-Springorum, "Einleitung," in *Deutsch-Jüdische Geschichte als Geschlechtergeschichte: Studien zum 19. und 20. Jahrhundert*, ed. Heinsohn and Schüler-Springorum (Göttingen: Wallstein, 2006), 7–24. Important contributions to this subject in general are provided by Julius Carlebach, "Family Structure and the Position of Jewish Women," in *Revolution and Evolution*, ed. Mosse et al., 157–188; Steven Martin Cohen and Paula Hyman, eds., *The Jewish Family: Myths and Reality* (New York: Holmes and Meier, 1986); Kaplan, "For Love or Money: The Marriage Strategies of Jews in Imperial Germany," *Leo Baeck Institute Year Book* 28 (1983), 263–300; Kaplan, "Tradition and Transition: The Acculturation, Assimilation and Integration of Jews in Imperial Germany," *Leo Baeck Institute Year Book* 27 (1982), 3–35; and Kaplan, *The Making of the Jewish Middle Class*.

107. An exception is the work of Baumann, in which female cattle traders are also the subject of investigation; see Baumann, *Zerstörte Nachbarschaften*, 41–42.

108. The range of years in the selection was determined by the accumulated data.

109. It should be noted that Jewish women who married Christian cattle traders do not show up in this data sample. Cattle-trading firms could only be reconstructed based on the (male) business owners, whose names may be found in classified directories and/or in trade office files.

110. Kaplan, "For Love or Money," 263ff. See also Mosse, "Jewish Marriage Strategies: The German Jewish Economic Elite," *Studia Rosenthaliana* XIX, no. 2 (1985): 188–202. This finding, however, also reflects the general trend for marriages between partners of Jewish and non-Jewish background. Thus, in 1927, some 26 percent of all Jewish men had married a non-Jewish wife and only 16 percent of Jewish women a non-Jewish husband; see Maurer, "From Everyday Life to a State of Emergency: Jews in Weimar and Nazi Germany," in *Jewish Daily Life in Germany, 1618–1945*, ed. Kaplan (Oxford: Oxford University Press, 2005), 284.

111. Kaplan, *The Making of the Jewish Middle Class*, 103.

112. Thus, for example, Gisela Roming emphasizes how Jewish women coming out of an urban milieu more frequently married "into the country," where they introduced an "urban" culture, see Roming, "Haushalt und Familie auf dem Lande im Spiegel südbadischer Nachlaßakten," in *Jüdisches Leben auf dem Lande*, ed. Rürup and Richarz, 270; Teuber, by contrast, argues that the majority of female Jewish marriage partners came from far-flung environs, though he does not offer proof for this assertion; see Teuber, *Jüdische Viehhändler in Ostfriesland*, 198.

113. Hyman, "The Modern Jewish Family: Image and Reality," in *The Jewish Family: Metaphor and Memory*, ed. David Charles Kraemer (New York: Oxford University Press, 1989), 184.

114. See also Roming, "Haushalt und Familie," 270.

115. It is asserted in the literature that Jewish women brought an urban culture to the countryside through the kind of clothing they wore and the fact that they came from other municipalities; see Lowenstein, "Alltag und Tradition: Eine fränkisch-jüdische Geographie," in *Die Juden in Franken*, ed. Brenner and Daniela F. Eisenstein (Munich: Oldenbourg 2012), 5–25; Jeggle, *Judendörfer in Württemberg*, 202–203. But the wives of Jewish cattle dealers largely came from localities of a similar size to those of their husbands and also from cattle-trading families, so their urban airs may be called into question. It may be assumed that as cattle traders' wives, they cultivated manners that were different from those of farmers' wives.

116. Mehler underpins this finding with a study of the Lower Franconian town Neustadt/Saale. For this small town, he compared the birthplaces of both partners in forty-seven marriages. Here, too, the majority of marriage partners, namely in thirty cases, came from localities of similar

size. Only in eleven cases could it be shown that the wife had been born in a locality larger than that of her husband. See Mehler, "Die Entstehung eines Bürgertums," 210.

117. In the case of South Baden, too, Baumann finds that cattle traders' wives frequently came from a cattle-trading household; see Baumann, *Zerstörte Nachbarschaften*, 42; see also Kaufmann, *Jüdische und christliche Viehhändler*, 92.

118. See Maurer, "Partnersuche und Lebensplanung: Heiratsannoncen als Quelle für die Sozial- und Mentalitätsgeschichte der Juden in Deutschland," in *Juden in Deutschland: Emanzipation, Integration, Verfolgung und Vernichtung*, ed. Peter Freimark et al. (Hamburg: H. Christians, 1991), 359.

119. See, for example, the testimony from these women: Affidavit by Zwi Schapira to the LEA, Tel Aviv, May 14, 1957; affidavit by Lina Eckmann to the LEA, Tel Aviv, March 24, 1957; both in BayHStA, BEG 53316, K-89; affidavit by Else Feldmann to the LEA, Buenos Aires, June 14, 1955, in BayHStA, BEG 11308, K-320. See also Baumann, *Zerstörte Nachbarschaften*, 41–42.

120. This division of labor between husband and wife was also customary among Christian cattle traders. The wife of Christian cattle trader Hans Stopfer from Ingolstadt also kept the accounts; see Tax records, Moritz Engel, 1934, in StAN, Finanzamt Gunzenhausen, no. 234. This division of labor was also customary in the pork trade; see Fritz Müller, *Der letzte Sau-Müller* (Gunzenhausen: Selbstverlag, 2007). This practice is also corroborated in conversations with contemporaries; Fischer, conversation with Felicita R., Burghaslach, 2008.

121. Affidavit by Zwi Schapira, Tel Aviv, May 14, 1957; affidavit by Lina Eckmann, Tel Aviv, March 24, 1957; both in BayHStA, BEG 53316 K-89. Rosa Schmalgrund from Uffenheim was also a self-employed co-owner; see Antrag "Schaden im wirtschaftlichen Fortkommen," Rosa Schmalgrund, ohne Ort, 22.09.1950 ("Damages in business advancement" application, Rosa Schmalgrund, n.d. [September 22, 1950]), in BayHStA, EG 99154, K-1211.

122. Affidavit by Julius Eckmann, Tel Aviv, March 23, 1959, in BayHStA, EG 55184, K-87.

123. Quotation from letter of the City of Erlangen to the LEA, June 30, 1959, in BayHStA, BEG 41373, K-037.

124. Email correspondence between Ilse Vogel and Fischer, July 2009; on the history of the Jews from Feuchtwagen, see Weiß, "Aus der Geschichte der jüdischen Gemeinde von Feuchtwangen." After the death of her husband, Salomon, Helene Löwensteiner also continued to manage the

cattle-trading business in Markt Berolzheim on her own account; see BayHStA, EG 26539, K-1955. Looking back as early as the eighteenth century, Barbara Rösch has shown that there were women self-employed as cattle traders, most of them presumably widows; see Rösch, *Der Judenweg: Jüdische Geschichte und Kulturgeschichte aus Sicht der Flurnamenforschung* (Göttingen: Vandenhoeck & Ruprecht, 2009), 205.

125. Fischer, conversation with Felicita R., Burghaslach, 2008. A further example of a woman trading in draperies is Eugenie Levite, who also was a self-employed trader in fabrics; see Hearing of Luzia Röder before Amtsgericht, Dinkelsbühl, March 10, 1964, in BayHStA, BEG 49839, A-185.

126. See also Baumann, *Zerstörte Nachbarschaften*, 42.

127. Cattle traders' wives' visits to livestock markets could not be verified, although peasant women are depicted in photographs of the local livestock market from the Gunzenhausen city archive. When their husbands were engaged in strenuous work in the fields, the peasant women drove to the livestock markets to buy cattle; see Stadtarchiv Gunzenhausen, Rep. XXV, Bildsammlung (picture collection).

128. In the category of housewives among the wives of cattle traders were, among others: Babette Aal from Ansbach, Selma Kohn from Wassertrüdingen, Lena Schneebalg from Erlangen, Recha Walz from Gunzenhausen, Rika Behr from Mönchsroth, Rosa Bermann from Markt Berolzheim, Ilse Heiligenbrunn from Hüttenbach, and Sophie Jochsberger from Leutershausen.

129. See also Carlebach, "Family Structure and the Position of Jewish Women," 172.

130. See Picard, "Childhood in the Village," 286; Maurer, "From Everyday Life," 277.

131. Fischer, conversation with Weinberg (née Hamburger), New York, NY, 2007.

132. Fischer, conversation with Weinberg (née Hamburger), New York, NY, 2007.

133. Fischer, conversation with Weinberg (née Hamburger), New York, NY, 2007.

134. Email correspondence between Jochsberger and Fischer, January 2008.

135. Kaplan, *The Making of the Jewish Middle Class*, 126ff.

136. See also Kaplan, *The Making of the Jewish Middle Class*, 206.

137. See chapter II.

138. Beate Bechtold-Comforty, "Jüdische Frauen auf dem Dorf—zwischen Eigenständigkeit und Integration," *Sowi, Sozialwissenschaftliche Informationen* 18, no. 3 (1989): 158ff. See also Kaplan, "Tradition and Transition," 11.

139. Email correspondence between Jochsberger and Fischer, January 2008; see also affidavit by Baumann, former maid for the family of Theodor Mann, Rothenburg o/T, March 11, 1958, in BayHStA, EG 46576, K-237.

140. Lisa Schaaf, "Schicksal und Lebensweg jüdischer Emigranten aus Gunzenhausen," Gunzenhausen (unpublished research paper), 2005; see also email correspondence between Jochsberger and Fischer, January 2008. Grete Weinberg, daughter of a Jewish cattle trader from Nördlingen, also took private piano lessons starting as a young child; Fischer, conversation with Weinberg (née. Hamburger), New York, NY, 2007. By contrast, no instance of musical instruction could be documented for any of the sons.

141. Wilfried Jung, "Die Juden in Altenmuhr," *Alt-Gunzenhausen* 44 (1988):173.

142. Walter Isaacson, *Kissinger: A Biography* (New York: Simon and Schuster, 1992), 20.

143. Bruce Mazlish, *Kissinger: The European Mind in American Policy* (New York: Basic Books, 1976); Isaacson, *Kissinger*.

144. Additional cases would be Dinah Grete Delpeint (née Mann) from Rothenburg o/T; Ingeborg Noah Bloomfield (née Aal) from Ansbach; and Fany Bergmann from Feuchtwangen. See Weiß, "Aus der Geschichte der jüdischen Gemeinde von Feuchtwangen," 41.

145. See affidavit by Baumann, Rothenburg o/T, February 1, 1957, in BayHStA, EG 121828, K-2720, 44. How important the arrangement of a marriage dowry was to facilitate a daughter's marriage with a husband who was at least befitting their station is demonstrated by several financial statements of Jewish cattle-trading families, one example of which is the financial statement of Leopold and Saly Weinmann from Treuchtlingen, who estimated the dowry for their daughter-in-law Irma Weinmann in calculating their property tax beginning in 1929; see property tax audit by Oberregierungsrat Ertl, Treuchtlingen, December 28, 1933, in StAN, Nachlass RA Herz, no. 1380.

146. See also Kaufmann, "Die Behejmeshändler," 17; Maurer, "From Everyday Life," 285.

147. Isaacson, *Kissinger*, 24.

148. A separate subchapter about the men born between 1870 and 1900 has not been provided, since this age cohort is the central focus of the entire book; their biographies and activities are explored in all the other chapters.

149. Kaufmann, "Die Behejmeshändler," 14; Kaplan, "Konsolidierung eines bürgerlichen Lebens," 286; Kohlmann, "'Die Viehbörse

Süddeutschlands'—Jüdische Pferde- und Viehhändler im Raum Horb," in *Jüdische Viehhändler zwischen Schwarzwald und Schwäbischer Alb*, ed. Kaufmann and Kohlmann, 22.

150. Richarz, "Viehhandel und Landjuden," 80; Baumann, *Zerstörte Nachbarschaften*, 44.

151. These firms include, among others, the Behr brothers from Mönchsroth, Julius Eckmann from Burghaslach, Louis Feldmann from Nuremberg, Karl Freising from Roth, Siegfried Kraus from Nuremberg, Justin Landecker from Nuremberg, Josef and Theodor Mann from Rothenburg ob der Tauber, the Walz brothers from Gunzenhausen, and Philipp Wassermann from Forth.

152. None of the younger sons were considered here, since their career paths were unable to develop freely owing to the persecution that set in after 1933.

153. On a critical note, it must be added that no statement can be made here about the brothers of the cattle traders born around 1871 and the sons of these brothers, since the data sample is fed by sociodemographic data from Jewish cattle traders who were born around 1871. That means that only the sons of cattle traders from these age groups could be examined.

154. Richarz, "Viehhandel und Landjuden," 79; Teuber, *Jüdische Viehhändler in Ostfriesland*, 71; Kaplan, "Konsolidierung eines bürgerlichen Lebens," 281; Gabeli, "'Die Männer der Gemeinde,'" 88.

155. Richarz, ed., *Jüdisches Leben in Deutschland*.

156. Affidavit by Karl Freising, New York, June 11, 1958, in BayHStA, BEG 35235, K-1379.

157. See Jung, "Die Juden in Altenmuhr," 166.

158. Affidavit by Hermann Behr to LEA, Brooklyn, NY, January 31, 1956, in BayHStA, BEG 8187, K-1109.

159. Richarz argues that the sons of Jewish cattle traders did not return to their home communities after successfully completing their training; see Richarz, "Viehhandel und Landjuden," 72. See also Gernot Römer, *Schwäbische Juden: Leben und Leistungen aus zwei Jahrhunderten in Selbstzeugnissen, Berichten und Bildern* (Augsburg: Presse-Dr.- und Verl., 1990), 152.

160. See Richarz, "Emancipation and Continuity," 97; Maurer, "From Everyday Life," 307.

161. See Richarz, "Emancipation and Continuity," 101. I associate myself here with the stance taken by Mehler, who criticizes how Jews were long viewed by historians as "full citizens" only once they were liberated from pre-emancipatory structures; see Mehler, "Die Entstehung eines Bürgertums," 194.

162. Lowenstein, "Suggestions for Study of the Mediene based on German,
French and English Models," *Studia Rosenthaliana* XIX, no. 2
(1985): 353; Lowenstein, "The Rural Community," 140. See also Ulmer,
"Bedeutung und Ende des jüdischen Viehhandels," 215.

163. Herzig, "Die westfälischen Juden im Modernisierungsprozeß," 103.

2. Trust and Cattle-Trading

1. LEA to RA Dr. Bayer, Munich, November 17, 1961, in BayHStA, BEG
77459, A-16.

2. Margot Grünberg, *Der deutsche Viehhandel* (Bottrop i. W.: Postberg,
1932), 7.

3. Only on the major cattle markets were cattle wagons used to determine
weight; in stables trades, the cattle's weight was estimated.

4. Fischer, conversation with Abe Gutman, Baltimore, MD, March 16,
2011. It was not until the postwar period that a labeling requirement was
introduced for commercially traded cattle. Today, in the European Union,
animals are labeled with plastic ear tags that contain the most important
information about the cattle (such as weight, age, and origin); see M. Zähner and E. Spiessl-Mayr, "Elektronische Kennzeichnung von Nutztieren,"
Agrarforschung 12, no. 2 (2005): 79–83.

5. Robert Uri Kaufmann, "Die Behejmeshändler: Oder der Alltag der
jüdischen Viehhändler in Zentraleuropa vor und nach der rechtlichen
Gleichstellung und dem Ausbau des Eisenbahnnetzes," *Geschichtswerkstatt* 15 (1988): 11.

6. Annette Baier, "Vertrauen und seine Grenzen," in *Vertrauen: Die Grundlage des sozialen Zusammenhalts*, ed. Martin Hartmann and Claus Offe
(Frankfurt am Main: Campus, 2001), 43.

7. Thomas Hobbes, "Leviathan, Or, the Matter, Form, and Power of a
Common Wealth, Ecclesiastical and Civil" (London: Printed for Andrew
Crooke, 1651). https://www.proquest.com/books/leviathan-matter-forme
-power-common-wealth/docview/2240945289/se-2.

8. Christian Hillen, "'Mit Gott'—Zum Verhältnis von Vertrauen und
Wirtschaftsgeschichte," in Hillen, *"Mit Gott": Zum Verhältnis von
Vertrauen und Wirtschaftsgeschichte* (Cologne: Stiftung Rheinisch-
Westfälisches Wirtschaftsarchiv, 2007), 13.

9. See Ute Frevert, "Vertrauen—eine historische Spurensuche," in *Vertrauen: Historische Annäherungen*, ed. Frevert (Göttingen: Vandenhoeck
und Ruprecht, 2003), 9.

10. Niklas Luhmann's reflections on trust mark the beginning of research
on the subject in the social sciences. See Luhmann, *Vertrauen: Ein*

Mechanismus der Reduktion sozialer Komplexität (Stuttgart: Lucius & Lucius, 2000). A compilation of the most important discussions from the aforementioned disciplines may be found in Hartmann and Offe, *Vertrauen*.

11. For an introduction to the historiography, see Sven Reichardt, *Soziales Kapital "im Zeitalter materieller Interessen": Konzeptionelle Überlegungen zum Vertrauen in der Zivil- und Marktgesellschaft des langen 19. Jahrhunderts (1780–1914)* (Berlin: Wissenschaftszentrum Berlin, 2003); Beate Krais and Gunter Gebauer, eds., *Habitus* (Bielefeld: Transcript, 2002); and Pierre Bourdieu, *Distinction: A Social Critique of the Judgement of Taste*, trans. Richard Nice (Cambridge, MA: Harvard University Press, 1984).

12. Niklas Luhmann, "Vertrautheit, Zuversicht, Vertrauen. Probleme und Alternativen," in Hartmann and Offe, *Vertrauen*, 143.

13. Reichardt, *Soziales Kapital*; see also Lothar Kolmer, *Geschichtstheorien* (Paderborn: Fink, 2008).

14. Frevert, "Vertrauen," 7–66.

15. Recently, Jan Philipp Reemtsma (searching for an answer to the question many Germans of his postwar generation asked: How is it possible that the murderers became our ordinary fathers?) grappled with the meaning of a special kind of political trust—"social trust"—which functions as a link between political institutions or systems and individuals. We will return to this issue in greater detail at another point in this book; see Reemtsma, *Vertrauen und Gewalt: Versuch über eine besondere Konstellation der Moderne* (Hamburg: Hamburger Edition, 2008).

16. Hillen, "'Mit Gott,'" 13; see also Frevert, "Vertrauen," 45.

17. Hillen, "'Mit Gott,'" 9.

18. Lynne Zucker, "Production of Trust: Institutional Sources of Economic Structure, 1840–1920," *Research in Organizational Behavior* 8 (1986): 53–111, esp. 60.

19. Zucker, "Production of Trust," 60.

20. Zucker, "Production of Trust," 57.

21. Gottfried Keller, "Kleider machen Leute," in Keller, *Sämtliche Werke: Historisch- kritische Ausgabe*, vol. 2 (Zurich: Stroemfeld, 2000), 11–62. One English translation of the story (by Harry Steinhauer) can be found in *The German Library*, vol. 44, *Gottfried Keller: Stories*, ed. Frank J. Ryder (New York: Continuum, 1982).

22. On the distinction between the clothing worn by the farming and the Jewish population, see Regina Schmid, *Verlorene Heimat. Gailingen – ein Dorf und seine jüdische Gemeinde in der Weimarer Zeit* (Konstanz: Arbeitskreis für Regionalgeschichte, 1988), 106–110; Monika Richarz, "Die soziale Stellung der jüdischen Händler auf dem Lande am Beispiel Südwestdeutschlands," in *Jüdische Unternehmer in Deutschland im 19. und 20.*

Jahrhundert, ed. Werner Eugen Mosse (Stuttgart: Steiner, 1992), 280; Utz Jeggle, *Judendörfer in Württemberg* (Tübingen: Tübinger Vereinigung für Volkskunde, 1999), 202; and Ulrich Baumann, *Zerstörte Nachbarschaften: Christen und Juden in badischen Landgemeinden 1862–1940* (Hamburg: Dölling und Galitz, 2000), 29–47.

23. Schmid, *Verlorene Heimat,* 106–110.

24. On the clothing of Jewish cattle traders, see Richarz, "Emancipation and Continuity: German Jews in the Rural Economy," in *Revolution and Evolution,* ed. Werner Eugen, Emil Mosse et al. (Tübingen: Mohr, 1981), 98; Martin Ulmer, "Bedeutung und Ende des jüdischen Viehhandels," in *Zerstörte Hoffnungen: Wege der Tübinger Juden,* ed. Geschichtswerkstatt Tübingen (Stuttgart: Theiss, 1995), 224. Oral tradition also stresses how the clothing worn by the Jewish cattle traders was strikingly different from how farmers dressed; see the email correspondence between Jerry Bechhöfer and Fischer, February 3, 2008.

25. In a report of his recollections, the son of one Jewish cattle trader, Fritz Franz, describes the clothing and appearance of the cattle traders in the village of Rexingen in Richarz, *Jüdisches Leben in Deutschland,* esp. 170; see also Erich Rosenthal, "Der Viehmarkt," *Der Morgen* 12 (1934/1935): 557.

26. One piece of evidence for the religiosity of Jewish cattle traders is that cattle markets did not take place on Jewish holidays and, for that very reason, were moved to a different day of the week, since otherwise there was hardly any activity on the markets. See Richarz, "Viehhandel und Landjuden im 19. Jahrhundert: Eine symbiotische Wirtschaftsbeziehung in Südwestdeutschland," in *Menora: Jahrbuch für deutsch-jüdische Geschichte,* ed. Julius H. Schoeps (Munich: Piper, 1990), 84–85; Ulmer, "Bedeutung und Ende des jüdischen Viehhandels," 218.

27. Fischer, conversation with Leonore E., Burghaslach, 2008.

28. See Clemens Zimmermann and Werner Troßbach, *Die Geschichte des Dorfes* (Stuttgart: Ulmer, 2006), 214–215.

29. It can be shown that, since the twelfth century, the merchant class developed a model of the "honorable merchant"—a lesson that was conveyed, among other ways, in merchants' journals. In his study of the honorable merchant, economic historian Daniel Klink examines the virtues and values that are associated with this concept; see Klink, "Der Ehrbare Kaufmann—Das ursprüngliche Leitbild der Betriebswirtschaftslehre und individuelle Grundlage für die CSR-Forschung," in *Corporate Social Responsibility,* special issue 3 of *Zeitschrift für Betriebswirtschaft* (*Journal of Business Economics*), ed. Joachim Schwalbach (Wiesbaden: Gabler, 2008), 57–79.

30. See Oswald Bauer, *Der ehrbare Kaufmann und sein Ansehen* (Stuttgart: Union, 1919), 80–81. This was also the advice given by Minister of State Johannes Wutzlhofer to cattle traders; see the minutes of the general assembly of the State Association of Bavarian Cattle Traders: "Protokoll der Generalversammlung des Landesverbandes bayerischer Viehhändler," n.d. [presumably October 28, 1919], in BayHStA, MWi 8073.

31. Bauer, *Der ehrbare Kaufmann und sein Ansehen*, 85, 101–102, 128–132.

32. Jewish cattle traders' nonrural style of clothing could also prompt mockery, as may be seen in numerous antisemitic depictions of Jewish cattle traders; see, for example, Jüdisches Museum Hohenems, ed., *Antijüdischer Nippes und populäre "Judenbilder": Die Sammlung Finkelstein* (Essen: Klartext, 2005). On the front page of the book *Hebräisch-deutscher Dolmetscher: Sammlung der gebräuchlichsten Handelsausdrücke der israel. Handelsleute auf Viehmärkten und im Privatverkehr* (Gunzenhausen: Leo Schwarzbeck's Buchhandlung, 1930), one such depiction may be found. See figure 16 at the end of the book.

33. As Frevert explained, trustworthiness is a fundamental precondition for being regarded as an "honorable merchant"; see Frevert, "Ehre—männlich/weiblich: Zu einem Identitätsbegriff des 19. Jahrhunderts," in *Tel Aviver Jahrbuch für deutsche Geschichte: Neuere Frauengeschichte*, vol. 21, ed. Institut für Deutsche Geschichte (Gerlingen: Bleicher, 1992), 25.

34. In his treatment of Jewish cattle traders' everyday life, Kaufmann is another historian who looks into the significance of the handshake in the cattle-trading business; see Kaufmann, "Die Behejmeshändler," esp. 11. See also Kaufmann, "Zum Viehhandel der Juden in Deutschland und der Schweiz – bisherige Ergebnisse und offene Fragen," in *Jüdische Viehhändler zwischen Schwarzwald und Schwäbischer Alb*, ed. Kaufmann and Carsten Kohlmann (Horb-Rexingen: Barbara Staudacher, 2008), esp. 22; Ulmer, "Bedeutung und Ende des jüdischen Viehhandels," 224; Helmut Gabeli, "'Die Männer der Gemeinde – fast alle Viehhändler': Jüdische Viehhändler im Raum Haigerloch," in *Jüdische Viehhändler zwischen Schwarzwald und Schwäbischer Alb*, 78.

35. See Kaufmann, *Jüdische und christliche Viehhändler in der Schweiz 1780–1930* (Zurich: Chronos, 1988), 36; Ulmer, "Bedeutung und Ende des jüdischen Viehhandels"; also Kaufmann, "Die Behejmeshändler," 11.

36. This trading procedure was confirmed in several conversations with contemporaries. See Fischer, conversation with Fritz Müller, Gunzenhausen, 2008; Fischer, conversation with Kurt B. and Oliver G., Mönchsroth, 2008; and Fischer, conversation with Yizachar Berman, Ellingen, 2009. See also Werner Teuber, *Jüdische Viehhändler in Ostfriesland und im*

nördlichen Emsland 1871–1942: Eine vergleichende Studie zu einer jüdischen Berufsgruppe in zwei wirtschaftlich und konfessionell unterschiedlichen Regionen (Cloppenburg: Runge, 1995), 75; Ulmer, "Bedeutung und Ende des jüdischen Viehhandels," 224.

37. Franz Kayser, *Die Ausbeutung des Bauernstandes durch die Juden* (Münster i. W.: Adolph Russel, 1894), 39–40, 17, quoted by Olaf Blaschke, "Antikapitalismus und Antisemitismus: Die Wirtschaftsmentalität der Katholiken im Wilhelminischen Deutschland," in *Shylock? Zinsverbot und Geldverleih in jüdischer und christlicher Tradition*, ed. Johannes Heil and Bernd Wacker (Munich: Fink, 1997), 133.

38. See Alexandra Binnenkade, *Kontaktzonen: Jüdisch-christlicher Alltag in Lengnau* (Cologne: Böhlau, 2009), 243–244; Clemens Escher, "Wucherjude," in *Handbuch des Antisemitismus. Begriffe, Ideologien, Theorien*, vol. 3, ed. Wolfgang Benz (Munich: K. G. Saur, 2010), 348–349.

39. This kind of trading procedure was confirmed by several contemporary witnesses; see Fischer, conversation with Fritz Müller, Gunzenhausen, 2008; Fischer, conversation with Kurt B. and Oliver G., Mönchsroth, 2008; Fischer, conversation with Yizachar Berman, Ellingen, 2009; Fischer, conversation with William Berman, Ellingen, 2009. See also Teuber, *Jüdische Viehhändler in Ostfriesland*, 75; Ulmer, "Bedeutung und Ende des jüdischen Viehhandels," 224.

40. On the importance of gossip in the cattle trade, see Rosenthal, "Der Viehmarkt," 558.

41. Fischer, conversation with Kurt B. and Oliver G., Mönchsroth, 2008. See also Elfie Labsch-Benz, *Die jüdische Gemeinde Nonnenweier: Jüdisches Leben und Brauchtum in einer badischen Landgemeinde zu Beginn des 20. Jahrhunderts* (Stuttgart: Landeszentrale für Politische Bildung Baden-Württemberg, 1980), esp. 66–67.

42. Gabeli, "'Die Männer der Gemeinde,'" 79.

43. Müller, *Der letzte Sau-Müller* (Gunzenhausen: Selbstverlag, 2007), 7; see also Georg Hörl, "Rechtsstreitigkeiten im Viehhandel: Untersuchungen von Fällen aus den Jahren 1949–1976" (PhD diss., Munich, 1981); Teuber, *Jüdische Viehhändler in Ostfriesland*, 76.

44. Müller, *Der letzte Sau-Müller*, 7.

45. Zucker, "Production of Trust," 56.

46. Mitteilung des Landesamts für Viehverkehr Nr. 37302, 22.07.1921 (Notice from State Office for Livestock Commerce, no. 37302, July 22, 1921), mentioned in Aktennotiz des Stadtrats Rothenburg o/T, Betreff: Ausübung des Pferdehandels neben dem Viehhandel, 29.07.1921 (Memorandum from the files of the Municipal Council of Rothenburg ob der Tauber, July 29, 1921), in Stadtarchiv Rothenburg o/T, Box 976.

47. Letter of the Auxiliary Police (Schutzmannschaft) Rothenburg o/T to Municipal Council (Stadtrat) Rothenburg o/T with heading "Betreff: unerlaubter Pferdehandel, 17.02.1923" ("Re: unauthorized horse trading, February 17, 1923"), Stadtarchiv Rothenburg o/T, Box 976.

48. Quoted in Rundschreiben V18 des Landesamts für Viehverkehr, München, 11.05.1922 (Circular V18 from the State Office for Livestock Commerce, May 11, 1922), in BayHStA, Sammlung Varia 378.

49. See also Ulmer, "Bedeutung und Ende des jüdischen Viehhandels," 224.

50. Bruno Buff, "Warum gehen wir 'auf die Bank'? Manfred Specht, Bäckermeister in Ellingen, berichtet über die Erzählungen seiner Großmutter," unpublished manuscript, Ellingen, 2011, private archive of Fischer, 1–2; see also Kaufmann, *Jüdische und christliche Viehhändler*, 35–45; Teuber, *Jüdische Viehhändler in Ostfriesland*, 75; Ulmer, "Bedeutung und Ende des jüdischen Viehhandels," 224.

51. Tax documents of Moritz Engel, 1934, in StAN, Finanzamt Gunzenhausen, no. 234.

52. Lorenz Eberle, "Das Problem der Handelsspanne, Referat gehalten auf der Generalversammlung des Bundes der Viehhändler in Deutschland e. V. am 27.11.1931" (Berlin: Bund der Viehhändler Deutschlands, 1933), 6; see also "Die Zizenhauser Tonfiguren," in *Antijüdischer Nippes und populäre "Judenbilder": Die Sammlung Finkelstein*, ed. Jüdisches Museum Hohenems (Essen: Klartext, 2005), 22–25.

53. See also the account given by teacher Karl Kußmaul (1871–1928), who, in the late 1920s, wrote a vivid portrait about a Jewish cattle trader from the area around Horb (on the Neckar river in the northern Black Forest) in which he provides a striking description of the trader's purse filled with a large amount of cash; see Kohlmann, "'Die Viehbörse Süddeutschlands' – Jüdische Pferde- und Viehhändler im Raum Horb," in *Jüdische Viehhändler zwischen Schwarzwald und Schwäbischer Alb*, 59.

54. Fischer, conversation with Fritz Müller, Gunzenhausen, 2008; see also Kaufmann, "Die Behejmeshändler," 8.

55. Fischer, conversation with Fritz Müller, Gunzenhausen, 2008.

56. Frevert, "Ehre," 25.

57. On farmers' serious cash shortage, see also the fortnightly report for March 1927 of the Central Franconian Regional Council from April 4, 1927: "Halbmonatsbericht für März 1927 des Regierungspräsidiums von Mittelfranken, 4.04.1927," in BayHStA, MA 102153; Heide Barmeyer, *Andreas Hermes und die Organisationen der deutschen Landwirtschaft: Christliche Bauernvereine, Reichslandbund, Grüne Front, Reichsnährstand 1928–1933* (Stuttgart: G. Fischer, 1971), 21; Richarz, "Viehhandel und Landjuden," 68.

58. Buff, "Warum gehen wir 'auf die Bank'?," 1–2; see also Kaufmann, *Jüdische und christliche Viehhändler*, 37ff.; Richarz, "Viehhandel und Landjuden," 81.

59. Anthony Giddens, *The Consequences of Modernity* (Cambridge, UK: Polity, 1991), 1–54, esp. 33.

60. See also Richarz, "Viehhandel und Landjuden," 79, 81.

61. Fischer, conversation with Robert Auernhammer, Oberhochstatt, 2008.

62. This event was depicted in a conversation with a contemporary and cannot be checked for its veracity; Fischer, conversation with Robert Auernhammer, Oberhochstatt, 2008.

63. Manfred Kittel, *Provinz zwischen Reich und Republik: Politischen Mentalitäten in Deutschland und Frankreich, 1918–1933/36* (Munich: Oldenbourg, 2000), 338; see also Steven M. Lowenstein, "The Struggle for Survival of Rural Jews in Germany 1933–1938: The Case of Bezirksamt Weissenburg, Mittelfranken," in *Die Juden im nationalsozialistischen Deutschland—The Jews in Nazi Germany, 1933–1943*, ed. Arnold Paucker (Tübingen: Mohr, 1986), 120.

64. "Kaufvertrag zwischen Maria Rottler und Andreas Auernhammer, Hausnummer 39, Oberhochstatt," 14.04.1927, in Privatarchiv Robert Auernhammer, Oberhochstatt (Bill of sale between Maria Rottler and Andreas Auernhammer, house number 39, Oberhochstatt, April 14, 1927, in private archive of Robert Auernhammer, Oberhochstatt).

65. Zucker, "Production of Trust," 56ff.

66. As Bronislaw Malinowsky explained, economic conduct is built on a kind of chain of mutual gifts that are constantly being given back but that, in the long run, need to be kept in balance and ultimately create a system of mutual obligations. Quoted in Zucker, "Production of Trust," 61.

67. See also Zucker, "Production of Trust," 56.

68. Frevert, "Vertrauen"; see also Gunilla-Friederike Budde, "Familienvertrauen—Selbstvertrauen—Gesellschaftsvertrauen: Pädagogische Ideale und Praxis im 19. Jahrhundert," in Frevert, ed., *Vertrauen: Historische Annäherungen*, 180.

69. On the significance of the "Medineh," see also Lowenstein, "Suggestions for Study of the Mediene Based on German, French and English Models," *Studia Rosenthaliana* XIX, no. 2 (1985): 344.

70. Fischer, conversation with William Berman, Ellingen, 2009; also Teuber, *Jüdische Viehhändler in Ostfriesland*, 74–75.

71. In an interview, Fritz Müller spoke about the drinking behavior of the peasants and the dangers this posed for the cattle trade; see Fischer, conversation with Fritz Müller, Gunzenhausen, 2008. This is also confirmed in Fischer, conversation with Abe Gutman, Baltimore, MD, 2011.

72. Those who adhered to kosher dietary laws brought their meals along in jars that were warmed up for them in taverns. One contemporary witness recalls how Jewish traders would heat up their meals there: "And the Jews arrived [in the tavern] and brought a noon lunch along, enclosed in a jug; they went out into the kitchen and said: 'May I warm this up a bit?' . . . Yes, they brought this along in a jug and stayed overnight in the Helfenberger inn. And, of course, there were a lot of children, servants too, and they [inaudible], a few wanted to look into the jug, but my grandmother forbade that strictly. 'That's their belief, ours is different. This is none of your business.'" From Fischer, conversation with Robert Auernhammer, Oberhochstatt, 2008; see also Gabeli, "'Die Männer der Gemeinde,'" 78.

73. See also Labsch-Benz, *Die jüdische Gemeinde Nonnenweier.* On the significance of visiting the tavern in the countryside more generally, see Heinrich Hacker, "Man gönnt sich ja sonst nichts: Beispiele für den oralen Luxus bei Ess-, Trink- und Rauchgewohnheiten der ländlichen Bevölkerung im nördlichen Unterfranken," in *Pracht, Prunk, Protz,* ed. Birgit Angerer et al. (Finsterau: Zweckverb Niederbayerische Freilichtmuseen, 2009), 83–92.

74. Labsch-Benz, *Die jüdische Gemeinde Nonnenweier,* 67.

75. Gilman objects to the common prejudice that Jews never indulged in excessive drinking; see Sander L. Gilman, "The Problem with Purim: Jews and Alcohol in the Modern Period," *Leo Baeck Institute Year Book* 50 (2005): 214–231.

76. Hillen, "'Mit Gott,'" 15.

77. Fischer, conversation with Grete Weinberg (née Hamburger), New York, NY, 2007; some contemporaries reported that non-Jewish employees also shared meals with Jewish families at home; see Fischer, "'Der hat irgendwie an Christen net den Hals abdreht': Erinnerungen an jüdische Viehhändler," *Alt-Gunzenhausen* 63 (2008): 226–246.

78. On the religious lifestyle of rural Jews, see Jacob Borut, "'Bin ich doch ein Israelit, ehre ich auch den Bischof mit': Village and Small-Town Jews within the Social Spheres of Western German Communities during the Weimar Period," in *Jüdisches Leben in der Weimarer Republik,* ed. Wolfgang Benz et al. (Tübingen: Mohr Siebeck, 1998), 17–133; but see also email correspondence between Hilde (Tzipora) Jochsberger and Fischer, January 13–14, 2008.

79. This mathematical aptitude is something confirmed by several contemporary witnesses. See Fischer, conversation with Fritz Müller, Gunzenhausen, 2008; Fischer, conversation with William Berman, Ellingen, 2009; Fischer, conversation with Yizachar Berman, Ellingen, 2009; see also Teuber, *Jüdische Viehhändler in Ostfriesland,* 71.

80. Teuber, *Jüdische Viehhändler in Ostfriesland*, 76ff.; Gabeli, "'Die Männer der Gemeinde,'" 79–80.

81. Fischer, conversation with William Berman, Ellingen, 2009. The son recounted further that he did not perform well at these tasks and, as a result, decided to become a veterinarian rather than a cattle trader. To this day, William Berman operates his own dairy farm in Florida; see Ari Daniel Shapiro and Amanda Kowalski, "The Frum Farmer," *Tablet Magazine. A New Read on Jewish Life* (2011), accessed March 2019, https://aridanielshapiro .wordpress.com/2011/06/07/farmer/.

82. Fischer, conversation with Yizachar Berman, Ellingen, 2009.

83. Fischer, conversation with Fritz Müller, Gunzenhausen, 2008.

84. See Labsch-Benz, *Die jüdische Gemeinde Nonnenweier*, 70.

85. See also Frevert, "Vertrauen"; Luhmann characterizes mistrust as a functional equivalent that can be said to have a lot in common with trust since, like trust, it helps "reduce social complexity." See Luhmann, *Vertrauen*, 92–100.

86. Zucker, "Production of Trust," 59.

87. Kaufmann discusses whether the cattle traders' language was a trade jargon or a secret language but does not arrive at any firm conclusion, since we still lack basic linguistic research about this; see Kaufmann, *Jüdische und christliche Viehhändler*, 98–100. Teuber and Gabeli, by contrast, are of the opinion that the cattle traders' language was not a secret language, but rather a trade jargon. See Teuber, *Jüdische Viehhändler in Ostfriesland*, 79; and Gabeli, "'Die Männer der Gemeinde,'" 79.

88. Werner Weinberg, *Die Reste des Jüdischdeutschen* (Stuttgart: Kohlhammer, 1973), 20–21.

89. See Franz J. Beranek, "Die fränkische Landschaft des Jiddischen," in *Festschrift Ernst Schwarz*, ed. Lothar Bauer and Ernst Schwarz (Kallmünz-Opf.: Michael Lassleben, 1961), 267–303; Edith Nierhaus-Knaus, *Geheimsprache in Franken—das Schillingsfürster Jenisch* (Rothenburg ob der Tauber: Peter, 1990); Helmut Weinacht, "Jiddisches im Ostfränkischen: Darstellung einer Forschungsproblematik," in *Dialekte im Wandel: Tagung zur Bayerisch-Österreichischen Dialektologie*, ed. Andreas Weiss (Göppingen: Kümmerle, 1992), 170–186; Othmar Meisinger, "Lothekolisch: Ein Beitrag zur Kenntnis der fränk. Händlersprache," *Zeitschrift für Hochdeutsche Mundarten* III (1992): 121–127; Alfred Klepsch, "Das Lachoudisch. Eine jiddische Sondersprache in Franken," in *Rotwelsch-Dialekte: Symposion, Münster, 10. bis 12. März 1995*, ed. Klaus Siewert (Wiesbaden: Harrassowitz, 1996), 81–93; Kohlmann, "'Die Viehbörse Süddeutschlands,'" 59.

90. The recordings made by the linguist Weinberg in the 1960s showed that Jüdisch-Deutsch was still widely used among the professional cattle

traders who came from Germany; see Weinberg, *Die Reste des Jüdisch-deutschen*, 15.

91. Shulamit Volkov, *Die Juden in Deutschland 1780–1918* (Munich: Oldenbourg, 2000), 116–117.

92. See Weinberg, *Die Reste des Jüdischdeutschen*, 15.

93. Weinberg, *Die Reste des Jüdischdeutschen*, 15–19; Gabeli, "'Die Männer der Gemeinde,'" 79.

94. Paul Spiegel, *Wieder zu Hause? Erinnerungen* (Berlin: Ullstein, 2001), 12; Müller, *Der letzte Sau-Müller*, 5.

95. Fischer, conversation with Fritz Müller, Gunzenhausen, 2008.

96. The only manuscript that could be located has no publication date. But since it includes a conversion table for exchanging karolins into marks, it can be roughly dated to the mid-nineteenth century (see fig. 16 at the end of the book). The karolin was initially a Bavarian coin between 1726 and 1738, but afterward it was regarded as having an invoice value of eleven "Gulden" (guilders). See Tyll Kroha, *Großes Lexikon der Numismatik* (Gütersloh: Bertelsmann Lexikon, 1997), 232; *Hebräisch-deutscher Dolmetscher: Sammlung der gebräuchlichsten Handelsausdrücke der israel. Handelsleute auf Viehmärkten und im Privatverkehr* (Gunzenhausen: Leo Schwarzbeck's Buchhandlung, 1930). In other regions, similar dictionaries for farmers were published, including: *Die geheime Geschäftssprache der Juden: Ein Hand- und Hilfsbuch für alle, welche mit Juden in Geschäftsverbindung stehen und der hebräischen Sprache (der sog. Marktsprache) unkundig sind* (Neustadt an der Aisch: Engelhardt, 1897); J. Wolff, *Die Geheimsprache der Handelsleute oder Dolmetscher und Wörterbuch zur Entzifferung aller beim Handel und Wandel vorkommenden jüdischen und jargonischen Wörter und Redensarten* (Leipzig: Grieben's, 1885). Teuber points out that the *Wörterbuch der jüdischen Geschäfts- und Umgangssprache* was still being published as late as 1995 by the Deutscher Vieh- und Fleischhandelsverband e.V. (the German Livestock and Meat Trade Association), headquartered in Bonn; see Teuber, *Jüdische Viehhändler in Ostfriesland*, 77; Fischer, "Das Lexicon der jüdischen Geschäfts- und Umgangs-Sprache (Itzig Feitel Stern, 1832)," in *Handbuch des Antisemitismus: Publikationen*, vol. 6, ed. Benz (Munich: De Gruyter Saur, 2013), 428–429.

97. Fischer, "Das Lexicon der jüdischen," 428–429.

98. Richarz, "Emancipation and Continuity," 115.

99. Weinberg, *Die Reste des Jüdischdeutschen*, 16.

100. *Hebräisch-deutscher Dolmetscher*.

101. Weinberg, *Die Reste des Jüdischdeutschen*, 16.

102. Weinberg, *Die Reste des Jüdischdeutschen*, 16.

103. Fischer, conversation with Fritz Müller, Gunzenhausen, 2008; Rosenthal draws attention to the role of humor as a bonding device among cattle traders; see Rosenthal, "Der Viehmarkt," 558.

104. Fischer, conversation with Felicita R., Burghaslach, 2008.

105. Fischer, conversation with Robert Auernhammer, Oberhochstatt, 2008; see also Gabeli, "'Die Männer der Gemeinde,'" 76.

106. Kaufmann, *Jüdische und christliche Viehhändler*.

107. Fischer, conversation with Yizachar Berman, Ellingen, 2009.

108. The elements of Rotwelsch, the old thieves' argot, in the cattle traders' language point to an exchange between these two groups and to the social status of many cattle traders, who were often earning just the amount of money they needed to make a living; see Siewert, *Rotwelsch-Dialekte*.

109. Rudolf Post, "Reste von Viehhändlersprachen in der Pfalz, in Baden und im Elsass," in *Geheimsprachen in Mittel- und Südosteuropa*, ed. Christian Efing and Corinna Leschber (Frankfurt am Main: Lang, 2009), 93.

110. See also Post, "Reste von Viehhändlersprachen."

111. Unpublished comment by a non-Jewish cattle trader and contemporary witness, presented at the conference "Jüdische Viehhändler zwischen Schwarzwald und Schwäbischer Alb," organized by the Arbeitsgemeinschaft Jüdische Gedenkstätten am Oberen Neckar, Horb-Rexingen, October 3, 2006. One indicator of how the cattle traders' language continues to be used today is the dictionary *Wörterbuch der jüdischen Geschäfts- und Umgangssprache*, distributed by the livestock breeding instrument firm Horn – Tierzuchtgeräte (Dülmen, 2013). I wish to thank Martina Edelmann, Veitshöchheim, for drawing my attention to this.

112. Kaufmann, "Die Behejmeshändler," 11; Pfarramtsarchiv (parish office archive) Mönchsroth; Jeggle, *Judendörfer in Württemberg*, 232.

113. Oliver G. about the practice of "cow tapering" in Fischer, conversation with Kurt B. und Oliver G., Mönchsroth, 2008.

114. Testimony by Fritz Weinberg, longtime herdsman for the Mann cattle-trading firm, given to BA Rothenburg o/T, July 10, 1935; Letter of Industrie- und Handelskammer Nürnberg-A to Regierung von Ober- und Mittelfranken (the government of Upper and Central Franconia), November 27, 1935, both in StAN, Rep. 270, Regierung, K.d.I, Abg. 1978, no. 3418.

115. Kaufmann, "Die Behejmeshändler," 11.

116. Thomas Hobbes, *Leviathan*, ed. Richard Tuck (Cambridge, UK: Cambridge University Press, 1991), 86–90; see also Hartmann, "Einleitung," in *Vertrauen*, ed. Hartmann and Offe, 12.

117. Baier, "Vertrauen und seine Grenzen," 43.

118. See Albert Ilien and Jeggle, "Die Dorfgemeinschaft als Not- und Terrorzusammenhang: Ein Beitrag zur Sozialgeschichte des Dorfes und zur Sozialpsychologie seiner Bewohner," in *Dorfpolitik: Fachwissenschaftl. Analysen u. didakt. Hilfen*, ed. Hans-Georg Wehling (Opladen: Leske und Budrich, 1978), 46; Katja Hürlimann, *Soziale Beziehungen im Dorf. Aspekte dörflicher Soziabilität in den Landvogteien Greifensee und Kyburg um 1500* (Zurich: Chronos, 2000), 65.

119. See introduction.

120. The concept of *honor* has been applied methodologically above all in research on the early modern era; the foundations for this were laid by Martin Dinges. See his chapter, "Ehre als Thema der historischen Anthropologie," in *Verletzte Ehre: Ehrkonflikte in Gesellschaften des Mittelalters und der Frühen Neuzeit*, ed. Klaus Schreiner (Cologne: Böhlau, 1995), 29–63; but also Richard van Dülmen, *Kultur und Alltag in der Frühen Neuzeit*, vol. 1, *Dorf und Stadt, 16.–18. Jahrhundert* (Munich: Beck, 1992), 196. Also working on conflicts of honor between Jews and Christian in the early modern era was Sabine Ullmann; see Ullmann, *Nachbarschaft und Konkurrenz: Juden und Christen in Dörfern der Markgrafschaft Burgau 1650 bis 1750* (Göttingen: Vandenhoeck und Ruprecht, 1999), 451–452. With the dissolution of the medieval estate-based society, the "concept of honor" lost significance as a "system of communication for the regulation of social relations"; see Sibylle Backmann and Hans-Jörg Künast, "Einführung," in *Ehrkonzepte in der frühen Neuzeit: Identitäten und Abgrenzungen*, ed. Backmann et al. (Berlin: Akademie, 1998), 15. As a result, the concept is no longer applied as an analytic category in more recent modern history. Nevertheless, *honor* retains relevance in interpersonal relations; hence, in this context, it must be understood as a synonym for human dignity or reputation.

121. In rural society, the assessment of the sexual behavior of others was a component of social manners; see Ilien and Jeggle, *Leben auf dem Dorf: Zur Sozialgeschichte des Dorfes und zur Sozialpsychologie seiner Bewohner* (Opladen: Westdeutscher, 1978), 175ff.; Frevert, *"Mann und Weib, und Weib und Mann": Geschlechter-Differenzen in der Moderne* (Munich: Beck, 1995), 212–217; Yvonne Wilms, *Ehre, Männlichkeit und Kriminalität* (Berlin: Lit, 2009), esp. 17–25. Hence, parties to a conflict were quick to justify their disapproval of an opponent by invoking the adversary's supposedly excessive sexual activity, or they would try to remedy an injury to their honor by slighting the opponent's potency. As numerous paternity suits in the records of the district courts from the Nuremberg state archives attest, these kinds of accusations were

widespread; in 1919, for example, fourteen out of a total of twenty civil trial litigations submitted had to do with paternity suits. See StAN, Rep. 235/30, AG Weißenburg, Zivilprozessakten, Jg. 1880–1952; see also Ilien and Jeggle, *Leben auf dem Dorf*, 80; Tanja Hommen, *Sittlichkeitsverbrechen: Sexuelle Gewalt im Kaiserreich* (Frankfurt am Main: Campus, 1999), 181–184.

122. See Jeggle, *Judendörfer in Württemberg*, 286–287.

123. Fischer, "'Der hat irgendwie an Christen net den Hals abdreht,'" 237–238.

124. Fischer, conversation with Fritz Müller, Gunzenhausen, 2008.

125. Fischer, conversation with Robert Auernhammer, Oberhochstatt, 2008.

126. See Friedrich Koch, *Sexuelle Denunziation: Die Sexualität in der politischen Auseinandersetzung* (Frankfurt am Main: Syndikat, 1986), 72–73; Gerhard Henschel, *Neidgeschrei: Antisemitismus und Sexualität* (Hamburg: Hoffmann und Campe, 2008); Alexandra Przyrembel, "'Rassenschande,'" in *Handbuch des Antisemitismus: Begriffe, Ideologien, Theorien*, ed. Benz, 273–275. On antisemitic representations of "lecherous Jewish men," see Thomas Gräfe, *Antisemitismus in Gesellschaft und Karikatur des Kaiserreichs: Glöß' politische Bilderbogen 1892–1901* (Norderstedt: Books on Demand, 2005), esp. 172–173.

127. RA Albert Pilland to mayor of Ellingen, Weißenburg/Bay., January 24, 1921, in Stadtarchiv Ellingen, no call number; see also Frevert, "Soldat, Staatsbürger: Überlegungen zur historischen Konstruktion von Männlichkeit," in *Männergeschichte—Geschlechtergeschichte: Männlichkeit im Wandel der Moderne*, ed. Thomas Kühne (Frankfurt am Main: Campus, 1996), 69–87.

128. From letter by Siegfried Weinmann to the Landgericht Eichstätt, Treuchtlingen, December 17, 1931, in StAN, Nachlass RA Herz, no. 1370.

129. Siegfried Weinmann to the Amtsgericht Mainburg, n.d. [presumably 1931], in StAN, Nachlass RA Herz, no. 1370.

130. This prejudice finds special expression in Werner Sombart's treatise on "the Jews and economic life"; see Sombart, *The Jews and Modern Capitalism*, trans. M. Epstein (Kitchener: Batoche Books, 2001), 89.

131. Letter from RA Dr. Max Schmidtmüller to the Landgericht Eichstätt, Landshut, January 18, 1932, in which he states that the cattle trader Weinmann was beaten in Mainburg on January 13, 1932, in StAN, Nachlass RA Herz, no. 1370.

132. On male combat rituals in general, see Lyndal Roper, "Männlichkeit und männliche Ehre," in *Frauengeschichte – Geschlechtergeschichte*, ed. Karin Hausen and Heide Wunder (Frankfurt am Main: Campus, 1992),

160–161; Frevert, "'Mann und Weib,'" 215. Since there is little available information on male combat rituals in a rural society at the beginning of the twentieth century, see the discussion about this in Bernhard Wirthmann-Müller, "Raufhändel: Gewalt und Ehre im Dorf," in *Kultur der einfachen Leute*, ed. Richard van Dülmen and Angelika Baumann (Munich: Beck, 1983), 79–111.

133. Fischer, conversation with Kurt B. and Oliver G., Mönchsroth, 2008. Among the written and unwritten laws of the cattle trade was the rule that once a trade had been started, it could not be interrupted, a norm prescribed, for example, by paragraph 8 of the Viehmarkt-Ordnung (Cattle Market Ordinance) of the city of Wassertrüdingen from 1926; see StAN, Rep. 270, IV, Regierung, K.d.I, Abg. 1968, Titel IX, no. 383. There is a reference to a 1930 brawl between cattle trader (Jakob) Rindsberg and farmer Johann Lang from Rennhofen in the letter from RA Dr. Levor to the Mayor of Nuremberg, Nürnberg (Nuremberg), May 4, 1936, in StAN, Rep. 270, Regierung, K.d.I, Abg. 1978, no. 3419. An additional reference to scuffles among Jewish cattle traders is provided by Gabeli, "'Die Männer der Gemeinde,'" 74.

134. This is the conclusion also reached by Ullmann, *Nachbarschaft und Konkurrenz*, 452–453.

135. The peasant population profited from the currency's devaluation, which helped them settle their debts; see Bernd Weisbrod, "Die Krise der Mitte oder: 'Der Bauer stund auf dem Lande,'" in *Bürgerliche Gesellschaft in Deutschland*, ed. Lutz Niethammer, 396–410 (Frankfurt am Main: Fischer, 1990); Detlev J. K. Peukert, *Die Weimarer Republik: Krisenjahre der klassischen Moderne* (Darmstadt: Wissenschaftliche Buchgesellschaft, 1997), 75. By contrast, the Jewish population suffered greatly from the effects of inflation, owing to its deep roots in capital-dependent professions; see Avraham Barkai, "Die Juden als sozio-ökonomische Minderheitsgruppe in der Weimarer Republik," in *Juden in der Weimarer Republik: Skizzen und Porträts*, ed. Walter Grab and Julius H. Schoeps (Stuttgart: Burg, 1986), 330; Donald L. Niewyk, "The Impact of Inflation and Depression on the German Jews," *Leo Baeck Institute Year Book* 28 (1983): 19–36.

136. See Ulrich Kluge, *Agrarwirtschaft und ländliche Gesellschaft im 20. Jahrhundert* (Munich: Oldenbourg, 2005), 22.

137. In the tax office files for the cattle trader Engel, several cases are listed in which livestock debts were converted into long-term debts—that is, into a mortgage on farm property; see these files in StAN, Finanzamt Gunzenhausen, no. 234, esp. p. 15.

138. Richarz, *Bürger auf Widerruf: Lebenszeugnisse deutscher Juden 1780–1945* (Munich: Beck, 1989), 257. One example of an antisemitic picture drawn of a "Jewish estate slaughterer" may be found in Gräfe, *Antisemitismus in Gesellschaft und Karikatur,* 76.

139. Grant of a debt-securing mortgage of 4,000 reichsmarks from the couple Josef and Elisabeth Höfelsauer to the merchant Siegfried Weinmann, October 17, 1930, in StAN, Nachlass RA Herz, no. 1383.

140. See introduction; but also Statistisches Reichsamt, *Statistik des Deutschen Reichs: Landwirtschaftliche Betriebszählung. Personal, Viehstand, Maschinenverwendung* (1929; repr., Berlin: Reimar Hobbing, 1978), 18–19, 372–373.

141. Fischer, conversation with Felicita R., Burghaslach, 2008; Buff, "Warum gehen wir 'auf die Bank'?," 1–2; see also Kittel, *Provinz zwischen Reich und Republik,* 478.

142. Anerkenntnisurteil (Consent decree) of the Amtsgerichts Mainburg, March 6, 1931, in StAN, Nachlass RA Herz, no. 1383.

143. See also Michael Wildt, *Geschichte des Nationalsozialismus* (Göttingen: Vandenhoeck & Ruprecht, 2008), 45–46. For an example of antisemitic images in the long tradition depicting the Jew as a "merciless estate slaughterer," see the portrait of a "cattle profiteer" in an illustrated broadsheet, shown in Gräfe, *Antisemitismus in Gesellschaft und Karikatur,* esp. 182.

144. Richarz, "Viehhandel und Landjuden," 77.

145. Siegfried Weinmann, quoted in RA Dr. Huss to Kriminal-Kommissär Zäch, Ingolstadt, June 12, 1933, in StAN, Nachlass RA Herz, no. 1385.

146. Siegfried Weinmann, quoted in RA Dr. Huss to Kriminal-Kommissär Zäch, Ingolstadt, June 12, 1933, in StAN, Nachlass RA Herz, no. 1385.

147. RA Dr. Huss to Kriminal-Kommissär Zäch, Ingolstadt, June 12, 1933, in StAN, Nachlass RA Herz, no. 1385.

148. Copy of the letter from RA Börner to the Amtsgericht Neuburg, Neuburg, October 22, 1936; Louis Feldmann to RA Dr. Levor, Buenos-Aires, June 10, 1936, and August 26, 1936, all in StAN, Nachlass RA Herz, no. 242.

3. Constituting Trust through Official Authority

1. Lynne Zucker, "Production of Trust: Institutional Sources of Economic Structure, 1840–1920," *Research in Organizational Behavior* 8 (1986): 68ff., 140.

2. George Frederick Warren, *Die Erzeugungs- und Absatzverhältnisse der deutschen Vieh- und Milchwirtschaft* (Berlin: P. Parey, 1929), 28–29.

3. Alfred Rudolph, "Der Absatz von Vieh in der Landwirtschaft: Freier Handel, Zwangswirtschaft oder gemeinsamer Vertrieb?" (PhD diss.,

Berlin, 1923), 43; Margot Grünberg, *Der deutsche Viehhandel* (Bottrop i. W.: Postberg, 1932), 60.

4. Rudolph, "Der Absatz von Vieh," 43.

5. Rudolph, "Der Absatz von Vieh," 43–44.

6. Excerpt from Münchner-Augsburger-Abendzeitung, February 28, 1922, no. 88, in StAN, Rep. 270, IV, Regierung, K.d.I, Abg. 1968, Titel IX, no. 402, 141.

7. Rudolph, "Der Absatz von Vieh," 46.

8. This accusation was made in, among other places, the pages of the Münchner-Augsburger-Abendzeitung, February 28, 1922, no. 88, in StAN, Rep. 270, IV, Regierung, K.d.I, Abg. 1968, Titel IX, no. 402.

9. Gesprächsnotiz über den Viehhandel (Memo about Cattle Trade), Munich, June 28, 1919, in BayHStA, MWi 8073; see also the article by the management of the State Association of Bavarian Cattle Traders: Die Verbandsleitung, "Der Kampf um Recht und Gerechtigkeit," *Der Bayerische Viehhändler* 4, no. 22 (May 30, 1924): 1.

10. Quoted in Gesprächsnotiz über den Viehhandel (Memo about Cattle Trade), Munich, June 28, 1919, in BayHStA, MWi 8073; see also Lorenz Eberle, "Das Problem der Handelsspanne, Referat gehalten auf der Genealversammlung des Bundes der Viehhändler in Deutschland e.V. am 27.11.1931" (Berlin, 1933), 16.

11. Grünberg, *Der deutsche Viehhandel*, 9.

12. Oswald Bauer, *Der ehrbare Kaufmann und sein Ansehen* (Dresden: Steinkopff & Springer, 1906), 7.

13. Bauer, *Der ehrbare Kaufmann und sein Ansehen*.

14. "Rundschreiben V 19 des Landesamts für Viehverkehr, 27 July 1922, Punkt III 'Bekämpfung des wilden Viehhandels,'" in StAN, Rep. 270, IV, Regierung, K.d.I, Abg. 1968, Titel IX, no. 402; and "Landesamt für Viehverkehr an die Bezirksverwaltungsbehörden," January 4, 1923, in StAN, Bayerische Landeswucherabwehrstelle, Zweigstelle Nürnberg, no. 63.

15. On the procedure for admitting non-Bavarian cattle traders in the Central Franconian district (Bezirk Mittelfranken), see all the cases in StAN, Regierung, K.d.I, Abg. 1968, Tit. IX, no. 405.

16. See "Wochenbericht des Regierungspräsidenten von Schwaben und Neuburg," October 21, 1919; "Protokoll über die Besprechung mit Oberregierungsrat Süßkind vom Landesamt für Viehverkehr, Betreff: Gewinne aus dem Viehhandel, München," June 7, 1921; both documents in BayHStA, MWi 8073.

17. Excerpt from the Münchner-Augsburger-Abendzeitung, February 28, 1922, no. 88, in StAN, Rep. 270, IV, Regierung, K.d.I, Abg. 1968, Titel IX, no. 402.

18. See excerpt from transcript "Neuregelung des Vieh- und Fleischverkehrs in Bayern," November 21, 1919, in BayHStA, MWi 8073.

19. Letter of Landesverband Bayerischer Viehhändler im Bunde der Viehhändler Deutschlands (Bavarian Cattle Traders' Association) to Staatsministerium für Handel, Gewerbe und Industrie (Bavarian Trade Ministry) in Munich, April 4, 1919; this view is also shared by the Nordwestdeutscher Viehhändlerverband (Northwest German Cattle Traders' Association) in a letter to the Reichsminister für Ernährung und Landwirtschaft (National Agricultural Ministry in Berlin), July 4, 1922; both communications in BayHStA, MWi 8073. Here it needs to be explained that buying up cattle was restricted to the cattle-trading associations and the official funding organizations on an equal footing with them. When controls were lifted on the economy, this regulation was rendered invalid, so there was a need to ensure "that even in the future only reliable persons, as far as possible in limited numbers, will then be admitted to the cattle trade." Quote from "Entwurf einer Verordnung über die Aufhebung kriegswirtschaftlicher Vorschriften auf dem Gebiete der öffentlichen Fleischversorgung," around August 18, 1920, in BayHStA, MWi 8073.

20. Excerpt from the transcript of "Neuregelung des Vieh- und Fleischverkehrs in Bayern," November 21, 1919, in BayHStA, MWi 8073.

21. From the transcript of "Neuregelung des Vieh- und Fleischverkehrs in Bayern," November 21, 1919, in BayHStA, MWi 8073; see also Zucker, "Production of Trust," 53. Niklas Luhmann, too, points to the significance of trust for reproducing social complexity; see Luhmann, *Vertrauen: Ein Mechanismus der Reduktion sozialer Komplexität* (Stuttgart: Lucius & Lucius, 2000), 27–37. Franchising in the cattle trade, moreover, was not new; it had already been introduced along with state controls on the economy in 1916. See Grünberg, *Der deutsche Viehhandel*, 64–67.

22. The Landesamt für Viehverkehr existed between 1920 and 1924. It was the successor organization to the Bayerische Fleischversorgungsstelle (Bavarian Meat Supply Office), which existed between 1916 and 1920. See Helmut Braun, "Kriegs- und Zwangswirtschaftsstellen, 1915–1924," in *Historisches Lexikon Bayerns*, November 8, 2009. On the reorganization of the cattle trade, see "Neuregelung des Vieh- und Fleischverkehrs in Bayern," November 21, 1919; and Rundschreiben (circular) from the Landesamt für Viehverkehr, Munich, October 20, 1920; both in BayHStA, MWi 8073.

23. Annette Baier, *Moral Prejudices: Essays on Ethics* (Cambridge, MA: Harvard University Press, 1996), 95–129, 99.

24. Even if, philosophically speaking, reliability cannot be equated with trust, it is nonetheless a key precondition for the production of trust. Someone

proven to be reliable can be granted trust. In contrast to trust that is tied to moral norms, reliability is regarded as morally neutral and is therefore potentially subject to bureaucratic interrogation and examination. See Baier, *Reflections on How We Live* (Oxford: Oxford University Press, 2010), Oxford Scholarship Online (2015), https://doi.org/10.1093/acprof:osobl /9780199570362.001.0001; see chapter entitled "Demoralization, Trust, and Virtues," 173–275.

25. These files, however, fell victim to the destruction of the Bayerisches Hauptstaatsarchiv (archives of the Bavarian State) and could not be consulted as a source for this analysis. It is unclear when and why the files were removed from the holdings of the Bayerisches Hauptstaatsarchiv. The only material that could be found was the aforementioned list of cattle traders resident in Bavaria between 1920 and 1925; see BayHStA, General-direktion der Staatl. Archive Bayerns 2677.

26. Zucker, "Production of Trust," 98.

27. Letter from Landesverband bayerischer Viehhändler (LBV) to the Sta-atsministerium für Landwirtschaft, January 31, 1927, in BayHStA, MWi 8074.

28. In a letter on May 15, 1924, the LBV complained to the Bavarian Justice Ministry about the purported bias of the courts toward the profession of cattle traders; it was alleged that the courts were too quick to condemn or pass judgment on cattle traders without an extensive presentation of evidence. See BayHStA, MWi 8073.

29. Dr. Graminger quoted according to an article in the *Münchner Neueste Nachrichten*, no. 161, April 15, 1923; this was also criticized by the branch of the Deutscher Fleischer-Verband (German Butchers' Association) from Köln-Kalk (the Kalk district of Cologne) in a letter on July 13, 1925, to the Handwerkskammer von Oberbayern (Upper Bavarian Chamber of Handicrafts) in Munich, pertaining to the Gesetz über den Verkehr mit Vieh und Fleisch (Law on Commerce with Cattle and Meat); both documents in BayHStA, MWi 8073. See also "Was bringt uns die völlige Wiederherstellung der Gewerbefreiheit?," in *Allgemeine Viehhandels-Zei-tung: Wochenschrift für Viehverkehr, Viehverwertung, Viehhaltung; offizielles Organ des Deutschen Viehhandels-Bundes und aller Viehhandels-Verbände im Bundesgebiet*, ed. Bund der Viehhändler Deutschlands. Beilage [supple-ment] 32 (Garmisch-Partenkirchen: Viehhandels-Verl., 1925).

30. From the circular "Rundschreiben V2 des Landesamts für Viehverkehr," October 20, 1920, in BayHStA, MWi 8073.

31. Quoted by Martin Hartmann, "Einleitung," in *Vertrauen: Die Grundlage des sozialen Zusammenhalts*, edited by Hartmann and Claus Offe (Frank-furt am Main: Campus, 2001), 15.

32. Excerpt from the 1929 annual conference of the Verbandstag des Landesverbandes Bayerischer Viehhändler (State Association of Bavarian Cattle
Traders), in BayHStA, MWi 7819. But inside the Jewish community, too,
youth vocational training was promoted; see Wilhelm Cohn, "Die Berufswahl der jüdischen Jugend," *Nürnberger-Fürther Israelitisches Gemeindeblatt* 8, no. 1 (1927): 1.

33. Zucker, "Production of Trust," 94.

34. As Wiebke Lisner emphasized, the process of professionalization in any
particular field is always accompanied by processes of social and political
negotiation, something also demonstrated here in the case of the cattle
trade; see Lisner, *"Hüterinnen der Nation": Hebammen im Nationalsozialismus* (Frankfurt am Main: Campus, 2006), 12.

35. The Bund der Viehhändler Deutschlands (Association of German Livestock
Traders) was founded in 1900, and one of its chairmen was Jewish cattle
trader Hermann Daniel (from 1910 to 1916, approximately). The national
association was divided into numerous smaller state and district branches,
and its official organ was the *Allgemeine Viehhandels-Zeitung*, published
starting in 1909. The main office, damaged by bombing during the Second
World War, was located in Berlin's Kochstraße. For more on the establishment of livestock traders' professional associations, see August Skalweit, ed.,
Die Viehhandelsverbände in der deutschen Kriegswirtschaft (Berlin: Verlag der
Beiträge zur Kriegswirtschaft Reimar Hobbing, 1917), 1–7.

36. The existence of a cattle traders' school is demonstrable only for the period
after 1945. At the beginning of the 1950s, a cattle traders' school existed
in Herrsching am Ammersee, according to telephone directory information from the town's municipal archivist. As early as its congress in June
1929, the Verbandstag des Landesverbandes Bayerischer Viehhändler was
already calling for "the establishment of an officially recognized registry
of apprentices and . . . the holding of voluntary courses with the chief aim
of commercial training," from "Entwurf eines Schreibens des Staatsministeriums für Wirtschaft an den Landesverband der Bayerischen Viehhändler," June 7, 1929, in BayHStA, MWi 7819.

37. See chapter I.

38. Excerpt from the circular "Rundschreiben V2 des Landesamts für Viehverkehr," October 20, 1920, in BayHStA, MWi 8073.

39. The government of Upper Palatinate (Oberpfalz) and Regensburg
expresses this view in a letter (June 30, 1921) to the other district governments, in StAN, Rep. 270, IV, Regierung, K.d.I, Abg. 1968, Titel IX,
no. 402.

40. See letter from Regierung der Oberpfalz und von Regensburg, Kammer
des Innern an die übrigen Regierungen, Kammern des Innern (Chamber

of the Interior of the Government of Upper Palatinate and Regensburg
to other chambers of the interior), June 20, 1921; see also the circular
from the State Office for Livestock Commerce, "Rundschreiben V19 des
Landesamts für Viehverkehr," July 27, 1922; both documents in StAN,
Rep. 270, IV, Regierung, K.d.I, Abg. 1968, Titel IX, no. 402.

41. "Staatsministerium für Landwirtschaft an die Bezirksverwaltungsbe-
hörden," Munich, December 28, 1921, in StAN, Rep. 270, IV, Regierung,
K.d.I, Abg. 1968, Titel IX, no. 402; see also another letter (July 21, 1923):
"Gewerbe- und Handelsverein, Marktredwitz u. Umgebung an das
Bayerische Handelsministerium, Marktredwitz, 21.07.1923, Betreff:
Handelserlaubnis mit Vieh für das Metzgergewerbe," in BayHStA,
MWi 8073.

42. That this regulation was criticized by the butchers and their representatives emerges from the statement made by Jakob Grabmair at the seven-
teenth meeting of the Bayerische Landesbauernkammer (Bavarian State
Chamber of Agriculture) on July 12, 1923, in BayHStA, MWi 8073.

43. See also chapter 2.

44. "Mitteilung des Landesamts für Viehverkehr Nr. 37302, 22.07.1921," mentioned in a memo from the city council of Rothenburg ob der Tauber with
the heading "Betreff: Ausübung des Pferdehandels neben dem Viehhandel," July 29, 1921, in Stadtarchiv Rothenburg o/T, Box 976.

45. But Christian traders also divided up the business of cattle and horse trading among each other, as did the brothers Fritz and Heinrich Kirchbaum
from Rothenburg ob der Tauber; see the file "Kirchbaum" in Stadtarchiv
Rothenburg o/T, Box 976.

46. One example would be the brothers Samson and Siegmund Wurzinger
from Rothenburg ob der Tauber; see the files "Wurzinger" in Stadtarchiv
Rothenburg o/T, Box 976. But the traders Hugo and Salomon Hausmann
from Ansbach were also affected by this regulation; see "Protokoll des
Stadtrats Ansbach vom 19.06.1921," in Stadtarchiv Ansbach, ABc
R12/22.

47. Bayerisches Staatsministerium für Landwirtschaft an die Bezirksverwaltungsbehörden, Munich, December 28, 1921, in StAN, Rep. 270, IV,
Regierung, K.d.I, Abg. 1968, Titel IX, no. 402; see also "Stellungnahme
von Landwirtschaftsrat Schwamberger bei der 17. Sitzung der bayerischen
Landesbauernkammer, 12.07.1923," in BayHStA, MWi 8073.

48. On Jewish horse traders, see Arno Herzig, "Die westfälischen Juden im
Modernisierungsprozeß," in *Deutsche Juden und die Moderne*, ed. Shulamit
Volkov (Munich: Oldenbourg, 1994), 108.

49. See minutes of Ansbach Municipal Council from June 19, 1921, "Protokoll des Stadtrats Ansbach vom 19.06.1921," in Stadtarchiv Ansbach,

ABcR12/22. The repeal of this prohibition was constantly being discussed anew, yet the ban stayed in place; see also this discussion in the minutes of the Bayerische Landesbauernkammer (Bavarian Chamber of Agriculture): "Protokoll der Bayerischen Landesbauernkammer, 17. Sitzung, 12.07.1923, Diskussion über die gleichzeitige Zulassung zum Vieh- und Pferdehandel," in BayHStA, MWi 8073.

50. Letter from Landesamt für Viehverkehr to the cattle and horse trader Samson Wurzinger, Rothenburg ob der Tauber, October 7, 1921, in Stadtarchiv Rothenburg o/T, Box 976.

51. All of the letters from the Landesamt für Viehverkehr (State Office for Livestock Commerce) and the Stadtrat (city council) of Rothenburg ob der Tauber in the Wurzinger case between 1922 and 1924 in Stadtarchiv Rothenburg o/T, Box 976.

52. Der Minister für Landwirtschaft, "Betreff: Buchführung im Viehhandel, Berlin, 29.01.1924," in BayHStA, MWi 8073.

53. Excerpt from the transcript of "Neuregelung des Vieh- und Fleischverkehrs in Bayern," November 21, 1919, in BayHStA, MWi 8073.

54. Statement, "Stellungnahme Steininger bei der 17. Sitzung der Bayerischen Landesbauernkammer, München, 12.07.1923," in BayHStA, MWi 8073.

55. Statement, "Stellungnahme Dr. Heim bei der 17. Sitzung der Bayerischen Landesbauernkammer, München, 12.07.1923," in BayHStA, MWi 8073.

56. See Protokoll der Bayerischen Landesbauernkammer, 17. Sitzung der Landesbauernkammer, München, 12.07.1923 (minutes of Bavarian Chamber of Agriculture meeting from July 12, 1923), in BayHStA, MWi 8073; see also Stephanie Merkenich, *Grüne Front gegen Weimar: Reichs-Landbund und agrarischer Lobbyismus 1918–1933* (Düsseldorf: Droste, 1998), 121–128; Martin Ulmer, "'Zuerst die Kuh, dann Hab und Gut, erpreßt der Advokat und Jud'—Über Agrarantisemitismus in Württemberg," in *Jüdische Viehhändler zwischen Schwarzwald und Schwäbischer Alb: Vorträge der Tagung der Arbeitsgemeinschaft Jüdische Gedenkstätten am Oberen Neckar am 3. Oktober 2006 in Horb-Rexingen*, ed. Robert Uri Kaufmann and Carsten Kohlmann, 131–155 (Horb-Rexingen: Barbara Staudacher, 2008).

57. Dr. Johann Attinger, "Die Bayerische Viehverwertung," *Süddeutsche Landwirtschaftliche Tierzucht* (Sonderdruck), no. 18, 1920, in BayHStA, MWi 8073; see also Elke Kimmel, *Methoden antisemitischer Propaganda im Ersten Weltkrieg: Die Presse des Bundes der Landwirte* (Berlin: Metropol, 2001), 164–165.

58. "Stellungnahme Jakob Grabmair auf der 17. Sitzung der Bayerischen Landesbauernkammer, München, 12.07.1923," in BayHStA, MWi 8073.

59. If deals were concluded below their actual value during the inflation, traders were able to make claims for revaluation against the buyer retroactively. Letter of member of the Bavarian Landtag [name illegible, and party membership not stated on the letter] to the Bavarian Justice Ministry, Munich, January 9, 1926; see also the much more measured reply from the Agriculture Ministry about how to proceed as a legal matter with attempts at revaluing livestock: "Staatsministerium für Landwirtschaft an die Bezirksverwaltungsbehörden, München, 5.03.1926." Both letters in BayHStA, MJu 15694. There was a similar reaction by the Württembergischer Bauern- und Weingärtnerbund (Württemberg Farmers and Vintners Association) to the revaluation applications of a Jewish cattle trader, which the association rejected as the "usurious demands of a Jewish cattle trader." See "Wie sich der Württ. Bauern- und Weingärtnerbund die Aufwertung alter Kaufpreis-Forderungen vorstellt!," *Württembergische Viehhandelszeitung* 1, no. 19 (1926): 1. See also the verdict "Urteil des Landgerichts Würzburg gegen den Viehhändler Sally Schwab aus Rimpar wegen Preiswuchers, 17.04.1924," in BayHStA, MJu 13207; also Merkenich, *Grüne Front gegen Weimar*, 121–128.

60. Kriminalbeamter Weigel an die Bayerische Landeswucherabwehrstelle, Nürnberg, 10.09.1923 (files for Nuremberg branch of Bavarian State Anti-Profiteering Authority), in StAN, Bayerische Landeswucherabwehrstelle, Zweigstelle Nürnberg, no. 64.

61. See also Eberle, "Das Problem der Handelsspanne," 17–18.

62. Jens Zinke, *Die Entwicklung der landwirtschaftlichen Genossenschaften in der Weimarer Republik: Unter besonderer Berücksichtigung der Änderungen des Genossenschaftsgesetzes* (Berlin: Inst. für Genossenschaftswesen, 1999), 21.

63. Ingrid Bauert-Keetman, *Friedrich Wilhelm Raiffeisen: Ein Leben für die Zukunft* (Hanover: Steinbock, 1987).

64. Heinrich Richter, "Friedrich Wilhelm Raiffeisen und die Entwicklung seiner Genossenschaftsidee" (PhD diss., Erlangen-Nürnberg, 1966).

65. Förderverein Hermann Schulze-Delitzsch, ed., *Hermann Schulze-Delitzsch: Weg—Werk—Wirkung* (Wiesbaden: Deutscher Genossenschafts, 2008).

66. Monika Richarz, "Viehhandel und Landjuden im 19. Jahrhundert: Eine symbiotische Wirtschaftsbeziehung in Südwestdeutschland," in *Menora: Jahrbuch für deutsch-jüdische Geschichte*, ed. Julius H. Schoeps, 66–88 (Munich: Piper, 1990), 82; see also Werner Teuber, *Jüdische Viehhändler in Ostfriesland und im nördlichen Emsland 1871–1942: Eine vergleichende Studie zu einer jüdischen Berufsgruppe in zwei wirtschaftlich und konfessionell unterschiedlichen Regionen* (Cloppenburg: Runge, 1995), 54–57.

67. See Ulrich Baumann, *Zerstörte Nachbarschaften: Christen und Juden in badischen Landgemeinden 1862–1940* (Hamburg: Dölling und Galitz, 2000), 39.

68. Verein für Socialpolitik, ed., *Der Wucher auf dem Lande: Berichte und Gutachten* (Leipzig: Duncker & Humblot, 1887).

69. Franz Bussen, *Das landwirtschaftliche Genossenschaftswesen, mit bes. Berücks. d. hannoverschen Verhältnisse* (Hanover: C. V. Engelhard, 1928), 8.

70. The liberal Hansa-Bund, established in 1909 to oppose the conservative Bund der Landwirte (Agrarian League), played a special role in lending moral support to the private cattle trade, whereas the governmental meat supply office advocated the introduction of a state monopoly in the cattle trade as a solution to the sector's problems. The Hansa-Bund (a modern pro-free-trade organization not to be confused with the medieval Hanseatic League after which it was named) regarded the private cattle trade as the only kind of "trustworthy cattle trade" (*"reellen Viehhandel"*). In the view of the Hansa-Bund, only the private cattle trade was in a position to bring excessive prices down and combat illicit trading. See the May 3, 1919, letter, "Schreiben vom Hansa-Bund für Gewerbe, Handel und Industrie, Landesverband Nordbayern, Zentrale Nürnberg, an das Handelsministerium, Bamberg, Nürnberg, 3.05.1919"; see also transcript excerpt "Auszug aus der Niederschrift der 163. Sitzung der Nationalversammlung, Anfrage No. 828, Dr. Böhme (Magdeburg), 16.04.1920." Both documents in BayHStA, MWi 8073.

71. From "Fleischverwertung und Viehhandel," *Münchner Neueste Nachrichten*, February 9, 1921, in BayHStA, MWi 8073.

72. "Fleischverwertung und Viehhandel," *Münchner Neueste Nachrichten*, February 9, 1921, in BayHStA, MWi 8073. Between 1922 and 1924, the Bayerische Landeswucherabwehrstelle (Bavarian State Anti-Profiteering Authority) was responsible for monitoring livestock commerce; it supervised how cattle was sent to regions outside Bavaria. See, for example, this report to its Nuremberg branch: "Bericht der Bayerischen Landeswucherabwehrstelle, München, 9.11.1923," in StAN, Bayerische Landeswucherabwehrstelle, Zweigstelle Nürnberg, no. 64.

73. *Fränkischer Kurier*, January 25, 1921, no. 40, in StAN, Rep. 270, Regierung, K.d.I, Abg. 1968, no. 409. See also "Fleischverwertung und Viehhandel," *Münchner Neueste Nachrichten*, February 9, 1921; file memo "Aktenvermerk bayerisches Staatsministerium für Wirtschaft," Munich, June 7, 1921. Both in BayHStA, MWi 8073. In addition, Hans Riedl points out that the cooperative was active selling only in regions with a surplus of cattle, so as to distribute this cattle to regions where there was a scarcity of beef cattle;

see Riedl, *Die genossenschaftliche Viehverwertung in Bayern* (Munich: Bayerische Viehverwertung, 1930), 58.

74. "Fleischverwertung und Viehhandel," Münchner Neueste Nachrichten, February 9, 1921, in BayHStA, MWi 8073. The discussion about cattle exports out of Bavaria was still on the minds of Nuremberg cattle traders in 1923. See the transcript "Niederschrift Sitzung vom 16.04.1923 und Sitzung vom 13.08.1923, Schlachthof Nürnberg," in Stadtarchiv Nürnberg, C69 001–006; also see the correspondence between the Bavarian Anti-Profiteering Authority and the State Office for Cattle Commerce in 1923 about the supervision of the Bavarian cattle markets in StAN, Bayerische Landeswucherabwehrstelle, Zweigstelle Nürnberg, no. 63.

75. "Fleischverwertung und Viehhandel," *Münchner Neueste Nachrichten,* February 9, 1921, in BayHStA, MWi 8073.

76. "Gendarmerie-Hauptstation Gunzenhausen an die Bayerische Landeswucherabwehrstelle, Zweigstelle Nürnberg, 16.09.1923," in StAN, Bayerische Landeswucherabwehrstelle, Zweigstelle Nürnberg, no. 64; see also the indictment for price gouging brought against Julius Mann, Rothenburg ob der Tauber, October 2, 1923, in Stadtarchiv Rothenburg o/T, Box 976.

77. Riedl, *Die genossenschaftliche Viehverwertung in Bayern*, 6; Franz Ruhwandl also lamented the low earnings garnered by farmers from the market proceeds. See Ruhwandl, "Die Aufgaben der Genossenschaften bei der Neugestaltung des landwirtschaftlichen Marktwesens: Mit besonderer Berücksichtigung der Verhältnisse in Bayern r.d. Rh" (PhD diss., Munich, 1932), 2; see also Warren, *Die Erzeugungs- und Absatzverhältnisse,* 110ff.

78. "Viehhändler-Gewinne," *Frankfurter Zeitung*, no. 394, May 3, 1921. Social Democratic Landtag Deputy Lina Ammon also joined in this chorus; see "Stenographische Berichte zu den öffentlichen Sitzungen 1922/23," vol. 7, of the "Sitzung des Bayerischen Landtags, 2.03.1923," 1013–1019. See also Eberle, "Das Problem der Handelsspanne," 12; Grünberg, *Der deutsche Viehhandel,* 67.

79. Riedl, *Die genossenschaftliche Viehverwertung in Bayern*, 5.

80. From the annual report of the Jahresbericht des LBV (State Association of Bavarian Cattle Traders), June 5, 1929, in BayHStA, MWi7819.

81. Eberle, "Das Problem der Handelsspanne," 13; also published in *Bayerischen Viehhändler,* no. 7 (1933).

82. Eberle, "Das Problem der Handelsspanne," 13; also published in *Bayerischen Viehhändler,* no. 7 (1933).

83. Cited by Eberle, "Das Problem der Handelsspanne," 13–14.

84. See Grünberg, *Der deutsche Viehhandel,* 13.

85. Riedl, *Die genossenschaftliche Viehverwertung in Bayern*, 6; Ruhwandl, "Die Aufgaben der Genossenschaften," 2.

86. Note from the Bayerische Landeswucherabwehrstelle with the subject heading "Handelsübliche Gewinnsätze im reellen, gewerbsmäßigen Viehhandel," Munich, May 3, 1923, in StAN, Bayerische Landeswucher-abwehrstelle, Zweigstelle Nürnberg, no. 63.

87. Ruhwandl, "Die Aufgaben der Genossenschaften," 24.

88. See also Bussen, *Das landwirtschaftliche Genossenschaftswesen*, 91.

89. "Die genossenschaftliche Viehverwertung in Bayern," in *Allgemeine Viehhandels-Zeitung. Wochenschrift für Viehverkehr, Viehverwertung, Viehhaltung; offizielles Organ des Deutschen Viehhandels-Bundes und aller Viehhandels-Verbände im Bundesgebiet* 43, no. 3, ed. Bund der Viehhändler Deutschlands; see also letter to the editor about an article in issue 99 of *Forchheimer Tagblatt*, reprinted in *Forchheimer Tagblatt*, no. 101, May 1, 1924, in BayHStA, MJu 13207.

90. "Die Landwirtschaft als Konkurrent des Viehhandels," in *Allgemeine Viehhandels-Zeitung. Wochenschrift für Viehverkehr, Viehverwertung, Viehhaltung; offizielles Organ des Deutschen Viehhandels-Bundes und aller Viehhandels-Verbände im Bundesgebiet*, ed. Bund der Viehhändler Deutschlands. Beilage [supplement] 17, no. 1 (Garmisch-Partenkirchen: Viehhandels-Verl., 1925).

91. From annual report "Jahresbericht des Landesverbandes bayerischer Viehhändler," June 5, 1929, in BayHStA, MWi 7819; the State Association of Bavarian Cattle Traders criticized the national livestock sales effort of the national government, using the subsidies that were part of Agricultural Minister Schiele's policy and that amounted to two million marks, as "artificially grafted"; see Landesverband Bayerischer Viehhändler e.V., "Im Kampf um Gerechtigkeit! Gegen die Monopolstellung der Reichsviehverwertung!," *Der Bayerische Viehhändler* 12, no. 52 (1932).

92. Attinger, "Die Bayerische Viehverwertung."

93. From Riedl's diagram, it is impossible to get readings of any exact figures; the only possible readout involves approximate groups of a thousand, used to calculate percentages.

94. Bussen, *Das landwirtschaftliche Genossenschaftswesen*, 12.

95. Attinger, "Die Bayerische Viehverwertung."

96. Attinger, "Die Bayerische Viehverwertung." During the First World War, the cooperatives were accused of having paid too little to the farmers for their products. See reply written by "Der Völkische Block" to an article in issue 99 of *Forchheimer Tagblatt* in *Forchheimer Tagblatt*, no. 101, May 1, 1924, in BayHStA, MJu 13207.

97. Excerpt from a lecture by U. Assel about "Zweck und Ziel der Bayer-ischen Viehverwertung GmbH & Co und ihre Aufgaben in der freien Wirtschaft," Munich, August 16, 1920, in BayHStA, MWi 8073; see also Grünberg, *Der deutsche Viehhandel*, 44–45.
98. Riedl, *Die genossenschaftliche Viehverwertung in Bayern*, 11.
99. Bussen, *Das landwirtschaftliche Genossenschaftswesen*, 96.
100. Attinger, "Die Bayerische Viehverwertung."
101. Riedl, *Die genossenschaftliche Viehverwertung in Bayern*, 21.
102. Excerpt from a lecture by Assel, "Zweck und Ziel der Bayerischen Viehverwertung GmbH & Co und ihre Aufgaben in der freien Wirtschaft," 14.
103. Ute Frevert characterizes trustees in addition as the "personification of mistrust"; see Frevert, "Vertrauen—eine historische Spurensuche," in *Vertrauen: Historische Annäherungen*, ed. Frevert, 7–66 (Göttingen: Vandenhoeck und Ruprecht, 2003), 45.
104. "Der Hanseat, Reichsverband der deutschen landwirtschaftlichen Genossenschaften," 1926, 24, in BayHStA, ML 1911; Richarz argued that Jewish cattle traders were able to hold their ground because they were very familiar with the commodities they were trading, expertise they were able to pass on from generation to generation; see Richarz, "Viehhandel und Landjuden," 79.
105. Eberle and Graminger, "Nieder mit dem Handel?," *Der Bayerische Viehhändler* 4, no. 22 (May 30, 1924).
106. Eberle and Graminger, "Nieder mit dem Handel?"
107. This is a view also endorsed by Bussen (speaking for the husbandry cooperatives); see Bussen, *Das landwirtschaftliche Genossenschaftswe-sen*, 92.
108. Kaufmann confirms this finding for Switzerland; see Kaufmann, *Jüdische und christliche Viehhändler in der Schweiz 1780–1930* (Zurich: Chronos, 1988), 121–122. Teuber does, as well, for Eastern Frisia; see Teuber, *Jüdische Viehhändler in Ostfriesland*, 54–57.
109. Falk Wiesemann draws attention to how the livestock husbandry cooperatives were also attempting to gain a foothold in the trade with domestic cattle for farm use; see Wiesemann, "Juden auf dem Lande: Die wirtschaftliche Ausgrenzung der jüdischen Viehhändler in Bayern," in *Die Reihen fast geschlossen*, ed. Jürgen Reulecke and Detlev Peukert, 381–396 (Wuppertal: Hammer, 1981), 392. See also Assel, "Zweck und Ziel der Bayerischen Viehverwertung GmbH & Co und ihre Aufgaben in der freien Wirtschaft."
110. "Der Hanseat, Reichsverband der deutschen landwirtschaftlichen Genossenschaften," 1926, 24, in BayHStA, ML 1911.

111. This was a result of eating habits among the German population, whose intake of meat was met by pork at a level up to more than 50 percent but covered by beef only up to 35 percent; see Statistisches Reichsamt, *Statistisches Jahrbuch für das Deutsche Reich*, 1924/25, 306. Bussen also stated that the livestock husbandry cooperatives were focused mainly on selling hogs and piglets but not on cattle for breeding and domestic farm use (that is, on the sale of cows); see Bussen, *Das landwirtschaftliche Genossenschaftswesen*, 92.

112. See Assel, "Zweck und Ziel der Bayerischen Viehverwertung GmbH & Co und ihre Aufgaben in der freien Wirtschaft," 13; see also Bussen, *Das landwirtschaftliche Genossenschaftswesen*, 92.

113. This finding is confirmed by Richarz, "Viehhandel und Landjuden," 82; and by Kaufmann, "Zum Viehhandel der Juden in Deutschland und der Schweiz – bisherige Ergebnisse und offene Fragen," in *Jüdische Viehhändler zwischen Schwarzwald und Schwäbischer Alb*, ed. Kaufmann and Kohlmann, 37.

114. Willi Wygodzinski, *Agrarwesen und Agrarpolitik: Kapital und Arbeit in der Landwirtschaft. Verwertung der landwirtschaftlichen Produkte. Organisation des landwirtschaftlichen Berufsstandes* (Berlin: Göschen, 1928), 84–85; Grünberg, *Der deutsche Viehhandel*, 10–12.

115. For example, the Bayerische Landeswucherabwehrstelle, Zweigstelle Nürnberg (Nuremberg branch of the Bavarian State Anti-Profiteering Authority), complains in a letter (April 26, 1923) to the main office of the Bayerische Landeswucherabwehrstelle in Munich that cities were recently registering significant losses because of lower revenues from cattle market fees; see StAN, Bayerische Landeswucherabwehrstelle, Zweigstelle Nürnberg, no. 64.

116. Erich Rosenthal draws attention to the social significance of the cattle markets: Rosenthal, "Der Viehmarkt," *Der Morgen* 12 (1934/1935): 556–559.

117. There is a reference to the link between the cattle-trading and marriage-brokering activities of cattle trader Josef Mann between 1924 and 1927 in a letter from RA Dr. Bayer to the city council of Rothenburg o/T, Ansbach, March 9, 1935, in StAN, Rep. 270, Regierung, K.d.I, Abg. 1978, no. 3417. See also Stefanie Fischer, conversation with Robert Auernhammer, Oberhochstatt, 2008; Marion A. Kaplan, "For Love or Money: The Marriage Strategies of Jews in Imperial Germany," *Leo Baeck Institute Year Book* 28 (1983): 287; Kaufmann, "Zum Viehhandel der Juden," 39.

118. See *Südfränkische Zeitung*, no. 59, March 11, 1927, in StAN, LRA Dinkelsbühl, Abg. 1976, no. 1506; Letter from Georg Soldner to the BA Rothenburg o/T, August 15, 1933, in StAN, LRA Rothenburg o/T, Abg. 1975, no. 4396.

119. Letter from Bezirkstierarzt für den Verwaltungsbezirk Weißenburg/Bay (District Veterinarian for the Administrative District Weißenburg/Bavaria) to the BA Weißenburg/Bay (Weißenburg District Office), February 14, 1925, in Stadtarchiv Ellingen, no call number. An excerpt from the minutes of the Sitzungsprotokoll des Stadtmagistrats Ellingen (Ellingen Municipal Authority) on May 29, 1914, shows that these accusations were part of a long tradition going back many years; see document in StAN, LRA Wbg., Abg. 1996, Titel VII, no. 3111.

120. See Bayerische Landeswucherabwehrstelle, Zweigstelle Nürnberg an die Bayerische Landeswucherabwehrstelle, 21.07.1924 (Letter from Nuremberg branch of Bavarian State Anti-Profiteering Authority to main office in Munich, July 21, 1924), in StAN, Bayerische Landeswucherabwehrstelle, Zweigstelle Nürnberg, no. 64.

121. See Bund der Viehhändler Deutschlands an den Reichsminister für Ernährung und Landwirtschaft, 29.06.1922 (Letter from Association of German Livestock Traders to Reich Agriculture Minister, June 29, 1922), in BayHStA, MWi 8073; Bayerische Bauernkammer, ed., *Agrar-Korrespondenz* (Munich, 1929/1930). See also Gutachten von Dr. Händel, Nürnberger Schlachthofdirektion, 7.11.1924 (report by Dr. Händel of the Nuremberg Slaughterhouse Management, November 7, 1924), in Stadtarchiv Nürnberg, C69, no. 3.

122. Dr. Haushofer, "Viehmarkthallen," *Agrar-Korrespondenz der Bayerischen Landesbauernkammer* 8, no. 34 (August 23, 1930).

123. Haushofer, "Viehmarkthallen."

124. Stadtrat Scheinfeld an das BA Scheinfeld, Scheinfeld, 22.05.1933 (Communication from Scheinfeld Municipal Council to Scheinfeld District Office, May 22, 1933), in StAN, LRA Scheinfeld, Abg. 1977, no. 1592.

125. In a letter from the Wassertrüdingen Municipal Council to the Dinkelsbühl District Office, undated (but presumably around February 16, 1926), the municipal council justifies its plan to reintroduce the cattle market by arguing that such markets work to regulate prices, since the farmer would get a better price in a public trade than in a stables trade; see StAN, LRA Dinkelsbühl, Abg. 1976, no. 1509. See also Warren, *Die Erzeugungs- und Absatzverhältnisse*, 110.

126. Adelheid von Saldern, *Mittelstand im 'Dritten Reich': Handwerker—Einzelhändler—Bauern* (Frankfurt am Main: Campus, 1985), 203; Merkenich, *Grüne Front gegen Weimar*, 13; Detlev Peukert, *Die Weimarer Republik*, 226–231.

127. On the discussion about reintroducing the municipal cattle markets, see Magistrat der bayerischen Kreishauptstadt Ansbach an die Regierung von Mittelfranken, Ansbach, 10.08.1921 (Communication from the

Town Council of the Bavarian County Seat Ansbach to the Central Franconian government's Chamber of the Interior, August 10, 1921), in StAN, Rep. 270, Regierung von Mittelfranken, K.d.I, Abg. 1968, Titel IX, no. 407.

128. Letter from Wassertrüdingen Municipal Council to Dinkelsbühl District Office, Wassertrüdingen, February 11, 1926, in StAN, LRA Dinkelsbühl, Abg. 1976, no. 1509. Other local governments also made an effort to reintroduce their cattle markets; see StAN, LRA Ansbach, Abg. 1961, no. 4290; StAN, LRA Dinkelsbühl, Abg. 1976, no. 1509; StAN, LRA Scheinfeld, Abg. 1977, no. 1599 & no. 1592; StAN, Rep. 270, Regierung von Mittelfranken, K.d.I, Abg. 1968, Titel IX, no. 404.

129. Helmut Genschel, *Die Verdrängung der Juden aus der Wirtschaft im Dritten Reich* (Göttingen: Muster-Schmidt, 1966), 32ff.; Rainer Hambrecht, *Der Aufstieg der NSDAP in Mittel- und Oberfranken, 1925–1933* (Nuremberg: Stadtarchiv Nürnberg, Korn u. Berg, 1976), 237–238; Manfred Kittel, *Provinz zwischen Reich und Republik: Politische Mentalitäten in Deutschland und Frankreich, 1918–1933/36* (Munich: Oldenbourg, 2000), 294ff.

130. See the document "Die Errichtung einer Markthalle," especially the letter by Salomon Strauß, Vorstand des mittelfr. Viehhändlervereins (chair of the Central Franconian Cattle Traders Association), to the Nuremberg City Council, September 28, 1921, in Stadtarchiv Nürnberg, C7/VIII KR, no. 6751; see also Teuber, *Jüdische Viehhändler in Ostfriesland*, 67–68.

131. Michael Wildt, *Geschichte des Nationalsozialismus* (Göttingen: Vandenhoeck & Ruprecht, 2008), 46.

132. Shifting to a favorable weekday is discussed in a letter of April 14, 1927, from the municipal council of Ansbach to the Central Franconian government's Chamber of the Interior; see Schreiben vom Stadtrat von Ansbach an die Regierung von Mittelfranken, Kammer des Innern, Ansbach, 14.04.1927, in StAN, Rep. 270, Regierung von Mittelfranken, K.d.I, Abg. 1968, Titel IX, no. 407. The municipal council of Greding, in a letter sent to the district veterinarian Dr. Englert on April 8, 1927, called for the cattle market to be shifted from Friday to another weekday, since Jewish traders would be absent on Friday owing to the start of Shabbat. See letter in StAN, LRA Hilpoltstein, Abg. 1971, no. 1668. As in Treuchtlingen, the cattle market regulations (Viehmarktordnung) in many localities contained a paragraph specifying that no market should be held on a Jewish holiday; see excerpt from minutes of meeting of the Treuchtlingen municipal council on December 22, 1926, Der Stadtrat beschliesst eine neue Viehmarktordnung, in StAN, LRA Wbg.,

Abg. 1996, Titel VII, no. 3111. See also Teuber, *Jüdische Viehhändler in Ostfriesland*, 64.

133. See the correspondence "Schlacht- und Viehhofdirektion an den Stadtrat Ansbach, Ansbach, 14.12.1926"; "Stadtrat Ansbach an die Betriebsinspektion Ansbach, 16.12.1926"; and "Stadtrat Ansbach an Ludwig Mohr, Ansbach, 5.01.1927"—all three letters in Stadtarchiv Ansbach, ABc R21/12. Previously, municipal decision-makers had always rejected similar requests, as illustrated by a letter of January 18, 1915, from the municipal council (Stadtmagistrat) Ellingen to its counterpart in Gunzenhausen, filed under "Ellingen, 18.01.1915," in Stadtarchiv Gunzenhausen, Rep. II, Fach 29, no. 6I.

134. See Hambrecht, *Der Aufstieg der NSDAP*, 240.

135. Memo from Gunzenhausen Municipal Councilor "Notiz des Stadtrats, J. V. Raab, Juni 1927," in Stadtarchiv Gunzenhausen, Rep. II, Fach 29, 6I; cases like this have also been recorded at this time at other places in the vicinity, as in Treuchtlingen. There, too, the municipal council complained in a letter of February 8, 1928, to the Weißenburg/Bayern District Office that handing out issues of the *Stürmer* was upsetting its efforts to get more cattle driven to the market there; see the letter in StAN, LRA Wbg., Abg. 1996, Titel VII, no. 3111. Beatrix Herlemann points out that this was not just a regional phenomenon. In Lower Saxony, incidents like this were already being noted as early as 1926. See Herlemann, *"Der Bauer klebt am Hergebrachten": Bäuerliche Verhaltensweisen unterm Nationalsozialismus auf dem Gebiet des heutigen Landes Niedersachsen* (Hanover: Hahn, 1993), 181.

136. In 1927, there were still no National Socialists represented on the Gunzenhausen Municipal Council. Yet as early as a year later, in the Reichstag election of May 20, 1928, the NSDAP got 16.4 percent of the vote. The nationwide average was merely 2.6 percent. See Gunnar Beutner, "Das Pogrom von Gunzenhausen 1934: Anfänge des NS-Terrors in Westmittelfranken," in *Was brauchen wir einen Befehl, wenn es gegen die Juden geht?": Das Pogrom von Gunzenhausen 1934*, ed. Heike Tagsold (Nuremberg: Antogo, 2006), 9. As an analysis of the cattle market records for 1922 reveals, there really was a majority of Jewish traders represented at the market in Gunzenhausen. For example, on August 22, 1922, there were twenty-eight purchases of cattle, twenty-six of which were by Jewish traders; see Stadtarchiv Gunzenhausen. Rep. VI 731/13.

137. Municipal council resolution (Stadtratsbeschluss) no. 496 from June 23, 1927, Gunzenhausen, in Stadtarchiv Gunzenhausen, Rep. II, Fach 29, 6I.

138. Fortnightly reports II (Halbmonatsberichte II), February 1927, for the governing committee (Regierungspräsidium) of Central Franconia,

March 3, 1927, in BayHStA, MA 102153; see also Hambrecht, *Der Aufstieg der NSDAP*, 294.

139. At its meeting on March 9, 1923, the municipal council of Ansbach decided to reintroduce and make improvements to the cattle market there. See StAN, Rep. 270, Regierung von Mittelfranken, K.d.I, Abg. 1968, Titel IX, no. 407. See also "Der Stadtrat, Ansbach, 15.07.1925," in Stadtarchiv Ansbach, ABc R21/12.

140. In order to stimulate trade on the modernized cattle market, the municipal council of Ansbach in November 1926 wrote specifically to traders who had previously supplied the market with cattle. Thirteen of the sixteen traders to whom the council wrote could be identified as Jewish; see "Schreiben des St. Bezirksarztes an den Stadtrat Ansbach, Ansbach, 6.11.1926," in Stadtarchiv Ansbach, R21/12.

141. Baruch Z. Ophir and Wiesemann, eds., *Die jüdischen Gemeinden in Bayern, 1918–1945: Geschichte und Zerstörung* (Munich: Oldenbourg, 1979), 158.

142. At the end of the nineteenth century, Hessian antisemite Otto Böckel had already attempted to introduce cattle markets that were "free of Jews," yet his effort failed owing to a lack of support from the rural population. See David Peal, "Antisemitism by Other Means? The Rural Cooperative Movement in Late Nineteenth-Century Germany," in *Leo Baeck Institute Year Book* 32 (1987), 135–153; Jacob Toury, "Antisemitismus auf dem Lande: Der Fall Hessen 1881–1895," in *Jüdisches Leben auf dem Lande: Studien zur deutsch-jüdischen Geschichte*, Monika Richarz and Rürup, 173–188, (Tübingen: Mohr Siebeck, 1997).

143. Dietrich Weiß, "Aus der Geschichte der jüdischen Gemeinde von Feuchtwangen, 1274–1938," in *Feuchtwanger Heimatgeschichte* (Feuchtwangen: Arbeitsgemeinschaft für Heimatgeschichte, 1991), 44.

144. Hambrecht, *Der Aufstieg der NSDAP*, 39; Dirk Walter, *Antisemitische Kriminalität und Gewalt: Judenfeindschaft in der Weimarer Republik* (Bonn: Dietz, 1999), 157–165.

145. Letter from Central Association (CV) to the Bavarian State Ministry for Justice, Nuremberg, February 12, 1924, in BayHStA, MJu 13207.

146. Wiesemann, "Einleitung: Zur Geschichte der jüdischen Gemeinden seit 1813," in *Die jüdischen Gemeinden in Bayern, 1918–1945*, ed. Ophir and Wiesemann, 20.

147. Letter from Central Association (CV) to the Bavarian State Ministry for Justice, Nuremberg, February 12, 1924, in BayHStA, MJu 13207.

148. Hambrecht, *Der Aufstieg der NSDAP*, 240. But this also has to be viewed in a nationwide context, since Hitler himself, at a meeting of Gauleiters in Weimar in November 1927, had proclaimed agitation among the rural population to be an aim of National Socialist propaganda; see Daniela

Münkel, *Nationalsozialistische Agrarpolitik und Bauernalltag* (Frankfurt am Main: Campus, 1996), 68.

149. Kittel, *Provinz zwischen Reich und Republik*, 589.

150. Thomas Greif, *Frankens braune Wallfahrt. Der Hesselberg im Dritten Reich* (Ansbach: Historischer Verein für Mittelfranken, 2007); also Siegfried Zelnhefer, *Die Reichsparteitage der NSDAP in Nürnberg* (Nuremberg: Museen der Stadt Nürnberg, 2002).

151. Hambrecht, *Der Aufstieg der NSDAP*, 305.

152. Hambrecht, *Der Aufstieg der NSDAP*, 307. This is also the conclusion drawn by Jürgen W. Falter, *Hitlers Wähler* (Munich: Beck, 1991), 55; Peukert also emphasizes the early acceptance of the NSDAP in the milieu of small-town Protestant Germany: Peukert, *Die Weimarer Republik*, 227–228.

153. Kittel, *Provinz zwischen Reich und Republik*, 587.

154. Kittel, *Provinz zwischen Reich und Republik*, 573, 616; Kittel, "Mentale Machtergreifung: Der frühe Anbruch des 'Dritten Reiches' in der evangelischen Agrarprovinz Frankens 1930– 1932," in *BilderLast: Franken im Nationalsozialismus*, ed. Hans-Christian Täubrich (Nuremberg: Dokumentationszentrum Reichsparteitagsgelände Nürnberg, 2008), 31.

155. Kittel, *Provinz zwischen Reich und Republik*, 556. Grünberg, *Der deutsche Viehhandel*, 59–62. Between 1930 and 1931, beef cattle prices fell by 29.3 percent; see Friedrich-Wilhelm Henning, *Landwirtschaft und ländliche Gesellschaft, 1750–1976* (Paderborn: Schöningh, 1985), 196.

156. Kittel, *Provinz zwischen Reich und Republik*, 556–557.

157. Kittel, *Provinz zwischen Reich und Republik*, 557.

158. While peasants were left out of earlier studies on the middle class, Adelheid von Saldern included farmers alongside artisans, small business, and retail trade as part of the middle class; see Saldern, *Mittelstand im 'Dritten Reich'*, 10.

159. "Bei den fränkischen Bauern am Hesselberg, 12. und 13. Juli 1930," *Illustrierter Beobachter* 5, no. 30 (1930), quoted by Greif, *Frankens braune Wallfahrt*, 159.

160. Hambrecht, *Der Aufstieg der NSDAP*, 242; Peukert, *Die Weimarer Republik*, 229.

161. Beutner, "Das Pogrom von Gunzenhausen 1934," 9.

162. Josef Schubert, "Die Zwangsversteigerungen land- und forstwirtschaftlicher Grundstücke in Bayern im Jahre 1931," *Zeitschrift des Bayerischen Statistischen Landesamts* 64 (1932), 265–267; also cited in Hambrecht, *Der Aufstieg der NSDAP*, 190.

163. Kittel, *Provinz zwischen Reich und Republik.*, 593. This development deserves attention beyond the borders of Central Franconia. In 1930, the NSDAP started building up an "agrarian politics apparatus" that was meant to be responsible for addressing rural voter groups nationwide; see Münkel, *Nationalsozialistische Agrarpolitik und Bauernalltag*, 70.

164. Kittel, *Provinz zwischen Reich und Republik*, 620.

165. Kittel, *Provinz zwischen Reich und Republik*, 591.

166. Kittel, *Provinz zwischen Reich und Republik*, 586–603, esp. 596.

167. For party members, a dense network of mutual support services and dependencies was created; for example, the staffs of entire factories were employed in order to manufacture party uniforms and badges. Public soup kitchens organized by the National Socialists administered to needy "national comrades," and party members received special consideration from Nazi physicians and lawyers. Party members also had conflicts regulated among themselves, without bringing in the police. See Hambrecht, *Der Aufstieg der NSDAP*, 315–316.

168. Hambrecht, *Der Aufstieg der NSDAP*, 242; Kittel, *Provinz zwischen Reich und Republik*, 593; Hambrecht, "Die Brücke Franken," in *BilderLast*, ed. Täubrich, 20.

169. Kittel, *Provinz zwischen Reich und Republik*, 594.

170. Hambrecht, *Der Aufstieg der NSDAP*, 304.

171. Wiesemann, "Einleitung," 20.

172. Hambrecht, *Der Aufstieg der NSDAP*, 252–253.

173. Weiß, "Aus der Geschichte der jüdischen Gemeinde von Feuchtwangen," 45; Christina von Braun, "Antisemitische Stereotype und Sexualphantasien," in *Die Macht der Bilder: Antisemitische Vorurteile und Mythen*, ed. Jüdisches Museum der Stadt Wien (Vienna: Picus, 1995), 183; Kittel, *Provinz zwischen Reich und Republik*, 248–249.

174. Friedrich Koch, *Sexuelle Denunziation: Die Sexualität in der politischen Auseinandersetzung* (Frankfurt am Main: Syndikat, 1986), 73–74.

175. Peter E. Becker, *Wege ins Dritte Reich* (Stuttgart: G. Thieme, 1990); Gregor Hufenreuter, "Rassenantisemitismus," in *Handbuch des Antisemitismus*, vol. 3, *Begriffe, Ideologien, Theorien*, ed. Wolfgang Benz (Munich: K. G. Saur, 2010), 272–273.

176. Fred Hahn and Günther Wagenlehner, *Lieber Stürmer: Leserbriefe an das NS- Kampfblatt 1924–1945* (Stuttgart: Seewald, 1978), 45–104; Greif, "Julius Streicher und Franken," in *BilderLast*, ed. Täubrich, 32.

177. Randall L. Bytwerk, *Julius Streicher: Nazi Editor of the Notorious Anti-Semitic Newspaper Der Stürmer* (New York: Cooper Square, 2001); Alexandra Przyrembel, *"Rassenschande": Reinheitsmythos und Vernichtungslegitimation im Nationalsozialismus* (Göttingen: Vandenhoeck und Ruprecht, 2003), 185–199.

178. Karl Holz, "Die Kipperjuden: Bauernschlächter und Frauenschänder in Leutershausen," *Der Stürmer* 8, no. 8 (1930): 1–2. Another accusation of the same kind is mentioned in "Lokales," *Nürnberg-Fürther Israelitisches Gemeindeblatt* 7, no. 12 (1927).

179. Walter Isaacson, *Kissinger: A Biography* (New York: Simon and Schuster, 1992).

180. The use of large drawings to illustrate articles characterizes the first phase of the *Stürmer* through 1933; only later did the *Stürmer* switch to photojournalism. See Przyrembel, *"Rassenschande,"* 192.

181. Verdict of Ansbach local court (Amtsgericht), Pr. Kl. Reg. 8/30, May 22, 1930, and letter of lawyer Dr. Bayer to Ansbach district court (Landgericht), Ansbach, September 29, 1930. Both documents in StAN, AG Ansbach, Abgabe 1947, no. 7.

182. Przyrembel, *"Rassenschande,"* 193–194.

183. Avraham Barkai, *Vom Boykott zur "Entjudung": Der wirtschaftliche Existenzkampf der Juden im Dritten Reich, 1933–1943* (Frankfurt am Main: Fischer, 1988), 15; see also Kaufmann, *Die Beerfeldener Juden 1691–1942* (Beerfelden: Stadt Beerfelden, 2003), 79–80.

184. Hambrecht, *Der Aufstieg der NSDAP*, 292.

185. Hambrecht, *Der Aufstieg der NSDAP*, 254. See also Hannah Ahlheim, *"Deutsche, kauft nicht bei Juden!": Antisemitismus und politischer Boykott in Deutschland 1924 bis 1935* (Göttingen: Wallstein, 2011), 214–229, esp. 220.

186. Hambrecht, *Der Aufstieg der NSDAP*, 230, 337; Barbara Eberhardt and Hans-Christof Haas, "Neustadt/Aisch," in *Mehr als Steine . . . Synagogen-Gedenkband Bayern*, Wolfgang Kraus et al. (Lindenberg im Allgäu: Kunstverlag Josef Fink, 2010), 457–458.

187. Witness examination before the local court (Amtsgericht) of Christian domestic servant for the Levite family, Luzia Röder, Dinkelsbühl, March 10, 1964, in BayHStA, BEG 49839, A-185; see too the application "E-Schaden im beruflichen Fortkommen," filed by Karl Steinberger and Ada Maier for Justin Steinberger, New York, February 9, 1961, in BayHStA, BEG 021315, K-0421, 55.

188. Wiesemann, "Einleitung," 20; Martin Liepach, *Das Wahlverhalten der jüdischen Bevölkerung: Zur politischen Orientierung der Juden in der Weimarer Republik* (Tübingen: Mohr, 1996), 150–151.

189. Robin Judd, *Contested Rituals: Circumcision, Kosher Butchering, and Jewish Political Life in Germany, 1843–1933* (Ithaca, NY: Cornell University Press, 2007), 1–8.

190. Judd, *Contested Rituals*, 218–220.

191. Theodor Fritsch, *Handbuch der Judenfrage* (Leipzig: Hammer, 1932), 147.

192. Judd, *Contested Rituals*, 218–220.

193. Fritsch, *Handbuch der Judenfrage*, 143–148; see also Shai Lavi, "Unequal Rites: Jews, Muslims and the History of Ritual Slaughter in Germany," in *Juden und Muslime in Deutschland: Recht, Religion, Identität*, ed. José Brunner and Lavi (Göttingen: Wallstein, 2009), 180ff.

194. Hambrecht, *Der Aufstieg der NSDAP*, 159.

195. In *Der Stürmer* 10 (1930).

196. In *Der Stürmer* 4 (1938).

197. Judd, *Contested Rituals*, 190–237.

198. Judd, *Contested Rituals*, 195.

199. Judd, *Contested Rituals*, 202.

200. Judd, *Contested Rituals*, 203.

201. "Gesetz über das Schlachten von Tieren," April 21, 1933, in RGBl. I, 1933, no. 39, 203; see also Trude Maurer, "Vom Alltag zum Ausnahmezustand: Juden in der Weimarer Republik und im Nationalsozialismus, 1918–1945," in *Geschichte des jüdischen Alltags in Deutschland*, ed. Kaplan (Munich: Beck, 2003), 355–356.

202. The number of Jews who were keeping kosher at this time is hard to ascertain. Maurer suspects that about 15 to 20 percent of the overall Jewish population at the time was adhering to the religious dietary laws; see Maurer, "From Everyday Life to a State of Emergency: Jews in Weimar and Nazi Germany," in *Jewish Daily Life in Germany, 1618–1945*, ed. Kaplan (Oxford: Oxford University Press, 2005), 277–278.

203. If one follows the research literature, one can assume that rural Jews in particular followed a kosher lifestyle; see Jacob Borut, "Religiöses Leben der Landjuden im westlichen Deutschland während der Weimarer Republik," in *Jüdisches Leben auf dem Lande*, Richarz and Rürup, 231–248.

204. Bayerische Rabbinerkonferenz, "An die bayerischen Juden!," *Nürnberg-Fürther Israelitisches Gemeindeblatt* 7 (March 1, 1930): 1.

205. Email correspondence between Hilde (Tzipora) Jochsberger and Fischer, January 13, 2008. On the impact that the ban on kosher slaughter promulgated in April 1933 had on the Jewish population, see Kaplan, *Between Dignity and Despair: Jewish Life in Nazi Germany* (New York: Oxford University Press, 1998), 34.

206. See chapter I.

207. Affidavit by David Levite to the LEA (June 27, 1955), in BayHStA, BEG 26698–26699, A-183. Shortly after the ban on kosher slaughter was issued, Adolf Fleischmann from Altenmuhr had to close his butcher's shop; see letter of Dr. H. Wolf to Dr. Walter Peters, n.d., in BayHStA, BEG 24946, K-861.

208. Bayerische Rabbinerkonferenz, "An die bayerischen Juden!," February 12, 1930, reprinted in *Nürnberg-Fürther Israelitisches Gemeindeblatt* 7 (March 1, 1930): 1; "Lokales," *Nürnberg-Fürther Israelitisches Gemeindeblatt* 2 (October 1, 1930): 24.

209. Between 1930 and 1933, the share of farmers among NSDAP members grew from 6.5 to 10 percent; see Hambrecht, *Der Aufstieg der NSDAP*, 306.

210. Hambrecht, *Der Aufstieg der NSDAP*, 252.

211. At this time, Stegmann was the Gausturmführer (holding the rank of district assault leader in the Nazi paramilitary) of Upper, Central, and Lower Franconia (September 1930 through April 13, 1932); see Joachim Lilla, "Stegmann, Wilhelm," in "Staatsminister, leitende Verwaltungs-beamte und (NS-)Funktionsträger in Bayern 1918 bis 1945," October 8, 2012, accessed November 2020, https://verwaltungshandbuch .bayerische-landesbibliothek-online.de/stegmann-wilhelm. See: *Ansbacher Zeitung*, 94, April 19, 1932, source cited in Hambrecht, *Der Aufstieg der NSDAP*, 253.

212. Hambrecht, *Der Aufstieg der NSDAP*, 253.

213. Hambrecht, *Der Aufstieg der NSDAP*, 252–253.

214. Hambrecht, *Der Aufstieg der NSDAP*, 253.

215. Hambrecht, *Der Aufstieg der NSDAP*, 294.

216. The number of compulsory auctions in Central Franconia was in the average range for Bavaria; numbers derived from Kittel, *Provinz zwischen Reich und Republik*, 559.

217. Kittel, *Provinz zwischen Reich und Republik*, 560.

218. Letter from Central-Verein Deutscher Staatsbürger jüdischen Glaubens to the government of Central Franconia, Ansbach, January 25, 1932, in StAN Reg. von Mfr. KdI, Tit. II, no. 692, source cited by Kittel, *Provinz zwischen Reich und Republik*, 616.

219. Kittel, *Provinz zwischen Reich und Republik*, 617. This incident was also exploited for propaganda purposes in the *Stürmer*; see *Der Stürmer* 10, no. 6 (1932): 5.

220. Subfolders "Zwangsversteigerung des Anwesens Ströbel in Colmberg," in StAN, LRA Ansbach, Abg. 1961, no. 3285.

221. Subfolders "Zwangsversteigerung des Anwesens Ströbel in Colmberg," in StAN, LRA Ansbach, Abg. 1961, no. 3285. Hofmann's first name is not mentioned in the source; presumably the reference was to (Johann) Hans Georg Hofmann, leader (*Führer*) of the SA-Obergruppe IV, the Nazi paramilitary division for the Bavarian Eastern March, Franconia, and the Bavarian Highlands (SA-Gruppen Bayerische Ostmark, Franken und Hochland). See Lilla, "Hofmann, (Johann) Hans," in "Staatsminis-ter, leitende Verwaltungsbeamte und (NS-)Funktionsträger in Bayern 1918 bis 1945," October 9, 2012, accessed November 2020, http://verwaltungshandbuch.bayerische-landesbibliothek-online .de/hofmann-johann.

222. Subfolders "Zwangsversteigerung des Anwesens Ströbel in Colmberg."

223. See various cases of suits by Jewish cattle traders against farmers in their attorney's papers. For example: StAN, Nachlass RA Herz, no. 1383; StAN, Nachlass RA Herz, no. 1370; StAN, Nachlass RA Herz, no. 1385; StAN, Nachlass RA Herz, no. 1379; StAN, Nachlass RA Herz, no. 1373. See the case of Leonhard Hübner in Staatsarchiv für Oberbayern, StAnW 3277. Similar cases are confirmed by Kaufman for the Hessian region in Menahem Kaufman, "The Daily Life of the Village and Country Jews in Hessen from Hitler's Ascent to Power to November 1938," *Yad Vashem Studies* 22 (1992): 156.

224. Ophir and Wiesemann, *Die jüdischen Gemeinden in Bayern*, 157; Greif, "Julius Streicher und Franken," 35.

225. Eckhart Dietzfelbinger, "Antisemitismus im 20. Jahrhundert," in *Antijudaismus und Antisemitismus in Franken*, vol. 3, ed. Andrea M. Kluxen and Julia Hecht (Ansbach: Bezirk Mittelfranken, 2008), 146.

226. Quoted by Axel Drecoll, *Der Fiskus als Verfolger: Die steuerliche Diskriminierung der Juden in Bayern, 1933–1941/42* (Munich: Oldenbourg, 2009), 267.

4. Destroying Trust by Force under Nazism

1. Michael Wildt, *Volksgemeinschaft als Selbstermächtigung: Gewalt gegen Juden in der deutschen Provinz 1919 bis 1939* (Hamburg: Hamburger Edition, 2007), 100.

2. This follows up on a point established by previous scholarship on the Nazi era; in his pioneering study on the expulsion of the Jews from the German economy, Helmut Genschel had already drawn attention to the asynchronous dynamic of this process. See Genschel, *Die Verdrängung der Juden aus der Wirtschaft im Dritten Reich* (Göttingen: Muster-Schmidt, 1966).

3. Wildt, "Violence against Jews in Germany 1933–1939," in *Probing the Depths of German Antisemitism: German Society and the Persecution of the Jews, 1933–1941*, ed. David Bankier (New York: Berghahn, 2000), 183; Wildt, *Volksgemeinschaft als Selbstermächtigung*, 115–137.

4. On the acts of violence against Jewish lawyers, see Reinhard Weber, *Das Schicksal der jüdischen Rechtsanwälte in Bayern nach 1933* (Munich: Oldenbourg, 2006); Wildt, *Volksgemeinschaft als Selbstermächtigung*, 109–110.

5. In depicting the initial years of antisemitic persecution, previous historical research has almost completely neglected the fate of rural Jews; among

the most prominent examples of this oversight are Peter Longerich, *Holocaust: The Nazi Persecution and Murder of the Jews* (Oxford: Oxford University Press, 2010), 29–52; Saul Friedländer and Orna Kenan, *Nazi Germany and the Jews, 1933–1945* (New York: Harper, 2009), 3–31.

6. See also Christhard Hoffmann, "Verfolgung und Alltagsleben der Landjuden im nationalsozialistischen Deutschland," in *Jüdisches Leben auf dem Lande: Studien zur deutsch-jüdischen Geschichte*, ed. Monika Richarz and Reinhard Rürup (Tübingen: Mohr Siebeck, 1997), 376–377; Menachem Kaufman, "The Daily Life of the Village and Country Jews in Hessen from Hitler's Ascent to Power to November 1938," *Yad Vashem Studies* 22 (1992): 158.

7. Wolf Gruner, *Öffentliche Wohlfahrt und Judenverfolgung: Wechselwirkungen lokaler und zentraler Politik im NS-Staat (1933–1942)* (Munich: Oldenbourg, 2002), 46.

8. RA Dr. Raff an das LEA, München (Lawyer Dr. Raff to the Bavarian State Compensation Office, Munich), January 3, 1956, in BayHStA, EG 121828, K-2720; see also "Halbmonatsbericht des Regierungspräsidenten von Ober- und Mittelfranken, 7.04.1933" ("Fortnightly Report of Upper and Central Franconian District President, April 7, 1933"), in *Bayern in der NS-Zeit: Soziale Lage und politisches Verhalten der Bevölkerung im Spiegel vertraulicher Berichte*, vol. 1, ed. Martin Broszat et al. (Munich: Oldenbourg, 1977), 434; Baruch Z. Ophir and Falk Wiesemann, *Die jüdischen Gemeinden in Bayern: Geschichte und Zerstörung* (Munich: Oldenbourg, 1979), 221; Wiesemann, "Juden auf dem Lande: Die wirtschaftliche Ausgrenzung der jüdischen Viehhändler in Bayern," in *Die Reihen fast geschlossen*, ed. Jürgen Reulecke and Detlev Peukert, 381–396 (Wuppertal: Hammer, 1981), 382.

9. RA Dr. Raff an das LEA, München.

10. Theodor Mann an den Bürgermeister der Stadt Rothenburg o/T, Rothenburg o/T (Theodor Mann to the Mayor of the City of Rothenburg ob der Tauber, Rothenburg), November 2, 1936, in StAN, Rep. 270, Regierung, K.d.I, Abg. 1978, no. 3420. Also RA Dr. Raff an das LEA, München; and Eidesstattliche Versicherung von Justizrat Dr. Bayer an das LEA, Ansbach (Affidavit or affirmation in lieu of oath from Counselor of Justice Dr. Bayer to the Bavarian State Compensation Office), October 12, 1954; both documents in BayHStA, EG 121828, K-2720.

11. Gendarmerie-Bezirk Rothenburg o/T an die Regierung von Ober- und Mittelfranken, Rothenburg o/T (Gendarmerie-District Rothenburg ob der Tauber to governing administration of Upper and Central Franconia, Rothenburg ob der Tauber), July 18, 1936, in StAN, Rep. 270, Regierung, K.d.I, Abg. 1978, no. 3420.

12. I. Anklageschrift zum Sondergericht für den Oberlandesgerichtsbezirk
    Nürnberg (1st indictment before special court for the Nuremberg higher
    regional court district), March 1933, Sg. II 4/33, in StAN, LRA Ansbach,
    Abg. 1961, no. 2225; characteristically, none of the Jewish cattle traders
    taken into protective custody were carried off to a concentration camp
    such as Dachau. Although, at the same time, in March 1933, three Jewish
    men—merchant Ernst Jakob Goldmann, PhD economist Rudolf Benario
    (both from Fürth), and student Arthur Kahn from Nuremberg—were
    arrested and deported on April 11, 1933, in the first prisoner transport from
    Franconia to Dachau, where they were shot on the following day. Since
    these three were prominent political activists, the extraordinary fact of
    their transfer to this early concentration camp may be explained by their
    highlighted enemy status. In addition, we have records from Hesse of
    Jewish cattle traders who were transported to the Osthofen concentra-
    tion camp after peasants had accused them of usury. For drawing my
    attention to these prominent cases, I thank Kim Wünschmann, author
    of *Before Auschwitz: Jewish Prisoners in the Prewar Concentration Camps*
    (Cambridge, MA: Harvard University Press, 2015). A possible explanation
    for the absence of concentration camp incarceration could be that local
    Nazi government decision-makers, by carrying out protective custody
    in local court jails like the one in Rothenburg, were trying to show off
    before the party leadership. In addition, it was still up in the air at this
    time as to whether a concentration camp would also be set up in North-
    ern Bavaria, so that Jewish prisoners in Franconia might be put there; see
    Günther Wieland and Klaus Drobisch, *System der NS-Konzentrationslager*
    (Berlin: Akademie, 1993), 32. For this reference, I also wish to thank
    Wünschmann.
13. Schreiben vom Polizeimeister von Neumarkt i.d. Opf. an das LEA (Letter
    from police constable of Neumarkt in der Oberpfalz to the Bavarian State
    Compensation Office), January 25, 1962, in BayHStA, BEG 43963; EG
    95832, K-119.
14. "Halbmonatsbericht des BAs Weißenburg/Bay, 2.04.1933" (Fortnightly
    report of Weißenburg/Bayern District Office, April 2, 1933), in *Bayern
    in der NS-Zeit*, vol. 1, Broszat et al., 433; Wiesemann, "Juden auf dem
    Lande," 383. On the antisemitic incidents in Ellingen in 1933, see also
    Hermann Seis, *Das Buch "Beacon of Light": Die Lebenserinnerungen der
    Ellinger Rabbinertochter Felice Poupko, als deutsches Kind: Felicitas Schuster*
    (Ellingen: Stadtarchiv Ellingen im ehemaligen Franziskanerkloster,
    2010), 14–15.
15. Hermann Fleischmann an die Wiedergutmachungskammer beim Landg-
    ericht Nürnberg-Fürth, Nürnberg (Hermann Fleischmann to Restitution

Chamber at regional court for Nuremberg-Fürth, Nuremberg),
August 11, 1952, in Staatsarchiv München, WB IIIa 2356; see also Ian
Kershaw, "Antisemitismus und Volksmeinung: Reaktionen auf die Juden-
verfolgung," in *Bayern in der NS-Zeit*, vol. 2, *Herrschaft und Gesellschaft im
Konflikt*, ed. Broszat and Elke Fröhlich, 281–348 (Munich: Oldenbourg,
1979), 297.

16. RA Dr. Bayer an das LEA, Ansbach (Attorney Dr. Bayer to Bavarian State
    Compensation Office, Ansbach), April 29, 1955, in BayHStA, BEG 77459,
    A-16.

17. Wildt, "Violence against Jews in Germany," 185; see also A. Goppelt an das
    BA Weißenburg/Bay., Treuchtlingen (A. Goppelt to the Weißenburg/Bay-
    ern District Office), April 27, 1934, in StAN, LRA Wbg., Abg. 1996, Titel IV,
    no. 217.

18. Ophir and Wiesemann, *Die jüdischen Gemeinden in Bayern*, 189; Gunnar
    Beutner, "Das Pogrom von Gunzenhausen 1934: Anfänge des NS-Terrors
    in Westmittelfranken," in *"Was brauchen wir einen Befehl, wenn es gegen
    die Juden geht?": Das Pogrom von Gunzenhausen 1934*, ed. Heike Tagsold,
    7–30 (Nuremberg: Antogo, 2006), 16. According to the memoirs of Felice
    Poupko, who grew up in nearby Ellingen, there was a violent antisemitic
    procession taking place in her hometown at the same time; see Seis, *Das
    Buch "Beacon of Light,"* 12.

19. To this day, it remains unclear whether the two Jewish men were killed
    during the pogrom or took their own lives out of fear of the rampaging
    mob. See Kershaw, "Antisemitismus und Volksmeinung," 295–296; Peter
    Zinke, "Der Strick mit dem Knoten—Suizid oder Mord bei Max Rosenau
    und Jakob Rosenfelder?," in *"Was brauchen wir einen Befehl,"* ed. Tagsold,
    31–44.

20. Salomon Walz an das LEA, New York (Salomon Walz to the Bavarian
    State Compensation Office, New York), October 14, 1953; RA Dr. Bayer an
    das LEA, Ansbach; both documents in BayHStA, BEG 77461, K-018.

21. Kershaw, *Hitler, the Germans, and the Final Solution* (New Haven, CT, and
    London: Yale University Press, 2008), 159.

22. Kershaw, *Hitler*, 295.

23. See also Klaus Hesse and Philipp Springer, *Vor aller Augen: Fotodoku-
    mente des nationalsozialistischen Terrors in der Provinz* (Essen: Klartext,
    2002).

24. There is no precise date mentioned in the interrogation files of the denazi-
    fication court for Gunzenhausen-Land. But from the context of the inter-
    rogation minutes, the conclusion may be drawn that the incident occurred
    around 1934; see Vernehmung des Zeugen Friedrich Franz vor der Sprk.
    Gunzenhausen-Land (Interrogation of the witness Friedrich Franz before

the denazification court of Gunzenhausen-Land), September 3, 1948, Wettelsheim, in StAN, Sprk. Gun-Land, K-70. This case is also confirmed by Georg Wurmthaler, from Mitteleschenbach, in the denazification court's written interrogation record ("Vernehmungsschrift der Sprk. Gunzenhausen-Land"), October 9, 1946, in StAN, Sprk. Gun-Land, R-37.

25. A. Goppelt an das BA Weißenburg/Bay., Treuchtlingen.

26. See Wildt, "Violence against Jews in Germany."

27. See also Kershaw, "The Persecution of the Jews and German Popular Opinion in the Third Reich," *Leo Baeck Institute Year Book 26* (1981): 268.

28. See Wildt, "Gewaltpolitik: Volksgemeinschaft und Judenverfolgung in der deutschen Provinz 1932–1935," in *WerkstattGeschichte* 11, no. 23 (2003): 42.

29. See Wildt, "Gewaltpolitik," 25; Frank Bajohr and Dieter Pohl, eds., *Der Holocaust als offenes Geheimnis: Die Deutschen, die NS-Führung und die Alliierten* (Munich: Beck, 2006), 8–19.

30. Only with the promulgation of the Nuremberg Laws in September 1935 does "racial defilement" (*Rassenschande*) become a statutory offense; see Alexandra Przyrembel, *"Rassenschande": Reinheitsmythos und Vernichtungslegitimation im Nationalsozialismus* (Göttingen: Vandenhoeck und Ruprecht, 2003), 127–148.

31. In the 1948 denazification procedure at which residents of Markt Berolzheim were charged with participating in the shaming procession, Löwensteiner's first name is not mentioned. Possibly, though, it was Abraham Löwensteiner; see testimony of witnesses in the denazification procedure for Ludwig Kögel, 1948, in StAN, Sprk. Gun-Land, K-74.

32. Przyrembel, *"Rassenschande,"* 70.

33. Zeugenaussage von Ludwig Kögel vor der Sprk. Gunzenhausen-Land (Testimony of Ludwig Kögel before the Gunzenhausen-Land denazification court), September 13, 1948, in StAN, Sprk. Gun-Land, K-74; Zeugenaussage von Karl Schreitmüller vor der Sprk. Gunzenhausen-Land (Testimony of Karl Schreitmüller before the Gunzenhausen-Land denazification court), September 6, 1946, in StAN, Sprk. Gun-Land, Sch-62; Zeugenaussage von Hans Kugler vor der Sprk. Gunzenhausen-Land (Testimony of Hans Kugler before the Gunzenhausen-Land denazification court), September 15, 1948, in StAN, Sprk. Gun-Land, C-5.

34. Przyrembel, *"Rassenschande,"* 63–83, esp. 70–71.

35. Przyrembel, *"Rassenschande,"* 71.

36. Przyrembel, *"Rassenschande,"* 77.

37. "Das Judentum im Kreisgebiete Hilpoltstein: Ein Halbjahrtausend Abwehrkampf gegen die jüdische Giftschlange" (Jewry in the

Hilpoltstein Area: A half century of defensive struggle against the poisonous Jewish snake [undated document without author]), Hilpoltstein, n.d., 48, in StAN, Rep. 503, NS-Mischbestand, Kreis Schwabach, no. 5.

38. RA Dr. Levor an den Oberbürgermeister der Stadt Nürnberg, Nürnberg, 4.05.1936, in Unterakte Theodor Rindsberg (Attorney Dr. Levor to mayor of the city of Nuremberg, Nuremberg, May 4, 1936, in subfiles Theodor Rindsberg), StAN, Rep. 270, Regierung, K.d.I, Abg. 1978, no. 3419. For the period after 1935, we have records of additional cases of Jewish cattle traders who were taken into protective custody. One of them was Max Gutmann from Ellingen, who was taken into protective custody in 1936 under the pretext of having falsely claimed that the NSDAP county leader had allowed him to trade with cattle in farming villages; see Max Gutmann an RA Dr. Josef Kern (Verteidiger von Rosa Bermann), Ellingen (Max Gutmann to attorney Dr. Josef Kern [defense lawyer for Rosa Bermann], Ellingen), July 15, 1950, in BayHStA, EG 92225, K-2242.

39. Gendarmeriestation Herrieden an die Gendarmerie-Hauptstation Ansbach (Gendarmerie Station Herrieden to gendarmerie-headquarters Ansbach), November 14, 1935, in StAN, LRA Ansbach, Abg. 1961, no. 2225. An additional example of a criminal complaint filed against a Jewish cattle trader is found in the "Bericht der Gendarmeriestation Ettenstatt an das BA Weißenburg/Bay., 14.07.1936, Betreff: Verhinderung von Ausschreitungen gegen die Juden" (Report of the Gendarmerie Station Ettenstatt to the Weißenburg/Bayern District Office, July 14, 1936, re: Prevention of Riots against the Jews), in StAN, LRA Wbg., Abg. 1996, Titel IV, no. 225. See also Avraham Barkai, *Vom Boykott zur "Entjudung": Der wirtschaftliche Existenzkampf der Juden im Dritten Reich, 1933–1943* (Frankfurt am Main: Fischer, 1988), 75.

40. See Wildt, "Gewaltpolitik," 31.

41. Barkai, "Population Decline and Economic Stagnation," in *German-Jewish History in Modern Times: Renewal and Destruction 1918–1945*, ed. Michael A. Meyer and Michael Brenner, 30–44 (New York: Columbia University Press: 1998), 201; Angelika Königseder, "Arierparagraph," in *Enzyklopädie des Nationalsozialismus*, ed. Wolfgang Benz et al. (Munich: Deutscher Taschenbuch, 2007), 415.

42. This aspect of the Third Reich's power structure is part of a historical debate for which Ernst Fraenkel provided the initial interpretive framework in Fraenkel, *The Dual State: A Contribution to the Theory of Dictatorship* (Oxford: Oxford University Press, 2017). Fraenkel's premise in this work was the juxtaposition of a "normative state" whose actions were tied to legal norms and a "prerogative state" without any norms. This explanatory

approach was followed by several historians who highlighted the blending of these two areas and conveyed the mixture conceptually by using the term *polycracy* (*Polykratie* in Greek-derived German)—that is, a system of rulers competing with each other. See Hans Mommsen, "'Nationalsozialismus oder Hitlerismus?,'" in *Persönlichkeit und Struktur in der Geschichte,* ed. Michael Bosch (Düsseldorf: Pädagogischer Verlag Schwann, 1977), 61–71. Yet the blending of the two opposing dualisms of state and party and the erosion of the normative state happened gradually; on this, see Benz, "Zum Verhältnis der NSDAP und staatlicher Verwaltung im Dritten Reich," in *Das Unrechtsregime: Internationale Forschung über den Nationalsozialismus,* ed. Ursula Büttner (Hamburg: Christians, 1986): 204–205. Axel Drecoll underlines how the normative state cannot be viewed from "the vantage point of the liberal legal system of the Weimar Republic" and emphasizes how "government offices working according to normative state criteria" participated early on in the persecution of the Jews; see Drecoll, *Der Fiskus als Verfolger: Die steuerliche Diskriminierung der Juden in Bayern, 1933–1941/42* (Munich: Oldenbourg, 2009), 186.

43. Cited by Daniela Münkel, *Bauern und Nationalsozialismus: Der Landkreis Celle im Dritten Reich* (Bielefeld: Verlag für Regionalgeschichte, 1991), 101.

44. Hellmuth Pohl, *Ratgeber des Viehverteilers: Ein Handb. f. d. prakt. Vieh- u. Pferdehändler über d. wichtigsten Berufsfragen d. tägl. Lebens* (Berlin: Allgemeine Viehhandels-Zeitung, 1936), 2–6; see also Beatrix Herlemann, *"Der Bauer klebt am Hergebrachten": Bäuerliche Verhaltensweisen unterm Nationalsozialismus auf dem Gebiet des heutigen Landes Niedersachsen* (Hanover: Hahn, 1993), 216–217.

45. Landesverband Bayerischer Viehhändler e.V. an seine Mitglieder (State Association of Bavarian Cattle Traders, registered association, to its members), March 12, 1933, in BayHStA, ML 3349.

46. Reichsverband des nationalen Viehhandels Deutschlands, Gau Bayern (Landesverband Bayerischer Viehhändler) an das Bayerische Staatsministerium für Wirtschaft, Abt. Landwirtschaft, München (Reich Association of National Cattle Trade of Germany, Gau Bavaria [State Association of Bavarian Cattle Traders] to Bavarian State Ministry for Economy, Agriculture Division, Munich), June 12, 1933; see also "Vermerk: Referat 7 Niklas an Herrn Regierungsrat Dr. Hofmann mit der Bitte um Entscheidung, München" ("Note: Department 7 Niklas to senior civil servant Dr. Hofmann with request for decision, Munich"), November 16, 1933; both documents in BayHStA, ML 3349.

47. Reichsverband des nationalen Viehhandels Deutschlands, Gau Bayern (Landesverband Bayerischer Viehhändler) an das Bayerische Staatsministerium für Wirtschaft, Abt. Landwirtschaft, München.

48. Reichsverband des nationalen Viehhandels Deutschlands, Gau Bayern, an das Staatsministerium für Wirtschaft, Abt. Landwirtschaft, München (Reich Association of National Cattle Trade of Germany, Gau Bavaria, to the State Ministry for Economy, Agriculture Division, Munich), March 9, 1934, in BayHStA, ML 3349; Stellungnahme des "Reichsbauernführers" zu der Frage "Reichsnährstand und Juden," Berlin (Position of the "Reich Farm Leader" on the question "Reich Food Corporation and Jews," Berlin), May 19, 1935, in BArch, R 16/I/2057. See also Günter Plum, "Wirtschaft und Erwerbsleben," in *Die Juden in Deutschland 1933–1945: Leben unter nationalsozialistischer Herrschaft*, ed. Benz (Munich: Beck, 1989), 299.

49. See Hannah Ahlheim, *"Deutsche, kauft nicht bei Juden!": Antisemitismus und politischer Boykott in Deutschland 1924 bis 1935* (Göttingen: Wallstein, 2011).

50. Historical scholarship has it that the Reich-wide summons to boycott Jewish businesses in April represented a reaction of the Nazi leadership to numerous individual antisemitic actions that were regional; see Barkai, *Vom Boykott zur "Entjudung,"* 33; Longerich, *Holocaust*, 32–33.

51. Uwe Dietrich Adam, *Judenpolitik im Dritten Reich* (Düsseldorf: Droste, 1972), 61; Maren Janetzko, *Die "Arisierung" mittelständischer jüdischer Unternehmen in Bayern 1933–1939: Ein interregionaler Vergleich* (Ansbach: Historischer Verein für Mittelfranken, 2012), 53.

52. Anordnung der NSDAP-Parteileitung, 28.03.1933 (Order of the NSDAP party leadership, March 28, 1933), cited by Barkai, *Vom Boykott zur "Entjudung,"* 27; Wildt, *Volksgemeinschaft als Selbstermächtigung*, 122.

53. On March 31, 1933, the title page of the *Altmühl-Bote*, a local newspaper, summoned local peasants to boycott Jewish cattle traders. See Honig, "Aufruf an die mittelfränkische Landwirtschaft," in *Der Altmühl-Bote* 86, no. 77 (March 31, 1933): 1; also "Aufruf zum April-Boykott im Altmühl-Boten der Stadt Gunzenhausen," April 1, 1933: 1.

54. Schreiben von RA Dr. Bayer an das LEA, Ansbach, A-16: 10.

55. Mommsen and Dieter Obst, "Die Reaktion der deutschen Bevölkerung auf die Verfolgung der Juden 1933–1943," in *Herrschaftsalltag im Dritten Reich: Studien und Texte*, ed. Mommsen and Susanne Willems (Düsseldorf: Schwann, 1988), 375; Drecoll, *Der Fiskus als Verfolger*, 63.

56. Wildt, "Gewaltpolitik," 33.

57. Bayerische Bauernschaft, Geschäftsstelle Bayreuth, an den Herrn Staatssekretär Georg Luber, Bayerisches Staatsministerium für Landwirtschaft (Bavarian Farmers' Association, Bayreuth branch office, to Undersecretary Georg Luber, Bavarian State Ministry for Agriculture), August 1, 1933, in BayHStA, ML 3341.

58. Bayerische Landesbauernkammer an das Staatsministerium für Wirtschaft, Abt. Landwirtschaft, München (Bavarian State Chamber of Agriculture to State Ministry for Economy, Agriculture Division, Munich), May 22, 1933, in BayHStA, ML 3349.

59. Staatsministerium für Wirtschaft, Abt. Landwirtschaft an die Bayerische Viehverwertung, München (State Ministry for Economy, Agriculture Division, to Bavarian [cooperative], Munich), August 12, 1933, in BayHStA, ML 3341; and memorandum by county leader Gerstner, Weißenburg/Bayern, May 8, 1934, in StAN, LRA Wbg., Abg. 1996, Titel IV, no. 217.

60. Drecoll, *Der Fiskus als Verfolger*, 60.

61. Karl Freising an das LEA, vermutlich New York, 12.05.1959 (Karl Freising to Bavarian State Compensation Office, presumably New York, May 12, 1959), in BayHStA, BEG 35235, K-1379.

62. From the Antrag auf Entschädigung für Schaden im wirtschaftlichen und gewerblichen Fortkommen von Salomon Walz aus Gunzenhausen (Application for restitution for damages to the economic and commercial career of Salomon Walz from Gunzenhausen), February 15, 1950, in BayHStA, BEG 77461, K-018.

63. Kershaw, "Antisemitismus und Volksmeinung," 302; see also Wiesemann, "Juden auf dem Lande," 383.

64. Kreisleitung Eichstätt, "Bericht für den Monat Juli 1935" (Nazi party county leadership, Eichstätt, "Report for the month of July 1935"), in StAN, Rep. 503, NS- Mischbestand, Kreisleitung Eichstätt, no. 7.

65. Cited by Kershaw, "Antisemitismus und Volksmeinung," 294.

66. "Reichsbauernführer" Richard Walther Darré an die Mitglieder des deutschen Reichsbauernrates ("Reich Farm Leader" Richard Walther Darré to the members of the German Reich Farmers' Council), Berlin, October 29, 1935, in BArch, R 16/I/2057. On March 26, 1934, after a complaint from the Association of Bavarian Israelite Communities, the Bavarian State Ministry for the Economy also called on the Ansbach Municipal Council to call off the virulent boycott measures; see Stadtarchiv Ansbach, ABc C3/16.

67. Gendarmeriestation Dentlein am Forst an die Schutzmannschaft Ansbach (Gendarmerie station Dentlein am Forst to Ansbach constabulary), August 20, 1936, in Stadtarchiv Ansbach, R12/41. We also have records from other regions about Jewish cattle traders collaborating with non-Jewish merchants in order to circumvent the rigorous boycott policy; see Landesbauernschaft Rheinland, Hauptabteilung III, Der Hauptabteilungsleiter Otto Breyer, M.d. L., an sämtliche Genossenschaften der Verbände Koblenz und Köln, Koblenz (State Farmers' Association Rhineland, Main Department III, Main Department Leader Otto Breyer, Member of the

Landtag, to all cooperatives of associations for Koblenz and Cologne, Koblenz), September 28, 1933, in BArch, R 3601/1803.

68. "Bericht der Gendarmeriestation Ettenstatt an das BA Weißenburg /Bay" ("Report of Ettenstatt Gendarmerie Station to Weißenburg/Bayern District Office"), July 14, 1936, in StAN, LRA Wbg., Abg. 1996, Titel IV, no. 225.

69. "Unterakte Simon Hutzler" (subfile Simon Hutzler), in StAN, BA Lauf, Abg. 1959, no. 404. Jakob Sommerich also moved his business activity to the Upper Palatinate after he was no longer to make any sales in Central Franconia; see NSDAP-Gauleitung Franken an das BA Lauf, Nürnberg (NSDAP Gau leadership to the Lauf District Office, Nuremberg), February 12, 1938, in StAN, BA Lauf, Abg. 1959, no. 404. Siegfried Behr complained that having to supply cattle markets outside Central Franconia resulted in huge expenses for him; see Siegfried Behr an das Finanzamt Dinkelsbühl (Siegfried Behr to the Dinkelsbühl revenue office), February 14, 1936, in StAN, Finanzamt Dinkelsbühl, Abg. 1996, 122 Est.

70. See chapter 3.

71. Bayerische Bauernschaft, Kreis Ansbach, "Wie kann der Bauer wieder mitbestimmend wirken an der Preisgestaltung des Viehmarktes?," *Fränkische Tageszeitung*, October 14, 1933; Hans Goetz, "Die neuen mittelfränkischen Nutzviehmärkte," written on behalf of the NS-Bauernschaft, Kreis Fürth, n.d. [presumably autumn 1933], in Stadtarchiv Scheinfeld, A-VIII 58.

72. "Stadtrat Ansbach" (Ansbach Municipal Council), April 8, 1933, in Stadtarchiv Ansbach, ABc C3/16; Wiesemann, "Juden auf dem Lande," 383–384. From the fortnightly report of the district president of Upper and Central Franconia on August 8, 1933, it emerges that the expulsion of Jewish traders from the Nuremberg cattle market had already been planned in August 1933; see Broszat et al., *Bayern in der NS-Zeit*, 435. In the Eastern Frisian town of Jever, Jewish cattle traders had already been blocked from access to the cattle market in February 1933; see Herlemann, *"Der Bauer klebt am Hergebrachten,"* 186.

73. Scheinfeld was among the municipalities trying to revive their cattle markets in 1933; see Stadtrat Scheinfeld an das BA Scheinfeld, Scheinfeld (Scheinfeld Municipal Council to Scheinfeld District Office), May 22, 1933, in StAN, LRA Scheinfeld, Abg. 1977, no. 1592. The list included the municipality of Burghaslach; see Marktgemeinde Burghaslach an die Kreisregierung von Mittelfranken, Burghaslach (Market town Bughaslach to county government of Central Franconia, Bughaslach), July 25, 1933, in StAN, LRA Scheinfeld, Abg. 1977, no. 1599. It also included Ellingen; see Stadtrat Ellingen an das BA Weißenburg/Bay. (Ellingen Municipal

Council to Weißenburg/Bayern District Office), April 12, 1933, in StAN, LRA Wbg, Abg. 1996, Titel VII, no. 3113.

74. Fritz Wissmüller an das Staatsministerium des Innern, Nürnberg (Fritz Wissmüller to the State Ministry of the Interior, Nuremberg), April 3, 1933; Schlachtviehhofdirektion an das Staatsministerium für Wirtschaft, Abt. Landwirtschaft, Nürnberg (Slaughterhouse management to the State Ministry for the Economy, Agriculture Division, Nuremberg), May 15, 1933; both documents in BayHStA, ML 3349. At the same time, SA Special Commissioner Hermann Ritter von Schöpf ordered the expulsion of Jewish traders from the municipal slaughterhouse in Catholic Augsburg (Swabia). There, too, non-Jewish merchants opposed any softening of this resolution. See Janetzko, *Die "Arisierung" mittelständischer jüdischer Unternehmen*, 63; see also Adelheid von Saldern, *Mittelstand im "Dritten Reich": Handwerker – Einzelhändler – Bauern* (Frankfurt am Main: Campus, 1985), 204.

75. "Stadtrat Scheinfeld, Lax, 1. Bürgermeister: ca. September 1933," in Stadtarchiv Scheinfeld, A-VIII 58. It is also not surprising that the poster was meant to appeal above all to young peasants. Even before 1933, the NSDAP was making significant inroads among this special demographic; see Manfred Kittel, *Provinz zwischen Reich und Republik: Politischen Mentalitäten in Deutschland und Frankreich, 1918–1933/36* (Munich: Oldenbourg, 2000), 596.

76. Bekanntmachung aus dem Altmühlboten, Nr. 237 (Announcement from the *Altmühlbote* newspaper), October 10, 1933; Bekanntmachung des Stadtrats Gunzenhausen (Announcement from the Gunzenhausen Municipal Council), September 29, 1933; "Richtlinie für die Einführung von Zucht- und Nutzviehmärkten" (Guideline for establishing breeding and farm livestock markets), n.d. [presumably autumn 1933]; all documents in Stadtarchiv Gunzenhausen, Rep IV, 842/8.

77. "Viehhandel ohne Juden. Genossenschaftliche Viehverwertung in Windsbach" (Cattle trade without Jews: Cooperative sales in Windsbach), newspaper article, no author, no indication of which newspaper, presumably September 1933. In the article, it is emphasized "that the delivery association is a free association, without compulsory delivery; that is, honest Christian trade will not be damaged in any way." Document in Stadtarchiv Gunzenhausen, Rep IV, 842/8.

78. Plum, "Wirtschaft und Erwerbsleben," 297–298.

79. Rede des "Reichsbauernführers" Richard Walter Darré mit dem Titel "Vom Friedenswillen der deutschen Bauern" (Speech of the "Reich Farm Leader" Richard Walter Darr with the title "Of the German Farmers' Desire for Peace"), May 14, 1933, in BArch, R 16/I/2051; see also Münkel,

Nationalsozialistische Agrarpolitik und Bauernalltag (Frankfurt am Main: Campus, 1994), 95–99.

80. Bayerische Viehverwertung an den Stadtrat Ellingen, München (Bavarian Livestock Husbandry to the Ellingen Municipal Council, Munich), September 7, 1933; Stadtrat Ellingen an die Bayerische Viehverwertung, Ellingen (Ellingen Municipal Council to Bavarian Livestock Husbandry), September 21, 1933; both letters in Stadtarchiv Ellingen, no call number.

81. Reporting about the exclusion of Jewish traders from fairgrounds but not about their banishment from cattle markets was Comité des Délégations Juives, ed., *Das Schwarzbuch: Tatsachen und Dokumente: Die Lage der Juden in Deutschland 1933* (Paris: Imprimerie "Pascal," 1934), 345–348; see also Gruner, *Öffentliche Wohlfahrt und Judenverfolgung*, 49.

82. Anordnung von Martin Bormann an alle Gauleitungen (Order from Martin Bormann to all Gau leaderships), September 12, 1933, reprinted in Mommsen and Willems, *Herrschaftsalltag im Dritten Reich*, 429. See also Gruner, *Öffentliche Wohlfahrt und Judenverfolgung*, 86. The Bayerischer Gemeindetag (Bavarian Association of Municipalities) also explained to its affiliates that non-Aryans could not, in principle, be refused access to markets; see Gemeindetag im Deutschen Gemeindetag an sämtliche Mitgliedsgemeinden (Association of Municipalities German Association of Municipalities to all affiliated municipalities), Munich, October 11, 1933, in BayHStA, MWi 846.

83. Ophir and Wiesemann, *Die jüdischen Gemeinden in Bayern*, 158. Similar developments have been noted for the town of Windsbach; see "Viehhandel ohne Juden" (Cattle trade without Jews), Windsbach, n.d., in Stadtarchiv Gunzenhausen, Rep IV, 842/8.

84. Bekanntmachung im Altmühl-Boten (Announcement in Altmühl-Bote newspaper), no. 237, October 10, 1933, Stadtarchiv Gunzenhausen, Rep IV, 842/8.

85. Quoted by Kershaw, "Antisemitismus und Volksmeinung," 300; see also Kaufman, "The Daily Life," 168–169.

86. A. Goppelt an das BA Weißenburg/Bay., Treuchtlingen. Moreover, in its first working report for 1934, the Zentralstelle für jüdische Wirtschaftshilfe (Central Office for Jewish Economic Assistance) reports a drastic collapse in cattle sales on livestock markets; see Plum, "Wirtschaft und Erwerbsleben," 297.

87. Michael Gerstner, Notiz vom 8.05.1934 zu dem Schreiben von A. Goppelt vom 27.04.1934 (Michael Gerstner, note from May 8, 1934, on the letter from A. Goppelt of April 27, 1934), in StAN, LRA Wbg., Abg. 1996, Titel IV, no. 217. [The term *Kulturstaat* refers to the state as the embodiment of a

nation's cultural legacy. Both Nazis and German conservatives preferred this term to the related Western notion of a "civilized society"—since *Zivilization* was regarded in these right-wing circles as overly liberal, Frenchified, and superficial in contrast to *Kultur* (supposedly more profound and more Germanic). But the term would also have been used by the more cosmopolitan cultural elites Michael Gerstner is mocking here.—Trans.]

88. David Peal, "Antisemitism by Other Means? The Rural Cooperative Movement in Late Nineteenth-Century Germany," *Leo Baeck Institute Year Book* 32 (1987): 135–153; Jacob Toury, "Antisemitismus auf dem Lande: Der Fall Hessen 1881–1895," in *Jüdisches Leben auf dem Lande*, ed. Richarz and Rürup, 173–188.

89. Bayerische Viehverwertung an den Herrn Ministerialrat Dr. Niklas, München (Bavarian Livestock Husbandry to Undersecretary Dr. Niklas, Munich), September 18, 1933, in BayHStA, ML 3349; Industrie- und Handelskammer Nürnberg an das BA Rothenburg o/T (Nuremberg Chamber of Industry and Commerce to the Rothenburg District Office), September 21, 1933, in StAN, LRA Rothenburg o/T, Abg. 1975, no. 4396. Bajohr also arrived at this conclusion in the case of Hamburg. He established that while the Chamber of Industry and Commerce did not actively take part in the exclusion (*Ausschaltung*) of Jewish firms, it only articulated any reservations when the exclusion of Jewish firms threatened its own position; see Bajohr, *Arianisation in Hamburg: The Economic Exclusion of Jews and the Confiscation of Their Property in Nazi Germany* (New York: Berghahn, 2002), 82; Drecoll, *Der Fiskus als Verfolger*, 108–109.

90. The idea of introducing "minimally sized markets" was rejected by the Scheinfeld District Chamber Of Agriculture; see Bezirksbauernkammer Scheinfeld an das BA Scheinfeld (Scheinfeld District Chamber Of Agriculture to Scheinfeld District Office), June 8, 1933, in StAN, LRA Scheinfeld, Abg. 1977, no. 1592.

91. "Tätigkeitsbericht der Gauamtsleitung für Kommunalpolitik, Gau-Franken, Nürnberg, an das Hauptamt für Kommunalpolitik, München" (Progress report from the Gau office management for local government policy, Gau of Franconia, Nuremberg, to the main office for local government policy, Munich), July 10, 1935, in BArch, NS 25/218, Bl. 272–350. I wish to thank Ralf Oberndörfer for drawing my attention to this source material.

92. "Tätigkeitsbericht der Gauamtsleitung für Kommunalpolitik," 272–350; see also Wiesemann, "Juden auf dem Lande," 384.

93. See also Wilfried Jung, "Die Juden in Altenmuhr," *Alt-Gunzenhausen* 44 (1988): 202.

94. "Tätigkeitsbericht der Gauamtsleitung für Kommunalpolitik,"
     272–350.

95. "Bericht der Schlacht- und Viehhofdirektion Nürnberg" (Report from
     the Slaughterhouse and Stockyard Administration), April 12, 1934, in
     Stadtarchiv Nürnberg, C69 016 001/2.

96. "Bericht der Schlacht- und Viehhofdirektion Nürnberg," in Stadtarchiv
     Nürnberg.

97. In the town of Norden in Eastern Frisia (Ostfriesland) during the
     summer of 1935, the mayor allotted separate sales lots to Jewish trad-
     ers on the livestock market; see Werner Teuber, *Jüdische Viehhändler
     in Ostfriesland und im nördlichen Emsland 1871–1942: Eine vergleichende
     Studie zu einer jüdischen Berufsgruppe in zwei wirtschaftlich und konfessio-
     nell unterschiedlichen Regionen* (Cloppenburg: Runge, 1995), 136. In other
     regions of Germany, Jewish traders were first denied access to livestock
     markets starting in 1936 (Cologne in the autumn of 1936 and Regensburg
     in November 1936 declared that their livestock markets were "Jew-free"
     [Judenfrei]); see Longerich, *Politik der Vernichtung: Eine Gesamtdarstel-
     lung der nationalsozialistischen Judenverfolgung* (Munich: Piper, 1998),
     122–123.

98. The expulsion of Jews from the German economy was regulated Reich-
     wide by paragraph 1 of "Verordnung zur Ausschaltung der Juden aus dem
     deutschen Wirtschaftsleben" (Decree on the elimination of the Jews
     from economic life), November 12, 1938, RGBl I, 1938, no. 189, 1580, which
     banned Jews from selling on markets. See Joseph Walk et al., eds., *Das
     Sonderrecht für die Juden im NS-Staat: Eine Sammlung der gesetzlichen
     Maßnahmen und Richtlinien; Inhalt und Bedeutung* (Heidelberg: Müller
     Juristischer, 1996), 254.

99. Das BA Ansbach an den Stadtrat Windsbach (Ansbach District Office to
     the Windsbach Municipal Council), August 16, 1934, in StAN, LRA An-
     sbach, Abg. 1961, no. 4289. See also Wiesemann, "Juden auf dem Lande,"
     390; Drecoll, *Der Fiskus als Verfolger*, 35. As early as April 1933, the state
     of Baden had already banned the cattle traders' language in the "Verord-
     nung zur Wiederherstellung der Ehrlichkeit im Viehhandel" (Decree on
     the restoration of honesty in the cattle trade); see Benz, *"Der ewige Jude"*
     (Berlin: Metropol, 2010), 54; also Hoffmann, "Verfolgung und Alltagsle-
     ben der Landjuden," 382.

100. Vermerk der Landesbauernschaft Bayern an das Staatsministerium für
      Wirtschaft, Abt. Landwirtschaft, München (Annotation from Bavarian
      State Farming Association to the State Ministry for Economy, Agricul-
      ture Division, Munich), June 23, 1936, in BayHStA, ML 3350.

101. See chapter 3.

102. Stefanie Fischer, interview with Fritz Müller (contemporary witness), Gunzenhausen, 2008; also Müller, *Der letzte Sau-Müller* (Gunzenhausen: Selbstverlag, 2007), 5.

103. Herbert Fleischmann an General Ritter von Epp, München, Apolda (Herbert Fleischmann to General Ritter von Epp, Munich, Apolda), April 18, 1933, in BayHStA, MWi 846; see also Staatsministerium für Wirtschaft, München, an M. Kellermann, Stuttgart (State Ministry for Economy, Munich to M. Kellermann, Stuttgart), July 13, 1934, in Bay-HStA, MWi 846; also Barkai, *Vom Boykott zur "Entjudung,"* 75; Hoffmann, "Verfolgung und Alltagsleben der Landjuden," 387.

104. Kreisbauernschaft Osterhofen an den Viehwirtschaftsverband Bayern (Osterhofen County Farmers' Association to the Bavarian Livestock Farming Association), November 10, 1936, in StAN, Reichsnährstand, Kreisbauernschaft Nürnberg, Rep. 267 IV, no. 173. The Aryan cattle distributors with whom Jakob Rindsberg collaborated had their trading permits revoked when the county farmers' association learned that they were doing business on behalf of Rindsberg. It does not emerge from the documents, however, what happened afterward to Rindsberg, who had also purchased cattle from Aryan cattle distributors without a valid trading permit; see also Kaufman, "The Daily Life," 168.

105. See also Kaufman, "The Daily Life," 165.

106. Antrag auf Entschädigung für Schaden im wirtschaftlichen und gewerblichen Fortkommen von Salomon Walz. Attorney Dr. Levor reported on the difficulties that arose from collaboration with non-Jewish cattle traders in a letter to the Feuchtwangen District Office, Nuremberg, May 16, 1936, in StAN, Rep. 270, Regierung, K.d.I, Abg. 1978, no. 3419.

107. Georg Fischer an die Militärregierung Ansbach, Leutershausen (Georg Fischer to the Ansbach Military Government Leutershausen), April 15, 1946, in StAN, BLVW, Ast. Nbg, no. 182.

108. "Tätigkeitsbericht der Gauamtsleitung für Kommunalpolitik," 272–350. From a different perspective, the collaboration of Jews and non-Jews in the rural trade to which Jews resorted so they could keep doing business while Jewish firms were subjected to persecution was also denounced by the Comité des Délégations Juives; see Comité des Délégations Juives, ed., *Das Schwarzbuch*, 364.

109. Wiesemann, "Juden auf dem Lande," 389.

110. Johann Eiffert und Georg Ebert an die Gendarmeriestation Colmberg, Buch am Wald (Johann Eiffert and Georg Ebert to the Colmberg Gendarmerie Station, Buch am Wald), August 28, 1934; Gendarmeriestation Colmberg an die Gendarmeriestation Schillingsfürst, Colmberg (Colmberg Gendarmerie Station Colmberg to Schillingsfürst Gendarmerie

Station, Colmberg), September 11, 1934; and Gendarmeriestation Schillingsfürst an das BA Ansbach (Schillingsfürst Gendarmerie Station to Ansbach District Office), October 18, 1934; all documents in StAN, LRA Ansbach, Abg. 1961, no. 2225.

111. Johann Eiffert und Georg Ebert an die Gendarmeriestation Colmberg, Buch am Wald (Johann Eiffert and Georg Ebert to Colmberg Gendarmerie Station, Buch am Wald), August 28, 1934; Gendarmeriestation Colmberg an die Gendarmeriestation Schillingsfürst, Colmberg (Colmberg Gendarmerie Station to Schillingsfürst Gendarmerie Station, Colmberg), September 11, 1934; and Gendarmeriestation Schillingsfürst an das BA Ansbach (Schillingsfürst Gendarmerie Station to Ansbach District Office), October 18, 1934; all correspondence in StAN, LRA Ansbach, Abg. 1961, no. 2225.

112. Landesbauernführer Bayern, Fritz Schuberth, an die Reichs-Verwaltungshauptabteilung des Reichsnährstands, München (Bavarian State Farm Leader, Fritz Schuberth, to Reich Main Administrative Department of the Reich Food Corporation, Munich), January 17, 1935, in BArch, R 16/I/2132. A similar incident had taken place in May 1935 in Weißenburg/Bayern; National Socialist municipal councilor Christian Schmoll had sold a sick cow to cattle trader Bermann from Ellingen. Under pressure from the party, Schmoll was forced to resign as municipal councilor. See Schreiben Michael Gerstner an Christian Schmoll, Weißenburg/Bay. (Letter of Michael Gerstner to Christian Schmoll, Weißenburg/Bayern), May 6, 1935; and Schreiben Christian Schmoll an Michael Gerstner, Weißenburg/Bay. (Letter of Christian Schmoll to Michael Gerstner, Weißenburg/Bayern), May 9, 1935; both letters in Stadtarchiv Weißenburg/Bay., Rep. III 141. Even in 1937, there were still party members conducting business with Jewish cattle traders. See Hans Mutzbauer, Pg., Metzgermeister, an die Kreisbauernschaft Nürnberg, Erlangen (Hans Mutzbauer, party member, master butcher, to the Nuremberg County Farmers' Association, Erlangen), November 22, 1937, in StAN, Reichsnährstand, Kreisbauernschaft Nürnberg, Rep. 267 IV, no. 172; see also Herlemann, *Der Bauer klebt am Hergebrachten*, 206–207.

113. In Günzburg, almost ten county provosts were unseated in 1935 because they were still approving the required certification of reliability a Jewish trader needed to practice his trade; see Gernot Römer, *Schwäbische Juden: Leben und Leistungen aus zwei Jahrhunderten in Selbstzeugnissen, Berichten und Bildern* (Augsburg: Presse-Dr.- und Verl., 1990), 155.

114. Wiesemann, "Juden auf dem Lande," 390.

115. Kaufman, "The Daily Life," 163.

116. See also Jan Philipp Reemtsma, *Vertrauen und Gewalt: Versuch über eine besondere Konstellation der Moderne* (Hamburg: Hamburger Edition, 2008), 21ff. Conversely, Wildt drew attention to how one need not have been an antisemite in order to feel "appealed to" by the "Volksgemeinschaft propaganda" of the Nazi regime. See Wildt, "Die Ungleichheit des Volkes: 'Volksgemeinschaft' in der politischen Kommunikation der Weimarer Republik," in *Volksgemeinschaft: Neue Forschungen zur Gesellschaft des Nationalsozialismus*, ed. Bajohr and Wildt (Frankfurt am Main: Fischer-Taschenbuch, 2009), 37.

117. On the significance of the local level for the persecution of rural Jews, see Steven M. Lowenstein, "The Struggle for Survival of Rural Jews in Germany 1933–1938: The Case of Bezirksamt Weissenburg, Mittelfranken," in *Die Juden im nationalsozialistischen Deutschland—The Jews in Nazi Germany, 1933–1943*, ed. Arnold Paucker, 115–124 (Tübingen: Mohr, 1986); and, in general, Gruner, "Die NS-Judenverfolgung und die Kommunen: Zur wechselseitigen Dynamisierung von zentraler und lokaler Politik, 1933–1941," *Vierteljahreshefte für Zeitgeschichte* 48, no. 1 (2000): 76–77.

118. Auszug aus dem Verzeichnis der für 1933 ausgestellten Gewerbelegitimationskarten (enth. die auf Viehhandel bezügl. Einträge) (Excerpt from the register of business licenses issued for 1933 [incl. entries related to cattle trade]), in StAN, LRA Ansbach Rep. 212/1, Abg. 1961, no. 4200.

119. See introduction for more on how these personal data were compiled.

120. Auszug aus dem Verzeichnis der für 1933 ausgestellten Gewerbelegitimationskarten (Excerpt from the register of business licenses issued for 1933), in StAN, LRA Ansbach Rep. 212/1, Abg. 1961, no. 4200.

121. BA Landau a.d. Isar an die Regierung von Niederbayern und der Oberpfalz, Kammer des Innern in Regensburg (Landau an der Isar District Office to the government of Lower Bavaria and Upper Palatinate, Chamber of the Interior in Regensburg), August 8, 1934, in BayHStA, ML 3349; *Regierungsanzeiger* (Government gazette) Nr. 31, August 4, 1934, in BayHStA, MF 68201.

122. Paragraph 57, Abs. 2a des "Gesetzes zur Änderung der Gewerbeordnung" vom 3.07.1934 (Paragraph 57, section 2a of "Law to Amend the Commercial Code" from July 3, 1934), RGBl. I, 1934, no. 74, 566. See also Drecoll, *Der Fiskus als Verfolger*, 110. This amendment also served the purpose of excluding other minorities the Nazis deemed undesirable, such as the Jehovah's Witnesses; see Detlef Garbe, *Zwischen Widerstand und Martyrium: Die Zeugen Jehovas im "Dritten Reich"* (Munich: Oldenbourg, 1993), 176. The Bavarian Gau affiliated with the Reich Association of the National Cattle Trade (Reichsverband des nationalen Viehhandels, Gau Bayern) was opposed to calls for a new legal regulation about certifying

and licensing the cattle trade, since existing regulations for "purging the cattle trade" (*Säuberung des Viehhandels*) were sufficient, in its opinion; see "Reichsverband des nationalen Viehhandels Deutschlands, Gau Bayern an das Staatsministerium für Wirtschaft, Abt. Landwirtschaft, München" (Reich Association of the National Cattle Trade, Gau Bavaria, to the State Ministry for the Economy, Agriculture Division, Munich), June 12, 1934, in BayHStA, ML 3349.

123. Unterakte Moritz Lehmann and Bescheid der Regierung von Ober- und Mittelfranken über die Verwerfung der Beschwerde von Moritz Lehmann (subfiles Moritz Lehmann and Decision of the government of Upper and Central Franconia on the dismissal of the complaint by Moritz Lehmann), August 26, 1937; both documents in StAN, Rep. 270, Regierung, K.d.I, Abg. 1978, no. 3420. Cattle trader Max Aal from Ansbach was also denied admission to trading on the pretext of having told a joke about the SA; see Max Aal an den Oberbürgermeister der Stadt Ansbach, Ansbach (Max Aal to the mayor of the city of Ansbach, Ansbach), February 4, 1937, in StAN, Rep. 270, Regierung, K.d.I, Abg. 1978, no. 3420.

124. Bescheid der Regierung von Ober- und Mittelfranken über die Verwerfung der Beschwerde von Moritz Lehmann (Decision of the government of Upper and Central Franconia on the dismissal of the complaint by Moritz Lehmann, Ansbach), August 26, 1937, in StAN, Rep. 270, Regierung, K.d.I, Abg. 1978, no. 3420.

125. Brief des Herrn Staatssekretärs (ohne Namensangabe) an den Herrn Staatsminister für Unterricht und Kultus Schemm, München (Letter of the Undersecretary [no name indicated] to the Undersecretary for Schools and Culture [Mr. Hans] Schemm, Munich), August 10, 1934, in BayHStA, ML 3349.

126. See, for example, StAN, Rep. 212/1, Abg. 1961, no. 161; StAN, LRA Ansbach Rep. 212/1, Abg. 1961, no. 4274; and StAN, LRA Hilpoltstein, Abg. 1971, no. 1253.

127. Reichsverband des nationalen Viehhandels Deutschlands, Gau Bayern, an das BA Ansbach, Nürnberg (Reich Association of the National Cattle Trade, Gau Bavaria, to the Ansbach District Office, Nuremberg), December 27, 1934, in StAN, LRA Ansbach Rep. 212/1, Abg. 1961, no. 4274. The fact that the county farmers' associations were interfering heavily in the district offices' powers to grant business licenses is also demonstrated by the following sources: Reichsnährstand, Kreisbauernschaft Ansbach, an das BA Ansbach (Reich Food Corporation, Ansbach County Farmers' Association, to the Ansbach District Office), December 21, 1935; and Kreisbauernschaft Ansbach an das BA Ansbach (Ansbach County Farmers'

Association to the Ansbach District Office), January 17, 1936, both documents in StAN, LRA Ansbach Rep. 212/1, Abg. 1961, no. 4274.

128. Gendarmeriestation Leutershausen an das BA Ansbach (Gendarmerie Station Leutershausen to the Ansbach District Office), January 28, 1935, in StAN, LRA Ansbach Rep. 212/1, Abg. 1961, no. 4274.

129. Gendarmeriestation Leutershausen an das BA Ansbach.

130. Bescheid der Regierung von Ober- und Mittelfranken, Kammer des Innern, Beschwerde des Josef Mann (Decision of the government of Upper and Central Franconia, Chamber of the Interior, complaint lodged by Josef Mann), May 2, 1935, in StAN, Rep. 270, Regierung, K.d.I, Abg. 1978, no. 3417.

131. Entschließung des Staatsministeriums für Wirtschaft, Abt. für Handel, Industrie und Gewerbe, München (Resolution of the State Ministry for the Economy, Div. for Trade, Industry, and Commerce, Munich), December 21, 1935, no. I C 23265, in BayHStA, MWi 799. See also the case of Philipp Wassermann, whom the Erlangen District Office wanted to deprive of his trading permit in 1935 because of his racial affiliation; the case proved unsuccessful before the Bavarian Higher Administrative Court. See Schreiben vom Generalstaatsanwalt des Bayerischen Verwaltungsgerichtshofs an das Staatsministerium für Wirtschaft, Abt. Handel, Industrie und Gewerbe, München (Letter of prosecutor general at the Bavarian Higher Administrative Court to the State Ministry for the Economy, Div. of Trade, Industry, and Commerce, Munich), July 17, 1935; and Schreiben vom Reichs- und Preußischen Wirtschaftsminister an das Bayerische Staatsministerium für Wirtschaft, Abt. Handel, Industrie und Gewerbe, Berlin (Letter from Reich and Prussian Economics Minister to the Bavarian State Ministry for the Economy, Div. of Trade, Industry, and Commerce, Berlin), August 15, 1935; both letters in BayHStA, MWi 799.

132. In 1933, Streicher had already criticized the civil service for posing an obstacle to the persecution of Jews, owing to the officials' "obstinacy." See Drecoll, *Der Fiskus als Verfolger*, 45.

133. Auszug aus dem Protokoll über die öffentliche Sitzung der Regierung von Ober- und Mittelfranken, Ansbach (Excerpt from the minutes of the public session of the government of Upper and Central Franconia, Ansbach), January 14, 1937, in StAN, Rep. 270, Regierung, K.d.I, Abg. 1978, no. 3420.

134. On the fiscal persecution of the Jewish population in Bavaria under Nazi rule, see Drecoll, *Der Fiskus als Verfolger*, 249–267; and Janetzko, *Die "Arisierung" mittelständischer jüdischer Unternehmen*.

135. Der Bürgermeister der Stadt Rothenburg o/T an die Regierung von Ober- und Mittelfranken, Rothenburg o/T (The mayor of the city Rothenburg ob der Tauber to the government of Upper and Central Franconia, Rothenburg ob der Tauber), December 16, 1937; and RA Dr. Bayer an die Regierung von Ober- und Mittelfranken, Ansbach (Attorney Dr. Bayer to the government of Upper and Central Franconia, Ansbach), December 24, 1937, both documents in StAN, Rep. 270, Regierung, K.d.I, Abg. 1978, no. 3420.

136. Herlemann, *"Der Bauer klebt am Hergebrachten,"* 198–199.

137. Bayerische Politische Polizei an alle Bezirksämter, München (Bavarian Political Police to all district offices, Munich), October 26, 1935, in StAN, LRA Ansbach Rep. 212/1, Abg. 1961, no. 2218.

138. Gendarmeriestation Colmberg an das BA Ansbach (Gendarmerie Station Comberg to the Ansbach District Office), November 8, 1935; and Gendarmeriestation Heilsbronn an das BA Ansbach (Gendarmerie Station Heilsbronn to the Ansbach District Office), November 7, 1935; both documents in StAN, LRA Ansbach Rep. 212/1, Abg. 1961, no. 2218. In other parts of the Reich, this even resulted in Jewish cattle traders being incarcerated in concentration camps; see Herlemann, *"Der Bauer klebt am Hergebrachten,"* 198.

139. Bayerische Politische Polizei an alle Bezirksämter (Bavarian Political Police to all district offices), October 18, 1935, in StAN, LRA Wbg, Abg. 1949, no. 2; also Wiesemann, "Juden auf dem Lande," 388.

140. Notiz der Gendarmeriestation Ellingen auf dem Schreiben der Bayrischen Politischen Polizei an alle Bezirksämter vom 18.10.1935 (Notice of Ellingen Gendarmerie Station on the letter of the Bavarian Political Police to all district offices from October 18, 1935), in StAN, LRA Wbg, Abg. 1949, no. 2.

141. The accusation of cruelty to animals was raised against Isaak Hutzler on July 29, 1936; taken from the Polizeiliches Führungszeugnis (police certificate) for Isaak Hutzler, Hüttenbach, October 3, 1938, in StAN, BA Lauf, Abg. 1959, no. 403.

142. Gendarmeriestation Dombühl an das BA Ansbach (Dombühl Gendarmerie Station to Ansbach District Office), September 5, 1935, in StAN, LRA Ansbach Rep. 212/1, Abg. 1961, no. 4274. An additional example of refusing a business license (a GLK, abbreviation for *Gewerbelegitimationskarte*) because of complaints lodged against a cattle trader from long ago is the case of Theodor Rindsberg; the city of Nuremberg refused to issue him a GLK in 1936 on the grounds that his dispute with a farmer over an ox back in 1930 had turned into a physical fight.

Ultimately, the government of Upper and Central Franconia rejected Rindsberg's own complaint while simultaneously stripping him of the certification as a reliable trader he needed to stay in business. See Bescheid der Regierung von Ober- und Mittelfranken, Ansbach (Decision of the government of Upper and Central Franconia, Ansbach), March 23, 1937, in Unterakte Theodor Rindsberg (subfiles Theodor Findsberg), StAN, Rep. 270, Regierung, K.d.I, Abg. 1978, no. 3420. In 1935, Josef Mann would also be refused admission to his trade owing to a suit going back years; see RA Dr. Bayer an den Stadtrat Rothenburg o/T, Ansbach (Attorney Dr. Bayer to the Rothenburg City Council, Ansbach), March 9, 1935, in StAN, Rep. 270, Regierung, K.d.I, Abg. 1978, no. 3417.

143. Gendarmeriestation Leutershausen an das BA Ansbach (Leutershausen Gendarmerie to Ansbach District Office), January 29, 1935; and Kreisbauernschaft Ansbach an das BA Ansbach (Ansbach County Farmers' Association to Ansbach District Office), August 14, 1935; both documents in StAN, LRA Ansbach Rep. 212/1, Abg. 1961, no. 4274. This confirms the view stated by Barkai, who pointed out that at the party level, it was the economic advisers to the Gauleiters (*Gauwirtschaftsberater*) who were in charge of expelling Jews from the economy; see Barkai, *Vom Boykott zur "Entjudung,"* 74.

144. BA Gunzenhausen an das Staatsministerium für Wirtschaft, Abt. für Handel, Industrie und Gewerbe (Gunzenhausen District Office to the State Ministry for the Economy, Div. for Trade, Industry, and Commerce), November 27, 1935, in BayHStA, MWi 799.

145. Staatsministerium für Wirtschaft, Abt. Landwirtschaft, an die Regierungen und Bezirksverwaltungsbehörden, München (State Ministry for the Economy, Div. Agriculture, to [Bavarian district] governments and district administrative authorities, Munich), December 24, 1935, in BayHStA, ML 3349.

146. A *Kalm* (in Frankish dialect) is a mature female cow that has not yet become pregnant.

147. Andreas Auernhammer, Geschäftsbuch, Oberhochstatt 1924–1935, in Familienarchiv Robert Auernhammer, Oberhochstatt (Andreas Auernhammer, account book, Oberhochstatt 1924–1935 in Robert Auernhammer family archive, Oberhochstatt).

148. This had been decided by the municipal council of Egenhausen (in the rural county of Uffenheim); see Ophir and Wiesemann, *Die jüdischen Gemeinden in Bayern*, 170, 202. See also *Bayerischer Staatsanzeiger*, no. 21, September 19, 1933, in BayHStA, MWi 846. On the repressive measures that threatened farmers if they were still trading with Jews, see also Hoffmann, "Verfolgung und Alltagsleben der Landjuden," 384.

149. Andreas Auernhammer, Geschäftsbuch, Oberhochstatt 1924–1935, in Familienarchiv Robert Auernhammer, Oberhochstatt (Andreas Auernhammer, account book, Oberhochstatt 1924–1935 in Robert Auernhammer family archive, Oberhochstatt).

150. "Bericht aus Ellingen, 10.08.1935" (Report from Ellingen, August 10, 1935), quoted by Lowenstein, "The Struggle for Survival," 121.

151. See Robert Gellately, *The Gestapo and German Society: Enforcing Racial Policy 1933–1945* (Oxford: Clarendon, 1990), 186.

152. See also Kershaw, "Antisemitismus und Volksmeinung," 291; Przyrembel, *"Rassenschande,"* 185–199.

153. Karl Schmidt produced evidence about one such case to exonerate himself before a postwar denazification tribunal; see his Verteidigungsschreiben an die Sprk. des Internierungslagers Regensburg, Unterwurmbach (Defense deposition to the denazification court at the Regensburg internment camp), December 10, 1947, in StAN, Sprk Gun- Land, K-30. See also Fred Hahn and Günther Wagenlehner, *Lieber Stürmer: Leserbriefe an das NS-Kampfblatt 1924–1945* (Stuttgart: Seewald, 1978), 228; and Kaufman, "The Daily Life," 163.

154. Staatsministerium für Wirtschaft, Abt. Landwirtschaft an den Schlachtviehverwertungsverband, Bayern, München (State Ministry for the Economy, Agriculture Div. to Beef Cattle Husbandry Association, Bavaria, Munich), April 23, 1936, in BayHStA, ML 3350.

155. See also Kershaw, "Antisemitismus und Volksmeinung," 296.

156. Gendarmeriestation Geslau an das BA Ansbach, Geslau (Gendarmerie Station Geslau to the Ansbach District Office, Geslau), September 15, 1935, in StAN, LRA Ansbach Rep. 212/1, Abg. 1961, no. 4274.

157. Gendarmeriestation Geslau an das BA Ansbach, Geslau.

158. Gendarmeriestation Geslau an das BA Ansbach, Geslau.

159. One of the cases pointing to this pattern of denunciation comes from the Gunzenhausen District Office. In 1937, innkeeper Karl Bergmann from Frickenfelden lodged a complaint at the main police station in Gunzenhausen concerning an accusation made in the *Stürmer* newspaper, in which he was reproached for doing business with cattle trader Hugo Walz in 1935. He alleged that August Krug from Frickenfelden had denounced him in the *Stürmer* because Krug was jealous of his business. See Gendarmerie-Hauptstation Gunzenhausen an das BA Gunzenhausen, Gunzenhausen (Gendarmerie main station Gunzenhausen to the Gunzenhausen District Office, Gunzenhausen), July 24, 1937, in StAN, LRA Gun, Abg. 1961, no. 658.

160. See also Gellately, *The Gestapo and German Society,* 186ff.

161. The card index was found in the first decade of the 2000s in the attic of
the Keitel family in the Württemberg town of Wiesenbach. According to
an oral account, American troops had left behind the card index, which
originated in Rothenburg ob der Tauber, in the house of the Keitel family when the troops withdrew after 1945. I wish to thank Hartwig Behr,
Bad Mergentheim, who is in possession of this card index and was kind
enough to provide me with a copy.

162. See also Drecoll, *Der Fiskus als Verfolger*, 31. Along these lines, confirmation is also provided for Barkai's thesis that there was never any such
thing as a closed season when it came to the expulsion of the Jews from
the German economy; see Barkai, "Population Decline and Economic
Stagnation," 205–210.

163. Abschrift eines Beschlusses zur "Säuberung des Viehhandels von unzu-
verlässigen Personen" des BA Weißenburg/Bay. (Copy of a resolution on
"Purging the cattle trade of unreliable persons" from the Weißenburg/
Bayern District Office), August 29, 1935; and Schreiben von RA Landen-
berger an das BA Weißenburg/Bay., Nürnberg (Letter from attorney
Landenberger to the Weißenburg/Bayern District Office, Nuremberg),
September 10, 1935; both documents in Staatsarchiv für Oberbayern,
StAnW 3277.

164. Schreiben von RA Landenberger an das BA Weißenburg/Bay, Nürnberg
(Letter from attorney Landenberger to the Weißenburg/Bayern District
Office, Nuremberg), September 10, 1935. See also Schreiben von RA
Landenberger an die Staatsanwaltschaft München, Nürnberg (Letter
from attorney Landenberger to the Munich public prosecutor's office,
Nuremberg), December 10, 1937. Both letters in Staatsarchiv für Ober-
bayern, StAnW 3277.

165. Gendarmeriestation Ettenstatt an das BA Weißenburg/Bay., 14.07.1936,
Betreff: Verhinderung von Ausschreitungen gegen die Juden (Gendarmerie Station Ettenstatt to the Weißenburg/Bayern District Office, July
14, 1936, re: prevention of riots against Jews), in StAN, LRA Wbg., Abg.
1996, Titel IV, no. 225.

166. Schutzhaftbefehl des BAs Weißenburg/Bay. (Protective custody arrest
warrant from Weißenburg/Bayern District Office), July 25, 1936, in
StAN, LRA Wbg., Abg. 1996, Titel IV, no. 225.

167. Schreiben der Bayerischen Politischen Polizei an den Herrn Vorstand des
BAs Weißenburg/Bay., München (Letter of Bavarian Political Police to
chair of Weißenburg/Bayern District Office), July 31, 1936, in StAN, LRA
Wbg., Abg. 1996, Titel IV, no. 225.

168. Schreiben von RA Landenberger an das BA Weißenburg/Bay., Nürnberg
(Letter from attorney Landenberger to the Weißenburg/Bayern District

Office, Nuremberg), April 27, 1937, in StAN, Rep. 270, Regierung, K.d.I, Abg. 1978, no. 3420.

169. Zeugenaussage von Michael Gerstner vor der Staatsanwaltschaft München (Testimony from Michael Gerstner before the Munich public prosecutor's office), n.d. [presumably January 1938], in Staatsarchiv für Oberbayern, StAnW 3277.

170. Notiz BA Hilpoltstein (Note Hilpoltstein District Office), February 1, 1937, in StAN, LRA Hilpoltstein, Abg. 1971, no. 1253. In Oberwurmbach (part of the Gunzenhausen muncipality), Georg Reichardt was relieved of his municipal service job because he had negotiated with Jewish cattle trader Gutmann for a calf. See "Monatsbericht der NSDAP, Gau Franken, Ortsgruppe Unterwurmbach" (Monthly report of NSDAP, Gau Franken, Unterwurmbach local party group), October 2, 1936, in StAN, Sprk Gun-Land, K-30. See also Ordnungsstrafe gegen das Parteimitglied Linsenmeier aus Dittenheim (Disciplinary sanction against party member Linsenmeier from Dittenheim). Linsenmeier was said to have negotiated with the Jewish cattle trader Engel for an ox as late as 1937. See Friedrich Linsenmeier an die Sprk. Gunzenhausen-Land, Dittenheim (Friedrich Linsenmeier to the denazification court for Gunzenhausen-Land, Dittenheim), February 22, 1948, in StAN, Sprk. Gun-Land, L-39.

171. Ausschnitt aus dem "Tätigkeitsbericht der Gauamtsleitung für Kommunalpolitik, Gau-Franken, an das Hauptamt für Kommunalpolitik, München, Nürnberg" (Excerpt from "Progress report of the Gau office head for local government policy, Gau of Franconia, to the Nazi party main office for local government policy, Munich, Nuremberg"), September 7, 1936, in BArch, NS 25/218, Bl. 343.

172. Ausschnitt aus dem Tätigkeitsbericht der Gauamtsleitung.

173. Ausschnitt aus dem Tätigkeitsbericht der Gauamtsleitung.

174. Gendarmeriestation Treuchtlingen an die Staatsanwaltschaft für den Landgerichtsbezirk München I, Treuchtlingen (Treuchtlingen Gendarmerie Station to the state prosecuting attorney for the regional court district Munich I, Treuchtlingen), November 19, 1937; and RA Landenberger an die Staatsanwaltschaft München, Nürnberg (Attorney Landenberger to the state prosecuting attorney Munich, Nuremberg), December 10, 1937; both documents in Staatsarchiv für Oberbayern, StAnW 3277. See Max Gutmann an RA Dr. Josef Kern (Max Gutmann to attorney Dr. Josef Kern), July 15, 1950, in BayHStA, EG 92225, K-2242. See also Ophir and Wiesemann, *Die jüdischen Gemeinden in Bayern*, 172.

175. "Jüdischer Mordanschlag: Der Jude Bärmann in Ellingen bietet für die Ermordung des Kreisleiters und des Kreisbauernführers 10000 Mark!"

(Jewish Murder Attempt: The Jew Bärmann in Ellingen offers 10,000 marks for the murder of county leader and county farm leader!), *Der Stürmer* 16, no. 49 (1937): 1–4.

176. RA Landenberger an die Geheime Staatspolizei, Leitstelle Bayern, München, Nürnberg (Attorney Landenberger to the Gestapo, Bavaria control center, Munich, Nuremberg), November 19, 1937, in Staatsarchiv für Oberbayern, StAnW 3277.

177. Schreiben von RA Dr. Levor an den Oberbürgermeister der Stadt Nürnberg, Nürnberg (Letter from attorney Dr. Levor to the Mayor of the City of Nuremberg, Nuremberg), May 4, 1936, in Unterakte Theodor Rindsberg, StAN, Rep. 270, Regierung, K.d.I, Abg. 1978, no. 3420.

178. Also arriving at the same conclusion is Janetzko, *Die "Arisierung" mittelständischer jüdischer Unternehmen*, 57–58.

179. See also Gruner, "Die NS-Judenverfolgung und die Kommunen," 88.

180. Barkai, *Vom Boykott zur "Entjudung,"* 74.

181. Ludwig Kohn, for example, records a note to the Bavarian State Compensation Office from November 7, 1956—"Schreiben an das LEA, 7.11.1956"—that is part of the document found under the descriptive title "Ende des Jahres 1934 allgem. Geschäftsrückgang und Verweigerung der Legitimationskarte (Handelserlaubnis zur Ausübung des Fachhandelsgeschäftes) d. den Bürgermeister Idermeier in Wassertrüdingen.... Verbot auf Verord. d. Kreisleiters Idermeier m. Juden zu handeln u. Verordng., dass d. Betreten d. Dörfer f. Juden auf eigene Gefahr war. 1933 ein Drittel Rückgang. 1934 völliger Stillstand." ("End of 1934 gen. downturn in business and refusal of business license [commercial permit for practicing a specialized trade business] via Mayor Idermeier in Wassertrüdingen . . . ban by directive from county leader Idermeier on dealing w. Jews and directive that entering villages for Jews was at their own peril. 1933 downturn by one third. 1934 complete standstill."), note and document in BayHStA, BEG 21874, K-1973. An additional example of a business that was abandoned in 1934 is that of merchant Simon Hutzler, who had to stop trading in the autumn of 1934; see Eidesstattliche Erklärung von Simon Hutzler an das LEA, New York (Affidavit by Simon Hutzler to the Bavarian State Compensation Office, New York), April 4, 1956, in BayHStA, BEG 13311, A-00359.

182. Kershaw, "Antisemitismus und Volksmeinung," 300–301.

183. As examples we may cite the cattle-trading firms of the Walz brothers (Gebrüder Walz) from Gunzenhausen, of Bermann & Oppenheimer from Ellingen, and of Steinberger from Colmberg, all of whom first gave up their businesses in 1938 under pressure from the party, before the Reich-wide ban.

184. The cattle-trading and real-estate business of Salomon and Hugo Walz had to dismiss two of three staff members owing to the intensity of the persecution measures; see Antrag auf Entschädigung für Schaden im wirtschaftlichen und gewerblichen Fortkommen von Salomon Walz.

185. Information about Hugo Walz's revenues taken from the Antrag auf Entschädigung für Schaden im wirtschaftlichen und gewerblichen Fortkommen von Salomon Walz.

186. The tax office files for Moritz Behr reveal a similar development; see Finanzamt Dinkelsbühl an das LEA München, Dinkelsbühl (Dinkelsbühl Tax Office to the Bavarian State Compensation Office in Munich, Dinkelsbühl), November 6, 1958, in BayHStA, BEG 57576, K-1138.

187. This has been pointed out in Bajohr, *Arianisation in Hamburg,"* 287.

188. In addition, Jewish traders in Gunzenhausen had already been banned in 1935 from trading in real estate; see BA Gunzenhausen über Einzelmaßnahmen gegen Juden, Gunzenhausen (Gunzenhausen District Office on individual measures against Jews, Gunzenhausen), November 28, 1935, in StAN, LRA Gun, Abg. 1961, no. 658; see also Ophir and Wiesemann, *Die jüdischen Gemeinden in Bayern*, 190.

189. Barkai, *Vom Boykott zur "Entjudung,"* 65.

190. Barkai, *Vom Boykott zur "Entjudung,"* 68.

191. "Vermerk des Staatssekretärs im Reichsministerium des Innern, Wilhelm Stuckart, über eine interministerielle Besprechung am 29. September 1936 über die 'grundsätzliche Richtung der gesamten Judenpolitik,'" reprinted in Mommsen and Willems, *Herrschaftsalltag im Dritten Reich*, 445–452; Longerich, *Politik der Vernichtung*, 118; and Gruner, "Die NS-Judenverfolgung und die Kommunen," 93.

192. Münkel, *Nationalsozialistische Agrarpolitik und Bauernalltag*, 94.

193. Dritte Verordnung zur Regelung des Verkehrs mit Schlachtvieh, RGBl. I, 1936, Nr. 39 (Third Decree Regulating Commerce with Beef Cattle, Reich Law Gazette [Reichsgesetzblatt] I, 1936, no. 39), 366; but also Zweite Verordnung zur Regelung des Verkehrs mit Schlachtvieh, RGBl. I, 1935, Nr. 84 (Second Decree Regulating Commerce with Beef Cattle, Reich Law Gazette I, 1935, no. 84), 1045. See also Herlemann, *"Der Bauer klebt am Hergebrachten,"* 215.

194. Herlemann, *"Der Bauer klebt am Hergebrachten,"* 216.

195. Reichsverband der deutschen landwirtschaftlichen Genossenschaften—Raiffeisen—an die Verbände, Berlin (Reich Association of German Agricultural Cooperatives—Raiffeisen—to its affiliated associations, Berlin), November 11, 1936, in BArch, R 3601/1946. As a report from the association of cooperatives from the Electorate of Hesse-Kassel (Kurhessen) demonstrates, most of the livestock husbandry cooperatives were

not in any position to finance livestock dues. See Kurhessischer Verband ländlicher Genossenschaften an die Darlehenskassen-Vereine, Kassel (Association of Electoral-Hessian Rural Cooperatives to the Loan Societies, Kassel), October 28, 1936, in BArch, R 3601/1946, 267.

196. Viehwirtschaftsverband Bayern an das BA Ansbach, München (Bavarian Livestock Farming Association to the Ansbach District Office, Munich), November 3, 1936, in StAN, LRA Ansbach Rep. 212/1, Abg. 1961, no. 4274.

197. Viehwirtschaftsverband Bayern an das BA Ansbach, München.

198. See the case of Johann Frauenschläger, especially the Schreiben der Kreisbauernschaft Ansbach an das BA Ansbach (Letter of the Ansbach County Farmers' Association to the Ansbach District Office), December 17, 1935, in StAN, LRA Ansbach Rep. 212/1, Abg. 1961, no. 4274. See also the case of Fritz Schörner, to whom the Rehau (Upper Franconia) District Office wanted to deny issuance of a business license (GLK) because of previous criminal offenses, although the Hof an der Saale County Farmers' Association then advocated issuing him a GLK. Details in Kreisbauernschaft Hof a/S an die Regierung von Ober- und Mittelfranken, Hof (Hof an der Saale County Farmers' Association to the government of Upper and Central Franconia, Hof), November 27, 1937 in StAN, Rep. 270, Regierung, K.d.I, Abg. 1978, no. 3420. See also the case of Max Sommerer, whom the peasant population was unable to trust because of his difficulties making payments. For details, see Gendarmerie-Station Kirchenlamitz an das BA Wunsiedel, Kirchenlamitz (Kirchenlamitz Gendarmerie Station to the Wunsiedel District Office, Kirchenlamitz), January 4, 1936, in BayHStA, ML 3347.

199. BA Uffenheim an die Regierung von Ober- und Mittelfranken (Uffenheim District Office to the government of Upper and Central Franconia), January 9, 1937, in StAN, Rep. 270, K.d.I, Abg. 1978, no. 3420.

200. BA Scheinfeld an die Regierung von Ober- und Mittelfranken (Scheinfeld District Office to the government of Upper and Central Franconia), January 20, 1937, in StAN, Rep. 270, K.d.I, Abg. 1978, no. 3420.

201. BA Scheinfeld an die Regierung von Ober- und Mittelfranken.

202. BA Scheinfeld an die Regierung von Ober- und Mittelfranken.

203. BA Scheinfeld an die Regierung von Ober- und Mittelfranken, January 23, 1937, in StAN, Rep. 270, K.d.I, Abg. 1978, no. 3420.

204. Verordnung über den Handel mit Vieh vom 25.01.1937 (Decree on trade with cattle from January 25, 1937), esp. paragraph 3, in RGBl. I, 1937, no. 7, 28–29.

205. BA Schwabach an die Regierung von Ober- und Mittelfranken, Schwa-
     bach (Schwabach District Office to the government of Upper and
     Central Franconia, Schwabach), March 27, 1937; and BA Schwabach an
     die Regierung von Ober- und Mittelfranken, Schwabach (Schwabach
     District Office to the government of Upper and Central Franconia,
     Schwabach), April 1, 1937; both documents in StAN, Rep. 270, K.d.I,
     Abg. 1978, no. 3420.

206. See both documents (March and April 1937 letters from Schwabach
     District Office to government of Upper and Central Franconia) cited in
     previous endnote, from StAN, Rep. 270, K.d.I, Abg. 1978, no. 3420. Some
     information about the lack of clarity that prevailed among the authori-
     ties affected by the decree of January 25, 1937, is provided by the written
     exchange between the Württemberg State Trade Office (Württember-
     gisches Landesgewerbeamt), the Württemberg Economics Minister
     (Württembergischer Wirtschaftsminister), and the Reich and Prussian
     Minister for Food and Agriculture (Reichs- und Preußischer Minister
     für Ernährung und Landwirtschaft) between March and August 1937 in
     BArch, R 3101/14135.

207. Vermerk Nr. 2401, Betreff: Jüdische Viehhändler, das BA Ansbach an
     den Herrn Oberbürgermeister der Stadt der Reichsparteitage Nürnberg
     (Note no. 2401, re: Jewish cattle traders, the Ansbach District Office to
     the Mayor of the City of the Reich Party Congresses, Nuremberg), n.d.
     [presumably 1937], in StAN, LRA Ansbach, Abg. 1961, no. 4196. Barkai
     has evidence of a similar case from 1938; see Barkai, *Vom Boykott zur
     "Entjudung,"* 75.

208. Lowenstein, "The Struggle for Survival," 122.

209. In *Der Stürmer* 15 (1937), nos. 8, 20, 21, 26, 28, 31, 32, 33, 34, and 44.

210. From the Antrag auf Entschädigung von Salomon Walz für Schaden
     im wirtschaftlichen und gewerblichen Fortkommen (Application for
     reconciliation by Salomon Walz for damages in economic and com-
     mercial career), January 15, 1950, in BayHStA, BEG 77461, K-018; RA
     Dr. Leo Beck an das LEA, Coburg (Attorney Dr. Leo Beck to Bavarian
     Compensation Office, Coburg), December 8, 1961, in BayHStA, BEG
     61371, K-302.

211. Georg Meyer an die Sprk. Gunzenhausen, Markt Berolzheim (Georg
     Meyer to Gunzenhausen denazification court, Markt Berolzheim),
     January 3, 1947; and affidavit by Ludwig Hüttinger for Georg Meyer to
     Gunzenhausen denazification court, n.d. [around 1947]; both docu-
     ments in StAN, Sprk. Gun-Land, M-43. Robert Uri Kaufmann also
     draws attention to this kind of secret cow deal in Hesse; see Kaufmann,
     "Zum Viehhandel der Juden in Deutschland und der Schweiz – bisherige

Ergebnisse und offene Fragen," in *Jüdische Viehhändler zwischen Schwarzwald und Schwäbischer Alb: Vorträge der Tagung der Arbeitsgemeinschaft Jüdische Gedenkstätten am Oberen Neckar am 3. Oktober 2006 in Horb-Rexingen*, ed. Kaufmann and Carsten Kohlmann, 17–41 (Horb-Rexingen: Barbara Staudacher, 2008), 40.

212. Quoted by Wiesemann, "Juden auf dem Lande," 391; see also Römer, *Schwäbische Juden*, 155.

213. Gendarmeriestation Treuchtlingen an die Staatsanwaltschaft für den Landgerichtsbezirk München I, Treuchtlingen (Treuchtlingen Gendarmerie Station to the state prosecuting attorney for the regional court district Munich I, Treuchtlingen), November 19, 1937; Zeugenaussagen von Max Gutmann, Simon Gutmann, Leonhard Hübner und Johann Seibold gegenüber der Gendarmeriestation Treuchtlingen (Testimony of Max Gutmann, Simon Gutmann, Leonhard Hübner, and Johann Seibold to the Treuchtlingen Gendarmerie Station), November 15, 1937; all statements in Staatsarchiv für Oberbayern, StAnW 3277.

214. Zeugenaussage von Bernhard Bermann, aber auch die Zeugenaussagen von Max Gutmann, Leonhard Hübner und Johann Seibold gegenüber der Gendarmeriestation Treuchtlingen (Testimony of Bernhard Bermann, but also testimony of Max Gutmann, Leonhard Hübner, and Johann Seibold to the Treuchtlingen Gendarmerie Station), November 15, 1937; Gendarmeriestation Treuchtlingen an die Staatsanwaltschaft für den Landgerichtsbezirk München I, Treuchtlingen (Treuchtlingen Gendarmerie Station to the state prosecuting attorney for the regional court district Munich I, Treuchtlingen), November 19, 1937; all documents in Staatsarchiv für Oberbayern, StAnW 3277.

215. Gellately describes this kind of behavior as "compliance through pressure"; see Gellately, *The Gestapo and German Society*, 186–187.

216. Zeugenaussagen von Bernhard Bermann und Leonhard Hübner gegenüber der Staatsanwaltschaft für den Landgerichtsbezirk München I (Testimony of Bernhard Bermann and Leonhard Hübner to the state prosecuting attorney for the regional court district Munich I), January 1938, Staatsarchiv für Oberbayern, StAnW 3277.

217. This is the conclusion drawn by Wiesemann, "Juden auf dem Lande," 389; Teuber, *Jüdische Viehhändler in Ostfriesland*, 132; and Hoffmann, "Verfolgung und Alltagsleben der Landjuden," 383.

218. Saldern, *Mittelstand im "Dritten Reich,"* 181; Gellately, *The Gestapo and German Society*, 167.

219. Münkel, *Nationalsozialistische Agrarpolitik und Bauernalltag*, 360.

220. See chapter 3.

221. Eidesstattliche Erklärung von Alfred Eckmann an das LEA, Tel Aviv (Affidavit by Alfred Eckmann to the Bavarian State Compensation Office, Tel Aviv), January 25, 1956, in BayHStA, BEG 3843, K-85. There is a report of a similar incident by Karl Freising from the town of Roth; see Karl Freising an das LEA, vermutlich New York, 12.05.1959.

222. Gendarmeriestation Markt Berolzheim an das BA Gunzenhausen (Markt Berolzheim Gendarmerie Station to the Gunzenhausen District Office), March 26, 1937, in StAN, LRA Gun, Abg. 1961, no. 658.

223. Quoted by Wiesemann, "Juden auf dem Lande," 391; see also Römer, *Schwäbische Juden*, 155.

224. In his study, Teuber compared the persecution of Jewish cattle traders in a heavily Protestant region with their harassment in a mostly Catholic region. He came to the conclusion that persecution was less intense in the largely Catholic region; see Teuber, *Jüdische Viehhändler in Ostfriesland*, 246ff. See also Anthony Kauders, *German Politics and the Jews: Düsseldorf and Nuremberg* (Oxford: Clarendon, 1996), 186ff.

225. Kershaw, "Antisemitismus und Volksmeinung," 292ff.

226. See Drecoll, *Der Fiskus als Verfolger*, 40–42.

227. Siegfried Weinmann aus Treuchtlingen, Schuldnerliste erstellt aus sämtlichen Akten im Nachlass Herz bezüglich Siegfried Weinmann (Siegfried Weinmann from Treuchtlingen, lists of debtors compiled from all the files in the Herz estate relating to Siegfried Weinmann), in StAN, Nachlass RA Herz.

228. Since the state of source material did not make it possible to determine the religious affiliation of every single debtor, a procedure was chosen in which a conclusion about the debtor's religious affiliation could be surmised based on the religious character of the town. This procedure may be methodologically problematic, yet it does seem plausible based on the religious topography of Central Franconia since, in the time period under investigation, these localities still had majorities that were either Protestant or Catholic that could be traced back to the impact of the Reformation. For example, in 1925, there were 1,013 Catholics and 17 Protestants in the town of Wolframs-Eschenbach, while in Unterwurmbach, there were 536 Protestants and 2 Catholics. Figures from Bayer. Statistisches Landesamt, *Gemeinde-Verzeichnis für den Freistaat Bayern: Nach der Volkszählung vom 16. Juni 1925 und dem Gebietsstand vom 1. Dezember 1925* (Munich: J. Lindauer, 1926), 188. Admittedly, there were also localities with a denominationally mixed population; these were excluded from the analysis because no conclusions could be drawn about the religious character of the debtor in these cases.

229. Figures derived from all correspondence between Attorney Herz and Louis Feldmann in StAN, Nachlass RA Herz, no. 242.

230. From the Antrag aus Entschädigung von Hugo Walz, Aufstellung zu Form. D "Schaden an Eigentum und Vermögen" III (Application for restitution by Hugo Walz, list for Form D "Damages to Property and Assets" III), February 22, 1950, in BayHStA, BEG 38426.

231. The large share of debtors from Catholic localities in the Medineh of Louis Feldmann might, however, indicate that Feldmann avoided heavily Protestant localities and preferred seeking out localities with a highly Catholic share of the population. On this, see Kershaw, "Antisemitismus und Volksmeinung," 336. Teuber also shows that there were fewer attacks on Jews in Catholic regions than in Protestant ones. This made Jews feel more secure in Catholic areas, where they typically decided to emigrate later than in Protestant regions. Frequently, however, that delayed decision meant it was then too late to find refuge abroad; see Teuber, *Jüdische Viehhändler in Ostfriesland.*

232. One such case is mentioned in the Schreiben von RA Dr. Bayer an das LEA, Ansbach (Letter of attorney Dr. Bayer to the Bavarian State Compensation Office, Ansbach), September 12, 1957, in BayHStA, BEG 77459, A-16. In Hesse, some cattle traders were sent to a concentration camp after being reported to the authorities by a farmer who wanted his debts deferred; see Kim Wünschmann, "Jüdische Häftlinge im KZ-Osthofen: Das frühe Konzentrationslager als Terrorinstrument der nationalsozialistischen Judenpolitik," in *Vor 75 Jahren: "Am Anfang stand die Gewalt . . . ,"* ed. Landeszentrale für Politische Bildung Rheinland-Pfalz (Mainz: LpB Rheinland-Pfalz, 2008), 25–26.

233. Zeugenvernehmung der Luzia Röder (ehemaliges Hausmädchen bei der Viehhändlerfamilie Eugenie und Herman Levite) vor dem Amtsgericht, Dinkelsbühl (Witness interrogation of Luzia Röder [former housemaid for the cattle-trading family of Eugenie and Herman Levite] before the district court, Dinkelsbühl), March 10, 1964, in BayHStA, BEG 49839, A-185; RA Dr. Levor an Louis Feldmann, Nürnberg (Attorney Dr. Levor to Louis Feldmann, Nuremberg), December 17, 1936; and Louis Feldmann an RA Dr. Levor, Buenos-Aires, Argentinien (Louis Feldmann to Attorney Dr. Levor, Buenos-Aires, Argentina), January 31, 1937; both sets of documents in StAN, Nachlass RA Herz, no. 242. See also Ophir and Wiesemann, *Die jüdischen Gemeinden in Bayern,* 197.

234. Ophir and Wiesemann, *Die jüdischen Gemeinden in Bayern,* 197.

235. "Kleine Nachrichten," *Der Stürmer* 15, no. 26 (1937): 8.

236. Eidesstattliche Versicherung von Justizrat Dr. Bayer, an das LEA, Ansbach; see also Hoffmann, "Verfolgung und Alltagsleben der Landjuden," 377.

237. "NSDAP-Kreisleitung Eichstätt, Monatsbericht 1935" (NSDAP Eichstätt county leadership, monthly report 1935), in StAN, Rep. 503, NS- Mischbestand, Kreisleitung Eichstätt, no. 7.

238. Gesetz über die Änderung der Gewerbeordnung für das Deutsche Reich (Law amending the Commercial Code for the German Reich), RGBl. I, 1938, no. 107, 823–824.

239. In January 1938, the Erfurt District Office and the Nuremberg and Schweinfurt county farmers' associations discussed one such case concerning the issuance of a trading permit for Jewish cattle trader Josef Uhlfelder fron Erlangen; see StAN, Reichsnährstand, Kreisbauernschaft Nürnberg, Rep. 267 IV, no. 172. After the Bavarian Livestock Farming Association (Viehwirtschaftsverband Bayern) had to uphold a complaint from Jewish traders, the Ansbach District Office issued them a trading permit; see Aktennotiz Nr. 2401, Betreff: Jüdische Viehhändler (File memorandum no. 2401, re: Jewish cattle traders), n.d. [presumably beginning of 1938], in StAN, LRA Ansbach, Abg. 1961, no. 4196.

240. Viehwirtschaftsverband Bayern an die Landesbauernschaft Bayern (Bavarian Livestock Farming Association to Bavarian State Farmers' Association), February 26, 1938, in BayHStA, ML 3350.

241. Der Oberbürgermeister der Stadt der Reichsparteitage Nürnberg an das BA Ansbach, Nürnberg (Mayor of Nuremberg, City of the Reich Party Congresses, to the Ansbach District Office, Nuremberg), March 29, 1938, in StAN, LRA Ansbach, Abg. 1961, no. 4196.

242. NSDAP Gauleitung Franken an das BA Lauf, Nürnberg (NSDAP Gau leadership Franconia to Lauf District Office, Nuremberg), February 12, 1938, in StAN, BA Lauf, Abg. 1959, no. 404.

243. "Monatsbericht der Kreisbauernschaft Weißenburg/Bay., Januar 1938" (Monthly report of Weißenburg/Bayern County Farmers' Association, January 1938), in StAN, Rep. 503, NS-Mischbestand, Kreisleitung Eichstätt, no. 7.

244. See also Lowenstein, "The Struggle for Survival," 122.

245. Janetzko, Die "Arisierung" mittelständischer jüdischer Unternehmen, 347.

246. See also Janetzko, Die "Arisierung" mittelständischer jüdischer Unternehmen, 127–143.

247. See chapter 3.

248. Fischer, conversation with contemporary witnesses, Kurt B. and Oliver G., Mönchsroth, 2008.

249. Wiesemann, "Juden auf dem Lande," 393.

250. On the Aryanization of the Mann brothers' firm, see StAN, WBIIIa 5244; Müller, *Der letzte Sau-Müller*; Auszug aus der Anmeldung zum Rückerstattungsverfahren für Max Gutmann, Baltimore, MD, USA an die WBIII (Excerpt from the application for restitution procedure for Max Gutmann, Baltimore, MD, USA, to the WBIII [Wiedergutmachungsbehörde III or Compensation Office III for Upper and Central Franconia]), December 9, 1948, in StAN, WB IIIa 4129. See also Bruno Buff, "Warum gehen wir 'auf die Bank'? Manfred Specht, Bäckermeister in Ellingen, berichtet über die Erzählungen seiner Großmutter," unpublished manuscript, Ellingen 2011, in private archive of Fischer, 1–2. Beginning sometime around 1935, non-Jewish cowherd Hans Hauptner from Nuremberg also worked as an independent cattle trader after his former employer, owing to the decline in sales resulting from persecution, could no longer employ him. Ssee RA Dr. Levor an die Regierung von Ober- und Mittelfranken, Nürnberg (Attorney Dr. Levor to the government of Upper and Central Franconia, Nuremberg), November 10, 1933 [*sic*, 1936], in StAN, Rep. 270, Regierung, K.d.I, Abg. 1978, no. 3419.

251. For the town of Gunzenhausen, Janetzko has impressively demonstrated that a high proportion of sales of Jewish properties took place without Nazi party offices getting involved, and at prices that were overwhelmingly reasonable, even though Gunzenhausen stands out for the intensity and frequency of violent antisemitic attacks; see Janetzko, *Die "Arisierung" mittelständischer jüdischer Unternehmen*, 138–139.

252. Hans Hofmann an die Kreisbauernschaft Nürnberg, Forth (Hans Hofmann to the county farmers' association in Nuremberg, Forth), January 20, 1938, in StAN, Reichsnährstand, Kreisbauernschaft Nürnberg, Rep. 267 IV, no. 173.

253. Additional cases may be found in StAN, Reichsnährstand, Kreisbauernschaft Nürnberg, Rep. 267 IV, no. 173. See also the "Ehrverfahren" des Reichsnährstands gegen den Kreisbauernführer der Kreisbauernschaft Nürnberg, Konrad Wagner (Action for slander [literally "honor proceeding"] of the Reich Food Corporation against the county farm leader for the county farmers' association in Nuremberg, Konrad Wagner), December 12, 1938, in BArch, R 16/I 2307.

254. Fischer, conversation with contemporary witnesses, Kurt B. und Oliver G., Mönchsroth, 2008; see also Helmut Gabeli, "'Die Männer der Gemeinde – fast alle Viehhändler': Jüdische Viehhändler im Raum Haigerloch," in *Jüdische Viehhändler zwischen Schwarzwald und Schwäbischer Alb*, ed. Kaufmann and Kohlmann, 87.

255. Kaufvertrag zwischen Falk Stern, Fanny Stern und Wilhelm Engelhardt, Haigerloch (Sales contract between Falk Stern, Fanny Stern, and

Wilhelm Engelhardt, Haigerloch), April 25, 1938, in StAN, BLVW, Ast. Nbg. no. 218; see also Wiedergutmachungsakte Hannchen Stern, Betty Bernheim, Paula Kissinger gegen Wilhelm Engelhardt (Restitution file Hannchen Stern, Betty Bernheim, Paula Kissinger versus Wilhelm Engelhardt), in StAN, WB III 3506.

256. Hermann Fleischmann an die Wiedergutmachungskammer beim Landgericht Nürnberg-Fürth, Nürnberg. A similar forced sale is confirmed by Karl Frey before the Restitution Chamber at the Nuremberg-Fürth regional court on January 27, 1954, in StAN, WB III 3874, vol. I.

257. How difficult it was for Jewish homeowners after 1933 to hire non-Jewish mechanics for maintenance work at their houses is confirmed by Johann Horn from Altenmuhr before the Restitution Chamber at the Nuremberg-Fürth regional court on January 27, 1954 in StAN, WB III 3874, vol. I.

258. Drecoll, *Der Fiskus als Verfolger*, 43.

259. Ophir and Wiesemann, *Die jüdischen Gemeinden in Bayern*, 211.

260. Ophir and Wiesemann, *Die jüdischen Gemeinden in Bayern*, 172, 195.

261. Ophir and Wiesemann, *Die jüdischen Gemeinden in Bayern*, 195. Similar atrocities also took place in Altenmuhr; see Ophir and Wiesemann, *Die jüdischen Gemeinden in Bayern*, 156.

262. Ophir and Wiesemann, *Die jüdischen Gemeinden in Bayern*, 242. Incidents like this are also reported for the town of Bechhofen; see Wildt, "Violence against Jews in Germany," 195.

263. Ophir and Wiesemann, *Die jüdischen Gemeinden in Bayern*, 221. There are reports of similar incidents from Windsbach; see Ophir and Wiesemann, *Die jüdischen Gemeinden in Bayern*, 241.

264. Zeugenaussage von Lisette Decker (Testimony by Lisette Decker), July 3, 1951, in StAN, WBIIIa 5244.

265. Zeugenaussage von Babette Baumann (Testimony by Babette Baumann), July 3, 1951, in StAN, WBIIIa 5244.

266. RA Dr. Bayer an das Zentralmeldeamt für Rückerstattung, Betreff: Antrag von Josef und Theodor Mann, Ansbach (Attorney Dr. Bayer to the Central Registration Office for Restitution, re: application from Josef and Theodor Mann), September 1, 1948, in StAN, WBIIIa 5244; Bundesarchiv Koblenz, ed., *Gedenkbuch Opfer der Verfolgung der Juden unter der nationalsozialistischen Gewaltherrschaft in Deutschland 1933–1945* (Koblenz: Bundesarchiv, 2006), 2237, 2239.

267. Ophir and Wiesemann, *Die jüdischen Gemeinden in Bayern*, 159.

268. Ophir and Wiesemann, *Die jüdischen Gemeinden in Bayern*, 159.

269. Schreiben von Martha Wassermann an das LEA, New York, NY (Letter from Martha Wassermann to the Bavarian State Compensation Office,

New York, NY), December 15, 1956, in BayHStA, BEG 24293, K-387; email information from the Archiv der Gedenkstätte Dachau, August 10, 2010.

270. See also Wildt, "Violence against Jews in Germany," 196.

271. Hoffmann, "Verfolgung und Alltagsleben der Landjuden," 389.

272. Ophir and Wiesemann, *Die jüdischen Gemeinden in Bayern*, 211.

273. Benz, "'Rasch und ohne besondere Reibungen zum Abschluß gebracht': Der Novemberpogrom 1938," in *"Es brennt!": Antijüdischer Terror im November 1938*, ed. Andreas Nachama et al. (Berlin: Stiftung Topographie des Terrors, 2008), 13.

274. Wildt, "Violence against Jews in Germany," 198.

275. Arnd Müller, *Geschichte der Juden in Nürnberg, 1146–1945* (Nuremberg: Stadtbibliothek Nürnberg, 1968), 243; Eckhart Dietzfelbinger, "Antisemitismus im 20. Jahrhundert," in *Antijudaismus und Antisemitismus in Franken*, vol. 3, ed. Andrea M. Kluxen and Julia Hecht, 141–155 (Ansbach: Bezirk Mittelfranken, 2008), 151.

276. Ophir and Wiesemann, *Die jüdischen Gemeinden in Bayern*, 196–197.

277. Nachama et al., *"Es brennt!,"* 42.

278. Zeugenaussage von Babette Oberndorfer vor der Staatsanwaltschaft Ansbach (Testimony from Babette Oberndorfer before the Ansbach state prosecuting attorney), n.d.; Zeugenaussage von Karl Schreitmüller vor der Staatsanwaltschaft Ansbach, Markt Berolzheim (Testimony by Karl Schreitmüller before the Ansbach state prosecuting attorney, Markt Berolzheim), September 6, 1946; Zeugenaussagen von Siegfried und Sofie Schönwalter, New York (Testimony by Siegfried and Sofie Schönwalter, New York), January 31, 1949; all statements in StAN, Staatsanwaltschaft Ansbach, no. 835.

279. Protokoll der Öffentlichen Sitzung der Sprk. Gunzenhausen-Land (Minutes of the Public Session for the Gunzenhausen-Land denazification court), September 13, 1948, in StAN, Sprk. Gun-Land, K-70; Rosa Bermann an das Büro der Militärregierung für Bayern, Buenos Aires (Rosa Bermann to the office of the military government for Bavaria, Buenos Aires), December 20, 1948, in StAN, Staatsanwaltschaft Ansbach, no. 835.

280. Zeugenaussage von Johannes Knoll vor der Sprk. Gunzenhausen-Land (Testimony from Johannes Knoll before the Gunzenhausen-Land denazification court), September 13, 1948, in StAN, Sprk. Gun-Land, K-70.

281. Zeugenaussage von Karl Loy vor der Staatsanwaltschaft Ansbach, Markt Berolzheim (Testimony by Karl Loy before the Ansbach state prosecuting attorney, Markt Berolzheim), September 5, 1946, in StAN, Staatsanwaltschaft Ansbach, no. 835; Spruch der Sprk. Gunzenhausen-Land für

den Angeklagten Johannes Knoll (Verdict of the Gunzenhausen-Land denazification court in the case of the accused Johannes Knoll), September 22, 1948, in StAN, Sprk. Gun-Land, K-70; Zeugenaussage von Friedrich Bickel vor der Sprk. Gunzenhausen-Land (Testimony by Friedrich Bickel before the Gunzenhauen-Land denazification court), September 13–16, 1948, in StAN, Sprk. Gun-Land, R-37.

282. Zeugenaussage von Karl Loy vor der Staatsanwaltschaft Ansbach, Markt Berolzheim.

283. Zeugenaussage von Karl Schreitmüller vor der Staatsanwaltschaft Ansbach, Markt Berolzheim; Zeugenaussage von Fritz Liebhardt vor der Staatsanwaltschaft Ansbach, Markt Berolzheim (Testimony by Fritz Liebhardt before the Ansbach state prosecuting attorney, Markt Berolzheim), September 7, 1946; both statements in StAN, Staatsanwaltschaft Ansbach, no. 835. See also Ophir and Wiesemann, *Die jüdischen Gemeinden in Bayern*, 197. On the participation of children in the November pogrom, see Fischer, "'Der hat irgendwie an Christen net den Hals abdreht': Erinnerungen an jüdische Viehhändler," *Alt-Gunzenhausen* 63 (2008): 239.

284. Ophir and Wiesemann, *Die jüdischen Gemeinden in Bayern*, 197.

285. Zeugenaussage von Fritz Liebhardt vor der Staatsanwaltschaft Ansbach, Markt Berolzheim.

286. Zeugenaussage von Karl Loy vor der Staatsanwaltschaft Ansbach, Markt Berolzheim; Bürgermeister von Markt Berolzheim an RA Felix Friedmann, Nürnberg (Mayor of Markt Berolzheim to attorney Felix Friedman, Nuremberg), July 17, 1958, in StAN, WB III N 3449.

287. Zeugenaussage von Karl Loy vor der Staatsanwaltschaft Ansbach, Markt Berolzheim. See also Fischer, "'Der hat irgendwie an Christen net den Hals abdreht,'" 241–242.

288. Zeugenaussage von Karl Loy vor der Staatsanwaltschaft Ansbach, Markt Berolzheim; Zeugenaussage von Fritz Ernst vor der Sprk. Gunzenhausen-Land (Testimony by Fritz Ernst before the Gunzenhausen-Land denazification court), September 13, 1948, in StAN, Sprk- Gun-Land, E-22; RA Dr. Josef Kern an das LEA, München (Attorney Dr. Josef Kern to the Bavarian State Compensation Office, Munich), October 29, 1956, in BayHStA, EG 093012, A-82.

289. Zeugenaussage von Babette Oberndorfer vor der Staatsanwaltschaft Ansbach; Zeugenaussage von Karl Schreitmüller vor der Staatsanwaltschaft Ansbach, Markt Berolzheim; both statements in StAN, Staatsanwaltschaft Ansbach, no. 835.

290. Zeugenaussage von Karl Schreitmüller vor der Staatsanwaltschaft Ansbach, Markt Berolzheim; Zeugenaussagen von Siegfried und Sofie

Schönwalter, New York; both statements in StAN, Staatsanwaltschaft Ansbach, no. 835.

291. Zeugenaussage von Karl Schreitmüller vor der Staatsanwaltschaft Ansbach, Markt Berolzheim; Zeugenaussage von Fritz Liebhardt vor der Staatsanwaltschaft Ansbach, Markt Berolzheim; Zeugenaussage von Sofie Schönwalter, New York (Testimony by Sofie Schönwalter, New York), January 31, 1949; all statements in StAN, Staatsanwaltschaft Ansbach, no. 835.

292. Zeugenaussage von Babette Oberndorfer vor der Staatsanwaltschaft Ansbach; Zeugenaussage von Karl Loy vor der Staatsanwaltschaft Ansbach, Markt Berolzheim; Zeugenaussage von Karl Schreitmüller vor der Staatsanwaltschaft Ansbach, Markt Berolzheim; all statements in StAN, Staatsanwaltschaft Ansbach, no. 835.

293. Zeugenaussage von Friedrich Kirsch vor der Staatsanwaltschaft Ansbach, Markt Berolzheim (Testimony by Friedrich Kirsch before the Ansbach state prosecuting attorney, Markt Berolzheim), September 6, 1946, in StAN, Staatsanwaltschaft Ansbach, no. 835.

294. StAN, Akten aus dem BLVW des Ehepaars Emanuel und Berta Engel mit den Nummern 277, 276, 274, 273, 272, 271, 266, 260, 259, 258, 683 und 703 (StAN, files from the Bavarian State Office for Asset Management and Restitution for the couple Emanuel and Berta Engel with numbers 277, 276, 274, 273, 272, 271, 266, 260, 259, 258, 683, and 703).

295. Vernehmung des Zeugen Ludwig Bauer von der Landpolizei Ober- und Mittelfranken, Krim.-Aussenstelle Ansbach, Markt Berolzheim (Interrogation of witness Ludwig Bauer before the state police for Upper and Central Franconia, Ansbach criminal branch, Markt Berolzheim), May 9, 1947, in StAN, Sprk. Gun-Land, B-23, 5.

296. Fischer, conversation with contemporary witness Leonore E., Burghaslach, 2008.

297. Fischer, conversation with contemporary witness Leonore E., Burghaslach, 2008.

298. Ophir and Wiesemann, *Die jüdischen Gemeinden in Bayern*, 190, 194.

299. Ophir and Wiesemann, *Die jüdischen Gemeinden in Bayern*, 194.

300. Kurt Pätzold, "Novemberpogrom," in *Enzyklopädie des Nationalsozialismus*, ed. Benz et al., 743.

301. Pätzold, "Novemberpogrom."

302. Benz, "'Rasch und ohne besondere Reibungen zum Abschluß gebracht,'" 15.

303. Der Stadtrat von Pappenheim an das BA Weißenburg/Bay. (Pappenheim Municipal Council to Weißenburg/Bayern District Office), September 22, 1936, in StAN, Juden (Sammelakt, allgemein), LRA Wbg., Abg. 1996, Titel IV, no. 218.

304. The total emigration quotient for Central Franconia—including the cities of Nuremberg and Fürth—was 65 percent; see Wiesemann, "Einleitung," 24.

305. Eidesstattliche Versicherung von Babette Baumann an das LEA (Affirmation in lieu of oath from Babette Baumann to the Bavarian State Compensation Office), September 18, 1956; Dinah G. Delpeint an das LEA, Paris (Dinah G. Delpeint to the Bavarian State Compensation Office, Paris), September 20, 1965; both testimony statements in BayHStA, EG 46576, K-237.

306. Fischer, conversation with contemporary witness Senta Bechhöfer, New York, NY, 2008.

307. Freie Vereinigung für die Interessen des orthodoxen Judentums an Max Gutmann, Frankfurt am Main (Free Association for the Interests of Orthodox Jewry to Max Gutmann, Frankfurt am Main), January 30, 193[6], in Stadtarchiv Ellingen, no call number.

308. Eidesstattliche Erklärung Frieda Eckmann an das LEA München (Affidavit by Frieda Eckmann to the Bavarian State Compensation Office, Munich), n.p., n.d., in BayHStA, BEG, K-Akt, no. 86 BEG 60441, 4.

309. Ärztliches Attest Dr. A. Grotto an das LEA München, Petach-Tikwah, 17. August 1962 (Medical report by Dr. A. Grotto to the Bavarian State Compensation Office in Munich, Petah Tikva, August 17, 1962), in BayHSTA, BEG, K-Akt, no. 86 BEG 60441, 9.

310. Ärztliches Attest Dr. A. Grotto an das LEA München, Petach-Tikwah, 17. August 1962.

311. Dr. med. W. Maier, Dr. med. E. Hoffmann, Ärztlicher Dienst (Medical Service), Bayerisches Landesentschädigungsamt, München, February 28, 1963, in BayHSTA, BEG, K-Akt, no. 86 BEG 60441, 20. The doctors use an abbreviation *MdE*—presumably meaning *Minderung der Erwerbsfähigkeit*—which is translated here as "reduction in earning capacity."

312. From the Antrag auf Entschädigung für Schaden im wirtschaftlichen und gewerblichen Fortkommen von Salomon Walz aus Gunzenhausen.

313. Adolf Fleischmann to Dr. H. Wolf and Dr. Walter Peters, in BayHSTA, Entschädigungsakte Adolf Fleischmann, LEA München K-Akt, BEG 24946, 33.

314. Eidesstattliche Erklärung des Julius Eckmann (Affidavit by Julius Eckmann), Tel Aviv, March 23, 1959, in BayHSTA, Entschädigungsakte Eckmann, Julius, EB 55184; K-87, 8.

315. Schreiben der Rosa Schmalgrund an Herrn Rödelsperger, Steuerberater (Letter of Rosa Schmalgrund to Herr Rödelsperger, tax accountant), Story, Wyoming, August 21, 1950, in BayHSTA,

Landesentschädigungsamt München. Entschädigungsakte Schmalgrund, Jakob, Geb. 19.11.1879 (Compensation files Schmalgrund, Jakob, born November 19, 1879); Schmalgrund, Rosa, Geb. 23.10.1902 (Schmalgrund, Rosa, born October 23, 1902], EG 99154; K-1211, 10.

316. Schreiben der Rosa Schmalgrund an Herrn Rödelsperger, Steuerberater (Letter of Rosa Schmalgrund to Herr Rödelsperger, tax accountant), Story, Wyoming, August 21, 1950, in BayHSTA, Landesentschädigungsamt München. Entschädigungsakte Schmalgrund, Jakob, Geb. 19.11.1879 (Compensation files Schmalgrund, Jakob, born November 19, 1879); Schmalgrund, Rosa, Geb. 23.10.1902 (Schmalgrund, Rosa, born October 23, 1902], EG 99154; K-1211, 10.

317. Eidesstattliche Versicherung der Jenny Bechhöfer an das LEA (Affidavit in lieu of oath by Jenny Bechhöfer to the Bavarian State Compensation Office), New York, January 4, 1956, in BayHSTA; Entschädigungsakte Hermann Bechhöfer, geb. 15.08.1882 (Compensation files Hermann Bechhöfer, born August 15, 1882), September 14, 1954, BEG 12034; K-1784, 9.

318. Ibid.

319. Fischer, conversation with contemporary witness Senta Bechhöfer, New York, NY, 2008.

320. Bruce Mazlish, *Kissinger: The European Mind in American Policy* (New York: Basic Books, 1976), 28.

321. Fischer, conversation with contemporary witness Henry Frankel, Edison, NJ, 2008; Gert Niers, "Neuanfang auf dem Lande: Die Hühnerzüchter von New Jersey," in *Das Exil der kleinen Leute: Alltagserfahrung deutscher Juden in der Emigration*, ed. Benz (Munich: Beck, 1991), 39–46.

322. Fischer, conversation with Abe Gutman, Baltimore, MD, 2011.

323. Margie Pensak, "Mishpacha Magazine: A Breed Apart," photos by Esky Cook, *Baltimore Jewish Life*, May 11, 2016, accessed May 10, 2022, https://baltimorejewishlife.com/news/news-detail.php?SECTION_ID=1&ARTICLE_ID=73648.

324. Pensak, "Mishpacha Magazine." Abe Gutman also refers to this incident in his conversation with the author, Fischer, Baltimore, MD, 2011.

325. Pensak, "Mishpacha Magazine."

326. Pensak, "Mishpacha Magazine."

327. Pensak, "Mishpacha Magazine."

328. Fischer, conversation with Abe Gutman, Baltimore, MD, 2011.

329. Daphna Berman, "Inheritance," *Tablet*, June 7, 2011, accessed May 10, 2022, https://www.tabletmag.com/sections/community/articles/inheritance-2.

330. Fischer, conversation with William (Bill) Berman, August 19, 2009, Ellingen.

331. Fischer, conversation with Abe Gutman, Baltimore, MD, 2011.

332. Rhonda F. Levine, *Class, Networks, and Identity: Replanting Jewish Lives from Nazi Germany to Rural New York* (Lanham, MD: Rowman & Littlefield, 2001).

333. Eidesstattliche Erklärung des David Levite an das LEA, Haifa (Testimony of David Levite to the Bavarian State Compensation Office, Haifa), June 27, 1955, in BayHStA, BEG 26698–26699, A-183.

334. See Heinz Högerle, ed., *Ort der Zuflucht und Verheißung: Shavei Zion 1938–2008* (Stuttgart: Theiss, 2008).

335. Peter Pulzer, "What Shall I Put in my Luggage? Reflecting Cultural Migration from Central Europe," in *Disseminating German Tradition: The Thyssen Lectures*, ed. Dan Diner and Moshe Zimmermann (Leipzig: Leipziger Universitätsverlag 2009), 81.

Conclusion

1. See, for example, Stefanie Schüler-Springorum, *Die jüdische Minderheit in Königsberg, Preußen: 1871–1945* (Göttingen: Vandenhoeck und Ruprecht, 1996); Anthony Kauders, *German Politics and the Jews: Düsseldorf and Nuremberg 1910–1933* (Oxford: Clarendon, 1996); Till van Rahden, *Jews and Other Germans: Civil Society, Religious Diversity, and Urban Politics in Breslau, 1860–1925* (Madison: University of Wisconsin Press, 2008); Nicola Wenge, *Integration und Ausgrenzung in der städtischen Gesellschaft: Eine jüdisch-nichtjüdische Beziehungsgeschichte Kölns 1918–1933* (Mainz: von Zabern, 2005).

2. Following Wolfram Pyta, this study deliberately avoids conceiving of the village community as the transfigured concept with *völkisch* and agrarian romantic connotations. Instead, it is understood as an analytical term demonstrating the "fissures and ruptures in the ways villagers work and live together" and facilitating insights into intravillage forms of social domination; see Pyta, *Dorfgemeinschaft und Parteipolitik 1918–1933: Die Verschränkung von Milieu und Parteien in den protestantischen Landgebieten Deutschlands in der Weimarer Republik* (Düsseldorf: Droste, 1996), 39–40.

3. See, for example, Monika Richarz, "Die soziale Stellung der jüdischen Händler auf dem Lande am Beispiel Südwestdeutschlands," in *Jüdische Unternehmer in Deutschland im 19. und 20. Jahrhundert*, ed. Werner Eugen Mosse, 271–283 (Stuttgart: Steiner, 1992); Utz Jeggle, *Judendörfer in Württemberg* (Tübingen: Tübinger Vereinigung für Volkskunde, 1999).

4. Van Rahden, *Juden und andere Breslauer: Die Beziehungen zwischen Juden, Protestanten und Katholiken in einer deutschen Großstadt von 1860 bis 1925* (Göttingen: Vandenhoeck & Ruprecht, 2000), 133–140.

5. One exception is the study by Ulrich Baumann; see Baumann, *Zerstörte Nachbarschaften: Christen und Juden in badischen Landgemeinden 1862–1940* (Hamburg: Dölling und Galitz, 2000).

6. See, for example, Pyta, *Dorfgemeinschaft und Parteipolitik*; Manfred Kittel, *Provinz zwischen Reich und Republik: Politischen Mentalitäten in Deutschland und Frankreich, 1918–1933/36* (Munich: Oldenbourg, 2000).

7. See Stefanie Fischer, "Ein Beispiel für Landjuden? Jüdische Viehhändler in Mittelfranken, 1919–1939," *Aschkenas: Zeitschrift für Geschichte und Kultur der Juden* 21, no. 1–2 (2013): 105–142.

8. On the softening of the rural Jewish population's strictly Orthodox lifestyle around the time of the Weimar Republic, see Jacob Borut, "'Bin ich doch ein Israelit, ehre ich auch den Bischof mit': Village and Small-Town Jews within the Social Spheres of Western German Communities during the Weimar Period," in *Jüdisches Leben in der Weimarer Republik*, ed. Wolfgang Benz et al., 117–133 (Tübingen: Mohr Siebeck, 1998).

9. The Jewish egg trade, which was mainly run by East European Jews, is not included here, since it was hardly entrenched in Germany's southwestern regions and was thus linked to other structural conditions than, for example, the trade in hops, cattle, or horses was. On Jewish egg traders in Berlin, see Karolin Steinke, *Simon Adler: Eierhändler in Berlin* (Berlin: Hentrich & Hentrich, 2011). How profitable a comparative European perspective can be for research on economic and political contexts is something to which William W. Hagen, among others, has drawn attention. See Hagen, "Before the 'Final Solution': Toward a Comparative Analysis of Political Anti-Semitism in Interwar Germany and Poland," *The Journal of Modern History* 68, no. 2 (1996): 356.

10. See Volker Rolf Berghahn, "Elitenforschung und Unternehmensgeschichte—Rückblick und Ausblick," in *Die deutsche Wirtschaftselite im 20. Jahrhundert: Kontinuität und Mentalität*, ed. Berghahn et al., 11–31 (Essen: Klartext, 2003); Martin Münzel, *Die jüdischen Mitglieder der deutschen Wirtschaftselite 1927–1955: Verdrängung—Emigration—Rückkehr* (Paderborn: Schöningh, 2006).

11. See Avraham Barkai, "Die Juden als sozio-ökonomische Minderheitsgruppe in der Weimarer Republik," in *Juden in der Weimarer Republik: Skizzen und Porträts*, ed. Walter Grab and Julius H. Schoeps, 330–346 (Stuttgart: Burg, 1986), 334; van Rahden, "Jews and the Ambivalences of Civil Society in Germany, 1800–1933: Assessment and Reassessment," *The Journal of Modern History* 77, no. 4 (2005): 1026; Derek J. Penslar, *Shylock's Children: Economics and Jewish Identity in Modern Europe* (Berkeley: University of California Press, 2001), 4.

12. Owing to the large-scale agrarian structure characteristic of the East
    Elbian regions, those large estates are not included here. Here, too, the
    Jewish population had a pattern of settlement and business activity that
    deviated from the Jewish minority in southwestern Germany.

13. See Robert Uri Kaufmann, *Jüdische und christliche Viehhändler in der Sch-
    weiz 1780–1930* (Zurich: Chronos, 1988); Werner Teuber, *Jüdische Viehhän-
    dler in Ostfriesland und im nördlichen Emsland 1871–1942: Eine vergleichende
    Studie zu einer jüdischen Berufsgruppe in zwei wirtschaftlich und konfessionell
    unterschiedlichen Regionen* (Cloppenburg: Runge, 1995); Paula Hyman,
    *The Emancipation of the Jews of Alsace: Acculturation and Tradition in the
    Nineteenth Century* (New Haven: Yale University Press, 1991).

14. Ernst Fraenkel, *The Dual State: A Contribution to the Theory of Dictatorship*
    (Oxford: Oxford University Press, 2017); see also chapter 4.

15. Adelheid von Saldern, *Mittelstand im "Dritten Reich": Handwerker – Einzel-
    händler – Bauern* (Frankfurt am Main: Campus, 1985), 206.

16. See chapter 4.

17. This is something Kauders has explained persuasively; see Kauders, *Ger-
    man Politics and the Jews*, 186ff. On this discussion, see also Helmut Baier,
    "Die Anfälligkeit des fränkischen Protestantismus gegenüber dem Nation-
    alsozialismus," in *Der Nationalsozialismus in Franken: Ein Land unter der
    Last seiner Geschichte*, ed. Evangelische Akademie Tutzing, 21–29 (Tutzing:
    Evangelische Akademie, 1979).

18. See also Falk Wiesemann, "Juden auf dem Lande: Die wirtschaftliche
    Ausgrenzung der jüdischen Viehhändler in Bayern," in *Die Reihen fast
    geschlossen*, ed. Jürgen Reulecke and Detlev Peukert, 381–396 (Wuppertal:
    Hammer, 1981).

19. Fischer, conversation with Abe Gutman, Baltimore, MD, March 16, 2011.

NOTE ON PRIMARY SOURCES CITED IN NOTES

Certain terms describing the kinds of materials cited in notes referring to archival documents, letters, interviews, and other primary sources have been translated for the benefit of English-speaking readers.

Frequently, these sources are also listed as untranslated titles, with quotation marks around the original German.

In some cases, the same source treated as a title in German is simultaneously described in English with square brackets surrounding the descriptive translation.

In untranslated German titles, the original German method of dating—DAY, MONTH, YEAR by number (e.g., 15.03.1932)—is retained. The descriptive English translations typically specify the month by name (e.g., March 15, 1932).

Researchers who wish to consult the primary sources cited are advised to find them as cited in the original German edition of this book:

Stefanie Fischer

Ökonomisches Vertrauen und antisemitische Gewalt:

Jüdische Viehhändler in Mittelfranken 1919–1939

(Göttingen: Wallstein-Verlag, 2014).

A searchable online file of the original German book has been made available by the Institut für die Geschichte der deutschen Juden in Hamburg:

https://www.igdj-hh.de/upload/fischer_vertrauen.pdf (Accessed July 2023)

BIBLIOGRAPHY

A. Unpublished Sources

Archives

Bayerisches Hauptstaatsarchiv München (BayHStA)
    Bayrisches Landesentschädigungsamt[1]
    Bundesarchiv Berlin-Lichterfelde (BArch)
    Generaldirektion der Staatl. Archive Bayerns 2677 MJu Staatsministerium für
        Justiz
    ML Staatsministerium des Innern und Staatsministerium für Landwirtschaft
    MWi Staatsministerium für Wirtschaft Sammlung Varia 378
    NS 25 Hauptamt für Kommunalpolitik
    R 16 und R 16/I Reichsnährstand
    R 17 Hauptvereinigung der Ernährungswirtschaft
    R 1501–1505 Reichsministerium des Innern
    R 3601 Reichsministerium für Ernährung und Landwirtschaft
    R 3101 Reichswirtschaftsministerium
Jüdisches Museum Fürth (Bibliothek und Archiv [Library and Archive])
    Gemeindeblatt der israelischen Kultusgemeinde
    Unveröffentlichte Literatur zur Geschichte der Juden in Franken (Unpub-
        lished literature on the history of the Jews in Franconia)
Leo Baeck Archive Berlin and New York
    Selbstzeugnisse (Personal testimonials)

---

1 The inventory of files from the Landesentschädigungsamt (LEA) was examined before it was transferred to the Bayrisches Hauptstaatsarchiv, so the call numbers (*Signaturen*) are the ones used by the LEA.

Private family archives of Lisa Aigen (Tiberias, Israel), Robert Auernhammer (Oberhochstatt), Jerry Bechhöfer (New York, NY), William Berman (Florida), Karin Eigenthaler (Scheinfeld), Stefanie Fischer (Berlin), Johann Fleischmann (Mühlhausen), Henry Frankel (NJ), Allan Hirsch (Baltimore, MD), Pfarramtsarchiv Mönchsroth, Oliver Gußmann (Rothenburg ob der Tauber), Heinrich Zoller (Wittelshofen).

Staatsarchiv Nürnberg (StAN)
    BA Lauf, Abgabe 1959 & 1969
    BA Weißenburg/Bay., Abg. 1948 und Abg. 1955, Abg. 1996
    Finanzamt Dinkelsbühl Finanzamt Gunzenhausen
    Handelsregisterakten
    Landeswucherabwehrstelle
    LRA Ansbach Rep. 212/1, Abg. 1961
    LRA Dinkelsbühl, Abg. 1976
    LRA Gun, Abg. 1961
    LRA Hersbruck, Rep. 212/10, Abg. 1976
    LRA Hilpoltstein, Abg. 1971
    LRA Rothenburg o/T, Abg. 1975
    LRA Scheinfeld, Abg. 1977
    Reichsnährstand, Kreisbauernschaft Nürnberg, Rep. 267 IV Akten der Spruchkammern sämtlicher Bezirksämter (Files from the restitution courts of all district offices)
    Rep. 270, Regierung von Ober- und Mittelfranken, Kammer des Innern
    Rep. 267 Reichsnährstand, Kreisbauernschaft
    Rep. 503, NS-Mischbestand
    Staatsanwaltschaft Ansbach
    Wiedergutmachungsbehörde III, Ober- und Mittelfranken HRA Amtsgericht Ansbach
Staatsarchiv München
    Pol. Dir. München
    Spruchkammer Weißenburg/Bay., Hauptkammer München
    Staatsarchiv für Oberbayern StAnW 3277
Stadtarchive von (Municipal archives from the following cities):
Ansbach, Ellingen, Gunzenhausen, Lauf/Pegnitz, Nürnberg, Rothenburg ob der Tauber, Scheinfeld und Weißenburg/Bay.
    Files from: Landesamt für Viehverkehr (State Office for Livestock Commerce), Viehmarktsakten (livestock market files), "Judenakten" ("Jewish files"), and others.
United States Holocaust Memorial Museum (USHMM) Photo Archives
YIVO, Institute for Jewisch Research, Center for Jewish History, New York
    Gregor Raskin Collection

Interviews with Contemporary Witnesses

(In this book, the names of contemporary witnesses were kept anonymous in all
  instances where there was no explicit authorization to reveal their full names.
  Names showing an abbreviated surname, such as Leonore E., are pseudonyms.)

Lisa Aigen: Granddaughter of a Jewish cattle and hops trader, Nuremberg,
  March 8, 2008.

Robert Auernhammer: Farmer, Oberhochstatt, April 9, 2008.

Kurt B.: Non-Jew, spent part of childhood in household of Jewish cattle traders
  where his mother worked, Mönchsroth, March 13, 2008.

Leonore E.: Daughter of a non-Jewish cattle driver, Burghaslach, March 9, 2008,
  and April 8, 2008.

Jerry Bechhöfer: Nephew of a Jewish cattle trader, New York, NY, July 28, 2008.

Senta Bechhöfer: Daughter of a Jewish cattle trader, New York, NY, August 4, 2008.

William Berman: Son of a Jewish cattle trader, Ellingen, August 19, 2009.

Yizachar Berman: Son of a Jewish cattle trader, Ellingen, August 19, 2009.

Bruno Buff: Veterinarian, Ellingen, February 22, 2011.

Gus Feissel: Son of a Jewish cattle trader, New York, NY, July 6, 2008.

Henry Frankel: Son of a Jewish cattle trader, Edison, NJ, July 12–13, 2008.

Oliver G.: Blacksmith, Mönchsroth, March 13, 2008.

Abe Gutman: Son of a Jewish cattle trader, Baltimore, MD, March 16, 2011.

Allan Hirsch: Descendent of Jewish cattle traders, Baltimore, MD, July 20, 2008.

Hilde (Tzipora) Jochsberger: Daughter of a Jewish cattle trader, Jerusalem,
  Israel, January 13–14, 2008.

Ruth Meier: Relative of Jewish cattle traders, New Rochelle, NY, July 6, 2008.

Max Meier: Son of a Jewish cattle trader, New Rochelle, NY, July 6, 2008.

Friedrich M.: Non-Jewish cattle trader, Gunzenhausen, April 10, 2008.

Nathan Reiss: Son of a Jewish cattle trader, Edison, NJ, July 13, 2008.

Felicita R.: Sister of a non-Jewish cattle trader, Burghaslach, March 9, 2008, and
  April 8, 2008.

Helmut S.: Former employee for a livestock husbandry cooperative, Mönchsroth, March 13, 2008.

Grete Weinberg (née Hamburger): Daughter of a Jewish cattle trader from
  Nördlingen, New York, NY, March 7, 2007.

Erwin Westinger: Farmer, Ellingen, April 7, 2008.

Herbert Z.: Farmer, Wittelshofen, March 13, 2008.

B. Printed Sources and Contemporary Publications

Bauer, Oswald. *Der ehrbare Kaufmann und sein Ansehen*. Dresden: Steinkopff &
  Springer, 1906.

———. *Der ehrbare Kaufmann und sein Ansehen*. Stuttgart: Union, 1919.

Bayerische Bauernkammer, ed. *Agrar-Korrespondenz*. Munich, 1929/1930.

Bayerische Industrie- und Handelskammer. *Bayerisches Landes-Adreßbuch für Industrie, Handel und Gewerbe: Bayernbuch*. Munich: Adreßbuchverlag der Industrie- und Handelskammer, 1929.

Bayerisches Statistisches Landesamt. *Gemeinde-Verzeichnis für den Freistaat Bayern: Nach der Volkszählung vom 16. Juni 1925 und dem Gebietsstand vom 1. Dezember 1925*. Munich: J. Lindauer, 1926.

Bischoff, Erich. *Wörterbuch der wichtigsten Geheim- und Berufssprachen*. Leipzig: T. Grieben, 1916.

Bussen, Franz. *Das landwirtschaftliche Genossenschaftswesen, mit bes. Berücks. d. hannoverschen Verhältnisse*. Hanover: C. V. Engelhard, 1928.

Comité des Délégations Juive, ed. *Das Schwarzbuch: Tatsachen und Dokumente: Die Lage der Juden in Deutschland 1933*. Paris: Imprimerie "Pascal," 1934.

Die geheime Geschäftssprache der Juden: Ein Hand- und Hilfsbuch für alle, welche mit Juden in Geschäftsverbindung stehen und der hebräischen Sprache (der sog. Marktsprache) unkundig sind. Neustadt/Aisch: Engelhardt, 1897.

Eberle, Lorenz. "Das Problem der Handelsspanne, Referat gehalten auf der Generalversammlung des Bundes der Viehhändler in Deutschland e.V. am 27.11.1931." Berlin 1933.

Fritsch, Theodor. *Handbuch der Judenfrage*. Leipzig: Hammer, 1932.

Grünberg, Margot. *Der deutsche Viehhandel*. Bottrop i. W.: Postberg, 1932.

Hebräisch-deutscher Dolmetscher: Sammlung der gebräuchlichsten Handelsausdrücke der israel. Handelsleute auf Viehmärkten und im Privatverkehr. Gunzenhausen: Leo Schwarzbeck's Buchhandlung, 1930.

Kayser, Franz. *Die Ausbeutung des Bauernstandes durch die Juden*. Münster i. W.: Adolph Russel, 1894.

Pohl, Hellmuth. *Ratgeber des Viehverteilers. Ein Handb. f. d. prakt. Vieh- u. Pferdehändler über d. wichtigsten Berufsfragen d. tägl. Lebens*. Berlin: Allgemeine Viehhandels-Zeitung, 1936.

Riedl, Hans. *Die genossenschaftliche Viehverwertung in Bayern*. Munich: Bayerische Viehverwertung, 1930.

Rudolph, Alfred. "Der Absatz von Vieh in der Landwirtschaft: Freier Handel, Zwangswirtschaft oder gemeinsamer Vertrieb?" PhD diss., Berlin, 1923.

Ruhwandl, Franz. "Die Aufgaben der Genossenschaften bei der Neugestaltung des landwirtschaftlichen Marktwesens: Mit besonderer Berücksichtigung der Verhältnisse in Bayern r.d. Rh." PhD diss., Munich, 1932.

Schubert, Josef. "Die Zwangsversteigerungen land- und forstwirtschaftlicher Grundstücke in Bayern im Jahre 1931." *Zeitschrift des Bayerischen Statistischen Landesamts* 64 (1932): 265–267.

Skalweit, August ed. *Die Viehhandelsverbände in der deutschen Kriegswirtschaft.*
    Berlin: Verlag der Beiträge zur Kriegswirtschaft Reimar Hobbing, 1917.
Sombart, Werner. *The Jews and Modern Capitalism.* Translated by M. Epstein.
    Kitchener: Batoche Books, 2001.
Statistisches Landesamt. *Gemeinde-Verzeichnis für das Königreich Bayern: Nach
    der Volkszählung vom 1. Dezember 1910 und dem Gebietsstand vom 1. Juni 1911.*
    Munich: J. Lindauer, 1911.
Statistisches Reichsamt. *Statistisches Jahrbuch für das deutsche Reich, 1924/25.*
    Berlin: Verlag für Politik und Wissenschaft, 1925.
"Stenographische Berichte zu den öffentlichen Sitzungen 1922/23." Vol. 7 of "Sit-
    zung des Bayerischen Landtags, 2.03.1923" (176th meeting of Bavarian Landtag,
    March 2, 1923): 1013–1019.
Verein für Socialpolitik. *Der Wucher auf dem Lande: Berichte und Gutachten.*
    Leipzig: Duncker & Humblot, 1887.
Warren, George Frederick. *Die Erzeugungs- und Absatzverhältnisse der deutschen
    Vieh- und Milchwirtschaft.* Berlin: P. Parey, 1929.
Wolff, J. *Die Geheimsprache der Handelsleute oder Dolmetscher und Wörterbuch
    zur Entzifferung aller beim Handel und Wandel vorkommenden jüdischen und
    jargonischen Wörter und Redensarten.* Leipzig: Grieben's Verlag, 1885.
Wygodzinski, Willi. *Agrarwesen und Agrarpolitik: Kapital und Arbeit in der Land-
    schaft. Verwertung der landwirtschaftlichen Produkte. Organisation des land-
    wirtschaftlichen Berufsstandes.* 3rd ed., rev. August Skalweit. Berlin: Göschen, 1928.

Newspapers

All Available Editions

Allgemeine Viehhandels-Zeitung
Der Bayerische Viehhändler
Nürnberg-Fürther Israelitisches Gemeindeblatt
Süddeutsche Viehhandels-Zeitung

Selected Annual Volumes

Der Stürmer (1933, 1934, and 1937)

Selected Newspaper Articles

"Die Landwirtschaft als Konkurrent des Viehhandels." In *Allgemeine Viehhandels-
    Zeitung. Wochenschrift für Viehverkehr, Viehverwertung, Viehhaltung; offizielles
    Organ des Deutschen Viehhandels-Bundes und aller Viehhandels-Verbände im
    Bundesgebiet.* Edited by Bund der Viehhändler Deutschlands. Beilage (supple-
    ment) 17th. Garmisch-Partenkirchen: Viehhandels, 1925.

"Die genossenschaftliche Viehverwertung in Bayern." In *Allgemeine Viehhandels-Zeitung. Wochenschrift für Viehverkehr, Viehverwertung, Viehhaltung; offizielles Organ des Deutschen Viehhandels-Bundes und aller Viehhandels-Verbände im Bundesgebiet* 43. Edited by Bund der Viehhändler Deutschlands.

"Jüdischer Mordanschlag: Der Jude Bärmann in Ellingen bietet für die Ermordung des Kreisleiters und des Kreisbauernführers 10000 Mark!" *Der Stürmer* 16, no. 49 (1937): 1–4.

"Lokales." *Nürnberg-Fürther Israelitisches Gemeindeblatt* 7, no. 12 (1927).

"Lokales." *Nürnberg-Fürther Israelitisches Gemeindeblatt* 2 (October 1, 1930): 24.

"Was bringt uns die völlige Wiederherstellung der Gewerbefreiheit?" In *Allgemeine Viehhandels-Zeitung: Wochenschrift für Viehverkehr, Viehverwertung, Viehhaltung; offizielles Organ des Deutschen Viehhandels-Bundes und aller Viehhandels-Verbände im Bundesgebiet*. Beilage (supplement) 32. Edited by Bund der Viehhändler Deutschlands.

Bayerische Rabbinerkonferenz. "An die bayerischen Juden!" *Nürnberg-Fürther Israelitisches Gemeindeblatt* 7 (March 1, 1930): 1.

Cohn, Wilhelm. "Die Berufswahl der jüdischen Jugend." *Nürnberger-Fürther Israelitisches Gemeindeblatt* 8, no. 1 (1927): 1.

Eberle and Graminger, "Nieder mit dem Handel?," *Der Bayerische Viehhändler* 4, no. 22 (May 30, 1924).

Holz, Karl. "'Die Kipperjuden' Bauernschlächter und Frauenschänder in Leutershausen." *Der Stürmer* 8, no. 8 (1930): 1–3.

Honig. "Aufruf an die mittelfränkische Landwirtschaft." *Der Altmühl-Bote* 86, no. 77 (March 31, 1933): 1.

———. "Aufruf zum April-Boykott." Der Altmühl-Bote, __no. __ (April 1, 1933): __.

Landesverband Bayerischer Viehhändler e.V. "Im Kampf um Gerechtigkeit! Gegen die Monopolstellung der Reichsviehverwertung!" *Der Bayerische Viehhändler* 12, no. 52 (1932).

Rosenthal, Erich. "Der Viehmarkt." *Der Morgen* 12 (1934/1935): 556–559.

"Wie sich der Württ. Bauern- und Weingärtnerbund die Aufwertung alter Kaufpreis-Forderungen vorstellt!" *Württembergische Viehhandelszeitung* 1, no. 19 (1926): 1.

C. Secondary Literature

Adam, Uwe Dietrich. *Judenpolitik im Dritten Reich*. Düsseldorf: Droste, 1972.

Ahlheim, Hannah. *"Deutsche, kauft nicht bei Juden!": Antisemitismus und politischer Boykott in Deutschland 1924 bis 1935*. Göttingen: Wallstein, 2011.

Angerer, Birgit, Jan Borgmann, Sabine Fechter, and Heinrich Hacker, eds. *Pracht, Prunk, Protz*. Finsterau: Zweckverband Niederbayerische Freilichtmuseen, 2009.

Arbeitsgemeinschaft für Heimatgeschichte, ed. *Feuchtwanger Heimatgeschichte.* Feuchtwangen: Arbeitsgemeinschaft für Heimatgeschichte, 1991.

Backmann, Sibylle, and Hans-Jörg Künast. "Einführung." In *Ehrkonzepte in der frühen Neuzeit,* edited by Sibylle Backmann, Hans-Jörg Kunast, Sabine Ullmann, and Ann B. Tlusty, 13–26. Berlin: Akademie, 1998.

Backmann, Sibylle, Hans-Jörg Künast, Sabine Ullmann, and Ann B. Tlusty, eds. *Ehrkonzepte in der frühen Neuzeit: Identitäten und Abgrenzungen.* Berlin: Akademie, 1998.

Baier, Annette. "Vertrauen und seine Grenzen." In *Vertrauen,* edited by Martin Hartmann and Claus Offe, 37–84. Frankfurt: Campus, 2001.

Baier, Annette. *Moral Prejudices: Essays on Ethics.* Cambridge, MA: Harvard University Press, 1996.

———. *Reflections on How We Live.* Oxford: Oxford University Press, 2010, https://academic.oup.com/book/5041.

Baier, Helmut. "Die Anfälligkeit des fränkischen Protestantismus gegenüber dem Nationalsozialismus." In *Der Nationalsozialismus in Franken,* edited by Evangelische Akademie Tutzing, 21–29. Tutzing, Tutzinger Studien, 1979.

Bajohr, Frank. *Arianisation in Hamburg: The Economic Exclusion of Jews and the Confiscation of Their Property in Nazi Germany.* New York: Berghahn, 2002.

Bajohr, Frank, and Dieter Pohl, eds. *Der Holocaust als offenes Geheimnis: Die Deutschen, die NS-Führung und die Alliierten.* Munich: Beck, 2006.

Bajohr, Frank, and Michael Wildt, eds. *Volksgemeinschaft: Neue Forschungen zur Gesellschaft des Nationalsozialismus.* Frankfurt am Main: Fischer-Taschenbuch, 2009.

Bankier, David, ed. *Probing the Depths of German Antisemitism: German Society and the Persecution of the Jews, 1933–1941.* New York: Berghahn, 2000.

Barkai, Avraham. "Die Juden als sozio-ökonomische Minderheitsgruppe in der Weimarer Republik." In *Juden in der Weimarer Republik,* edited by Walter Grab and Julius H. Schoeps, 330–346. Stuttgart: Burg Verlag, 1986.

———. "The German Jews at the Start of Industrialisation: Structural Change and Mobility, 1835–1869." In *Revolution and Evolution,* edited by Werner Mosse, Arnold Paucker, Reinhard Rürup, and Robert Weltsch, 123–150. Tübingen: Mohr, 1981.

———. "Population Decline and Economic Stagnation." In *German-Jewish History in Modern Times: Renewal and Destruction 1918–1945,* edited by Michael A. Meyer and Michael Brenner, 30–44. New York: Columbia University Press, 1998.

———. *Vom Boykott zur "Entjudung": Der wirtschaftliche Existenzkampf der Juden im Dritten Reich, 1933–1943.* Frankfurt am Main: Fischer, 1988.

Barmeyer, Heide. *Andreas Hermes und die Organisationen der deutschen Landwirtschaft: Christliche Bauernvereine, Reichslandbund, Grüne Front, Reichsnährstand 1928–1933.* Stuttgart: G. Fischer, 1971.

Bauer, Lothar, and Ernst Schwarz, eds. *Festschrift Ernst Schwarz.* Kallmünz-Opf.: Michael Lassleben, 1961.

Bauert-Keetman, Ingrid. *Friedrich Wilhelm Raiffeisen: Ein Leben für die Zukunft.* Hanover: Steinbock, 1987.

Baumann, Ulrich. *Zerstörte Nachbarschaften: Christen und Juden in badischen Landgemeinden 1862–1940.* Hamburg: Dölling und Galitz, 2000.

Bechtold-Comforty, Beate. "Jüdische Frauen auf dem Dorf—zwischen Eigenständigkeit und Integration." *Sowi, Sozialwissenschaftliche Informationen* 18, no. 3 (1989): 157–162.

Becker, Peter E. *Wege ins Dritte Reich.* Stuttgart: G. Thieme, 1990.

Bennewitz, Susanne. "All Talk or Business as Usual? Brokerage and Schmoozing in a Swiss Urban Society in the Early Nineteenth Century." In *The Economy in Jewish History*, edited by Gideon Reuveni and Sarah Wobick-Segev, 79–93. New York: Berghahn, 2011.

Benz, Wolfgang, ed. *Das Exil der kleinen Leute: Alltagserfahrung deutscher Juden in der Emigration.* Munich: Beck, 1991.

———. *"Der ewige Jude."* Berlin: Metropol, 2010.

———, ed. *Die Juden in Deutschland 1933–1945: Leben unter nationalsozialistischer Herrschaft.* Munich: Beck, 1989.

———, ed. *Handbuch des Antisemitismus.* Vol. 3. *Begriffe, Ideologien, Theorien.* Berlin: De Gruyter Saur, 2010.

———, ed. *Handbuch des Antisemitismus.* Vol. 6. *Publikationen.* Berlin: De Gruyter Saur, 2013.

———. "'Rasch und ohne besondere Reibungen zum Abschluß gebracht': Der Novemberpogrom 1938." In *"Es brennt!": Antijüdischer Terror im November 1938*, edited by Andreas Nachama, Uwe Neumärker, and Hermann Simon, 11–17. Berlin: Stiftung Topographie des Terrors, 2008.

———. "Zum Verhältnis der NSDAP und staatlicher Verwaltung im Dritten Reich." In *Das Unrechtsregime: Internationale Forschung über den Nationalsozialismus*, edited by Ursula Büttner, 203–218. Hamburg: Christians, 1986.

Benz, Wolfgang, Arnold Paucker, and Peter Pulzer, eds. *Jüdisches Leben in der Weimarer Republik.* Tübingen: Mohr Siebeck, 1998.

Benz, Wolfgang, Hermann Graml, and Hermann Weiß, eds. *Enzyklopädie des Nationalsozialismus.* Munich: Deutscher Taschenbuch, 2007.

Beranek, Franz J. "Die fränkische Landschaft des Jiddischen." In *Festschrift Ernst Schwarz*, edited by Lothar Bauer and Ernst Schwarz, 267–303. Kallmünz-Opf.: Michael Lassleben, 1961.

Berghahn, Volker Rolf. "Elitenforschung und Unternehmensgeschichte – Rückblick und Ausblick." In *Die deutsche Wirtschaftselite im 20. Jahrhundert*, edited by Volker Rolf Berghahn, Stefan Unger, and Dieter Ziegler, 11–31. Essen: Klartext, 2003.

Berghahn, Volker Rolf, Stefan Unger, and Dieter Ziegler, eds. *Die deutsche Wirtschaftselite im 20. Jahrhundert: Kontinuität und Mentalität*. Essen: Klartext, 2003.

Bergmann, Klaus. *Agrarromantik und Großstadtfeindschaft*. Meisenheim am Glan: Hain, 1970.

Berman, Daphna. "Inheritance." *Tablet*, June 7, 2011, accessed May 10, 2022 https://www.tabletmag.com/sections/community/articles/inheritance-2.

Beutner, Gunnar. "Das Pogrom von Gunzenhausen 1934: Anfänge des NS-Terrors in Westmittelfranken." In *"Was brauchen wir einen Befehl, wenn es gegen die Juden geht?": Das Pogrom von Gunzenhausen 1934*, edited by Heike Tagsold, 7–30. Nuremberg: Antogo-Verlag, 2006.

Binnenkade, Alexandra. *Kontaktzonen: Jüdisch-christlicher Alltag in Lengnau*. Cologne: Böhlau, 2009.

Bischoff, Frank M., and Hans-Jürgen Höötmann. "Wiedergutmachung: Erschließung von Entschädigungsakten im Staatsarchiv Münster." *Der Archivar - Mitteilungsblatt für deutsches Archivwesen* 51, no. 3 (1998): 425–438.

Blaschke, Olaf. "Antikapitalismus und Antisemitismus. Die Wirtschaftsmentalität der Katholiken im Wilhelminischen Deutschland." In *Shylock? Zinsverbot und Geldverleih in jüdischer und christlicher Tradition*, edited by Johannes Heil and Bernd Wacker, 113–146. Munich: Fink, 1997.

Borut, Jacob. "'Bin ich doch ein Israelit, ehre ich auch den Bischof mit': Village and Small-Town Jews within the Social Spheres of Western German Communities during the Weimar Period." In *Jüdisches Leben in der Weimarer Republik*, edited by Wolfgang Benz, Arnold Paucker, and Peter Pulzer, 117–133. Tübingen: Mohr Siebeck, 1998.

———. "Religiöses Leben der Landjuden im westlichen Deutschland während der Weimarer Republik." In *Jüdisches Leben auf dem Lande*, edited by Reinhard Rürup and Monika Richarz, 231–248. Tübingen: Mohr Siebeck, 1997.

Bosch, Michael, ed. *Persönlichkeit und Struktur in der Geschichte*. Düsseldorf: Pädagogischer Schwann, 1977.

Bourdieu, Pierre. *Distinction: A Social Critique of the Judgement of Taste*. Translated by Richard Nice. Cambridge, MA: Harvard University Press, 1984.

Braun, Christina von. "Antisemitische Stereotype und Sexualphantasien." In *Die Macht der Bilder*, edited by Jüdisches Museum der Stadt Wien, 180–191. Vienna: Pincus-Verlag, 1995.

Braun, Helmut. "Kriegs- und Zwangswirtschaftsstellen, 1915–1924." *Historisches Lexikon Bayerns*, November 8, 2009, accessed August 5, 2020. https://www

.historisches-lexikon-bayerns.de/Lexikon/Kriegs-_und
   _Zwangswirtschaftsstellen,_1915-1924.

Brenner, Michael, and Daniela F. Eisenstein, eds. *Die Juden in Franken*. Munich:
   Oldenbourg, 2012.

Bringéus, Nils-Arvid, and Günter Wiegelmann, eds. *Wandel der Volkskultur in
   Europa: Festschrift für Günter Wiegelmann zum 60. Geburtstag*. Münster: Coppenrath, 1988.

Brockhaus Enzyklopädie in 30 Bänden. Leipzig: Brockhaus, 2006.

Broszat, Martin, and Elke Fröhlich, eds. *Bayern in der NS-Zeit*. Vol. 2. *Herrschaft
   und Gesellschaft im Konflikt*. Munich: Oldenbourg, 1979.

Broszat, Martin, Elke Fröhlich, and Falk Wiesemann, eds. *Bayern in der NS-Zeit*.
   Vol. 1. *Soziale Lage und politisches Verhalten der Bevölkerung im Spiegel vertraulicher Berichte*. Munich: Oldenbourg, 1977.

Brüdermann, Stefan, and Anikó Szabó. "Tiefenerschließung von Entschädigungsakten." *Archiv-Nachrichten Niedersachsen* 2 (1998): 35–38.

Brunner, José, and Shai Lavi, eds. *Juden und Muslime in Deutschland: Recht, Religion, Identität*. Göttingen: Wallstein, 2009.

Buchner, Siglinde. *Ellinger Hausbesitzer zwischen 1536 und 1820*. Ellingen: Stadtarchiv, 1998.

Budde, Gunilla-Friederike. "Familienvertrauen – Selbstvertrauen – Gesellschafts-
   vertrauen: Pädagogische Ideale und Praxis im 19. Jahrhundert." In *Vertrauen:
   Historische Annäherungen*, edited by Ute Frevert, 152–184. Vandenhoeck und
   Ruprecht, 2003.

Bundesarchiv Koblenz, ed. *Gedenkbuch Opfer der Verfolgung der Juden unter der
   nationalsozialistischen Gewaltherrschaft in Deutschland 1933–1945*. Koblenz:
   Bundesarchiv, 2006.

Büttner, Ursula, ed. *Das Unrechtsregime. Internationale Forschung über den Nationalsozialismus*. Hamburg: Christians, 1986.

Bytwerk, Randall L. *Julius Streicher: Nazi Editor of the Notorious Anti-Semitic
   Newspaper Der Stürmer*. New York: Cooper Square, 2001.

Cahnman, Werner Jacob. "Village and Small Town Jews in Germany: A Typological Study." *Leo Baeck Institute Year Book* 19 (1974): 107–130.

Caputo, Nina and Mitchell B. Hart. "Introduction: On the Word of a Jew, or
   Trusting Jewish History." In *On the Word of a Jew: Religion, Reliability, and
   the Dynamics of Trust*, edited by Nina Caputo and Mitchell B. Hart, 1-16 .
   Bloomington: Indiana University Press, 2019.

Chamberlin, Edward Hastings. *The Theory of Monopolistic Competition: A Re-orientation of the Theory of Value*. Cambridge, MA: Harvard University Press, 1965.

Cohen, Steven Martin, and Paula Hyman, eds. *The Jewish Family: Myths and
   Reality*. New York: Holmes and Meier, 1986.

Daxelmüller, Christoph. *Jüdische Kultur in Franken.* Würzburg: Echter, 1988.

———. "Kulturvermittlung und Gütermobilität: Anmerkung zur Bedeutung des jüdischen Handels für die ländliche und kleinstädtische Kultur." In *Wandel der Volkskultur in Europa,* vol. 1, edited by Nils-Arvid Bringéus and Günter Wiegelmann, 233–253. Münster: Coppenrath, 1988.

Deneke, Bernhard. "Fragen zur Rezeption bürgerlicher Sachkultur bei der ländlichen Bevölkerung." In *Kultureller Wandel im 19. Jahrhundert,* edited by Günter Wiegelmann and Dietmar Sauermann, 50–71. Göttingen: Vandenhoeck und Ruprecht, 1973.

Dietzfelbinger, Eckhart. "Antisemitismus im 20. Jahrhundert." In *Antijudaismus und Antisemitismus in Franken,* vol. 3, edited by Andrea M. Kluxen and Julia Hecht, 141–155. Ansbach: Bezirk Mittelfranken, 2008.

Dinges, Martin. "Ehre als Thema der historischen Anthropologie." In *Verletzte Ehre,* edited by Klaus Schreiner, 29–63. Cologne: Böhlau, 1995.

Dippold, Günter. *Eisenbahn und Kleinstadt: Auswirkungen des Knotenpunktes auf Lichtenfels im frühen 19. und 20. Jahrhundert.* Bayreuth: Regierung von Oberfranken, 2001.

Drecoll, Axel. *Der Fiskus als Verfolger: Die steuerliche Diskriminierung der Juden in Bayern, 1933–1941/42.* Munich: Oldenbourg, 2009.

Dülmen, Richard van. *Kultur und Alltag in der Frühen Neuzeit.* Vol. 2, *Dorf und Stadt, 16.–18. Jahrhundert.* Munich: Beck, 1992.

Dülmen, Richard van, and Angelika Baumann, eds. *Kultur der einfachen Leute: Bayerisches Volksleben vom 16. bis zum 19. Jahrhundert.* Munich: Beck, 1983.

Dynners, Glenn. *Men of Silk: The Hasidic Conquest of Polish Society.* Oxford: Oxford University Press, 2006.

Eberhardt, Barbara, and Frank Purrmann. "Fürth." In *Mehr als Steine,* edited by Wolfgang Kraus, Berndt Hamm, and Meier Schwarz, 266–333. Lindenberg im Allgäu: Kunstverlag Josef Fink, 2010.

Eberhardt, Barbara, and Hans-Christof Haas. "Neustadt/Aisch." In *Mehr als Steine,* edited by Wolfgang Kraus, Berndt Hamm, and Meier Schwarz, 448–465. Lindenberg im Allgäu: Kunstverlag Josef Fink, 2010.

———. "Schnaittach." In *Mehr als Steine,* edited by Wolfgang Kraus, Berndt Hamm, and Meier Schwarz, 575–596. Lindenberg im Allgäu: Kunstverlag Josef Fink, 2010.

Efing, Christian, and Corinna Leschber, eds. *Geheimsprachen in Mittel- und Südosteuropa.* Frankfurt am Main: Lang, 2009.

Eibach, Joachim, ed. *Kompass der Geschichtswissenschaft: Ein Handbuch.* Göttingen: Vandenhoeck und Ruprecht, 2006.

Eisenstadt, Shmuel N. "Multiple Modernities." *Daedalus* 129, no. 1 (2000), 1–29.

————. *Multiple Modernities.* New Brunswick, N.J.: Transaction, 2002.

Endelman, Todd M. "New Turns in Jewish Historiography?" *Jewish Quarterly Review* 103, no. 2 (2013): 589–598.

Escher, Clemens. "Wucherjude." In *Handbuch des Antisemitismus.* Vol. 3, *Begriffe, Ideologien, Theorien,* edited by Wolfgang Benz, 348–349. Berlin: de Gruyter Saur, 2010.

Evangelische Akademie Tutzing, ed. *Der Nationalsozialismus in Franken: Ein Land unter der Last seiner Geschichte.* Tutzing: Evangelische Akademie, 1979.

Falter, Jürgen W. *Hitlers Wähler.* Munich: Beck, 1991.

Fiedler, Martin. "Vertrauen ist gut, Kontrolle ist teuer: Vertrauen als Schlüsselkategorie wirtschaftlichen Handelns," *Geschichte und Gesellschaft* 27 (2001): 576–592.

Fischer, Stefanie. "Ökonomisches Vertrauen und antisemitische Gewalt. Jüdische Viehhändler in Mittelfranken, 1919–1939." Göttingen: Wallstein, 2014.

————. "Das Lexicon der jüdischen Geschäfts- und Umgangs-Sprache (Itzig Feitel Stern, 1832)." In *Handbuch des Antisemitismus.* Vol. 6, *Publikationen,* edited by Wolfgang Benz, 428–429. Berlin: De Gruyter Saur, 2013.

————. "'Der hat irgendwie an Christen net den Hals abdreht': Erinnerungen an jüdische Viehhändler." *Alt-Gunzenhausen* 63 (2008): 226–246.

————. "Ein Beispiel für Landjuden? Jüdische Viehhändler in Mittelfranken, 1919–1939." *Aschkenas: Zeitschrift für Geschichte und Kultur der Juden* 21, no. 1–2 (2013): 105–142.

Förderverein Hermann Schulze-Delitzsch, ed. *Hermann Schulze-Delitzsch: Weg – Werk – Wirkung.* Wiesbaden: Deutscher Genossenschafts, 2008.

Fraenkel, Ernst. *The Dual State: A Contribution to the Theory of Dictatorship.* Oxford: Oxford University Press: 2017.

Frank, Fritz. "Selbstzeugnis." In *Jüdisches Leben in Deutschland: Selbstzeugnisse zur Sozialgeschichte im Kaiserreich,* edited by Monika Richarz, 169–180. Stuttgart: Deutsche Verlags-Anstalt, 1979.

Frank, Julius. "Selbstzeugnis." In *Jüdisches Leben in Deutschland: Selbstzeugnisse zur Sozialgeschichte im Kaiserreich,* edited by Monika Richarz, 190–200. Stuttgart: Deutsche Verlags-Anstalt, 1979.

Freimark, Peter, Alice Jankowski, and Ina S. Lorenz, eds. *Juden in Deutschland: Emanzipation, Integration, Verfolgung und Vernichtung.* Hamburg: H. Christians, 1991.

Frevert, Ute. "Bürgerliche Familie und Geschlechterrolle: Modelle und Wirklichkeit." In *Bürgerliche Gesellschaft in Deutschland,* edited by Lutz Niethammer, 90–100. Frankfurt am Main: Fischer, 1990.

————. "Ehre—männlich/weiblich: Zu einem Identitätsbegriff des 19. Jahrhunderts." In *Tel Aviver Jahrbuch für deutsche Geschichte.* Vol. 21, *Neuere*

Frauengeschichte, edited by Institut für Deutsche Geschichte, 21–68. Gerlingen: Bleicher, 1992.

———. *"Mann und Weib, und Weib und Mann": Geschlechter-Differenzen in der Moderne.* Munich: Beck, 1995.

———. *"Soldat, Staatsbürger: Überlegungen zur historischen Konstruktion von Männlichkeit."* In *Männergeschichte – Geschlechtergeschichte*, edited by Thomas Kühne, 69–87. Frankfurt am Main: Campus, 1996.

———. *"Vertrauen—eine historische Spurensuche."* In *Vertrauen: Historische Annäherungen*, edited by Ute Frevert, 7–66.

———, ed. *Vertrauen: Historische Annäherungen.* Göttingen: Vandenhoeck und Ruprecht, 2003.

Friedländer, Saul, and Orna Kenan. *Nazi Germany and the Jews, 1933–1945.* New York: Harper, 2009.

Gabeli, Helmut. *"'Die Männer der Gemeinde—fast alle Viehhändler': Jüdische Viehhändler im Raum Haigerloch."* In *Jüdische Viehhändler zwischen Schwarzwald und Schwäbischer Alb*, edited by Robert Uri Kaufmann and Carsten Kohlmann, 70–106. Horb-Rexingen: Barbara Staudacher Verlag, 2008.

Garbe, Detlef. *Zwischen Widerstand und Martyrium: Die Zeugen Jehovas im "Dritten Reich."* Munich: Oldenbourg, 1993.

Gellately, Robert. *The Gestapo and German Society: Enforcing Racial Policy 1933–1945.* Oxford: Clarendon, 1990.

Genschel, Helmut. *Die Verdrängung der Juden aus der Wirtschaft im Dritten Reich.* Göttingen: Muster-Schmidt, 1966.

Geschichtswerkstatt Tübingen, ed. *Zerstörte Hoffnungen: Wege der Tübinger Juden.* Stuttgart: Theiss, 1995.

Giddens, Anthony. *The Consequences of Modernity.* Cambridge, UK: Polity, 1991.

Gilman, Sander L. *"The Problem with Purim: Jews and Alcohol in the Modern Period."* *Leo Baeck Institute Year Book* 50 (2005): 214–231.

Gotzmann, Andreas, Till van Rahden, and Rainer Liedtke, eds. *Juden, Bürger, Deutsche: Zur Geschichte von Vielfalt und Differenz 1800–1933.* Tübingen: Mohr, 2001.

Grab, Walter, and Julius H. Schoeps, eds. *Juden in der Weimarer Republik: Skizzen und Porträts.* Stuttgart: Burg, 1986.

Gräfe, Thomas. *Antisemitismus in Gesellschaft und Karikatur des Kaiserreichs: Glöß' politische Bilderbogen 1892–1901.* Norderstedt: Books on Demand, 2005.

Grau, Bernhard. *"Entschädigungs- und Rückerstattungsakten als neue Quelle der Zeitgeschichtsforschung am Beispiel Bayerns."* *Zeitenblicke* 3, no. 2 (2004). Accessed January 10, 2014. http://www.zeitenblicke.de/2004/02/grau/index .html.

Greif, Thomas. *Frankens braune Wallfahrt: Der Hesselberg im Dritten Reich*. Ansbach: Historischer Verein für Mittelfranken, 2007.

———. "Julius Streicher und Franken." In *BilderLast*, edited by Hans-Christian Täubrich, 32–39. Nuremberg: Dokumentationszentrum Reichsparteitagsgelände Nürnberg, 2008.

Gruner, Wolf. "Die NS-Judenverfolgung und die Kommunen. Zur wechselseitigen Dynamisierung von zentraler und lokaler Politik, 1933–1941." *Vierteljahrshefte für Zeitgeschichte* 48, no. 1 (2000): 75–126.

———. *Öffentliche Wohlfahrt und Judenverfolgung: Wechselwirkungen lokaler und zentraler Politik im NS-Staat (1933–1942)*. Munich: Oldenbourg, 2002.

Hacker, Heinrich. "Man gönnt sich ja sonst nichts: Beispiele für den oralen Luxus bei Ess-, Trink- und Rauchgewohnheiten der ländlichen Bevölkerung im nördlichen Unterfranken." In *Pracht, Prunk, Protz*, edited by Birgit Angerer, Jan Borgmann, Sabine Fechter, and Heinrich Hacker, 83–92. Finsterau: Zweckverb. Niederbayerische Freilichtmuseen, 2009.

Hagen, William W. "Before the 'Final Solution': Toward a Comparative Analysis of Political Anti-Semitism in Interwar Germany and Poland." *The Journal of Modern History* 68, no. 2 (1996): 351–381.

Hahn, Fred, and Günther Wagenlehner. *Lieber Stürmer: Leserbriefe an das NS-Kampfblatt 1924–1945*. Stuttgart: Seewald, 1978.

Hambrecht, Rainer. *Der Aufstieg der NSDAP in Mittel- und Oberfranken, 1925–1933*. Nuremberg: Stadtarchiv Nürnberg, Korn u. Berg, 1976.

———. "Die Brücke Franken." In *BilderLast*, edited by Hans-Christian Täubrich, 16–23.

Hartmann, Martin. "Einleitung." In *Vertrauen*, edited by Hartmann and Claus Offe, 7–37. Frankfurt am Main: Campus, 2001.

Hartmann, Martin, and Claus Offe, eds. *Vertrauen: Die Grundlage des sozialen Zusammenhalts*. Frankfurt am Main: Campus, 2001.

Hausen, Karin, and Heide Wunder, eds. *Frauengeschichte – Geschlechtergeschichte*. Frankfurt am Main: Campus, 1992.

Hecht, Julia, ed. *Juden in Franken 1806 bis heute*. Ansbach: Bezirk Mittelfranken 2007.

Hedwig, Andreas, ed. *"Auf eisernen Schienen, so schnell wie der Blitz": Regionale und überregionale Aspekte der Eisenbahngeschichte*. Marburg: Staatsarchiv Marburg, 2008.

Heil, Johannes, and Bernd Wacker, eds. *Shylock? Zinsverbot und Geldverleih in jüdischer und christlicher Tradition*. Munich: Fink, 1997.

Heinsohn, Kirsten, and Stefanie Schüler-Springorum, eds. *Deutsch-Jüdische Geschichte als Geschlechtergeschichte: Studien zum 19. und 20. Jahrhundert*. Göttingen: Wallstein, 2006.

Heinsohn, Kirsten, and Stefanie Schüler-Springorum. "Einleitung." In *Deutsch-Jüdische Geschichte als Geschlechtergeschichte*, edited by Kirsten Heinsohn and Stefanie Schüler-Springorum, 7–24.

Heller, Hartmut. "Juden in Franken im 19. Jahrhundert." In *Juden in Franken 1806 bis heute*, edited by Julia Hecht, 37–52.

Henning, Friedrich-Wilhelm. *Landwirtschaft und ländliche Gesellschaft, 1750–1976*. Paderborn: Schöningh, 1985.

Henschel, Gerhard. *Neidgeschrei: Antisemitismus und Sexualität*. Hamburg: Hoffmann und Campe, 2008.

Herlemann, Beatrix. *"Der Bauer klebt am Hergebrachten": Bäuerliche Verhaltensweisen unterm Nationalsozialismus auf dem Gebiet des heutigen Landes Niedersachsen*. Hanover: Hahn, 1993.

Herzig, Arno. "Die westfälischen Juden im Modernisierungsprozeß." In *Deutsche Juden und die Moderne*, edited by Shulamit Volkov, 95–118.

Hesse, Klaus, and Philipp Springer. *Vor aller Augen: Fotodokumente des nationalsozialistischen Terrors in der Provinz*. Essen: Klartext, 2002.

Hillen, Christian, ed. *"Mit Gott": Zum Verhältnis von Vertrauen und Wirtschaftsgeschichte*. Cologne: Stiftung Rheinisch-Westfälisches Wirtschaftsarchiv, 2007.

———. "'Mit Gott' – Zum Verhältnis von Vertrauen und Wirtschaftsgeschichte." In *"Mit Gott": Zum Verhältnis von Vertrauen und Wirtschaftsgeschichte*, edited by Christian Hillen, 7–17.

Hobbes, Thomas. *Leviathan*. Edited by Richard Tuck. Cambridge, UK: Cambridge University Press, 1991.

———. "Leviathan, Or, the Matter, Form, and Power of a Common Wealth, Ecclesiastical and Civil" (London: Printed for Andrew Crooke, 1651). https://www.proquest.com/books/leviathan-matter-forme-power-common-wealth/docview/2240945289/se-2.

Hoffmann, Christhard. "Verfolgung und Alltagsleben der Landjuden im nationalsozialistischen Deutschland." In *Jüdisches Leben auf dem Lande*, edited by Monika Richarz and Reinhard Rürup, 373–398. Tübingen: Mohr Siebeck, 1997.

Högerle, Heinz, ed. *Ort der Zuflucht und Verheißung: Shavei Zion 1938–2008*. Stuttgart: Theiss, 2008.

Hommen, Tanja. *Sittlichkeitsverbrechen: Sexuelle Gewalt im Kaiserreich*. Frankfurt am Main: Campus, 1999.

Hörl, Georg. "Rechtsstreitigkeiten im Viehhandel: Untersuchungen von Fällen aus den Jahren 1949–1976." PhD diss., Munich, 1981.

Hufenreuter, Gregor. "Rassenantisemitismus." In *Handbuch des Antisemitismus*. Vol. 3, *Begriffe, Ideologien, Theorien*, edited by Wolfgang Benz, 272–273, Berlin: De Gruyter Saur, 2013.

Hürlimann, Katja. *Soziale Beziehungen im Dorf: Aspekte dörflicher Soziabilität in den Landvogteien Greifensee und Kyburg um 1500.* Zürich: Chronos, 2000.

Hüttenmeister, Forwald Gil. "Die Genisot als Geschichtsquelle." In *Jüdisches Leben auf dem Lande,* edited by Monika Richarz and Reinhard Rürup, 207–218, übingen: Mohr Siebeck, 1997.

Hyman, Paula. *The Emancipation of the Jews of Alsace: Acculturation and Tradition in the Nineteenth Century.* New Haven: Yale University Press, 1991.

———. "The Modern Jewish Family: Image and Reality." In *The Jewish Family,* edited by David Charles Kraemer, 179–193, New York: Oxford University Press, 1989.

Ilien, Albert, and Utz Jeggle. "Die Dorfgemeinschaft als Not- und Terrorzusammenhang: Ein Beitrag zur Sozialgeschichte des Dorfes und zur Sozialpsychologie seiner Bewohner." In *Dorfpolitik,* edited by Hans-Georg Wehling, 38–53, Opladen: Leske, 1978.

———. *Leben auf dem Dorf: Zur Sozialgeschichte des Dorfes und zur Sozialpsychologie seiner Bewohner.* Opladen: Westdeutscher, 1978.

Institut für Deutsche Geschichte, ed. *Tel Aviver Jahrbuch für deutsche Geschichte.* Vol. 21, *Neuere Frauengeschichte.* Gerlingen: Bleicher, 1992.

Isaacson, Walter. *Kissinger: A Biography.* New York: Simon and Schuster, 1992.

Janetzko, Maren. *Die "Arisierung" mittelständischer jüdischer Unternehmen in Bayern 1933–1939: Ein interregionaler Vergleich.* Ansbach: Historischer Verein für Mittelfranken, 2012.

Jeggle, Utz. *Judendörfer in Württemberg.* Tübingen: Tübinger Vereinigung für Volkskunde, 1999.

Judd, Robin. *Contested Rituals: Circumcision, Kosher Butchering, and Jewish Political Life in Germany, 1843–1933.* Ithaca, NY: Cornell University Press, 2007.

Jüdisches Museum der Stadt Wien, ed. *Die Macht der Bilder: Antisemitische Vorurteile und Mythen.* Vienna: Pincus, 1995.

Jüdisches Museum Hohenems, ed. *Antijüdischer Nippes und populäre "Judenbilder": Die Sammlung Finkelstein.* Essen: Klartext, 2005.

Jung, Wilfried. "Die Juden in Altenmuhr." *Alt-Gunzenhausen* 44 (1988): 133–212.

Kaplan, Marion A. *Between Dignity and Despair: Jewish Life in Nazi Germany.* New York: Oxford University Press, 1998.

———. "For Love or Money: The Marriage Strategies of Jews in Imperial Germany." *Leo Baeck Institute Year Book* 28 (1983): S. 263–300.

———, ed. *Geschichte des jüdischen Alltags in Deutschland: Vom 17. Jahrhundert bis 1945.* Munich: Beck, 2003.

———, ed. *Jewish Daily Life in Germany, 1618–1945.* Oxford: Oxford University Press, 2005.

———. "Konsolidierung eines bürgerlichen Lebens im kaiserlichen Deutschland, 1871–1918." In *Geschichte des jüdischen Alltags in Deutschland,* edited by Marion A. Kaplan, 226–346. Munich: Beck, 2003.

———. *The Making of the Jewish Middle Class: Women, Family, and Identity in Imperial Germany.* New York: Oxford University Press, 1991.

———. "Tradition and Transition: The Acculturation, Assimilation and Integration of Jews in Imperial Germany." *Leo Baeck Institute Year Book* 27 (1982): 3–35.

Karp, Jonathan. "An 'Economic Turn' in Jewish Studies?" AJS Perspectives, Fall 2009: 10.

Kauders, Anthony. *German Politics and the Jews: Düsseldorf and Nuremberg 1910–1933.* Oxford: Clarendon, 1996.

Kaufman, Menahem. "The Daily Life of the Village and Country Jews in Hessen from Hitler's Ascent to Power to November 1938." *Yad Vashem Studies* 22 (1992): 147–198.

Kaufmann, Robert Uri. *Die Beerfeldener Juden 1691–1942.* Beerfelden: Stadt Beerfelden, 2003.

———. "Die Behejmeshändler: Oder der Alltag der jüdischen Viehhändler in Zentraleuropa vor und nach der rechtlichen Gleichstellung und dem Ausbau des Eisenbahnnetzes." *Geschichtswerkstatt* 15 (1988): 7–18.

———. *Jüdische und christliche Viehhändler in der Schweiz 1780–1930.* Zurich: Chronos, 1988.

———. "Zum Viehhandel der Juden in Deutschland und der Schweiz – bisherige Ergebnisse und offene Fragen." In *Jüdische Viehhändler zwischen Schwarzwald und Schwäbischer Alb,* edited by Robert Uri Kaufmann and Carsten Kohlmann, 17–41. Rexingen: Barbara Staudacher, 2008.

Kaufmann, Robert Uri, and Carsten Kohlmann, eds. *Jüdische Viehhändler zwischen Schwarzwald und Schwäbischer Alb: Vorträge der Tagung der Arbeitsgemeinschaft Jüdische Gedenkstätten am Oberen Neckar am 3. Oktober 2006 in Horb-Rexingen.* Horb-Rexingen: Barbara Staudacher, 2008.

Keller, Gottfried. "Kleider machen Leute." In *Sämtliche Werke.* Vol. 2, 11–62. English translation by Harry Steinhauer. *Gottfried Keller: Stories.* Vol. 44 of *The German Library,* edited by Frank J. Ryder. New York: Continuum, 1982.

———. *Sämtliche Werke: Historisch-kritische Ausgabe.* Zurich: Stroemfeld, 2000.

Kershaw, Ian. "Antisemitismus und Volksmeinung: Reaktionen auf die Judenverfolgung." In *Bayern in der NS-Zeit.* Vol. 2, *Herrschaft und Gesellschaft im Konflikt,* edited by Martin Broszat and Elke Fröhlich, 281–348. Munich: Oldenbourg, 1979.

————. *Hitler, the Germans, and the Final Solution.* New Haven: Yale University Press, 2008.

————. "The Persecution of the Jews and German Popular Opinion in the Third Reich." *Leo Baeck Institute Year Book* 26 (1981): 261–289.

Kimmel, Elke. *Methoden antisemitischer Propaganda im Ersten Weltkrieg: Die Presse des Bundes der Landwirte.* Berlin: Metropol, 2001.

Kittel, Manfred. "Mentale Machtergreifung: Der frühe Anbruch des »Dritten Reiches« in der evangelischen Agrarprovinz Frankens 1930–1932." In *Bilder-Last*, edited by Hans-Christian Täubrich, 24–31. Nuremberg: Dokumentation-szentrum Reichsparteitagsgelände Nürnberg, 2008.

————. *Provinz zwischen Reich und Republik: Politischen Mentalitäten in Deutschland und Frankreich, 1918–1933/36.* Munich: Oldenbourg, 2000.

Klepsch, Alfred. "Das Lachoudisch. Eine jiddische Sondersprache in Franken." In *Rotwelsch-Dialekte*, edited by Klaus Siewert, 81–93. Wiesbaden: Harrassow-itz, 1996.

Klink, Daniel. "Der Ehrbare Kaufmann – Das ursprüngliche Leitbild der Betriebswirtschaftslehre und individuelle Grundlage für die CSR-Forschung." In *Corporate Social Responsibility.* Special issue 3, *Zeitschrift für Betriebswirtschaft* (*Journal of Business Economics*), edited by Joachim Schwalbach, 57–79. Wies-baden: Gabler, 2008.

Kluge, Ulrich. *Agrarwirtschaft und ländliche Gesellschaft im 20. Jahrhundert.* Munich: Oldenbourg, 2005.

Kluxen, Andrea M., and Julia Hecht, eds. *Antijudaismus und Antisemitismus in Franken.* Ansbach: Bezirk Mittelfranken, 2008.

Koch, Friedrich. *Sexuelle Denunziation: Die Sexualität in der politischen Ausein-andersetzung.* Frankfurt am Main: Syndikat, 1986.

Kohlmann, Carsten. "'Die Viehbörse Süddeutschlands'—Jüdische Pferde—und Viehhändler im Raum Horb." In *Jüdische Viehhändler zwischen Schwarzwald und Schwäbischer Alb*, edited by Robert Uri Kaufmann and Carsten Kohl-mann, 42–69. Horb-Rexingen: Barbara Staudacher Verlag, 2008.

Kolmer, Lothar. *Geschichtstheorien.* Paderborn: Fink, 2008.

Königseder, Angelika. "Arierparagraph." In *Enzyklopädie des Nationalsozialis-mus*, edited by Wolfgang Benz, Hermann Graml, and Hermann Weiß, 415. Munich: Deutscher Taschenbuch Verlag, 2007.

Kraemer, David-Charles, ed. *The Jewish Family: Metaphor and Memory.* New York: Oxford University Press, 1989.

Krais, Beate, and Gunter Gebauer, eds. *Habitus.* Bielefeld: Transcript, 2002.

Kraus, Wolfgang, Berndt Hamm, and Meier Schwarz, eds. *Mehr als Steine: Syna-gogen-Gedenkband Bayern.* Lindenberg im Allgäu: Kunstverlag Josef Fink, 2010.

Kroder, Karl, and Birgit Kroder-Gumann. *Schnaittacher Häuserchronik: "Seit unfürdenklichen Zeiten . . ."* Nuremberg: Ges. für Familienforschung in Franken, 2002.

Kroha, Tyll. *Großes Lexikon der Numismatik.* Gütersloh: Bertelsmann Lexikon, 1997.

Kühne, Thomas, ed. *Männergeschichte—Geschlechtergeschichte: Männlichkeit im Wandel der Moderne.* Frankfurt am Main: Campus, 1996.

Labsch-Benz, Elfie. *Die jüdische Gemeinde Nonnenweier: Jüdisches Leben und Brauchtum in einer badischen Landgemeinde zu Beginn des 20. Jahrhundert.* Stuttgart: Landeszentrale für Politische Bildung Baden-Württemberg, 1980.

Landeszentrale für Politische Bildung Rheinland-Pfalz, ed. *Vor 75 Jahren: "Am Anfang stand die Gewalt . . ."* Mainz: LpB Rheinland-Pfalz, 2008.

Lavi, Shai. "Unequal Rites: Jews, Muslims and the History of Ritual Slaughter in Germany." In *Juden und Muslime in Deutschland: Recht, Religion, Identität,* edited by José Brunner and Shai Lavi, 164–184. Göttingen: Wallstein, 2009.

Levine, Rhonda F. *Class, Networks, and Identity: Replanting Jewish Lives from Nazi Germany to Rural New York.* Lanham, MD: Rowman & Littelfield, 2001.

Liebeschütz, Hans, and Arnold Paucker, eds. *Das Judentum in der Deutschen Umwelt 1800–1850: Studien zur Frühgeschichte der Emanzipation.* Tübingen: J. C. B. Mohr, 1977.

Liepach, Martin. *Das Wahlverhalten der jüdischen Bevölkerung: Zur politischen Orientierung der Juden in der Weimarer Republik.* Tübingen: Mohr, 1996.

Lilla, Joachim. "Hofmann, (Johann) Hans." In "Staatsminister, leitende Verwaltungsbeamte und (NS-)Funktionsträger in Bayern 1918 bis 1945." October 9, 2012, accessed November 2020. http://verwaltungshandbuch.bayerische-landesbibliothek-online.de/hofmann-johann.

———. "Stegmann, Wilhelm." In "Staatsminister, leitende Verwaltungsbeamte und (NS-)Funktionsträger in Bayern 1918 bis 1945." October 8, 2012, accessed November 2020. http://verwaltungshandbuch.bayerische-landesbibliothek-online.de/stegmann-wilhelm.

Lisner, Wiebke. *"Hüterinnen der Nation": Hebammen im Nationalsozialismus.* Frankfurt am Main: Campus, 2006.

Longerich, Peter. *Holocaust: The Nazi Persecution and Murder of the Jews.* Oxford: Oxford University Press, 2010.

———. *Politik der Vernichtung: Eine Gesamtdarstellung der nationalsozialistischen Judenverfolgung.* Munich: Piper, 1998.

Lowenstein, Steven M. "Alltag und Tradition: Eine fränkisch-jüdische Geographie." In *Die Juden in Franken,* edited by Michael Brenner and Daniela F. Eisenstein, 5–25. Munich: Oldenbourg, 2012.

———, ed. *The Mechanics of Change: Essays in the Social History of German Jewry* Atlanta, GA: Scholars Press, 1992.

———. "The Pace of Modernisation of German Jewry in the Nineteenth Century." In *The Mechanics of Change*, edited by Steven M. Lowenstein, 9–28. Atlanta, GA: Scholars Press, 1992.

———. "The Rural Community and the Urbanisation of German Jewry." In *The Mechanics of Change*, edited by Steven M. Lowenstein, 133–151. Atlanta, GA: Scholars Press, 1992.

———. "The Struggle for Survival of Rural Jews in Germany 1933–1938: The Case of Bezirksamt Weissenburg, Mittelfranken." In *Die Juden im nationalsozialistischen Deutschland*, edited by Arnold Paucker, 115–124. Tübingen: Mohr, 1986.

———. "Suggestions for Study of the Mediene Based on German, French and English Models." *Studia Rosenthaliana* XIX, no. 2 (1985): 342–354.

Lüdtke, Alf. "Eisenbahnfahren und Eisenbahnbau." In *Bürgerliche Gesellschaft in Deutschland*, edited by Lutz Niethammer, 101–119. Frankfurt am Main: Fischer, 1990.

Luhmann, Niklas. *Vertrauen: Ein Mechanismus der Reduktion sozialer Komplexität*. Stuttgart: Lucius & Lucius, 2000.

———. "Vertrautheit, Zuversicht, Vertrauen: Probleme und Alternativen." In *Vertrauen*, edited by Martin Hartmann and Claus Offe, 143–160. Frankfurt am Main: Campus, 2001.

Maurer, Trude. "From Everyday Life to a State of Emergency: Jews in Weimar and Nazi Germany." In *Jewish Daily Life in Germany*, edited by Marion A. Kaplan, 271–374. Oxford: Oxford University Press, 2005.

———. "Partnersuche und Lebensplanung: Heiratsannoncen als Quelle für die Sozial- und Mentalitätsgeschichte der Juden in Deutschland." In *Juden in Deutschland*, edited by Peter Freimark, Alice Jankowski, and Ina S. Lorenz, 344–374. Munich: H. Christians Verlag, 1991.

———. "Vom Alltag zum Ausnahmezustand: Juden in der Weimarer Republik und im Nationalsozialismus, 1918–1945." In *Geschichte des jüdischen Alltags in Deutschland*, edited by Marion A. Kaplan, 347–472. Munich: Beck, 2003.

Mazlish, Bruce. *Kissinger: The European Mind in American Policy*. New York: Basic Books, 1976.

Mehler, Richard. "Auf dem Weg in die Moderne: Die fränkischen Landjuden vom frühen 19. Jahrhundert bis zum Ende der 'Weimarer Republik.'" In *Juden in Franken 1806 bis heute*, edited by Julia Hecht, 67–98. Ansbach: Bezirk Mittelfranken 2007.

———. "Die Entstehung eines Bürgertums unter den Landjuden in der bayerischen Rhön vor dem Ersten Weltkrieg." In *Juden, Bürger, Deutsche: Zur Geschichte von Vielfalt und Differenz 1800–1933*, edited by Andreas Gotzmann, Till van Rahden, and Rainer Liedtcke, 193–216. Tübingen: Mohr, 2001.

Meisinger, Othmar. "Lothekolisch: Ein Beitrag zur Kenntnis der fränk. Händlersprache." *Zeitschrift für Hochdeutsche Mundarten* III (1992): 121–127.

Mergel, Thomas. "Geht es weiterhin voran? Die Modernisierungstheorie auf dem Weg zu einer Theorie der Moderne." In *Geschichte zwischen Kultur und Gesellschaft*, edited by Thomas Mergel and Thomas Welskopp, 203–232. Munich: Beck, 1997.

Mergel, Thomas, and Thomas Welskopp, eds. *Geschichte zwischen Kultur und Gesellschaft: Beiträge zur Theoriedebatte.* Munich: Beck, 1997.

Merkenich, Stephanie. *Grüne Front gegen Weimar. Reichs-Landbund und agrarischer Lobbyismus 1918–1933.* Düsseldorf: Droste, 1998.

Metz, Karl H. *Ursprünge der Zukunft: Die Geschichte der Technik in der westlichen Zivilisation.* Paderborn: Schöningh, 2006.

Meyer, Michael A., and Michael Brenner, eds. *German-Jewish History in Modern Times: Renewal and Destruction 1918–1945.* New York: Columbia University Press: 1998.

Mommsen, Hans. "'Nationalsozialismus oder Hitlerismus?'" In *Persönlichkeit und Struktur in der Geschichte*, edited by Michael Bosch, 61–71. Düsseldorf: Pädagogischer Verlag Schwann, 1977.

Mommsen, Hans, and Dieter Obst. "Die Reaktion der deutschen Bevölkerung auf die Verfolgung der Juden 1933–1943." In *Herrschaftsalltag im Dritten Reich*, edited by Hans Mommsen and Susanne Willems, 374–426. Düsseldorf: Schwann, 1988.

Mommsen, Hans, and Susanne Willems. *Herrschaftsalltag im Dritten Reich: Studien und Texte.* Düsseldorf: Schwann, 1988.

Mosse, Werner Eugen. "Jewish Marriage Strategies: The German Jewish Economic Elite." *Studia Rosenthaliana* XIX, no. 2 (1985): 188–202.

———, ed. *Jüdische Unternehmer in Deutschland im 19. und 20. Jahrhundert.* Stuttgart: Steiner, 1992.

Mosse, Werner Eugen, Arnold Paucker, Reinhard Rürup, and Robert Weltsch, eds. *Revolution and Evolution: 1848 in German-Jewish History: Robert Weltsch on his 90th Birthday in Grateful Appreciation.* Tübingen: Mohr, 1981.

Müller, Arnd. *Geschichte der Juden in Nürnberg, 1146–1945.* Nuremberg: Stadtbibliothek Nürnberg, 1968.

Müller, Fritz. *Der letzte Sau-Müller.* Gunzenhausen: Selbstverlag, 2007.

Münkel, Daniela. *Bauern und Nationalsozialismus: Der Landkreis Celle im Dritten Reich.* Bielefeld: Verlag für Regionalgeschichte, 1991.

———. *Nationalsozialistische Agrarpolitik und Bauernalltag.* Frankfurt am Main: Campus, 1996.

Münzel, Martin. *Die jüdischen Mitglieder der deutschen Wirtschaftselite 1927–1955: Verdrängung—Emigration—Rückkehr.* Paderborn: Schöningh, 2006.

Nachama, Andreas, Uwe Neumärker, and Hermann Simon, eds. *"Es brennt!":
Antijüdischer Terror im November 1938*. Berlin: Stiftung Topographie des Terrors, 2008.

Nierhaus-Knaus, Edith. *Geheimsprache in Franken—Das Schillingsfürster Jenisch*.
Rothenburg ob der Tauber: Peter, 1990.

Niers, Gert. "Neuanfang auf dem Lande: Die Hühnerzüchter von New Jersey." In
Das Exil der kleinen Leute, edited by Wolfgang Benz, 39–46. Munich: Beck, 1991.

Niethammer, Lutz. *Bürgerliche Gesellschaft in Deutschland: Historische Einblicke,
Fragen, Perspektiven*. Frankfurt am Main: Fischer, 1990.

Niewyk, Donald L. "The Impact of Inflation and Depression on the German
Jews." *Leo Baeck Institute Year Book* 28 (1983): 19–36.

Ophir, Baruch Z., and Falk Wiesemann, eds. *Die jüdischen Gemeinden in Bayern,
1918–1945: Geschichte und Zerstörung*. Munich: Oldenbourg, 1979.

Ott, Simone, Evelyn Pfliegel, and Hermann Seis, eds. *Juden in Ellingen 1540–1938*.
Ellingen: Hermann Seis, 2008.

Pätzold, Kurt. "Novemberpogrom." In *Enzyklopädie des Nationalsozialismus*,
edited by Wolfgang Benz, Hermann Graml, and Hermann Weiß, 742–743.
Munich: Deutscher Taschenbuch Verlag, 2007.

Paucker, Arnold. "Die Abwehr des Antisemitismus in den Jahren 1893–1933." In
Antisemitismus, edited by Herbert A. Strauss and Norbert Kampe, 143–171.
Bonn: Bundeszentrale für politische Bildung, 1988.

———, ed. *Die Juden im nationalsozialistischen Deutschland—The Jews in Nazi
Germany, 1933–1943*. Tübingen: Mohr, 1986.

Peal, David. "Antisemitism by Other Means? The Rural Cooperative Movement
in Late Nineteenth-Century Germany." *Leo Baeck Institute Year Book* 32 (1987):
135–153.

Pensak, Margie. "Mishpacha Magazine: A Breed Apart," photos by Esky
Cook, Baltimore Jewish Life, May 11, 2016, accessed May 10, 2022, https://
baltimorejewishlife.com/news/news-detail.php?SECTION_ID
=1&ARTICLE_ID=73648.

Penslar, Derek J. *Shylock's Children: Economics and Jewish Identity in Modern
Europe*. Berkeley: University of California Press, 2001.

Peukert, Detlev J. K. *Die Weimarer Republik: Krisenjahre der klassischen Moderne*.
Darmstadt: Wissenschaftliche Buchgesellschaft, 1997.

Picard, Jacob. "Childhood in the Village: Fragment of an Autobiography." *Leo
Baeck Institute Year Book* 4 (1959): 275–295.

Plum, Günter. "Wirtschaft und Erwerbsleben." In *Die Juden in Deutschland
1933–1945*, edited by Wolfgang Benz, 268–313. Munich: Beck, 1989.

Post, Rudolf. "Reste von Viehhändlersprachen in der Pfalz, in Baden und im Elsass." In *Geheimsprachen in Mittel- und Südosteuropa*, edited by Christian Efing
and Corinna Leschber, 89–98. Berlin: Peter Lang, 2009.

Przyrembel, Alexandra. "'Rassenschande.'" In *Handbuch des Antisemitismus*. Vol. 3, *Begriffe, Ideologien, Theorien*, edited by Wolfgang Benz, 273–275. Berlin: De Gruyter. Saur, 2010.

———. *"Rassenschande": Reinheitsmythos und Vernichtungslegitimation im Nationalsozialismus*. Göttingen: Vandenhoeck und Ruprecht, 2003.

Pulzer, Peter. "What Shall I Put in My Luggage? Reflecting Cultural Migration from Central Europe." In *Disseminating German Tradition: The Thyssen Lectures*, edited by Dan Diner and Moshe Zimmermann, 81–100. Leipzig: Leipziger Universitätsverlag, 2009.

Pyta, Wolfram. *Dorfgemeinschaft und Parteipolitik 1918–1933: Die Verschränkung von Milieu und Parteien in den protestantischen Landgebieten Deutschlands in der Weimarer Republik*. Düsseldorf: Droste, 1996.

Rahden, Till van. *Jews and Other Germans: Civil Society, Religious Diversity, and Urban Politics in Breslau, 1860–1925*. Madison: University of Wisconsin Press, 2008.

———. "Jews and the Ambivalences of Civil Society in Germany, 1800–1933: Assessment and Reassessment." *The Journal of Modern History* 77, no. 4 (2005): 1024–1047.

———. *Juden und andere Breslauer: Die Beziehungen zwischen Juden, Protestanten und Katholiken in einer deutschen Großstadt von 1860 bis 1925*. Göttingen: Vandenhoeck & Ruprecht, 2000.

Rechter, Gerhard. "Die Judenmatrikel 1813 bis 1861 in Mittelfranken." In *Juden in Franken 1806 bis heute*, edited by Julia Hecht, 53–66. Ansbach: Bezirk Mittelfranken, 2007.

Reemtsma, Jan Philipp. *Vertrauen und Gewalt: Versuch über eine besondere Konstellation der Moderne*. Hamburg: Hamburger Edition, 2008.

Reichardt, Sven. *Soziales Kapital "im Zeitalter materieller Interessen": Konzeptionelle Überlegungen zum Vertrauen in der Zivil- und Marktgesellschaft des langen 19. Jahrhunderts (1780–1914)*. Berlin: Wissenschaftszentrum Berlin, 2003. https://nbn-resolving.org/urn:nbn:de:0168-ssoar-111591.

Renda, Gerhard. "Fürth, das 'bayerische Jerusalem.'" In *Geschichte und Kultur der Juden in Bayern*, edited by Manfred Treml and Josef Kirmeier, 225–236. Munich: Haus der bayerischen Geschichte, 1988.

Reulecke, Jürgen, and Detlev Peukert, eds. *Die Reihen fast geschlossen: Beiträge zur Geschichte des Alltags unterm Nationalsozialismus*. Wuppertal: Hammer, 1981.

Reuveni, Gideon. "Prolegomena to an 'Economic Turn' Jewish History." In *The Economy in Jewish History*, edited by Gideon Reuveni and Sarah Wobick-Segev, 1–22. New York: Berghahn, 2011.

Reuveni, Gideon, and Sarah Wobick-Segev, eds. *The Economy in Jewish History: New Perspectives on the Interrelationship between Ethnicity and Economic Life*. New York: Berghahn, 2011.

Revel, Jacques. "Die Annales." In *Kompass der Geschichtswissenschaft*, edited by Joachim Eibach, 23–37. Göttingen: Vandenhoeck und Ruprecht, 2006.

Richarz, Monika. *Bürger auf Widerruf: Lebenszeugnisse deutscher Juden 1780–1945.* Munich: Beck, 1989.

———. "Die soziale Stellung der jüdischen Händler auf dem Lande am Beispiel Südwestdeutschlands." In *Jüdische Unternehmer in Deutschland im 19. und 20. Jahrhundert*, edited by Werner Eugen Mosse, 271–283. Stuttgart: Steiner, 1992.

———. "Emancipation and Continuity: German Jews in the Rural Economy." In *Revolution and Evolution*, edited by Werner Eugen, Emil Mosse, and Arnold Paucker, Reinhard Rürup, and Robert Weltsch, 95–116. Tübingen: Mohr, 1981.

———, ed. *Jüdisches Leben in Deutschland: Selbstzeugnisse zur Sozialgeschichte 1780–1871.* Stuttgart: Deutsche Verlags-Anstalt, 1976.

———, ed. *Jüdisches Leben in Deutschland: Selbstzeugnisse zur Sozialgeschichte im Kaiserreich.* Stuttgart: Deutsche Verlags-Anstalt, 1979.

———, ed. *Jüdisches Leben in Deutschland: Selbstzeugnisse zur Sozialgeschichte 1918–1933.* Stuttgart: Deutsche Verlags-Anstalt, 1982.

———. "Landjuden und Wirtschaft: Jüdische Schlachter und Viehhändler im deutschen und internationalen Viehhandel des 19. Jahrhunderts (Kurzfassung)." *Studia Rosenthaliana* XIX, no. 2 (1985): 357.

———. "Ländliches Judentum als Problem der Forschung." In *Jüdisches Leben auf dem Lande*, edited by Monika Richarz and Reinhard Rürup, 1–8. Tübingen: Mohr Siebeck, 1997.

———. "Viehhandel und Landjuden im 19. Jahrhundert: Eine symbiotische Wirtschaftsbeziehung in Südwestdeutschland." In *Menora: Jahrbuch für deutsch-jüdische Geschichte*, edited by Julius H. Schoeps, 66–88. Munich: Piper, 1990.

Richter, Heinrich. "Friedrich Wilhelm Raiffeisen und die Entwicklung seiner Genossenschaftsidee." PhD diss., Erlangen/Nürnberg, 1966.

Römer, Gernot. *Schwäbische Juden: Leben und Leistungen aus zwei Jahrhunderten in Selbstzeugnissen, Berichten und Bildern.* Augsburg: Presse-Dr.- und Verl., 1990.

Roming, Gisela. "Haushalt und Familie auf dem Lande im Spiegel südbadischer Nachlaßakten." In *Jüdisches Leben auf dem Lande*, edited by Reinhard Rürup and Monika Richarz, 269–291. Tübingen: Mohr Siebeck, 1997.

Roper, Lyndal. "Männlichkeit und männliche Ehre." In *Frauengeschichte – Geschlechtergeschichte*, edited by Karin Hausen and Heide Wunder, 154–172. Frankfurt am Main: Campus, 1992.

Rösch, Barbara. *Der Judenweg: Jüdische Geschichte und Kulturgeschichte aus Sicht der Flurnamenforschung.* Göttingen: Vandenhoeck & Ruprecht, 2009.

Roth, Ralf. "Die Eisenbahn und ihre Folgen für die Mobilität im 19. Jahrhundert." In *"Auf eisernen Schienen, so schnell wie der Blitz": Regionale und überregionale Aspekte der Eisenbahngeschichte*, edited by Andreas Hedwig, 1–16. Marburg: Hessisches Staatsarchiv Marburg, 2008.

Rürup, Reinhard, and Monika Richarz, eds. *Jüdisches Leben auf dem Lande: Studien zur deutsch-jüdischen Geschichte*. Tübingen: Mohr Siebeck, 1997.

Saldern, Adelheid von. *Mittelstand im "Dritten Reich": Handwerker—Einzelhändler—Bauern*. Frankfurt am Main: Campus, 1985.

Schaaf, Lisa. "Schicksal und Lebensweg jüdischer Emigranten aus Gunzenhausen." Unpublished research paper, Gunzenhausen, 2005.

Schmid, Regina. *Verlorene Heimat. Gailingen – ein Dorf und seine jüdische Gemeinde in der Weimarer Zeit*. Konstanz: Arbeitskreis für Regionalgeschichte, 1988.

Schoeps, Julius H. *Menora: Jahrbuch für deutsch-jüdische Geschichte*. Munich: Piper, 1990.

Schreiner, Klaus, ed. *Verletzte Ehre: Ehrkonflikte in Gesellschaften des Mittelalters und der Frühen Neuzeit*. Cologne: Böhlau, 1995.

Schüler-Springorum, Stefanie. *Die jüdische Minderheit in Königsberg, Preußen: 1871–1945*. Göttingen: Vandenhoeck und Ruprecht, 1996.

Schwab, Hermann. *Jewish Rural Communities in Germany*. London: Cooper, 1956.

Schwarz, Stefan. *Die Juden in Bayern im Wandel der Zeiten*. Munich: Olzog, 1980.

Seis, Hermann. *Das Buch "Beacon of Light": Die Lebenserinnerungen der Ellinger Rabbinertochter Felice Poupko, als deutsches Kind: Felicitas Schuster*. Ellingen: Stadtarchiv Ellingen im ehemaligen Franziskanerkloster, 2010.

Shapiro, Ari Daniel, and Amanda Kowalski. "The Frum Farmer." *Tablet Magazine: A New Read on Jewish Life*, June 6, 2011. Accessed March 2019. https://aridanielshapiro.wordpress.com/2011/06/07/farmer/.

Siewert, Klaus, ed. *Rotwelsch-Dialekte: Symposion, Münster, 10. bis 12. März 1995*. Wiesbaden: Harrassowitz, 1996.

Slezkine, Yuri. *The Jewish Century*. Princeton: Princeton University Press, 2004.

Spiegel, Paul. *Wieder zu Hause? Erinnerungen*. Berlin: Ullstein, 2001.

Statistisches Reichsamt. *Die Bevölkerung des Deutschen Reichs nach den Ergebnissen der Volkszählung 1925*. 1929. Reprint, Berlin: Reimar Hobbing, 1978.

———. *Statistik des Deutschen Reichs: Landwirtschaftliche Betriebszählung. Personal, Viehstand, Maschinenverwendung*. 1929. Reprint, Berlin: Reimar Hobbing, 1978.

Staudacher, Barbara. "Rexingen." In *Ort der Zuflucht und Verheißung*, edited by Heinz Högerle, 8–20. Stuttgart: Theiss, 2008.

Steinke, Karolin. *Simon Adler: Eierhändler in Berlin*. Berlin: Hentrich & Hentrich 2011.

Steinmetz, Horst, and Helmut Hofmann. *Die Juden in Windsheim nach 1871*. Bad Windsheim: Die Autoren, 1994.

Switalski, Martina. *Shalom Forth: Jüdisches Dorfleben in Franken*. Münster: Theiss, 2012.

Tagsold, Heike, ed. *"Was brauchen wir einen Befehl, wenn es gegen die Juden geht?":* *Das Pogrom von Gunzenhausen 1934.* Nuremberg: Antogo, 2006.

Täubrich, Hans-Christian, ed. *BilderLast: Franken im Nationalsozialismus.* Nuremberg: Dokumentationszentrum Reichsparteitagsgelände Nürnberg, 2008.

Teuber, Werner. *Jüdische Viehhändler in Ostfriesland und im nördlichen Emsland 1871–1942: Eine vergleichende Studie zu einer jüdischen Berufsgruppe in zwei wirtschaftlich und konfessionell unterschiedlichen Regionen.* Cloppenburg: Runge, 1995.

Teuteberg, Hans-Jürgen, and Cornelius Neutsch, eds. *Vom Flügeltelegraphen zum Internet: Geschichte der modernen Telekommunikation.* Stuttgart: Steiner, 1998.

Tilly, Richard H. *Vertrauen = Trust.* Berlin: Akademie, 2005.

Toury, Jacob. "Antisemitismus auf dem Lande: Der Fall Hessen 1881–1895." In *Jüdisches Leben auf dem Lande,* edited by Reinhard Rürup and Monika Richarz, 173–188. Tübingen: Mohr Siebeck, 1997.

———. "Der Eintritt der Juden ins deutsche Bürgertum." In *Das Judentum in der Deutschen Umwelt 1800–1850,* edited by Hans Liebeschütz and Arnold Paucker, 227–241. Tübingen: J.C.B. Mohr, 1977.

Treml, Manfred, and Josef Kirmeier, ed. *Geschichte und Kultur der Juden in Bayern: Aufsätze.* Munich: Haus der bayerischen Geschichte, 1988.

Ullmann, Sabine. *Nachbarschaft und Konkurrenz: Juden und Christen in Dörfern der Markgrafschaft Burgau 1650 bis 1750.* Göttingen: Vandenhoeck und Ruprecht, 1999.

Ulmer, Martin. "Bedeutung und Ende des jüdischen Viehhandels." In *Zerstörte Hoffnungen,* edited by Geschichtswerkstatt Tübingen, 215–233. Stuttgart: Theiss, 1995.

———. "'Zuerst die Kuh, dann Hab und Gut, erpreßt der Advokat und Jud'— Über Agrarantisemitismus in Württemberg." In *Jüdische Viehhändler zwischen Schwarzwald und Schwäbischer Alb,* edited by Robert Uri Kaufmann and Carsten Kohlmann, 131–155. Horb-Rexingen: Barbara Staudacher Verlag, 2008.

Volkov, Shulamit, ed. *Deutsche Juden und die Moderne.* Munich: Oldenbourg, 1994.

———. *Die Juden in Deutschland 1780–1918.* Munich: Oldenbourg, 2000.

———. "Zur Einführung." In *Deutsche Juden und die Moderne,* edited by Shulamit Volkov, vii–xxiii. Munich: Oldenbourg, 1994.

Walk, Joseph, Daniel Cil Brecher, and Robert M. W. Kempner, eds. *Das Sonderrecht für die Juden im NS-Staat: Eine Sammlung der gesetzlichen Maßnahmen und Richtlinien; Inhalt und Bedeutung.* Heidelberg: Müller Juristischer, 1996.

Walter, Dirk. *Antisemitische Kriminalität und Gewalt: Judenfeindschaft in der Weimarer Republik.* Bonn: Dietz, 1999.

Weber, Reinhard. *Das Schicksal der jüdischen Rechtsanwälte in Bayern nach 1933.* Munich: Oldenbourg, 2006.

Wehling, Hans-Georg, ed. *Dorfpolitik: Fachwissenschaftl. Analysen u. didakt. Hilfen.* Opladen: Leske und Budrich, 1978.

Weinacht, Helmut. "Jiddisches im Ostfränkischen: Darstellung einer Forschungsproblematik." In *Dialekte im Wandel,* edited by Andreas Weiss, 170–186. Göppingen: Kümmerle, 1992.

Weinberg, Werner. *Die Reste des Jüdischdeutschen.* Stuttgart: Kohlhammer, 1973.

Weisbrod, Bernd. "Die Krise der Mitte oder: 'Der Bauer stund auf dem Lande.'" In *Bürgerliche Gesellschaft in Deutschland,* edited by Lutz Niethammer, 396–410. Frankfurt am Main: Fischer, 1990.

Weiss, Andreas, ed. *Dialekte im Wandel: Tagung zur Bayerisch-Österreichischen Dialektologie.* Göppingen: Kümmerle, 1992.

Weiß, Dietrich. "Aus der Geschichte der jüdischen Gemeinde von Feuchtwangen, 1274–1938." In *Feuchtwanger Heimatgeschichte,* edited by Arbeitsgemeinschaft für Heimatgeschichte, 9–107. Feuchtwangen: Arbeitsgemeinschaft für Heimatgeschichte, 1991.

Wenge, Nicola. *Integration und Ausgrenzung in der städtischen Gesellschaft: Eine jüdisch-nichtjüdische Beziehungsgeschichte Kölns 1918–1933.* Mainz: von Zabern, 2005.

Wessel, Horst A. "Die Verbreitung des Telephons bis zur Gegenwart." In *Vom Flügeltelegraphen zum Internet,* edited by Hans-Jürgen Teuteberg and Cornelius Neutsch, 67–112. Feuchtwangen: Arbeitsgemeinschaft für Heimatgeschichte, 1991.

Wiegelmann, Günter, and Dietmar Sauermann, eds. *Kultureller Wandel im 19. Jahrhundert.* Göttingen: Vandenhoeck und Ruprecht, 1973.

Wieland, Günther, and Klaus Drobisch. *System der NS-Konzentrationslager.* Berlin: Akademie, 1993.

Wierling, Dorothee. "Mit Rohkaffee handeln: Hamburger Importeure im 20. Jahrhundert," In *Kaffeewelten: Historische Perspektiven auf eine globale Ware im 20. Jahrhundert,* edited by Christiane Berth et al., 105–128. Göttingen: V & R unipress, 2015.

Wiesemann, Falk. "Einleitung: Zur Geschichte der jüdischen Gemeinden seit 1813." In *Die jüdischen Gemeinden in Bayern, 1918–1945,* edited by Baruch Z. Ophir and Falk Wiesemann, 13–29. Munich: Oldenbourg, 1979.

———, ed. *Genizah, Hidden Legacies of the German Village Jews.* Gütersloh: Bertelsmann, 1992.

———. "Juden auf dem Lande: Die wirtschaftliche Ausgrenzung der jüdischen Viehhändler in Bayern." In *Die Reihen fast geschlossen,* edited by Jürgen Reulecke and Detlev Peukert, 381–396. Wuppertal: Hammer, 1981.

————. "'Verborgene Zeugnisse' der deutschen Landjuden: Eine Einführung in die Ausstellung." In *Genizah, Hidden Legacies of the German Village*, edited by Falk Wiesemann, 15–32. Gütersloh: Bertelsmann, 1992.

Wildt, Michael. "Die Ungleichheit des Volkes: 'Volksgemeinschaft' in der politischen Kommunikation der Weimarer Republik." In *Volksgemeinschaft*, edited by Frank Bajohr and Michael Wildt, 24–40. Frankfurt am Main: Fischer-Taschenbuch-Verlag, 2009.

————. *Geschichte des Nationalsozialismus*. Göttingen: Vandenhoeck & Ruprecht, 2008.

————. "Gewaltpolitik: Volksgemeinschaft und Judenverfolgung in der deutschen Provinz 1932–1935." *WerkstattGeschichte* 11, no. 35 (2003): 23–43.

————. "Violence against Jews in Germany 1933–1939." In *Probing the Depths of German Antisemitism*, edited by David Bankier, 181–212. New York: Berghahn, 2000.

————. *Volksgemeinschaft als Selbstermächtigung: Gewalt gegen Juden in der deutschen Provinz 1919 bis 1939*. Hamburg: Hamburger Edition, 2007.

Wilms, Yvonne. *Ehre, Männlichkeit und Kriminalität*. Berlin: Lit, 2009.

Wirthmann-Müller, Bernhard. "Raufhändel: Gewalt und Ehre im Dorf." In *Kultur der einfachen Leute*, edited by Richard van Dülmen and Angelika Baumann, 79–111. Munich: Beck, 1983.

Wörterbuch der jüdischen Geschäfts- und Umgangssprache. Dülmen: Horn—Tierzuchtgeräte, 2013. Author's personal copy. A fascimile edition by Klaus Siewert was later published under the same title. Münster: Geheimsprachen, 2018.

Wünschmann, Kim. *Before Auschwitz: Jewish Prisoners in the Prewar Concentration Camps*. Cambridge, MA: Harvard University Press, 2015.

————. "Jüische Häftlinge im KZ-Osthofen: Das frühe Konzentrationslager als Terrorinstrument der nationalsozialistischen Judenpolitik." In *Vor 75 Jahren: "Am Anfang stand die Gewalt . . . ,"* edited by Landeszentrale für Politische Bildung Rheinland-Pfalz, 18–33, Mainz: Landeszentrale für politische Bildung, 2008.

Zähner, M., and E. Spiessl-Mayr. *Elektronische Kennzeichnung von Nutztieren*. *Agrarforschung* 12, no. 2 (2005): 79–83.

Zelnhefer, Siegfried. *Die Reichsparteitage der NSDAP in Nürnberg*. Nuremberg: Museen der Stadt Nürnberg, 2002.

Zimmermann, Clemens, and Werner Troßbach. *Die Geschichte des Dorfes*. Stuttgart: Ulmer, 2006.

Zinke, Jens. *Die Entwicklung der landwirtschaftlichen Genossenschaften in der Weimarer Republik: Unter besonderer Berücksichtigung der Änderungen des Genossenschaftsgesetzes*. Berlin: Inst. für Genossenschaftswesen, 1999.

Zinke, Peter. "Der Strick mit dem Knoten – Suizid oder Mord bei Max Rosenau und Jakob Rosenfelder?" In *Was brauchen wir einen Befehl, wenn es gegen die Juden geht?": Das Pogrom von Gunzenhausen 1934*, edited by Heike Tagsold, 31–44. Nuremberg: Antogo-Verlag, 2006.

Zucker, Lynne. "Production of Trust: Institutional Sources of Economic Structure, 1840–1920." *Research in Organizational Behavior* 8 (1986): 53–111.

INDEX OF PERSONS

INDEX OF PLACES

Italicized page numbers refer to illustrations, such as maps

Liechtenstein, 189
London, 166, 194, 197
Lower Saxony, 259n135

Mainburg, 89, 91, 242n131
Mannheim, 46
Margarethentann, 90
Markt Berolzheim, *21*, 22, 31–33, 35,
 41, 43, 53, 71, 90, 138, 172, 175, 177,
 185–187, 217n32, 219n58, 221n68,
 227n124, 227n128, 270n31
Mönchsroth, *21*, 23–25, 27, 42, 57, 84,
 89, 128, 227n128, 229n151
Munich, 19, 22, 30, 43, 113, 134, 183,
 185, 189

Netherlands, 189
Neuburg, 144, 172
Neuendorf, 119
Neustadt/Aisch, *21*, 126, 131, 170–171,
 225n116
New York (City), 10, 190, 192,
 194–195; New York State (upstate
 New York), 198
Nördlingen, 41, 50, 172, 228n140
Nuremberg, 16, 19–20, *21*, 28, 30,
 38, *45*, 46, 47, 51, 57–58, 86, 92,
 105, 113, 119, 122–123, 126, 128,
 135, 138, 147–148, 150–152, 166,
 176–178, 180–182, 184, 216n16,
 217n32, 229n151, 241n121 , 253n74,
 268n12, 275n72, 285n142, 297n239,
 298n250, 303n304. *See also* Nuremberg Laws under Index of Subjects

Oberhochstatt, 73, 161
Old Bavaria, 43
Ostfriesland. *See* East Frisia, Eastern
 Frisia.
Osthofen concentration camp,
 268n12

Palestine (Mandate or Mandatory
 Palestine), 189, 191, 193, 198
Pappenheim, 189
Poland, 190
Pomerania, 110
Prussia, 2; East Prussia, 211n14

Regensburg, 107, 248n39, 279n97
Reichmannsdorf, 174
Rennhofen, 243n133
Rexingen, 198, 232n25
Rhineland, 105
Roth, *21*, 57, 144, 218n37, 229n151,
 295n221
Rothenburg-Land (electoral district),
 122
Rothenburg ob der Tauber, 18, 20,
 21, 23, 41, 53, 70, 100, 114, 122,
 129–130, 134–135, 156, 158–159,
 163–164, 170–171, 180, 182–183,
 189, 229n151, 249nn45–46,
 268n12, 288n161

Sachsenhausen concentration
 camp, 188
Saxony, 105
Scheinfeld, *21*, 119, 147, 170–171,
 275n73, 278n90
Schillingsfürst, 119
Schnaittach, *21*, 33
Schwabach, *21*, 171,
Schwaben-Neuburg government
 district, 172
South Africa, 189
Sugenheim, *21*, 119

Thalmässing, *21*, 138
Theresienstadt concentration camp,
 183, 190
Treblinka extermination camp,
 183

Stefanie Fischer holds a PhD from the Technical University of Berlin. She is a faculty member at the Center for Antisemitism Research at TU Berlin. Her fields of scholarly research are German Jewish history and Holocaust Studies. Fischer is coauthor of *Oberbrechen: A German Village Confronts its Nazi Past* (2024) and has published numerous articles on German-Jewish history and culture.

Jeremiah Riemer (PhD, Cornell 1983) taught comparative politics at several universities in the United States and Germany between 1981 and 2012. Since 1996, he has translated more than a dozen books and numerous scholarly articles on history, politics, psychology, architecture, and Jewish studies. His most recent translation was *In Hitler's Munich: Jews, the Revolution, and the Rise of Nazism* (2022) by Michael Brenner.

For Indiana University Press

Tony Brewer, Artist and Book Designer

Brian Carroll, Rights Manager

Gary Dunham, Acquisitions Editor and Director

Anna Francis, Assistant Acquisitions Editor

Brenna Hosman, Production Coordinator

Katie Huggins, Production Manager

Nancy Lightfoot, Project Editor and Manager

Dan Pyle, Online Publishing Manager

Pamela Rude, Senior Artist and Book Designer

Stephen Williams, Marketing and Publicity Manager